MW00563017

PATTERNS
of EVIDENCE

EXODUS

A FILMMAKER'S JOURNEY

TIMOTHY P. MAHONY

with STEVEN LAW

THINKING MAN MEDIA

For further information visit:
http://www.PatternsOfEvidence.com

Mahoney, Timothy P., 1957-

Patterns of Evidence: Exodus, A Filmmaker's Journey
/ Timothy P. Mahoney ; with Steven Law.
St. Louis Park, MN : Thinking Man Media, [2015]
392 pages; 3.5 cm.
ISBN: 978-0-9864310-0-5

"You never know where a crisis of faith will lead you."– Back Cover
Includes bibliographical references.

Summary:
In 2002, filmmaker Timothy Mahoney went to Egypt looking for an
answer to one fundamental question: Did the Exodus story as written in
the Bible really happen? During the course of his 12-year project, he
reviews accepted archaeological viewpoints, compares biblical references to evidence, and presents alternative theories that support the
validity of the event called the Exodus. This book tells the story about the
creation of his feature documentary film, also titled *Patterns of Evidence:
The Exodus*. It's not only a visual companion to the film, giving scenes
and diagrams; it's also a narration of his ongoing journey of research
and travel, giving perspectives of some of the leading archaeologists,
Egyptologists, and political and cultural influencers as they talk about
the story of the Exodus. – Publisher

1. Exodus, The. 2. Exodus, The–Biblical teaching. 3. Excavations
(Archaeology)–Egypt. 4. Egypt–In the Bible. 5. Bible. Exodus–Evidence,
authority, etc. 6. Bible. Exodus–Criticism, interpretation, etc. 7. Moses
(Biblical leader) 8. Ten Commandments–Criticism, interpretation, etc.
9. Jews–History–To 1200 BC. 10. Religion. I. Law, Steven. II. Title.

BS1199.E93 M34 2015

222.12/09505–dc23   1504

First Published in the USA in 2015 by
Thinking Man Media
6900 West Lake Street
St. Louis Park, MN 55426

Book Design: Kevin O'Neill, www.KevinOneill.com
Typeset in Garamond ITC Pro and Franklin ITC Pro.
Printed in Canada by Friesens Corp.

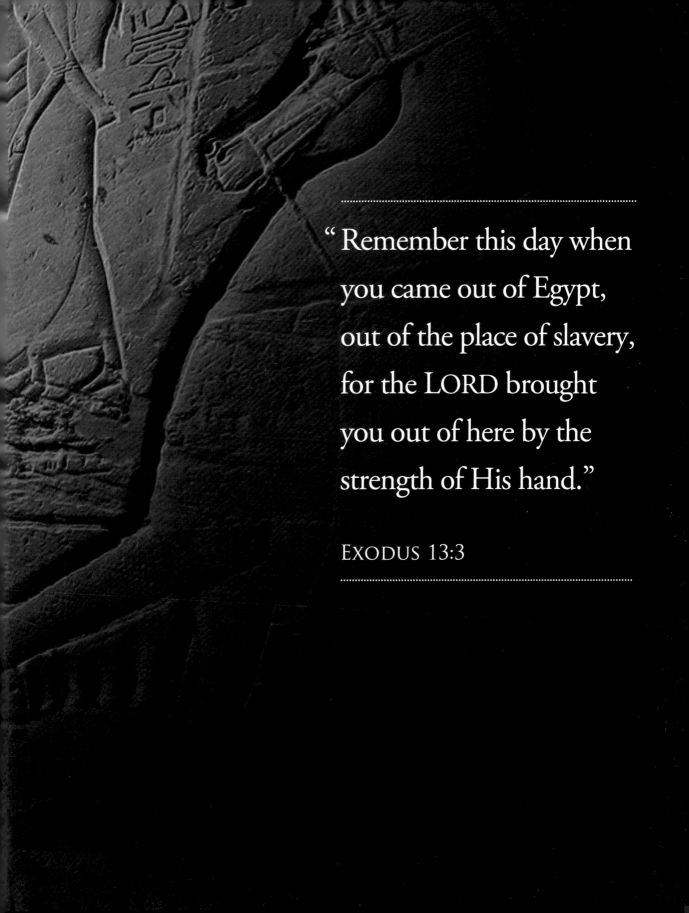

" Remember this day when
you came out of Egypt,
out of the place of slavery,
for the LORD brought
you out of here by the
strength of His hand."

EXODUS 13:3

FOREWORD

When Timothy Mahoney asked Nobel laureate and former President of the State of Israel, Shimon Peres, a person whose life has been devoted to the building of that nation, to characterize the legacy of the Exodus, he replied with no reservation that it was the experience at Sinai. "Take away the Ten Commandments and we are out of business." And we can add, take away the Exodus and we lose Sinai and with that the basis for all the absolute authority of those ten world-shaping concepts. So crucial are they to the fabric of humanity that they are engraved on the walls of the United Nations.

I have often heard the naive argument that there are no absolutes. Even in nature, the argument goes, we have the laws of relativity. Really? Are you not aware that the laws of relativity are entirely based on an absolute: the constant speed of light? Absolutes abound in nature and they also need abound in human relationships.

....

Humanity has the habit of not learning
from history, and so it repeats itself.

....

Take away the Exodus and with it the Ten Commandments and humanity is "out of business." We've seen that failed experiment time and again. The French Revolution embodied the warped wisdom of the Enlightenment that human reason alone is supreme. In doing so, it abandoned those absolutes and in their place instituted what was referred to as the "cult of reason." Within a decade of that debacle, the Revolution devoured its own leaders and thousands of others. Records from that awful era of terror relate the attempt to develop a poison gas that would make the killing of counter-revolutionaries more efficient. Humanity has the habit of not learning from history, and so it repeats itself.

Moses Maimonides, the 12th century theologian philosopher, taught in his youth that all must believe in a God that is active in the universe. In his later years he realized that belief is inadequate and taught that all must know that God is active in our lives, and can know this truth by observing events in the world.

This project, aptly titled *Patterns of Evidence,* is a game changer. It changes belief in the validity of the biblical Exodus into knowledge of that historic event. It does this by abandoning unquestioned "accepted wisdom" and replacing it with actual data gleaned from the era in question. When those data fall into a pattern, truth emerges. In this case, the Exodus. This is exactly the scientific method.

Scientific discovery is based on observing patterns in nature. I drop an apple; it falls to the ground. I drop a feather; it falls to the ground. I pour water; it flows down. I've discovered an invisible, ubiquitous force in nature – gravity. I cannot see gravity, but its effect is consistent and predictable. That becomes a known law of nature. Matter in any form attracts matter in any form.

In parallel logic, Mahoney and his colleagues have studied biblical passages and compared them with archaeological discoveries. Point after point revealed an absence of evidence for an Exodus in the era of Ramesses ll. And yet as is often quoted in archaeo-logical research, absence of evidence is not evidence of absence. So perhaps Ramesses was the pharaoh of the Exodus, but the evidence was lost or destroyed. That might have been their conclusion until this team abandoned that ill-conceived and preconceived notion and looked elsewhere in history. There, data point by data point revealed concordance between biblical wisdom and archaeological discoveries. No longer was there an absence of evidence.

In the fifth book of the Bible, Deuteronomy, chapter 32 verse 7, Moses urges us to consider two sets of evidence, the patterns of which demonstrate the presence of a Force, call it God if you like, that is active in this magnificent universe within which we dwell. Moses tells us to "remember the days of old; consider the years generation by genera-tion." Remember the days of old: all ancient commentary relates this to the flow from the creation of the universe as a burst of energy to the appearance of humankind. Then the second half of Moses' charge to us: consider the years generation by generation: look for patterns of a God active in human history, generation by generation.

I see these as two sets of evidence, each representing half of the cup that when full will establish the validity of many biblical claims. The first half of the cup is filled with scientific discovery, the second half with the study of human history.

The first half of the cup: NASA has published in a single diagram the condensed knowledge of the scientific community as to how we thinking, self-aware, conscious beings, we humans, developed from the burst of exquisitely hot energy that marked the Big Bang creation of our universe. That NASA diagram is likely the strongest theological statement that science has ever made, though my guess is that those individuals who produced this work did not do so for theological reasons. The key is the creating force shown thereon.

We are shown that via the laws of nature, in this case quantum fluctuations and the laws of relativity, an expanding universe can be created from absolute nothing. Since our concept of time begins with the creation of the universe, and since the laws of nature create the universe from nothing, then by logic, the laws of nature must exist prior to the universe. That is, they pre-date time as we understand time. They are outside of time. The laws of nature are not physical; they are not made of matter or energy. They are forces that act on the physical. So putting this together, we have a force or forces that are not physical, that are outside of time, that created the universe from nothing. This is science. But it is also the biblical description of the God of the Bible. And even avowed atheists have said that if you want to call it God, do so, but it would be a deist God, a God not active or interested in the universe It created. We need the second half of the cup if we are to go beyond the deist God of science. Still a half full cup is a huge theological leap.

The second half of the cup has several markers that point toward a Force active in the world, guiding but not always controlling the flow from the Big Bang creation to the world in which we currently live. If you believe that the energy of the Big Bang creation can, via totally random processes, morph and morph and morph again and eventually become alive and self-aware, conscious of the emotions that make us human, then you don't need a Guide. That would be the purely scientific view. I personally doubt that a super-powerful burst of energy (and energy is all that the creation brought into being) could have become alive by random events, even with fourteen billion years to accomplish this. How does a light beam have the hutzpah to feel love, joy, wonder? The wonder is not whether Creation took six biblical days (Genesis chapter one) or 14 billion years. The wonder is that it happened. Scientific endeavor has shown that it happened. How it happened has not been shown simply because randomness fails as an adequate explanation.

The biblical Exodus, when proven to be fact and not myth, is indeed a game changer, a game changer not only in establishing the validity of the march toward Sinai but, equally important, in establishing that the Force that created this universe remains active and interested in the creation It brought into being. The cup will then be full, awaiting our consumption.

Werner Heisenberg, Noble laureate in physics, 1932, stated it perfectly: "The first swallow from the cup of the natural sciences makes atheists, but at the bottom of the cup God is waiting."

Gerald L. Schroeder, PhD (M.I.T.)
5 December 2014

PREFACE

There are many films made from books. This is a book that tells the story about the creation of a film, *Patterns of Evidence: The Exodus*. It's not only a visual companion, giving you scenes and diagrams from this feature documentary; it's also my attempt to narrate my ongoing journey of research and travel, allowing you to hear the perspectives of some of the leading archaeologists, Egyptologists, and political and cultural influencers as they talk about the story of the Exodus.

There are 17 interviews featured in the film. In this book I've been able to expand them and add other experts whose insights and contributions are very important to the conversation at hand. I wanted to offer a diversity of viewpoints so that you can more clearly understand the debate and make your own decisions about the validity of the Exodus. For me, examining this issue through an open exchange of ideas was more valuable than just focusing on narrow arguments. I certainly haven't included all the opinions on this subject but I've tried to give you a broad introduction.

The book, like the film, doesn't sequentially trace every step I took in this investigation. Instead, I found that it was more effective to document the search in a way that follows the chronology of the Bible's story. During this inquiry I was pursuing foundational questions: Did the Exodus out of Egypt really happen? Is there a pattern of evidence for this in history?

I hope you enjoy this expedition into the ancient past of Egypt and the Bible as much as I have. I invite you now to stop a while and examine the possibilities found here. The name of our film company is Thinking Man Films. It is our desire to gain a better understanding of significant and complex topics by exploring the world with those who are curious.

May this book give you many hours of inspired thinking.

Timothy P. Mahoney   Thinking Man Films
Director/Producer   Minneapolis, Minnesota
Patterns of Evidence: The Exodus   October 2014

CONTENTS

IX   STEP FIVE: EVIDENCE OF THE EXODUS? 218

X   STEP SIX: EVIDENCE OF THE CONQUEST?..............................230

XI: A PATTERN AMONG THE RAGS AND TATTERS 262

XII: HOW DID THE PROBLEM GET STARTED? 276

FOR OVER 1,500 YEARS

WESTERN CIVILIZATION ACCEPTED

THE TRUTH OF THE BIBLE.

AFTER THE 1950s, HOWEVER,

SKEPTICISM GREW WHEN

ARCHAEOLOGISTS FOUND

MOUNTING EVIDENCE

THAT APPEARED TO CONTRADICT

THE EARLY HISTORY IN THE BIBLE.

TODAY THAT SKEPTICISM

HAS ONLY INCREASED.

INTRODUCTION: THE BACKSTORY

I. My Personal Journey

Filmmaker Timothy Mahoney in Saint Paul, Minnesota.

I never would have thought I'd be caught up in a story such as this one because I live on the other side of the world. On the one hand, it was exciting to be making a film that searches for the truth about the Exodus. On the other hand, I was a reluctant participant. I never wanted to go to the Middle East or to be involved in controversy. Embarking on this journey would lead me to challenge the giants of archaeology, history, religion, and culture. What was ultimately uncovered would test the very foundations upon which these giants stand, and it would bring me personally to a place of uncertainty and apprehension. What I've found might shock and surprise you. I'll let you decide if it changes you as it has changed me.

My name is Timothy Mahoney, and I'm a filmmaker from Minneapolis, Minnesota. As a young adult, I thought I would become a musician, not a filmmaker. I have a good ear for music and can play many stringed instruments. In high school this led me to play pedal steel guitar with folk rock bands. It was during this time I started songwriting. Many of my songs told stories, and I loved a good story.

In 1985 I began making TV commercials and corporate videos. They paid the bills but didn't fully satisfy my creative interests. What I really wanted to do was to make films that explored the big questions I had about the world: Where do we come from? Is what we've been taught to believe really true?

I guess it was only natural that I would become a documentary filmmaker because true stories had much more power and influence over me than fiction. I had been raised as a Christian and remember hearing amazing stories from the Bible as a child, and I believed them. But as I grew older, I was challenged to lose those beliefs. I often wondered if there was any evidence to support them. After all, the stories were so fantastic.

Now I just wanted to know the truth.

In 2002 I launched my journey to investigate archaeology related to the stories of the Bible. I was excited to start a new project that was at the core of so many of my own questions. I was to film amateur Exodus explorers in the Sinai Peninsula as they searched for the route the ancient Israelites might have taken after their Exodus from Egypt. The prospect of uncovering events from the distant past fascinated me. As I set out to interview professional archaeologists about this search, I was surprised when one of them said, "What's the point of looking for the route if the Israelites never existed in Egypt in the first place?" I couldn't shake that remark. It troubled me. Like so many people, I didn't realize that the events of the Exodus were for the most part dismissed by mainstream scholars. Whether I liked it or not, I would have to be true to my nature and delve into this topic, searching for answers to this 3,500-year-old mystery.

II. A Brief Overview of the Exodus Story

The story of the Exodus began with Abraham.

The Exodus is one of the most important and foundational stories in the Bible. From the twelfth chapter of Genesis onward, this early history of the people of Israel occupies the first six books of the Bible, and establishes the basis for every book that follows. These stories are about a family of shepherds, Jacob and his 12 sons, who were descendants of Abraham. Jacob's name would be changed to Israel, and that is why his descendants were called the "children of Israel," the "sons of Israel," or "Israelites."

Joseph, the great-grandson of Abraham, was Jacob's favorite son. He was sold by his jealous brothers to slave traders who took him down to Egypt. There, in an extraordinary turn of events, he helped the people of that land prepare for a coming famine by interpreting the dreams of Pharaoh. Because of his insight, which he credited to God, Joseph was made a ruler over all of Egypt.

The ancient lands of the Exodus.

During this famine, Joseph's father and brothers were allowed to move from their homeland of Canaan and freely settle in Goshen, the best land in Egypt's Nile Delta. Over time, the descendants of this family grew so numerous that they threatened the Egyptians. Consequently, they were enslaved by a new pharaoh who did not remember Joseph, and for generations they toiled, making bricks from mud and straw.

The biblical account says that at this time God chose a man named Moses to deliver the children of Israel out of their bondage. Moses commanded Pharaoh to let the people go, but Pharaoh refused. God then instructed Moses to confront Pharaoh with a series of plagues. After the tenth plague Pharaoh finally let his slave force go but later changed his mind and pursued Moses and the Israelites with his army, trapping them at the sea. The Bible next describes how God miraculously parted the waters and created a pathway for the children of Israel to escape through the sea on dry ground. As the Egyptians followed, God destroyed their entire army by closing the waters at just the right time, drowning them in the sea.

The story in the Bible continues by telling how God led Moses and the Israelites across the desert to a mountain where he met them and gave them commandments to live by. At that mountain God also established a Covenant (a formal promise) with Moses and the Israelites to make them his people and to lead them in their return to the land he had promised to their forefather Abraham. Despite God's promise, the Israelites were afraid of the inhabitants of the land and their many high-walled cities, so they wandered in the desert for 40 years until that generation died. This left the next generation, led by Joshua, to enter and conquer the Promised Land of Canaan. This Promised Land would become known around the world as the Holy Land, and at its center resides the ancient city of Jerusalem, which means "City of Peace." Ironically, for thousands of years this city has known little peace.

Jerusalem, the center of the Holy Land.

III. The Journey: From Idea to Film

I knew before I ever started this film that the story of the Exodus is the basis for Judaism and a central pillar of Christianity. Perhaps many Christians and Jews would be surprised to learn that Islam also accepts the Exodus as a historical reality, since it is mentioned several times in the Koran. What I didn't know in 2002 is that it would be a 12-year process of interviewing both experts and amateur explorers before things came together and I could finish the film.

I would make numerous trips halfway across the world to explore whether there was *any* hard evidence for the Exodus at all. I thought it best to begin the investigation by going to Egypt. I had been planning several months in advance, but a week before leaving, the American production company I had hired pulled out. It was just seven months after 9/11, and being cautious, they decided not to get involved.

A few days before I was to leave for Egypt, my wife, Jill, the mother of our four children, came and stood in front of me. Taking both of my hands in hers, she looked up. Her face was serious.

"Are you 100 percent sure you should be doing this?"

"What do you mean?" I knew all too well what she meant.

"I need to know in my heart that this is something you are absolutely convinced you have to do. Because if something happens to you, I can't have any doubts."

"Yes, I'm convinced."

"All right," she said. "I can live with that."

Although I was certain I should be doing this and had purchased the tickets, I really wasn't sure how our team would be navigating in a foreign country without the aid of an in-country producer. Fortunately, just a couple days before we left, an Egyptian film company became interested in the project and agreed to meet with me once we arrived in Egypt.

We landed in Cairo late in the evening. It was after midnight before we got through customs. Even so, I was up early the next morning. The hotel we were staying at was in the middle of the city near Tahrir Square. As I stepped out of the elevator into the lobby, I

During the 12-year investigation Mahoney gathered information in Egypt, Israel, and around the world.

saw businessmen from all over the Middle East moving about. Some wore suits and some were dressed in the traditional robes of their country. Today we were meeting with the new production company, so my crew and I went outside the hotel to wait for our ride. The doormen were military personnel who also served as security for the location. From the steps I could see the city was alive with taxis, bicycles, trucks, and people weaving their way through busy intersections.

Our driver finally arrived and whisked us by van through this bustle of traffic and humanity. After ten minutes he turned off the main boulevard into a Cairo neighborhood of narrow streets. We wound our way past playing children, women dressed in black, and shops with their doors flung wide open. We finally stopped in front of a white stucco building. Getting out of the van, I heard for the first time the call to worship from a local mosque. I hesitated for a moment and questioned if I should really go through with the filming. The world was in a crazy place at this time, and I wasn't sure whom I could trust.

Dr. Lennart Möller, Swedish DNA research scientist and author of "The Exodus Case".

We climbed a steep flight of stairs to their offices. I stepped through the doorway into a large dark room filled with smoke, streaked by shafts of light streaming in through the blinds. It was surprisingly cool inside. A ceiling fan lazily stroked the air. As we sat at a table, my host smoked his cigarette, his fingers relaxed, his palm held upright like some old European film star. I told him why I was there, that I was searching for the stories of the Bible.

He smiled. "Of course. No problem."

I was assigned two field producers, both with the name Muhammad. We became friends. They said I was quite different from the Americans they had seen on TV shows. We laughed, and I told them, "Don't believe everything you see on TV."

This first encounter taught me a lot about people who come from a culture other than my own. It also taught me how similar we all are. My new Egyptian friends were invaluable in helping me secure interviews, location permits, and additional crew. Our goal during the next month was to film many of the key archaeological sites in Egypt and the Sinai Peninsula that related to the stories of the Bible.

I made this first trip with Dr. Lennart Möller, a DNA scientist from Stockholm, Sweden. Beginning in 1995, Dr. Möller had pursued evidence for the route Moses and the Israelites might have taken after leaving Egypt. Eventually, he included all of this research in his book *The Exodus Case*. Möller's approach was to go to the original sources and see for himself the locations, artifacts, and documents pertaining to the Exodus story. Even though he knew others had already made various interpretations of these findings, as a scientist he wanted to look at the data with fresh eyes and form his own conclusions.

Although I was intrigued with Möller's work, I also wanted to understand what archaeologists believed about these matters. As the years of working on this project went by, I became increasingly aware of the significance and complexity of the Exodus. The story was massive, spanning almost 500 years, and covering a geographical region that includes parts of six modern countries: Turkey, Syria, Israel, Egypt, Saudi Arabia, and Jordan.

Modern borders in the Middle East.

The question of the historical reality of the Exodus is very complicated, and I can't tell you how many times I wrestled with the investigation process and the multitude of filming challenges associated with it. I felt very alone because in the beginning of this project, I only had my family, my executive producer David Wessner, and the Swedish explorer Lennart Möller as encouragers. Early on, I played all the parts – director, producer, writer, and editor – and the size of the venture at times intimidated and discouraged me.

One year I bought a camping trailer just to get away and think. I spent almost every weekend from early May to mid-November camping in the north woods as a means of escape. As I looked into those dying campfires late into the night, I pondered how all of this would play out. Would I ever be able to finish the film? All I knew then was that I had a passion to explore this story but I didn't have all the pieces to tell it. I didn't even know where to find them.

There is a popular movie, *The Karate Kid,* where a handyman/karate expert (Pat Morita) teaches a young bullied boy (Ralph Macchio) lessons in karate and, more importantly, lessons about life. The student thought his master's style of instruction was strange because it involved waxing the karate teacher's car. Wax on with one hand and wax off with the other. Frustrated by this continual repetition, the young student didn't understand that he was building the stamina and coordination for karate competition.

As the years progressed, I often felt that I too was involved in fruitless repetition. All I was doing was amassing numerous theories and ideas, each in conflict with the others. There was controversy over the date of the Exodus, disputes over the interpretation of archaeological finds, and competing theories about where all the events took place. Then there was the wide division of religious and philosophical ideas about what it all means and if it's even right to look for evidence of these stories of faith in the first place. Some people maintained it is impossible to find traces of the Exodus after 3,500 years. Whether it was expert archaeologists, historians, religious leaders, or just interested friends – everybody had a different opinion on most of these issues.

Untangling the web seemed hopeless. It was wax on, wax off, wax on, wax off. I didn't see how it all connected, and I didn't have a framework to organize the information. But now in hindsight I can see that I was being trained in a broad way, and that all those theories and ideas have become vital to the project.

Eventually, I was able to build a team of talented people who also shared a similar drive to investigate the Exodus story. Typically, films and television programs don't cover the subject matter very extensively because they might lose their audience. But we knew we had to risk digging deeper into this topic if we ever hoped to find any real solutions. And this would mean more time and money without any guarantee of a finished film or a successful outcome.

As we examined the subject more closely, we gradually understood the issues surrounding the Exodus and were able to connect the dots. It was challenging to expand the research to such a large scale. The process became more and more unwieldy, but that's what my instincts were telling me to do. We needed to take on more, not less, and hear from a broad spectrum of experts because no one person could know everything. Often when we talked with someone new, we uncovered another piece of the puzzle, and that gave us hope that we were making progress. Sometimes it took a while to recognize the importance of something we had found, but the mosaic continued to grow and come to life with each additional bit of information. One pivotal moment came when our team, following the suggestions of some of the scholars we interviewed, first considered the possibility that the Exodus occurred much earlier than most people would imagine. When that new idea was kept in view, an extraordinary pattern of evidence began to emerge from the archaeology and writings of ancient Egypt and Canaan:

An Egyptian palace and tomb that fit the story of Joseph in a remarkable way.
An Egyptian slave list with Hebrew names that seem to come right out of the Bible.
An Egyptian scribe's account of chaos and trouble that bears an uncanny resemblance to the plagues of the Exodus.
And evidence that the walls of Jericho fell down just as described in the biblical account.

Were these the remains of the actual events recorded in the Bible? Throughout the pages of this book you can read about these and many more amazing finds. You can determine for yourself if they hold any promise for solving this age-old question.

Over the years our team would shoot over 1,200 hours of footage, take thousands of still photographs, and recreate several 3D digital models of biblical cities based on actual dig surveys. We gained access to old maps and early archaeological field books. But most importantly, I was able to travel extensively and film over 50 in-depth interviews with leading scholars, archaeologists, and Exodus explorers in the United States, Europe, North Africa, New Zealand, and the Middle East. These rare and priceless interviews joined all the other content to create an invaluable resource library. This process of gathering information continues today.

The result of all this research became the feature documentary film, *Patterns of Evidence: The Exodus.* It still amazes me that this project developed into one of the most comprehensive investigations of the Exodus ever filmed. I am not going to suggest that this endeavor got everything right or exhausts all theories and information, but I believe it does present enough substantial patterns of evidence to be worth serious consideration. So let's begin.

I: Asking the Big Question

The Exodus story tells the origins of the Jewish people, and over the centuries its themes of liberty and freedom have universally resonated among people from around the world. What I wanted was an honest conversation with those who cared about this story, as well as with those who dismiss it. To do that, I would hear from archaeologists, Egyptologists, and historians, along with current cultural and political leaders.

Some would be sympathetic, others would be more skeptical, and some would ridicule the very idea that there was any historical truth to the stories of the Bible. All these viewpoints were crucial to my inquiry and helped me consider one of the biggest questions:

Did the Exodus out of Egypt really happen?

I decided to create a setting where I could film a lively debate, and asked the popular radio talk show host and film critic Michael Medved to participate in these debates. Medved is Jewish and believes that the Exodus is "one of the most influential and important stories in all of world history." My first introduction to Medved was watching him from my living room as he co-hosted *Sneak Previews,* a weekly movie review show on PBS. I think many aspiring filmmakers watch such shows, hoping that someday their own film will be the one positively reviewed.

I also knew that Medved had moved on in his career to host a national radio talk show where he fairly and amiably debates cultural ideas with a wide range of people. I think my relationship with him started when he came to host his show live at the Minnesota State Fair. It was during one of those visits that we connected, and he agreed to help me with several interviews and to narrate an early version of the film.

I. Vincent Bugliosi

The first person I had Medved debate was Vincent Bugliosi, an attorney and author, best known for prosecuting cult leader and serial killer Charles Manson, and for co-authoring the book *Helter Skelter.* Coincidentally, Bugliosi grew up in my home state of Minnesota. I was interested in his latest book, *Divinity of Doubt: The God Question.* As an agnostic, Bugliosi has a unique perspective: he doesn't deny the existence of God like an atheist; he's just not sure of God's existence and has many questions. I was very happy when he decided to participate, because he represents a segment of people out there who have the same questions.

Bugliosi is an interesting mix. He is a high-powered prosecutor but still very approachable. His Minnesotan friendliness showed through. He told me that email doesn't work very well for him since he never uses a computer.

"How can you not use a computer?" I asked.

"I don't need one," he replied. "I still write all my books out in longhand with a pencil and paper."

We met in a studio in Los Angeles, California. I seated Medved and Bugliosi on tall stools across from each other in front of a round table. I was looking forward to them exploring the big question. The lighting was low. Three cameras were rolling, and I pushed the intercom. "Ready, everyone. Action."

Vincent Bugliosi claims there is no evidence for the Exodus.

With enthusiasm Medved looked across the table. "Vincent Bugliosi, in your fascinating book, *Divinity of Doubt,* you write about aspects of religious faith that you think are frankly preposterous, and other aspects of religious faith that you take more seriously. The Exodus is obviously one of the core events of the entire biblical narrative. The existence of Israel, of the Jewish people, of the Jewish religion is based upon it. Did it happen?"

Bugliosi replied, "Well, as you know, there are many prominent people as well as I who say it did not. Egyptian Egyptologist Zahi Hawass, as recently as 2007, said that there is no evidence, no archaeological evidence of the Exodus, that it's just a pure myth."

Medved returned to his side of the argument. "Whether you choose to believe in it or not, the Exodus, and so much else in the Bible, is presented as history. That's the way the Bible lays it out. Now history may be all true, it may be all false, or it may be some combination of the two, but you have to acknowledge that it's presented as history. And in the Exodus story, it's presented as history with a purpose to give a very clear example – a flagrant, flamboyant example – of God intervening in human affairs, intervening in the destiny of nations, plucking a nation out of slavery, and through various miraculous interventions, bringing that nation to a very different place both spiritually and physically, and transforming it utterly."

Medved then asked, "Vincent Bugliosi, you don't believe, do you, that there is any reason to disbelieve – to disregard the Exodus story?"

Bugliosi said, "No, absolutely not. No, I think there's circumstantial evidence going in both directions. Neither side, the theists or the atheists, meets its burden of proof; so almost by default, the rational position to take is 'I don't know,' and, by the way, if Einstein said, 'I don't know,' I don't feel too bad saying that, because he was a rather bright guy."

Bugliosi then put the focus on the evidence. "I'm not a scholar on the Exodus or an authority, but apparently Egyptian historical records make no reference to a Jewish settlement around the time of the Exodus, which would have been around 13th century BC. They can find no reference to the ten plagues or to Pharaoh and his entire army drowning in the Red Sea. There are some problems, obviously, if they don't. Because the entire legitimacy of the Old Testament is in question if the Exodus – which is the central event, I think you'll agree, of the Old Testament – did not take place."

Medved agreed. "Absolutely!" Then he probed. "Is it significant in your life if God exists or not? Does it make a difference to you, Vincent?"

Bugliosi admitted, "Well, it would make a difference. Of course it would, of course it would. And I would like to believe, but the evidence is just simply not there."

II. Christopher Hitchens, Richard Dawkins, and the New Atheists

There are also people who do more than just question the stories in the Bible. They openly ridicule them. Among these skeptics is a group of best-selling authors and popular speakers known as the New Atheists, who have become very aggressive in arguing against the validity of the Bible because of the lack of evidence for major events such as the Exodus. They see religion as a delusion and mock the claim that the Bible could be a record of God acting in history. They go further to argue that it is foolish and harmful to believe in the biblical stories.

One person from this group I had wanted to interview but couldn't was the late author and journalist, Christopher Hitchens, who was Jewish. In his book *God is Not Great: How Religion Poisons Everything,* he said the following: "It goes without saying that none of the gruesome, disordered events described in Exodus ever took place. Israeli archaeologists are among the most professional in the world, even if their scholarship has sometimes been inflicted with a wish to prove that the 'covenant' between god and Moses was founded on some basis in fact. . . . These men regard the 'Hebrew Bible' or Pentateuch as beautiful, and the story of modern Israel as an all-around inspiration, in which respects I humbly beg to differ. But their conclusion is final, and the more creditable for asserting evidence over self-interest. There was no flight from Egypt, no wandering in the desert (let alone for the incredible four-decade length of time mentioned in the Pentateuch), and no dramatic conquest of the Promised Land. It was all, quite simply and very ineptly, made up at a much later date." [1]

Earlier in the same book he wrote that "God did not create man in his own image. Evidently, it was the other way about, which is the painless explanation for the profusion of gods and religions, and the fratricide both between and among faiths, that we see all about us and that has so retarded the development of civilization." [2]

Another popular member of the New Atheists is evolutionary biologist Richard Dawkins. In a speech given at the Edinburgh International Science Festival in 1992, he said, "Faith is the great cop-out, the great excuse to evade the need to think and evaluate evidence. Faith is the belief in spite of, even perhaps because of, the lack of evidence." In his book, *The God Delusion,* Dawkins critiqued the Bible: "To be fair, much of the Bible is not systematically evil but just plain weird, as you would expect of a chaotically cobbled-together anthology of disjointed documents, composed, revised, translated, distorted and 'improved' by hundreds of anonymous authors, editors and copyists, unknown to us and mostly unknown to each other, spanning nine centuries." [3]

Some might want to dismiss these claims against the Bible as extreme. But the provocative reality is that some of the arguments of Hitchens, Dawkins, and other New Atheists against the Bible's historical credibility seem to be supported by the findings of modern archaeology. Are these New Atheists right in saying that the stories in the Bible are just a myth? Now I wanted to hear what other important scholars had to say concerning the archaeological findings.

III. Kenneth Kitchen

In the spring of 2002, during a layover outside London, my producer Rick Garside suggested we contact the British Museum, which has one of the largest repositories of Egyptian artifacts in the world. Even though it was not a part of our plan, we devoted the early morning to filming this impressive collection. The afternoon was spent at an antiquities dealer off a London bystreet, where Dr. Möller and our crew filmed rare and ancient maps that have caused speculation about the geography and the routes of the Exodus. Often these detours have yielded priceless and amazing interviews and footage. Although exhausting at times, they have been well worth pursuing and have inspired a personal filmmaking principle: take advantage of unexpected opportunities while shooting the film.

Upon learning of the project, Nigel Cooke, an acquaintance and film producer, suggested he could arrange a meeting with one of the leading Egyptologists in the world, Professor Kenneth Kitchen from the University of Liverpool. Professor Kitchen wrote the book on Egyptian chronology for the Third Intermediate Period. His work has gathered and synthesized all data relevant to this period of Egypt's history. Mainstream scholars follow his established standard for their dating of Egypt's past.

Cooke told me that if we'd travel four hours to Liverpool that very evening, Kitchen would be able to meet in the morning. Although completely spent from traveling, I knew this was a rare chance I couldn't pass up. I figured Kitchen would know more than most and get me started on the right path. Professor Kitchen is unique in that he is both an Egyptologist at the very top of his field and also an evangelical Christian who vigorously defends the historical reality of the Exodus. Today most Egyptologists ignore the story altogether.

It was a beautiful sunny day when we arrived at the University of Liverpool, but inside the Garstang Museum of Archaeology where I met Kitchen, it was dark. I usually prefer it that way because then I can light it just the way I like. I positioned Kitchen in the center of the room. Behind him were two upright Egyptian sarcophagi. They set the mood perfectly.

I put forward the big question. "Did these stories really happen? Just how reliable is the book of Exodus?"

He replied in his very British accent, "I think the story of the book of Exodus, as we have it in the Hebrew Bible, is a very ancient story, written long before the surviving manuscripts, and the record that is preserved is likely to be a very reliable record. At points where we can check it against evidence from ancient Egypt and other aspects from the ancient world, it is very consistent. It fits very well with the period late in the second millennium BC (2000 - 1000 BC), and I see no reason to suppose that it was composed at a later date."

I was curious. "Is there evidence that there was an Exodus?" I wanted to know because I had heard that there was an absence of Egyptian records supporting what would have been a big event in Egypt.

Kitchen responded, "Egypt doesn't record an Exodus for the simple reason that the Exodus was a defeat. First of all, the literary records, the papyrus records, don't exist anyway. Secondly, no pharaoh ever records a defeat. That would bring them disfavor with the gods and then the people of Egypt. Pharaoh is always shown in a victorious pose, charging his chariot, defeating the enemy, tramping them down, sacrificing them before the gods. He is never shown losing his people in the sea, cowering back in amazement. He is never shown in defeat. You're never going to get a military record of a successful Exodus out of Egypt to the pharaoh's detriment. That would never happen. You're not going to get an Egyptian reference to the Exodus on the temple walls."

The British Museum in London houses some of the greatest artifacts from ancient Egypt.

Professor Kenneth Kitchen, University of Liverpool.

"What about any records that might be speaking about Moses or the early Israelites from the area where they were said to have lived – the Nile Delta region?"

"The Delta is made of flat mud. It produces no stone and it rots papyrus. Put a cigarette pack in the Delta, and it would be gone in a year or two in the water and the mud. That's true of papyrus as well. At one time, if there was such a man named Moses, he would feature in the documents. But we have no archives at all from Egypt in this period from the swamps of the Delta. It's all gone."

For thousands of years the banks of the Nile and the Delta basin have been covered with an annual flood. Kitchen then told me about a lecture he had heard by another professor of Egyptology who estimated that 98 percent of Egyptian papyri have been

Papyrus

The ancient Egyptians used papyrus for writing material. They made it from a common shoreline plant of the same name.

Below: Remains of a papyrus in the Brooklyn Museum.

destroyed by natural causes. "Three thousand years of administration, history, religion, everything else have disappeared into the mud or been eaten by the ants in the desert, and if only two percent survived, it is not coming from the Delta."

Annual flooding on the Nile River.

If what Kitchen was saying is true, then any written records in papyri that might have pointed to the Israelites' existence in the Delta have been lost due to the flooding of the Nile. This could be another logical reason why no such records for the Exodus have been found in Egypt's history, but it was not entirely satisfying because it still left me without evidence for the Exodus. The Bible states the early Israelites were given the land of Goshen where they lived and raised their flocks and herds. I asked myself, *Could there be physical evidence of their presence, such as the remains of pottery, homes, tools, and graves, in this area?*

IV. Hershel Shanks

Early on in my investigation I also met Hershel Shanks, the founder and editor of the *Biblical Archaeology Review* magazine. Shanks is another knowledgeable person in the field who is sympathetic to the historical reality of the Exodus. I met him at his lovely historic home in Washington, D.C. Sitting in his parlor, I asked, "How did you get interested in the Bible?"

He smiled. "I went to graduate school and law school, and I was curious about the Bible. So I joined a little group, and we would meet regularly and discuss it. Different people would take different viewpoints. I took the archaeological viewpoint. So that's how I got into it. A very amateur way. I never took a course in college or graduate school or law school in archaeology or in the Bible. But in this group I started reading the Old Testament, the Hebrew Bible, and from that I took a television course in the New Testament, which I had not read. That's the background that I had."

"What happened next?"

"My wife and I spent a year in Israel, and I got into the archaeological community there and wrote a book about Jerusalem while I was there. It got rave reviews in the *Jerusalem Post,* so I was off and running. That's how I started *Biblical Archaeology Review,* as a kind of an avocation."

"How long have you published?"

"Well, it's almost 30 years. A long time."

"You've had quite an education."

Shanks nodded. "I should say that I have learned about the Bible and archaeology from the greatest teachers in the world."

I took a risk and asked, "Is biblical archaeology a credible field?"

Hershel Shanks at his home in Washington, D.C.

Shanks replied, "I think there is a divide among professionals. Among some of them, biblical archaeology has a bad name. They don't like it. They think it's nonprofessional. They think it has a history of some scholars trying to use archaeology to prove the Bible, which no archaeologist does today. Then there are others, of whom I am one, who are very interested in the Bible and who want to know what illumination we can get about that text from archaeology. Archaeology provides a context. It shows how people lived and what they did and their motives. And it enlightens the texts. Now it doesn't prove or disprove the text very often. It is very rare that you would find a one-for-one correspondence between archaeology and the Bible."

"Is the Bible myth or a true historical account?"

Shanks answered immediately. "There is history, I believe, in the book of Exodus. There are many miracles in Exodus. Now, whether you accept these is a matter of faith. Archaeology cannot prove or disprove a miracle. That depends on things that aren't subject to rational inquiry. So I put that aside because archaeology can have nothing to say about these miracles, whether they happened or not."

He went on, "Some scholars do say that the Exodus, as a whole, is a myth. I think they are throwing out the baby with the bath. It's a gross exaggeration. It really is an example of a violation of a well-known principle, and that is that the absence of evidence is not the evidence of absence."

What Shanks said caught my attention. He acknowledged the principle that the absence of evidence doesn't prove that an event didn't happen. The absence of evidence just means that nothing's been found or recognized yet.

He continued, "The people who say that the Exodus is a myth don't depend on archaeology very much. What they are really saying is that if you look at this story, it is the kind of legendary account that people construct to explain their origins. It's because of the genre, not the evidence. There's no evidence that conflicts with the Exodus, but it's legendary, more than mythical, I think, and I really don't have an answer to this. We do have a lot of legends, or myths if you wish, about foundations and creations of people, but this is the only one that traces our origins back to slaves, not to princes and kings but to slaves. This gives it a ring of truth, and I'm not ready to throw this out."

"So what do you think was the reason they told the story of the Exodus?"

"The purpose of the book of Exodus is not to write a historical account. It is to tell a theological account of God's intervention in history. Now, some of the details, I believe, are historical, and I believe archaeology can make a contribution toward understanding this history. Can we prove it? No! Can we disprove it? No! But what we do know from archaeology is that the basic story is a very plausible one."

Shanks had pointed out that, although some people completely dismiss the Exodus as mere legend, they have no physical evidence to support those claims. But from my perspective as an outsider looking in, I felt Shanks as well wasn't really providing significant detail or tangible evidence for examination. I would need to continue the search.

V. Jim Phillips

Finding experts to interview near my home in Minnesota was rare. One of the closest was seven hours away in Chicago. I went to see paleoanthropologist Jim Phillips, a curator at Chicago's prestigious Field Museum of Natural History. Although Phillips' specialty is anthropology, his early training was in biblical archaeology.

Jim Phillips at the Field Museum in Chicago.

The location we chose for filming was in the archaeology department of the Field Museum. In the high-ceilinged workroom we were surrounded by shelves of artifacts and pottery shards in various stages of being cleaned and assembled.

Sitting across from Philips, I asked, "Has your work affected your beliefs?"

He folded his arms and leaned back. "My work, as far as I can tell right now, has really not affected my belief system in the sense that I am Jewish. I always have been Jewish, I always will be Jewish, and I believe in the tradition of Judaism. Do I think of the Bible as the word of God? No, I don't. Do I think of stories in the Bible as having been real and as having happened? Yes, I do."

"What made you choose anthropology?"

Mount Sinai in Midian?

"My research work in anthropology was dictated by my interest in the Bible and in biblical archaeology, and I began as a biblical archaeologist the first two years of graduate school. Eventually, I started shifting back in time and now work in the time periods that are much earlier."

Phillips' main area of investigation has been the Sinai-Levant Basin, which includes Israel. He has spent a great deal of time in the areas where the Israelites might have wandered after their Exodus from Egypt.

I decided to probe him on the big question. "Do you believe that the Exodus occurred as it is written in the Old Testament – do you believe it was a miraculous event with God intervening?"

Phillips responded with a smile. "No, I don't. Do I believe the event may have happened? Yep. Sure I do. But do I believe that there was a miraculous event with God intervening? I don't believe it." He paused for a moment, looking directly at me, and said, "But I'm willing to be shown."

I appreciated his openness and thought I could be open as well. I was wondering if he thought there was any point to looking for evidence since the events happened more than 3,000 years ago, so I asked, "What do you think about trying to find the events of the Exodus in the archaeological record?"

He leaned forward in his chair, resting his arms on the table. "I am happy for the people who are trying to prove the Exodus, in the sense that it's an adventure. But it's a goal that is, in my opinion, unachievable in one's lifetime. No one else has been able to do it over the last 2,000 years. I don't know if there's any physical evidence that might even be available today – because of erosion, because of political systems, because of what's been happening over the last 3,000 or so years – that an individual would be able to use to back up completely, factually, any of the Old Testament stories."

As I sat across from him I realized that Philips was politely telling me that our search for the events of the Exodus was an impossible mission. Why could I not accept that for an answer? Why did I need to search for the truth about this matter? By this point, I had already invested a year and a half in time and resources, working on the project and trying to understand the dynamics of this story.

What had originally caught my attention was hearing about the possibility of new physical evidence found by amateur Exodus explorers. These explorers were suggesting that the Red Sea crossing site was at the Gulf of Aqaba and that Mount Sinai was located in the biblical land of Midian, the northwestern part of present day Saudi Arabia. It made me curious. I wondered, as many others did, if these amateur explorers really had found evidence for the Exodus.

So I asked Phillips, "Do you think it's strange that ordinary people could find what might be evidence for the Exodus?"

He said, "Anybody can find an archaeological site. Look in your backyard. You might find a tomb if you live next to a river in North America because that's where Native Americans were. Many archaeological sites across the globe – in fact the majority of archaeological sites – have been found not by professional archaeologists but by laypeople or nonprofessionals."

"Does this pose a problem for a nonprofessional?"

Phillips nodded yes. "Interpreting what they find is another story."

Driving back from the interview in Chicago, I reflected on all that Phillips had told

Mount Sinai in Midian

Moses met God at the burning bush on Mount Sinai during his time in Midian. References to Moses living in Midian can be seen in the book of Exodus 2:15, 3:1, 3:12, and 4:19.

me. One of the most extraordinary and significant finds in archaeology was made by a Bedouin shepherd boy. The Dead Sea scrolls, which numbered nearly 1,000 ancient documents, were stumbled upon quite by accident. Today many consider the Dead Sea scrolls the most important archaeological discovery of the 20th century. They contain early Jewish writings, including portions of 18 different copies of the book of Exodus.

This gave me hope. If a shepherd boy could find ancient texts, maybe a filmmaker could find answers to the question of the Exodus story.

VI. Rabbi David Wolpe

Named by *Newsweek* magazine as the most influential rabbi in America, Rabbi David Wolpe challenged the historical reality of the Exodus in his famous 2001 Passover sermon. I called Rabbi Wolpe sometime around 2007 to talk about his opinions on the Exodus. As I recall, he told me that his views were influenced by the work of Israel Finkelstein, the famous Israeli archaeologist.

Several years later I contacted him again, and he agreed to participate in a filmed interview with Michael Medved on the same day as the Vincent Bugliosi interview. Wolpe cleared his busy schedule and arrived a little ahead of time. Unfortunately, Medved was held up at his radio station and was running late – how late I wasn't sure. There we were, the two of us, anxious for Medved's arrival. We were sitting on a sofa, staring at the blank, celery green walls of the studio waiting room. There was an old soda pop machine against one of the walls and a little pantry at the end of the room. Perhaps this green room was an attempt to calm its occupants, but so far it wasn't working. My mind was racing, trying to think of topics related to the project without getting into the content of the interview. I wanted to keep that fresh for the filming. Wolpe had told me that he was on a tight schedule and had another meeting to get to. As he checked his phone for emails, I knew I had to do something to engage him.

"How did you become a rabbi?"

He looked up from his phone. "I've always known I would be a rabbi. My father is Rabbi Gerald Wolpe. He is a wonderful man, and I admire him very much. So I've always wanted to be a rabbi."

"So you are close to your father?"

Rabbi David Wolpe during the Los Angeles interview.

"Yes, very close."

"It must be wonderful to have a father that you can talk with and be mentored by."

He nodded. "Yes, it's been priceless to have this type of relationship. He is a very kind and wise man."

He then asked, "How about your family?"

"Well, my story is different. My parents separated when I was 11. I never knew my father growing up." I could see that Wolpe was saddened by my loss. I continued, "I really didn't see him for about 25 years."

Just then the door opened, and it was Medved. "Sorry, I'm late. I got hung up."

I smiled, relieved. "It's okay." I yelled to the crew, "We're all here. Let's do it."

I ushered them into the darkened studio to their places in front of a round, black table. I had chosen several vintage RCA microphones that had been used in radio for decades. These working props completed the "old school" attitude I was after for the interview. As I looked through the window of the control room into the scene, the atmosphere seemed perfect. I could feel their anticipation of a lively debate.

Positioned next to the engineer, I pressed the intercom. "Roll camera." I paused for a second. "Ready, Michael?" He nodded yes. This was the moment for which I had worked so hard. "Action!"

Medved smiled and began to speak. "Rabbi Wolpe, one of the things that fascinate me is, about a decade ago, you gave a sermon in your synagogue, one of the largest conservative synagogues in the country, and that sermon became hugely controversial."

Wolpe nodded. "Yes."

"What did you say?"

"I said that the Exodus certainly didn't happen the way the Bible depicts it, assuming that it was a historical event in any description. But you also have to understand that your faith isn't based on splitting seas or archaeological digs. It's based on something much deeper."

"Why did you say that?"

"I said it for two reasons. One was because I knew that these students and others would go off to college and hear people talk about biblical archaeology and comparative religion, and I wanted them to know that that was not a frightening topic. That belief was apart from what you uncover with a spade. The second part of it was, if you make a historical claim, then you have to be willing to let history look at it. What I meant to do was to try to tell people that no single fact or event was the pivot of faith. It was faith that was the pivot of faith."

Medved leaned forward. "I'm sure you heard from people who said, 'Wait a minute. You haven't considered this evidence or that evidence about the historicity of the Exodus.'"

Wolpe agreed.

Medved then asked, "Did any of those contacts lead you to reconsider your assumptions?"

"Well, they led me not so much to reconsider my assumptions that it didn't happen the way the Bible said. If you look at it scientifically, it's virtually indefensible to make the Bible's case. But I am persuaded that the Jewish people have some origin in the land of Egypt, although I also think that it is possible that the fleeing Jews from Egypt, when they came to Canaan, met up with people from the same background who were also an indigenous people in the land of Canaan from long before that. That is a possibility, but were you to ask me, 'Were Jews ever in Egypt?' I think I would put a lot of money on it

that the Jews were in Egypt."

Medved countered, "But if these are not facts, if this is a fairy story, if this is somehow fabricated, doesn't that undermine its religious meaning? In other words, doesn't that change things?"

"The extent to which the Exodus story has a historical core is very hard to say, but my deeper conviction about it is that it's a story that whether it *was* true, it *is* true. And those are two different things," Wolpe answered.

Medved seemed unconvinced. "That seems to be evading —"

Wolpe broke in. "Well, there are things that aren't facts that can be truths." Wolpe's skepticism concerning the historical reality of the Bible persisted. "The idea of the Exodus and the revelation at Mount Sinai, however you can figure it, is central to the Jewish tradition, but I think that doesn't mean that you have to believe that the Torah gives a historical account of it. I don't think the Torah is a book of facts. It's a book of meaning."

Medved paused, taken aback, and then asked, "Given that the Torah is a book of meaning and given your acknowledgement that there was almost certainly some kind of

Michael Medved pressing Rabbi Wolpe on his views about the history found in the Torah.

43

ancient Jewish presence in Egypt, then a departure from Egypt – what part of the Torah would you grant to be based upon historical reality?"

Wolpe seemed hesitant for a moment and then boldly replied, "I can't tell you. I don't know. I don't know and, although it may irk people, I don't care."

"So you're not an Exodus denier, you're an Exodus agnostic," Medved added.

"I suppose in a way I'm an Exodus agnostic, but I'm something more than that. No one would say I don't know whether God exists or not and it doesn't really matter. I'm saying, I don't know who went out, how they went out, but that's not the point. The point is not the fact of the matter but the truth of the matter. And there are endless, deep spiritual truths that we haven't succeeded completely in mining in that story, and that matters much more than whether we can find – I mean, people put so much effort in finding 'it was this sea they crossed, it was that sea they crossed' as though if they find it, it's going to give them religious meaning. But the fact doesn't give you religious meaning. It's the wrong search."

As I sat in the control room listening to Wolpe's reasons for his famous Passover message, I was not only intrigued but also sympathetic because I was raised with the understanding that faith was trusting in something even though you didn't have all the answers. However, I was also troubled because I thought that if you did believe these stories, wasn't it important to think that the events actually happened in history?

What makes something true if it didn't happen? And if this foundational story of the Bible didn't happen – which atheists, agnostics, skeptical archaeologists, and even some rabbis like Wolpe are suggesting – wouldn't that mean that the two religions of the Bible, Judaism and Christianity, are both based on a gigantic lie? ψ

II: A CHANGE OF PLANS

The Magen David, or Star of David, is a comparatively new symbol that today we often associate with Judaism. Its shape is said to represent the actual Shield of King David, or an emblem on it, but that is not verifiable.

When I first began researching locations for filming, I didn't intend to go to Israel because I didn't think that this area was a part of the story. During a marketing meeting in 2007, our team was discussing future promotional events to release what we thought was close to being a finished film about the journey that Moses and the Israelites might have taken after they left Egypt. We had a crazy idea to stage a publicity reenactment for the route of the Exodus. We were going to do this in Texas and call it the "Texodus."

One of the PR guys got up and suggested that if the film was to be promoted, it should be promoted in Israel. After all, that was the final destination of the Exodus. Dr. Möller was in the meeting, and he agreed. "Yes, Israel." It was at that moment when all discussion ceased. We just sat there for what seemed like minutes as we pondered a dramatic shift in direction. I felt a strong sense that the film was not finished. I had only been looking at the departure of the Israelites from Egypt, I hadn't given any thought to looking for evidence of their arrival in Israel. But how would I explain this to the investors? And what would we do in Israel? Where would we go? What would we film? Who could I interview to help me answer the next big question?

I went to discuss this change of direction with the executive producer of the film. David Wessner was the visionary leader of a large health organization. On the weekends he pursued music, and that is how we became friends. What we originally had in common was that we both played the pedal steel guitar. I would bring my guitar over to his home on the bay of a beautiful lake. For several hours we'd jam. I'd sing my original songs, and he with his very good ear would pick up the tunes immediately while accompanying me on the Dobro resonator guitar, slide guitar, or pedal steel. When he learned about the Exodus project, he was the first person to support it. And he would need a lot of vision and patience because the project was more than a film. It was becoming a mammoth research endeavor. By this time I had already edited an early version of the film.

David and I met for breakfast. What I had to tell him needed to be said face to face. After the usual pleasantries I got down to business. "I don't think we're done filming."

"Really? Why is that?"

"I think there is more here. I can't exactly explain it, but I think we need to go to Israel. There's more to this story, and we need to pursue it."

"Do you know what you'd do in Israel?"

"The Israelites ended up there. I'd like to ask Israeli archaeologists on both sides of the debate if there is any evidence of that. We also need reenactments of the biblical story with people that look more ethnically authentic. I can't easily find them in Minnesota. And we don't have a good desert here," I said jokingly.

He smiled. "You're right about that."

"After all, this is a story about the heritage of the Jewish people, so it makes sense to ask some of their leaders about it. And it would be a good opportunity to learn how the Exodus has impacted history."

"Well, I'm used to managing things, and this project seems to be one that keeps getting bigger."

"I know. I'm sorry. It does seem to have a life of its own. But, if we follow the leads, I think we could find answers that have never been fully considered. The film could be a breakthrough."

David doesn't spend a lot of time talking because he's usually thinking. This was one of those times. After a long pause he said, "Do what you think is best."

It was amazing the trust he gave me. This wouldn't be the last time.

Pete Windahl, our co-producer and the manager of the project, was at that same marketing meeting where filming in Israel was proposed. Pete and I were on a high school ski jumping team together, but at the time we were only acquaintances. He went to college and was interested in archaeology but pursued business instead. We met again through our children 30 years later. It was around the midpoint of this project when Pete joined the team. He loved the challenge of what we were doing and took a big risk by leaving a stable job. If I am Frodo from *The Lord of the Rings* on an impossible quest, Pete is Samwise, my faithful companion. He will do whatever he's asked to do. His strengths are his belief in an idea and his positive attitude. Pete also has the gift of finding things, people, and places – a very important gift in our business.

Within a few weeks of that planning meeting, I walked past Pete's office. He looked up from his computer and said, "You got a minute?"

"Sure."

"I think I found our Israeli production company."

Co-Producer Pete Windahl in Jerusalem.

47

"Who are they?"

"It's called Biblical Productions. It's in Jerusalem, headed by a producer, Sharon Schaveet."

"Are they good?"

Israeli producer Sharon Schaveet with Mahoney in Jerusalem.

"Yes, talented, experienced, and connected with all aspects of biblical film production in the Holy Land. They know what they are doing."

Pete was right. Biblical Productions was a great choice. Producer Sharon Schaveet and her family had lived in this region for generations. People like her who are born in Israel are known as "Sabra." Their name comes from a cactus, known commonly as a prickly pear. Like the desert plant, their persona is thorny, but on the inside they are very warm and sweet.

In Jerusalem, our team stayed in affordable and quality accommodations on the Palestinian side of the city. Looking out from the balcony of my hotel room, I thought about the trouble this piece of land has known for centuries. Below were vehicles that had their tops marked with large UN symbols, a reminder of the on-going international attempts to keep peace in the region. Apparently, UN workers also used the hotel.

"One minute. I'm just arranging some of our crew for the week."

I could see she was a woman who took authority. She could get things done. Just what I needed. Her call ended.

"Tim, it's so good to finally meet you." She was attractive and, I guessed, in her mid-30s.

"It's great to meet you as well."

She motioned for us to sit and then got right to business. "What do you want to accomplish here in Israel? Who do you want to talk to?"

I wasn't sure how to answer that question because Pete Windahl was still working on a list. "I would like to talk with Israeli archaeologists to hear what they believe about the historical credibility of the Exodus."

"Which ones?"

Again I wasn't so sure, but I knew she had filmed at different archaeological sites so I said, "I want to talk with all the archaeologists you might suggest. Oh, and also famous rabbis, and I'd even like to try for leaders like Benjamin Netanyahu, Shimon Peres, and Natan Sharansky."

She looked at me without even blinking. "Okay, I will see what I can do."

Jill Mahoney working as a production assistant during the shoot in Israel.

Nothing ventured, nothing gained, I thought. *Why not try for the impossible?* Since I had left for Israel so quickly I hadn't fully researched all the possibilities of who I might interview. I was just trying to get the rest of the story. What I didn't grasp then was that this trip would become the basis for an entirely new dimension to this ever-growing investigation.

We discussed locations, talent, and what type of historical reenactments would be needed to tell the story.

"How many camels do you need?"

I don't know," I replied.

"One? Two? Three?"

I could tell she was in a hurry to get everything moving. "I need five camels. It needs to look like a caravan."

"Five? Are you sure?"

"Yes, five. Is that a problem? Is five too much?" I paused. "How much are five camels?"

"No, it's not a problem. You can have five camels. It's not too much."

I had been in the Middle East for less than 48 hours, and already I had negotiated for five camels, a herd of sheep, one ram, one altar, a tent with fire, and bargained for a list of biblical characters, Abraham, Isaac, Ishmael, Sarah, Hagar, Joseph, and a band of Midianite traders.

We finished compiling the list of people I wanted to interview, and she sent them official requests. Much to my astonishment, over the next few weeks almost everyone on that list permitted an interview.

I. Norma Franklin

In the 1950s the biblical account was discredited in the eyes of many as archaeologists found mounting evidence that contradicted the story of the Israelites conquering the Promised Land. Particularly significant was the evidence uncovered by British archaeologist Kathleen Kenyon at Jericho, the first city the Israelites were said to have defeated. She found that there was no destruction of the city at the time the events were presumed to have happened. In Canaan, archaeologists also knew they should find a new Israelite culture moving in, along with a number of specifically named, strongly fortified cities that were then dramatically destroyed. They did not.

Noted Israeli archaeologist Israel Finkelstein and his associate Norma Franklin have been a part of these excavations, and their conclusions have led them to be very skeptical of how the Bible came to be written. Finkelstein is a huge figure in this debate, and I knew I had to include him in this investigation. I was seeking the answer to the next big question:

Did the Israelites conquer the Promised Land?

I began the day of interviews in the hill country of Israel, talking with Norma Franklin. It was springtime. As we walked along the hillside, birds chirped from a cliff above as a herd of sheep grazed peacefully in the green meadow below. Yellow flowers dotted the grass on each side of our path, and the intense blue of the sky made them more beautiful and vibrant. I noticed two large stones nearby.

"I think this is a good place to sit."

Franklin pleasantly agreed. She was very sweet and wore an attractive, wide-brimmed hat, which I'm sure she often used as a seasoned archaeologist.

I turned and said, "Tell me about your work."

"Basically, I'm an archaeologist. I deal with the biblical period. So, although we don't

Archaeologist Norma Franklin
in the hill country of Israel.

like to call ourselves biblical archaeologists, that's what I am. In the main, I deal with the 10th, 9th, and 8th century BC (900s, 800s, and 700s BC) and my real hope as far as archaeology is concerned is Megiddo, Tel Megiddo, and biblical Armageddon. I've been excavating there together with Tel Aviv University and Israel Finkelstein since 1992."

I asked her, "So was there an Exodus?"

"My easy answer to you, as an archaeologist, would be to say it didn't happen. Not in the way it's written down in the Bible. In the old days, of course, most archaeologists read the Bible as an archaeological guide to the Holy Land. We don't do that now. Everything that we know now is based on excavations, on surveys, on data."

"How do we answer those questions about the Exodus according to your work?"

"If we didn't have the Bible, we would never, as archaeologists or as Egyptologists, be able to say this happened. A mass exodus of people from one nation with a long journey of 40 years? Of course, you wouldn't have 40 years – I mean 40 years is more than a lifetime. People would have died, people would have been born, a different generation. People didn't live, necessarily, for 40 years in those days. And arriving in the Promised Land? We have no evidence of it whatsoever. But as archaeologists, we say, 'Absence of evidence is not necessarily evidence of absence.' But I wouldn't like to take a bet that we find that evidence."

I wanted to understand how Professor Franklin could reconcile this lack of evidence with her personal experience. "The Exodus, according to the tradition of Israel, is a very important event."

She nodded in agreement as she listened.

I continued, "Well, when you challenge that idea, it upsets a lot of people's understanding of how the Bible can be true." I could tell she was thinking, so I put forward a challenging question. "How do you cope with the difference between what we find in the archaeology and what is written in the Bible stories?"

A little surprised by the question, she explained, "How do I cope with the differences? Well, for me, the Bible is the Bible. I'm Jewish, and I like to sit down at a Seder meal and enjoy recounting the Exodus. But that's a tradition. That makes me who I am culturally. As an archaeologist, we do not see this happening as a one-off event. Perhaps it's a story that encapsulates many exoduses, many journeys, migrations from Egypt into the land of Israel and from the land of Israel down to Egypt of course. You have to get to Egypt first in order to come back. And we know about this historically. We see it archaeologically. There was always a link between the land of Israel and Egypt, especially the eastern side of the Nile Delta. But I don't believe there was a single event that we can call the Exodus, archaeologically or historically."

For a moment I contemplated what Franklin was saying. She was very comfortable with the tradition of the Exodus, but from her scientific point of view it never really happened as written in the Bible. I was anxious to hear how Finkelstein would expand on these comments.

II. Israel Finkelstein

The lack of physical evidence for the events of the Exodus has led Israel Finkelstein to a theory that explains how the Bible came to be written. He lays out this theory in his book, *The Bible Unearthed*, co-authored with Neil Asher Silberman. Very influential in the popular culture, their book has reinforced mainstream academia's skepticism about the Exodus by adding a missing archaeological piece. Some people look at Finkelstein as only an enemy of the Bible, but I wanted to get past this overly simplistic view and meet the real person face to face.

When I arrived at Tel Aviv University, my Israeli producer Sharon Schaveet was concerned that my interview with Israel Finkelstein might not go well. Based on her past experience, an interview with Finkelstein could be cut very short, especially if the interviewer wasn't prepared or if Finkelstein didn't like where the conversation was going.

When Finkelstein came to meet us in the lobby of the archaeology building, I have to admit I was a little nervous. I saw a tall, athletic man in his early 60s. He said, "Hello, it's good to meet you."

"It's a pleasure to meet you, Professor Finkelstein."

"I understand you've been out filming in the Judean hills."

"Yes, earlier with Norma Franklin."

He was handsome and carried himself well. My producer had told me that Finkelstein has been described as the George Clooney of Israel.

Interview with Professor Israel Finkelstein at Tel Aviv University.

53

He suggested we go off to his office to talk. I learned later that Schaveet then went into a panic, concerned that what might be discussed would end the interview before it even got off the ground. As I followed Finkelstein down the hallway I had the impression that he was planning to investigate me and the subject matter before going on camera.

His office had a high ceiling lit by fluorescents. There was a graduate student in a nearby central room rebuilding an ancient pot. His focus was intense as he carefully glued back into place one more missing piece of the massive pottery puzzle.

Finkelstein sat back in his chair. "Tell me about this project."

"Well, I've been investigating the story of the Exodus for years. I've been to Egypt and England and talked with Ken Kitchen and Jim Phillips and a number of other archaeologists."

"Good," he said.

"Since I've gotten this far, I wanted to include as many viewpoints as I could. That's why I've come to see you. Your ideas are very important to the dialogue." He seemed to relax when I shared my personal effort to understand the stories of the Bible. In our own ways we were both trying to accomplish the same task.

"How did you get started in archaeology?"

His eyes lit up. "It was very early in my career. A major part of Israel – Judea and Samaria and their territories – had reopened for the first time. During the late '70s and early '80s, I organized archaeological surveys into those areas, especially in the highlands. These areas were in the heart of biblical Israel, and we were eager to learn about the archaeology and to understand Israel's ancient history."

"Was this safe?" I asked.

"At times the political tensions in the areas made it very dangerous work. There were snipers, and one of our people was shot and killed. But we continued, and for seven years our team of volunteers walked in all types of weather, picking up pottery shards and recording the data, trying to locate where the peaks of the population were and where the population started to disappear."

"That was an amazing undertaking."

He nodded in agreement. "At that time we all believed, and rightly so, that by achieving a better understanding of the settlement patterns, especially in the highlands, we would be able to achieve a better understanding of the historical processes. The surveys helped me a lot in that they made it possible to present a different understanding of the rise of ancient Israel in Canaan. By simply understanding the settlement pattern, it was possible either to reject past theories or to present more elaborate views regarding a novel reconstruction of the events."

I would later understand just how different Finkelstein's reconstruction was from the Bible's account of these events.

When we came out of his office, laughing, my producer Sharon Schaveet was greatly relieved. Finkelstein led me and my crew to a large workroom where the interview would be held. In the workroom was a 30-foot table, scattered with more pieces of pottery and several large vases held up by frames that assisted the assembly.

The pottery room at Tel Aviv University.

Going into the interview, I remember having a very clear idea of how I should approach it. I wasn't to bring any notes. I needed to sit as close as possible and look him straight in the eyes. I was there to listen and have a respectful and meaningful dialogue. As I listened to Finkelstein, I felt he cared very deeply about finding answers for the history of the Bible. After all, he had risked his life at times to find those answers. The camera was set, the soundman had us mic'd up, and Schaveet had silenced her ever-present cell phone.

I opened our conversation. "Well, let's start with the easy questions, Israel. Why did you become an archaeologist?"

Smiling, Finkelstein said, "Oh, I can't remember anymore. I became an archaeologist because I had a very strong interest in history, I suppose, from the days of at least high school. I have always been on the side of history. My profession is history. I am a historian practicing archaeology, which means I work in archaeology, but my goal is to reconstruct history."

"Let's go to the question of the Exodus then. Did the Exodus happen?"

He kindly replied, "The way that you posed the question – which is okay, I'm not criticizing you – is difficult to answer because I usually refrain from giving a yes-no answer, black and white. I would say the following, 'Exodus did not happen in the way it is described in the text of the Bible on the background of the 13th century BC.' Okay? This does not mean that there is no germ of a memory in the text which comes from very early times."

Most scholars place the Exodus in the 13th century BC and the Israelites' Conquest of the Promised Land 40 years later. Finkelstein's archaeological surveys did not turn up evidence for a large influx of people coming into Israel during this time period, and this is one of the main reasons he says the Exodus didn't happen and the story described in the Bible is not an eyewitness account by Moses and Joshua who followed him. However, if these stories were not written by Moses, why would other writers, centuries later, tell such a tale?

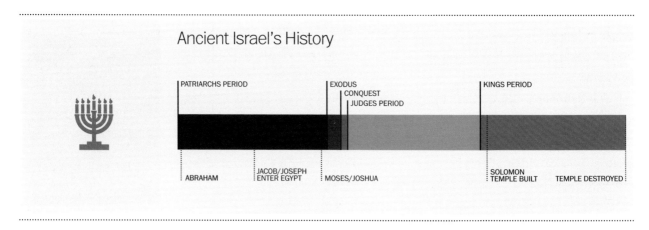

Ancient Israel's History

The main segments of history for the people of Israel from Abraham through the kings – a period of more than 1,300 years.

Etiology

An etiology is a mythical story crafted for the purpose of explaining the origins of something.

So I asked, "Why would they invent such a history of being slaves?"

Finkelstein said, "I don't think they invented history, first of all. The word *invent* cannot be used, in my opinion, regarding the Hebrew Bible because I don't think in antiquity people invented stories. There were enough stories around them to pick up, you know, and use them in order to convey what they wanted to tell the people."

I asked, "So you're saying that you think there is truth to that part of the story?"

He lowered his head but continued to make eye contact with me. "*Truth* is also a word that cannot be used. Neither *truth* nor *invent*. We are dealing with traditions. Let's say that the author of this or that part of the Hebrew Bible sits in Jerusalem. And people have traditions. Grandpa says this and Grandma says another story, and there is one tradition of this village and another tradition of that family, that clan and this tribe and so on and so forth. So they collect all these traditional stories, myths, etiological stories, and so forth, and then they sort them out because it would be naive to think that everything they collected was immediately put in writing. I mean, they looked to the stories and said, 'Well, this fits us and this does not.' As we said, they did not invent traditions.

56

They collected all sorts of stories, memories, myths, tales, you know. And they put them together in such a way that transmits an idea."

In other words, Finkelstein was suggesting that the early books of the Bible were written around 600 BC, many centuries after the events of the Exodus were supposed to have happened. These stories were constructed from memories and tales, giving the people of Israel an epic origin known as the Exodus. The authors of the Bible, according to Finkelstein, used these mainly mythical stories to control people religiously and politically.

This is strikingly different from what the Bible says about its own origins. The Bible implies that Moses was the author of its earliest books and that he was inspired by God to record historical events. So are the stories of the Bible a constructed myth or an accurate account of ancient history? Is there a pattern of evidence that favors one of these two opposing views?

The Source of the Bible

The Bible claims that the God of Abraham, Isaac, and Jacob worked through various human authors to record his message from the time of Moses onward. In other words, the Bible claims that its text is the product of divine intention. That Moses was the author of the early writings is pointed to in the book of Exodus 17:14. The book of 2 Samuel 23:2-3 says that King David's writings were inspired by God. Exodus 31:18 stipulates that the words of the Ten Commandments, recorded on two stone tablets, were a result of God writing with his own finger.

III. Ze'ev Herzog

During one of my conversations with Michael Medved, he strongly recommended that I get an interview with another famous Israeli archaeologist, Ze'ev Herzog. It just so happened that Herzog also taught at the University of Tel Aviv, which made it very convenient to film him as well. Herzog was one of the first voices in his field to openly discount the early events recorded in the Bible. In 1999 Israel's oldest newspaper, *Haaretz*, featured a cover page article by Herzog titled "Deconstructing the Walls of Jericho." It touched off a firestorm of controversy. In this article Herzog wrote that "the Israelites were never in Egypt, did not wander in the desert, did not conquer the land in a military campaign and did not pass it on to the 12 tribes of Israel."

The university halls were empty except for the occasional student who walked past me as I stood leaning against a wall, waiting to meet Professor Herzog. Given the bold statements he had made, I was concerned about what his temperament might be. How would he accept my questions when he was so strong in his declarations against the Bible's historical accounts?

After a few minutes a short man in his 60s came around the corner and smiled.

"Tim?"

"Yes."

He held out his hand. "I'm Professor Herzog."

At that moment I realized I had nothing to worry about. The man who had shaken the world of biblical archaeology was kind and soft-spoken. His once reddish hair had now faded to a light auburn. He motioned for me to follow. "Come in here to this room. Will this work out for you?"

Ze'ev Herzog at Tel Aviv University.

The room had a number of ancient pots arrayed on a large vertical frame against one side. On the other side were several work tables and chairs. It was a teaching lab with dark cabinets for storing supplies along two of the walls. At the front of the classroom was a black and much worn chalkboard. I guess I wasn't surprised to see more pots. That's one of the prizes that archaeologists get for their work. It's one of the main tools they use to date history.

"Yes, this will work very well."

"Good. I will be back in 20 minutes after you have set up your equipment."

"Great. See you then." It's always a race to get the gear set up before the subject returns.

After 15 minutes the camera and the lights were in position. Suddenly my Israeli cameraman came to me. "I've been looking all over, and these rooms only have one electrical outlet. We can't light the scene."

"What? You're kidding! How could they build a room with only one outlet?"

He shrugged.

I knew Herzog would be coming back any minute. I had to make a quick decision, and I decided to get creative with the use of reflectors and only one light.

He arrived. "Where would you like me to sit?"

"Right here would be good." I sat him in front of the array of rebuilt pots. They were dimly lit behind him. It was not what I had planned, but it would have to do. I took a deep breath, looked at the reflector I had creatively positioned a foot from Herzog's face, and hoped it would not fall during the interview. The setting inspired me to ask my first question. "The world of digging – digging up vases, digging up pots, and digging up history – is that what interested you?"

Herzog gave a little boyish grin. "Well, I started my interest in archaeology already as a youngster. It was part of my interest in the land, in our connection to the land, and I looked for the roots of our people, our nation. So from this interest I moved into archaeology, became attracted to the very digging and the exposure, the finding of new objects. This is what attracted me."

"What did your parents think about you going into archaeology? Did they want you to be a doctor or something else?"

"No, actually they were probably surprised because this is not a very popular job. But they were happy that I was going to study at the university. And later I continued in this process, so they were really pleased. No. There was no problem."

"What area have you been drawn to most in archaeology? Some people like to dig, and others like to research and analyze."

Herzog nodded. "Well, field archaeology, digging, was the most exciting part, and I liked it very much. I did almost 30 seasons of fieldwork all over the country. And then I realized that this is the easiest part because the interpretation, the analysis, the study of the objects – that is the harder one, which I have been doing for many years and am still doing. And as I used to tell my students, archaeology is about 10 percent data and

59

90 percent interpretation. And this is why I'd say it is controversial in many aspects and open to different opinions."

What Herzog was telling me was something important. If interpretation is 90 percent of the process, there will always be more than one interpretation.

"Archaeology is about 10 percent data and 90 percent interpretation."

– Ze'ev Herzog

Since he knew why I was there, I raised the controversial question. "You believe the Exodus and the Conquest are legendary stories? You don't see them in the archaeology, is that right?"

"No, we don't see them at all. We see something different. Many times people tell us absence of evidence is not evidence of absence, but the point is, as I used to say, paradoxically, the more information we have on biblical matters, the more contradictions we've found. And the evidence that we do have is very rich. Palestine, or the land of Israel, is the most excavated place in the world, in comparison to its size. And we have hundreds of sites now of different periods and millions of objects which indicate an archaeological reality. And this reality says the Israelites did not come from outside the land of Canaan. They did not conquer the land. They simply evolved from within the local community to a new phase of economic and social organization, which later developed into the state of Israel. So, the process was entirely different than described in the Bible."

Just like Finkelstein, Herzog believes the Bible was compiled and written down many centuries after the Exodus events. It seemed that Tel Aviv University had at some point reached a new consensus about how the Bible was written.

Both of us were more relaxed, so I pressed on. "What's fascinating about the Jewish legend, if that's what you like to call it, is that many Christians and Jewish people would believe that it's a historical truth. It has attracted so many people to it. I mean, there are not many people following the Greek gods, are there?"

"Right. Well, yes, I agree with that. The Old Testament became the basis for the three monotheistic periods. I published an article in Harvard about ten years ago in which I collected all of these new ideas in archaeology, about the scientific revolution in archaeology. And one of my students here, he was an Arabic Muslim from Israel, a student of archaeology. And I asked him, 'What will they tell you in your village about this article?' And he said, 'They will ask,' and a week later he came and he said, 'Everything you wrote about Moses and about Solomon, this is wrong.' I said, 'Why?' 'Because all these stories are written in the Koran, and ones that are written in the Koran, they must be true.' Well, this is fine. It is obviously a common heritage of the three monotheistic beliefs, and I very much appreciate it. But I have to believe we have to separate between belief and scientific analysis. And those are two spheres which, in my opinion, should be separate."

I asked him, "Can you take these ideas and summarize them, so I can use them more easily in the film?"

He paused for a moment and said, "The Exodus story is a very important and interesting legend about the people of Israel, but it has no real historical basis."

"How long have you felt this way?"

"In my own experience there were two phases. And as students and as young scholars, we considered the biblical stories as historical events and we tried to – as the founders of biblical archaeology science – we made our best effort to find the realities: 'Is there material evidence to exhibit and to illustrate the biblical history?' This was the case I would say until the '80s of the 20th century, when accumulation of data in many aspects

Palestine

When most archaeologists use the word *Palestine* in a geographic sense, they mean the territory of ancient Israel, or Canaan, or what many call the Holy Land. This generally includes the land around the Jordan River down to the Dead Sea and westward to the Mediterranean Sea.

of archaeology led us to what I call a revolution scientifically – to realize that what we did until then was to find excuses to explain why the material does not fit the biblical stories. And once we realized this point we said, 'We'll stop. We have to see what the archaeology tells us if we did not have the biblical history, just as we interpret periods in other lands or in other periods when we have no Bible for the period. We will interpret the history and the society which we uncover from the archaeological material.' Once we came to this realization, we concluded that the history which we find in the archaeological record is entirely different from what is described in the Bible."

After the interview we drove back from the seacoast of Tel Aviv, our vehicle making the long climb up the winding heights to Jerusalem. As I sat in the back of the van, my thoughts returned again and again to what I had just heard. It surprised me that early in their careers these archaeologists had a belief, a hope of finding evidence for the biblical account. Since they could not reconcile the evidence they found with the Bible, they abandoned their quest as intellectually futile and lost their faith in the story.

I had known beforehand that there was a lot of skepticism about the Exodus and the biblical events that followed, but after talking with these Israeli archaeologists, the weight of the strong case against the Bible was finally settling on me.

IV. Natan Sharansky

I never imagined I would actually have a chance to meet with Israel's political leaders, but then to my delight I heard that Sharon Schaveet had successfully secured my first high-level interview. It would take place in just a few days with Natan Sharansky, the Soviet dissident whose defiance of Communist leaders had won him world acclaim. His perseverance under hardship was recognized with the Congressional Gold Medal as well as the Presidential Medal of Freedom. My team and I usually prepare for weeks before going on a scheduled interview. This preparation helps me know the questions well, keep eye contact, and stay connected with the people I'm talking to. I didn't get much of a chance to prepare this time.

Sharansky's story started when he discovered that he was Jewish and wanted to know more about his heritage. Upon hearing the story of the Exodus, he longed to emigrate to

Natan Sharansky, a former Soviet dissident, at the Shalem Center in Jerusalem.

Israel. After one of his protests, he was arrested as a Soviet dissident and served nine years (including five years in solitary confinement) in the Gulag, one of the worst prisons in the world. It was his wife, Avital, who kept Sharansky's plight in front of the world, which eventually helped win his release. Under intense political pressure, the Soviets finally agreed to let Sharansky go, although they insisted that his release be included as part of an exchange for a pair of convicted Soviet spies.

On February 11, 1986, Sharansky arrived at a checkpoint bridge between the divided cities of East and West Berlin. He was told by his captors to walk straight towards his freedom. In a final act of resistance, he walked in a zigzag instead.

I went to see Sharansky and the other political leaders because I wanted to ask them a significant question:

What impact has the Exodus had on the world?

In Jerusalem, we traveled through the German quarter to a lovely three-story building housing Sharansky's office. The street was quiet except for the chirping birds that had made their nests in hidden crevices and ledges.

Sharansky was a short man, balding, with a very wide and genuine smile. His Russian accent added a colorful dimension to our conversation. Even though he was not big in stature, from what I had learned, he was gigantic in courage and principle. Sharansky is broadly acclaimed for his work on human rights, freedom, and democracy. His office wall was filled with photographs of him standing with world leaders.

I introduced the topic of the interview. "Tell me about your story and how it relates to the Exodus."

"Well, I was born in the Soviet Union. I was absolutely a dissimulated Soviet Jew because the policy of the Soviet Communist regime was to deprive people of their identity, of their religion, and of their nationality."

"So you weren't raised with any Jewish traditions or history?"

He leaned back in his chair. "We knew practically nothing about our tradition, about our history, about our holidays. The only reason we knew we were Jews was because there was official anti-Semitism. There were official restrictions put on you as a Jew. That's how I knew I was Jewish. I had restrictions on me."

"So these restrictions were just because you were Jewish?"

"Yes. Then I realized I needed to know what it meant to be a Jew. I wanted to go back to my roots, so I began to study Hebrew in the underground."

"Why couldn't you study openly?"

"Because many people had gone to prison for being Hebrew teachers. We were studying the history of Exodus and the history of our people. But it had to be in secret."

"When did you begin to protest in the freedom movement?"

"It was the moment when I realized that I believed in the history of the Exodus. In fact, what was happening to us was the continuation of the story of the Exodus from Egypt. It was at that moment that I felt myself strong enough to raise my voice against my being in that country. My being a slave, and others being slaves, held in bondage of a country we were not free to leave."

"What sorts of things did you do to protest?"

"We were organizing demonstrations, successful demonstrations of five to seven people, standing in the center of the law school with the slogan, 'Let us go to Israel,' and after two or three minutes we were arrested. I was an official spokesman of the human rights movement."

"So the story of the Exodus impacted you greatly?"

"We knew very little about our history, but it was so easy for us to imagine that situation. It was so clear to us what is the Egypt of today – the Soviet Union – and what made all these forces of KGB, who were with us practically every day and watching every minute of our activity. So I felt I was an active participant of the Exodus, and we knew, because we succeeded 3,000 years ago, we would succeed today."

"Do you think the ideas that came from Exodus have impacted the rest of the world?"

He leaned forward, putting both elbows on the desk. As he talked, he gestured with his hands. "No doubt. The principles of modern democracy go back to what was given at Mount Sinai. And many of today's activists of the movement of human rights would be surprised to know that the two basic principles, which are defining and giving legitimacy to their activity, are both coming from that Covenant. 'It is in the image of God, I am creating man,' and that's the basis of equality because we are all created in the same image of God. And, as our great teacher said, 'If you want in one line the wisdom of the Jewish law, don't do to others what you don't want done to you.' And that is the basis of today's demand for equality and democracy and human rights.

V. Benjamin Netanyahu

It was maybe a week later when I had my next interview, this time with Benjamin Netanyahu. In Jerusalem I traveled to the Knesset, the legislative branch of the Israeli government. After 90 minutes and multiple layers of security, the film crew and I were allowed 15 minutes for the interview. At the time of our meeting, Netanyahu had not yet entered his second term as Prime Minister.

I was a little nervous as we set up the cameras in his office and waited for him to arrive. When he entered, he looked me in the eye and asked me the first question in his deep baritone voice. "What's this all about?"

I told him, "I am making a very important film about the Exodus, and I believe a lot of people are going to see it!"

He nodded his head, affirming, and said, "Let's begin."

I asked him, "When did you first hear about the story of the Exodus?"

Prime Minister Benjamin Netanyahu at the Knesset in Jerusalem.

With a slight smile he replied, "With my mother's milk, I think. I mean, every Jewish child absorbs that story. It's a formative one."

"Why are these stories important?"

"The stories in the Bible are the most powerful narrative stories ever told. It's not a coincidence that this book has held the imagination of mankind for thousands of years because the stories are remarkable. The story of Joseph and his brothers, the story of the Exodus from Egypt, the story of Moses and the tablets – they are just remarkable stories. They fire a child's imagination. They certainly did fire my imagination from a very, very early age."

"Tell me about the effect the Exodus has had upon civilizations in the last 3,000 years."

"Moses was the greatest revolutionary of all time. Remember that in antiquity there were grand empires that were based on one principle: slavery. Moses challenged that twice. He challenged it by taking his people, who were slaves in bondage in Egypt, freeing them, and taking them to their Promised Land. But Moses also challenged the empires of the world by providing a moral code for mankind that said it is not the king or the emperor who decides the law. There is a higher law. These were absolutely revolutionary ideas."

It was obvious Netanyahu passionately believes that these age-old events established the heritage of Israel and a moral code for both the Jewish people and all mankind, and that this code and the abolishment of slavery were the two major legacies of the Exodus that had greatly impacted the world.

I had a feeling I was asking him the kinds of questions he did not typically encounter during an interview. He did seem to enjoy himself as he told me about his upbringing. Maybe it was his engagement and interest in this topic that made our interview go three times longer than it was supposed to, much to my delight and to the dismay of the news crew that was waiting outside his office to film him next.

VI. Shimon Peres

It was four o'clock Easter morning when our vehicles left the hotel for the Dead Sea area. We were going there before sunrise to film a series of reenactments beginning with the story of Abraham. My entire cast was Palestinian, and my film crew was a mix of Americans, Israelis, and Palestinians. We communicated in three languages – English, Hebrew, and Arabic. The only person who made me a little nervous was the local Imam who came to watch the production. I hadn't been around an Imam before, and I wasn't sure how he would respond to the biblical content of what I was filming. As the day went on, we were served hot tea by a member of the cast of Midianite traders. It was one of those moments when I looked around and appreciated how privileged I was to have this opportunity to film such an intriguing story in the Holy Land. I knew my experience was rare.

At lunch I got to know the Imam a little better. By late afternoon he was acting like my assistant director, helping guide the actors, translating my Minnesotan English into Arabic. Eventually, I got my five-camel caravan of Midianite traders leading Joseph off to Egypt to be sold as a slave. As the sun set, we captured one of the most amazing scenes in the film, a shot of Abraham tending sheep as he pondered the Covenant that God had made with him. It was around this time that we received an important approval. The former Prime Minister and future President of Israel, Shimon Peres, had consented to an interview.

It was windy the day I walked up the steps of the President's building in Tel Aviv. Warm breezes were coming off the Mediterranean Sea and blowing into the coastal city.

His office was large and very comfortable. A beautiful bookcase lined one wall, filled over the years with books, sculptures and mementos of a public life, and gifts from around the world. I could have stayed there for weeks just reading. The problem with filming is that you can make a quick mess of a nice office with lights, stands, cables, and cameras. That was the case when Peres entered the room that was now turned into a film set. But he was very gracious, and I am sure he had seen it all before.

Sometimes I like to ask the people I interview questions about their earliest memories of a topic. Their answers can help me understand what shaped them and made them the individual they've become. This personal approach worked so well with Netanyahu that I tried it again with Peres. We were both seated in front of his bookcase. "When was the first time you heard this wonderful story of the Exodus?"

He smiled. "Probably when I was three or so, when I was a child."

Curious, I asked him, "Who told you this story?"

President Shimon Peres at his office in Tel Aviv.

"My grandfather. It was educated in me, and then I went to school, and those were the first chapters we learned. The creation of the world and then the Exodus."

"What is significant about the Exodus story?"

He paused and thought for a moment. "Well, the story has several chapters. One is clearly the view of Moses. He remains, without any competition, the greatest legislator of all time. And as for the Ten Commandments that he brought down from Sinai, it is the foundation of our civilization."

When I talked with Shimon Peres, as well as other leaders, there was a charisma about them that I have rarely experienced with anyone else. I felt that presence during this first trip to Israel in 2007. I could see why these men had become the leaders of their nation. Peres had been there from the beginning of the State of Israel in 1948.

Great leadership is what Peres recognized in Moses. It was interesting to me that he saw Moses as a real person in history and thought the legacy of the Exodus had substantially shaped Western civilization. Could the success of our civilization and its underlying principles of law and democracy be evidence that the Exodus had really happened?

Peres, whose life has been filled with building a nation, then said something very simple but profound. "Take away the Ten Commandments, and we are out of business!"

VII. The Oldest Copies of Exodus

We spent our last day in Israel filming in the Negev. It was a beautiful desert location that contained numerous sites thought to have biblical connections. It was a day well spent, and yet as we drove back, I was grateful to be out of the heat and inside the air conditioned van. As the road climbed its way back to Jerusalem, out the window I saw a sign for the turnoff to Qumran National Park, the place where they found the Dead Sea scrolls, which contain the oldest known copies of books from the Hebrew Bible. Immediately my sense of accomplishment faded as I realized I had overlooked one of the most important archaeological sites in Israel. How could I have missed such an opportunity? And now it was too late; we would be heading back to the States in the morning. I felt terrible. It would be a year before I could come back to Israel and film again.

Whether this story is true or not, I still wanted to find out more about the oldest copies of the Bible. I hoped this would lead me to better understand the events that were recorded in these documents. Would they hold any clues to the mystery of the Exodus?

After I was back in Minnesota for a while, I asked Pete Windahl, our co-producer, to help me find a Dead Sea Scroll specialist. I knew I didn't want to miss another opportunity to explore Qumran. A few days later he returned with good news.

"I think I've got a good candidate for filming."

"Good. Who is it?"

"Dr. Jodi Magness, a professor from the University of North Carolina, and the author of the book, *The Archaeology of Qumran and the Dead Sea Scrolls.*"

"She sounds perfect. You know, some of those scrolls include records of the Exodus."

"Exactly." As usual, Pete had taken care of the details. "She's agreed to meet us at a vista overlooking the northwestern shore of the Dead Sea. Then we'll go on to Qumran. I've arranged everything with Sharon and the crew."

"Perfect!"

Later that year, we arrived at our first location in the pitch dark before dawn. Most people are accustomed to walking on smooth surfaces. The challenge of setting up camera gear at a rocky site like this, especially in the dark, is that it involves more stumbling than walking. Off in the distance the sun was beginning to rise over the dull mirror of the salty sea. We were standing at a vantage point that has been unchanged for thousands of years. What notable people throughout the ages have seen this same view? Did Abraham ever stand here? Or Joshua? Or King David? History says that Roman legions swept through this area on their way to destroy Masada.

Professor Magness arrived just after sunrise. We greeted each other and began to walk along the crest of the high ridge above the Dead Sea.

"It's quite amazing," I said, "that just below us is the lowest point on earth."

She smiled, knowing the curiosity of a newcomer. "It is an amazing place."

"Aren't there a number of biblical traditions associated with this region?"

"That's right. In fact, according to biblical tradition, Moses viewed the Promised Land, which he was not allowed to enter, from the top of a mountain called Mount Nebo, which is located at the northern end of the Dead Sea in modern Jordan."

After a slight stumble, I realized I couldn't continue eye contact and keep my balance. Watching my next steps, I said, "I recall that the Israelites also crossed into the Promised Land not far from here."

"That's exactly right. Biblical tradition says that the Israelites entered the Promised Land near Jericho, which is the area that Mount Nebo overlooks."

We stopped to take in the sea. "This area is not only rich with minerals, but it's also

The Dead Sea, also called the Salt Sea, is a salt lake that lies in the Jordan Rift Valley. Its main tributary is the Jordan River. Jericho is just to the north.

The surface and shores of the Dead Sea are 429 meters (1,407 feet) below sea level, the lowest land elevation on Earth. Its water is 9.6 times saltier than the ocean.

Sunrise over the Dead Sea.

rich with a lot of history."

"Yes, that's right. There are other traditions associated with the Dead Sea. For example, King David reportedly fled from Saul and hid out in this area."

Professor Jodi Magness and Timothy Mahoney walking above the Dead Sea.

The sun had climbed above the mountains of Jordan as Magness, the crew, and I went on to Qumran National Park. It was surprising – no, it was a bit shocking – to note how quickly the temperature was rising from the cool of the dawn. I was afraid that the heat would shut the camera down, and it was only midmorning. I knew we had to hurry with the interview before it became unbearable for humans and equipment.

At the far end of the park is a steep hillside filled with caves. Walking along an adjacent ridge, separated from the hillside by a valley, I continued the interview. "Tell me about the significance of the caves surrounding Qumran and their connection to the Exodus."

Magness pointed across to the hillside. "This is where the Dead Sea scrolls were found. The caves that yielded the Dead Sea scrolls literally ringed the site of Qumran, including the terrace on which the site sits, which is immediately below us here; and the cliffs behind the site contain some caves in which scrolls were found. In fact, we are overlooking now the cave that yielded the lion's share of the Dead Sea scrolls. Over 500 different scrolls were found in this cave alone."

As I surveyed the mouth of the entrance, I could see it would take a difficult and dangerous climb to reach it. "This must have been an incredible find."

"Oh, it was," she said. "In fact, the discovery of the Dead Sea scrolls has been described

Hidden in this cave for almost 2,000 years were over 500 of the Dead Sea scrolls.

as the most important archaeological discovery of the 20th century."

"They had no idea at the time, did they?"

"No, of course not. Nobody knew what they were."

"How were they found?"

She paused. "Well, the scrolls were originally discovered by accident in early 1947, when a Bedouin boy wandered into the first cave – Cave One – and found a row of tall ceramic cylindrical jars covered with bowl-shaped lids. He opened up most of the jars and found them empty. But in at least a couple of the jars he found ancient scrolls, and these ancient scrolls turned out to be the first of the Dead Sea scrolls that were ever found."

"Why are the Dead Sea scrolls significant to this story of the Exodus?"

"Among other things, the Dead Sea scrolls contain early copies of the Hebrew Bible, dating as far back as the third and second centuries BC. These copies of the Hebrew Bible include copies of the book of Exodus, which shows us that already by that time the story of the Exodus was an ancient tradition."

"Who deposited the scrolls in these caves?" I asked.

"It was the community that lived here at Qumran that deposited the scrolls in the caves. This community was a Jewish sect, which many scholars identify with the Essenes."

"What happened to these people?"

"Well, in 68 AD the Roman army destroyed the site of Qumran during the first Jewish revolt against the Romans. Some, if not most, of the people who lived here were killed at the time of the destruction of the site. That's the same revolt that culminated two years later with the destruction of the Second Temple in Jerusalem."

Scholars believe these scrolls were hidden just before the Temple was destroyed. The surviving Jewish population was scattered by the Romans. After the destruction of Jerusalem, the nation of Israel did not exist for almost 2,000 years – until 1948, when it was again recognized as a nation.

It was now 106 degrees. We were starting to cook as the sweat beaded on our foreheads but just as quickly evaporated into the desert air. It was time to take a break.

As I gazed across the valley to the hillside, it fascinated me to think that for nearly 2,000 years these important texts lay hidden in the caves above Qumran, only to be found by a shepherd boy aimlessly throwing stones in the desert. So it is possible for ordinary people to find significant evidence. As we continued this investigation, little did I comprehend what patterns of evidence would be uncovered as we reexamined the details of the story. It would be like throwing stones into forgotten caves. ♔

Opposite page: One of the Dead Sea scrolls, a collection of around 981 different texts discovered between 1946 and 1956 in 11 caves near the ancient settlement at Khirbet Qumran in the West Bank.

Professor Jodi Magness resting in the shade.

III: Investigating With the Standard Approach

I. Off to Egypt

Filming the pyramids of Giza.

As I listened to everyone I had interviewed, I could see the debate was broad and passionate and there was much at stake. But the time had now come to go to the next phase of the investigation and search for answers myself. This would mean traveling back to Egypt, the very place that the Bible says it happened. On this trip, however, I would not be focusing on the route but on the big question. Was there evidence for the presence of early Israelites and the Exodus in the legendary land of the pharaohs?

On the first day of filming we headed for the Great Pyramid of Giza. If you're going to film in Egypt, you have to film the pyramids. Some people have even suggested that the early Israelites built them during their time of slavery. These iconic wonders filled the horizon. Until I actually stood beside one of them, I didn't appreciate how massive they really are or how much ingenuity and manpower it must have taken to build them.

We filmed a distant line of camels and their riders as they might have been seen for millennia carving a winding path between the pyramids. Hot desert winds swept fine sand into our eyes and cameras as the Egyptian sun burned high over our heads. It was the first time I had been this close to the equator, and I had never before experienced the sun's rays bearing directly down on top of me.

But solving this 3,500-year-old mystery would require more than filming grand landscapes. Sensing that there was much more waiting to be told, I wanted to go deeper.

Midway down the Nile were some of Egypt's most important archaeological sites surrounding the city of Luxor. I was eager to explore the magnificent past of this land.

As I walked through the impressive temples of the Ramesseum, Medinet Habu, and Karnak, dwarfed by the pillars and walls of these massive structures, I was awed by the capability and vision of these ancient people. It's hard to imagine how they built these colossal and beautiful memorials that recorded the deeds and exploits of the pharaohs. It humbled me when I compared their staggering feats with our modern buildings made with sophisticated technology. I wondered what these temples must have looked like in their glory. Were there any connections to the stories of the Bible here?

I had come for an Egyptian perspective on the Exodus, so one morning I went to see Mansour Boraik, Director General of Antiquities at the Karnak Temple complex in Luxor. I hoped he could tell me about any evidence for the Exodus in Egypt.

Boraik had traveled by train down from Cairo the previous night. I'm sure he was tired, but he didn't show it. He was trim, I would guess in his mid-50s. He wore a light-colored shirt that looked good against his deep tan and brown eyes. I didn't know immediately how well our conversation would go, but when he started to talk, his intensity and energy were very evident. I remember his interview as one of my favorites. All of my interviews have been good, but Boraik spoke with the most passion.

Mansour Boraik, Director General of Antiquities at the Karnak Temple Complex in Luxor.

Discussing the Exodus at the Temple of Khonsu in Karnak.

To find the perfect backdrop for the interview, we walked to an area known as the Temple of Khonsu. It was several hundred yards away from the main Karnak complex. We entered through a small side opening that acted as a doorway to the inside of the temple. I followed him as he led the way to the center of the building. On each side of us were massive pillars reaching 40 to 50 feet in height and extending the length of the timeworn hall. At one end there was scaffolding along each of the pillars, and at their bases were buckets and masonry tools. Long sheets of plastic hung from the ceiling. We stopped for a moment while Boraik spoke to some of the workmen in Arabic. I could see they were just finishing up and starting to leave.

I asked, "What is happening here?"

He turned. "We are in the restoration process of this site."

"The hieroglyphics are beautiful."

"Yes, they are very impressive." The images were deeply cut into the stone, protected through the ages from the wind and sand by the interior walls of the temple. I followed him down the center of the columns through a large archway.

"I want to show you something," he said. We approached an entrance that had a metal grid door with a padlock. Taking out a set of keys, he opened the lock and swung the door open wide. I followed him into the chamber. Ambient sunrays pierced the dust rising off our footsteps in the dirt floor. The walls and the ceiling were dark as if painted with black coal. One of Boraik's workmen passed us and disappeared into another chamber. A moment later several light bulbs hanging from the ceiling flicked on to reveal more scaffolding against the far wall. He motioned. "Look up at the ceiling."

We lifted our eyes and to my amazement beheld intensely vivid paintings. Apparently, a team of archaeologists had been uncovering them from beneath the grime.

"They're wonderful. The colors are so rich," I said with awe. "What is the black material you're removing from these walls?"

Boraik explained, "Later in the history of Egypt, people lived in this temple, and this chamber became a kitchen. Over the years smoke from cooking blackened the walls and ceilings."

"So under that layer of soot was all this beauty?"

"Yes, beauty that has been hidden for centuries upon centuries."

The restoration was hard work, and I could see he was proud of it. We walked into the sunlight of a small hall near the front of the temple. The stone here was grayer than the columns, and the deep, dark cuts of the hieroglyphs were more striking in their artistry. These walls were telling the stories of ancient Egypt.

We set up the cameras and started the interview. "The events of the Exodus, would they have been recorded in Egypt?"

"Never," Boraik replied. "The Egyptians never mentioned bad things in the reliefs of the temples."

"Can we find any evidence for the Exodus in Egypt?"

He was cautious but open-minded. "Nobody knows what the sands of Egypt can tell of secrets. Maybe in the excavations we will find some evidence, but so far there's not any documented evidence about the Exodus. We know the story from the holy books only. It's mentioned in the Holy Koran more than seven times. It's in the Holy Bible. But in the ground, we have no evidence. We think that it was during the Ramesside time. But nobody can tell exactly which pharaoh was the hero of the Exodus."

I smiled at Boraik's comment that Pharaoh was the hero of the Exodus. I guess I did come for an Egyptian perspective, and I got one.

II. The Wall of Time: Understanding Egypt's History

It became clear to me that I would need to better understand the terms and concepts of Egyptology and archaeology if I was going to continue to pursue this investigation. Since I am not a historian but a visual storyteller, I had to find a way to visualize how the history of ancient Egypt related to the events of the Bible.

I first imagined a vertical device, a Tower of Time, since in the world of archaeology, time is measured by the depth of the various layers of earth. The farther down you go, the older the layer. The tower had levels like floors in a building, and we constructed a large-scale version out of cardboard boxes and set it up in one of our offices. It stood for over a year as a reminder of my clever visual aid.

When people came over, they'd ask, "What's that?"

"Oh, that's the Tower of Time," I'd proudly explain.

One day in a meeting David Wessner said, "I don't get it. I just can't seem to wrap my mind around a vertical time tower."

"Really?" I said with some unbelief.

"Well," he continued, "I think all that people really need is a simple graphical understanding, and I'm just used to seeing something like this in a horizontal presentation."

I went home a little deflated and spent the rest of the weekend thinking about what he had said. I have always tried to be open to suggestions and yet still retain strong creative oversight. By Monday, I had decided to lay out a Wall of Time version. *Who knows?* I thought. *This could work. But it has to be visually interesting. Could it be a Wall coming from the ancient past through a valley of some kind? What type of valley? A lush one? Will there be streams? No, on second thought it should be a Wall of Time through a mysterious desert valley. It will cross in front of age-old mountains that cast deep shadows across the landscape. It will be epic.*

The first attempts at putting graphics on the Wall of Time were terrible. It was a confusing mess of information. Finally, Kevin O'Neill, our creative director, suggested a much simpler approach, one that would use six bold colors to indicate the six key steps of the investigation. As we began to work with the different events on the Wall of Time, I started to see how simply and effectively it displayed complex archaeological ideas.

In its final form, the Wall stretched back to the earliest moments of civilization. On the Wall's first level, I placed Egyptian history, and on its second level, the events recorded in the Bible. At the base was a timeline of absolute or BC dates, an immovable reference to gauge the events of history, with great pylons marking every 1,000 years.

Scholars who study this area of the world have created several approaches for dividing its history. Their first approach identifies the great kingdoms of ancient Egypt. Over the course of 2,000 years, Egypt experienced three of these great kingdoms, each lasting for hundreds of years. The first period was the Old Kingdom with its great pyramids of stone. Next was the Middle Kingdom, the high point of art and literature. Finally, the New Kingdom emerged with its vast empires that dominated foreign lands.

Each of these three great periods of power was followed by a dark age, a stretch of time in which scholars have found less clearly defined activity in the archaeology. These dark ages are known as the First, Second, and Third Intermediate Periods, when the power of Egypt collapsed and the nation experienced many troubles. During these times the pharaohs usually lacked the wealth and stability to build great tombs, monuments, or temples.

In their second way of defining Egypt's history, scholars break the stretch of time

Medinet Habu, the inspiration for the Wall of Time.

Opposite page: The Wall of Time with fixed dates marked on the bottom, Egyptian history on the first level, and biblical events on the middle level.

into smaller units by identifying the different dynasties that reigned over Egypt. A dynasty generally consists of generations of pharaohs from the same family. For example, Ramesses I (Ramesses the First) initiated the 19th Dynasty. Next to reign was his son Seti I, who was followed by Ramesses' grandson, Ramesses II. A total of 30 dynasties have been recognized, and each one of the three great kingdom periods included several powerful dynasties that ruled a unified Egypt, one after the other. However, in the more chaotic Intermediate Periods there could be multiple dynasties ruling at the same time in different regions of Egypt.

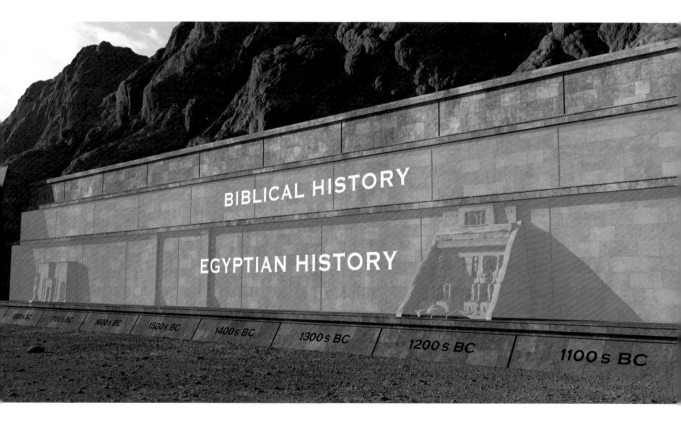

In their third approach to organizing events in history, scholars use pottery styles to classify broad periods of ancient history. The terms the experts have adopted (Stone Age, Bronze Age, and Iron Age) loosely match the materials people have taken to fashion their implements and weapons. But generally it's not stone, bronze, or iron that designates a group of finds to the proper time period. To assign a date, archaeologists instead use the different styles of the more abundant ceramic pottery that is present among the artifacts.

Each of these three approaches has unique dates attached to the various periods of history that are outlined, and early on in my investigation I was often faced with scholars who used all three of these approaches in one sentence. It took me some time to really understand what they were talking about. On top of this, it was sometimes confusing to work with the BC dates they were using because they move in the opposite direction to modern AD dates. The farther back in time you go, the bigger the BC number; with modern dates when you go farther back in time you get smaller numbers.

The terms BC and AD are used to designate the two halves of the timeline of the world's dates that meet at the birth of Jesus Christ. BC stands for Before Christ, and AD is an abbreviation of *Anno Domini*, a Latin phrase meaning "Year of Our Lord." The two halves of the timeline have recently been designated by some as BCE, for Before the Common Era, and CE, for Common Era.

Unlike AD dates, numbers for BC dates grow larger as you travel further back in time.

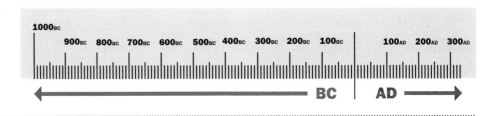

I decided that the simplest way to proceed was to primarily use the three great kingdom periods (Old, Middle, and New) to depict Egypt's history. After they were placed on the Wall of Time, I could get more familiar with their associated BC dates and with how things related to each other.

....

Below: The three major kingdom periods of Egyptian history, each followed by dark periods of weakness and instability (also known as intermediate periods). The Ramesses Exodus Theory places the date for the Exodus at around 1250 BC.

III. The Ramesses Exodus Theory

Ramesses II was a pharaoh of the New Kingdom who ruled a grand empire and, as Egypt's greatest builder king, filled Egypt with his monuments, including a city that bore his name. Millions are familiar with this famous pharaoh from the classic Cecil B. DeMille film *The Ten Commandments* (1956), where Charlton Heston's Moses confronts Ramesses, played by Yul Brynner. DeMille chose Ramesses as his pharaoh because he knew that most scholars believe the Exodus occurred during his reign. Disney's animated film, *The Prince of Egypt* (1998) continued the trend, and Sir Ridley Scott, the director of the 2014 film *Exodus: Gods and Kings*, also went with the idea that Ramesses was the pharaoh of the biblical story. In this recent version Christian Bale takes on the role of Moses opposing Ramesses, played by Joel Edgerton.

This identification of the pharaoh of the Exodus with Ramesses II is what I call the Ramesses Exodus Theory. When I was at the University of Liverpool in England, I questioned Professor Kitchen concerning the predominate view that connects the Exodus to Ramesses II. "Based on your research, when do you think the Exodus happened?"

Kitchen replied, "I think myself, on the evidence that we've got, that it would have to be about 1250, 1260 BC, in the heart of the reign of Ramesses. This is in the 19th Dynasty of ancient Egypt, the first dynasty of the Ramesses kings. Ramesses II is the biggest man in every sense of the word. He reigned for 66 years, eight principal wives, 100 children, monuments the length of Egypt. He was a big fellow."

Identifying the pharaoh is so important because it helps to determine the date of the Exodus. Since so many experts had said there was no evidence during the time of Ramesses around 1250 BC, I was puzzled why scholars like Kitchen still regarded him as the pharaoh of the Exodus.

James K. Hoffmeier, Egyptologist from Trinity Evangelical Divinity School, discusses the Ramesses Exodus Theory.

To help answer that question, I traveled to Chicago to interview Professor James Hoffmeier, one of the few Egyptologists who has written extensively on the biblical Exodus. Hoffmeier has an interesting connection to Professor Kitchen. As a child, James grew up in Egypt, where his parents worked at a mission. Professor Kitchen learned about this young boy at his church in England and began a correspondence with him that resulted in a lifetime friendship and ultimately influenced Hoffmeier's decision to become an Egyptologist.

The room where we met was part of a recent expansion at the university. It was light and bright, something you would expect in a new classroom. However, the stark fluorescent lights were not conducive to filming, so we turned them off and lit the scene with a softbox. It gave a warm, wrapping light that many cinematographers prefer. We moved the tables out and set up two chairs towards the back of the room for us to use as we talked. He wore a suit and the well-groomed salt and pepper beard of a scholar.

I asked Hoffmeier, "Why is it that so many people hold to the Ramesses Exodus Theory?"

"Key to that theory is the building of the city of Ramesses mentioned in Exodus 1:11. The Hebrews are making bricks to build this city of Ramesses or to construct the storage facilities of Ramesses," he said.

"Has this city been found in the archaeology?"

Ramesses in Exodus 1:11

This crucial verse is the foundation for the Ramesses Exodus Theory, which dates the Exodus to the time of Pharaoh Ramesses II. It says that the Israelites built the city of Ramesses, and archaeologists know that a city by that name was built by Ramesses II.

So the Egyptians assigned taskmasters over the Israelites to oppress them with forced labor. They built Pithom and Rameses as supply cities for Pharaoh.
(Exodus 1:11)

The short, 200-year period of activity for the city of Ramesses.

"This important city, which we know Ramesses II built, is being excavated even as we speak and continues to be studied. It has a very brief history. It was expanded into the world's largest city back in the 13th century BC. By around 1100 BC the city is gone. It has a very narrow history of no more than 200 years."

Scholars connect this city built by Ramesses II with the one mentioned in the book of Exodus because Ramesses II's grandfather, Ramesses I, was a very minor pharaoh who reigned about two years and is not known to have built anything significant. [4] In contrast, Ramesses II was perhaps the most famous king in Egypt's history and built a huge city named after him. Since Egyptologists have found no other city named Ramesses, most scholars believe that the Ramesses mentioned in Exodus 1:11 must be referring to the city built by Ramesses II.

Chronology

Chronology is an important science within the discipline of history. It arranges events in their proper order and assigns dates to each. A proper chronology is necessary to understand history rightly. In order to reconstruct the chronology of the BC period, historians have added the lengths of kings' reigns together, working back from the known to the unknown.

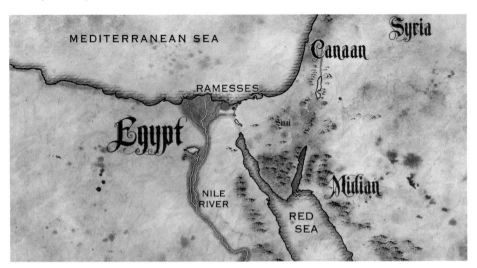

The Nile Delta region of Egypt highlighting the city built by Pharaoh Ramesses II.

Hoffmeier went on, "If this building project that the Israelites are involved in is Ramesses II's Delta residence, then we have no escape but to say that this is an important chronological marker and that the Exodus can only be somewhere in the 13th century BC."

Although I was beginning to understand why scholars have made the connection between the time of Ramesses II and the story of the Exodus, I wanted to know more. "Lately, the Bible has been greatly challenged by people like Israel Finkelstein. He claims that the 'Exodus did not happen in the way that it is described in the text.' Tell me what's going on here?"

Hoffmeier explained, "Well, there will always be those who challenge the Bible. There always have been; there always will be. And archaeologists have come to play an important role in challenging the Bible and in confirming the Bible at the same time. So we have these two competing views of the Bible. The Bible, or any text or narrative we read, requires a certain amount of interpretation or sophistication in reading. Similarly, archaeological data is not neutral. It has to be read, it has to be interpreted, and on any kind of scientific data, there are going to be differences of perspective, differences of viewpoint of how one looks at things. I can look at the same thing and see something in a positive way, and somebody else can come at it from a different perspective and see it in a negative way. So one's assumptions influence greatly how one views archaeological data."

IV. The Crisis: A Turning Point

Although Hoffmeier and Finkelstein both locate the Exodus at the time of Ramesses II, why have they reached such opposite conclusions? According to Hoffmeier, it's about perspective and interpretation. So far he hadn't given me archaeological evidence that was very specific, but if the Exodus actually happened, there should be some physical evidence of Semites, the cultural group that the Israelites were a part of, migrating down to Egypt from a land called Canaan and growing into a large population. However, there are no archaeological remains of a large group of Semites living in the city built by Ramesses II. Yet part of me was still hopeful of finding some clue of their existence in the ruins of this magnificent civilization.

Ramesses II in the Cairo Museum.

Then I heard some astonishing news. New archaeological discoveries had been made at the ancient city of Ramesses, modern Tell el-Dab'a, the very location where the Bible places the Israelites. A city and a people had been uncovered that appeared to match the biblical story. I knew I had to go to the Tell el-Dab'a dig site in the eastern Nile Delta to try to find Professor Manfred Bietak, an Austrian and one of the world's most respected Egyptologists.

My Egyptian producer Muhammad said, "No problem, no problem. We can find the site."

We left Cairo around six o'clock in the morning and made our way toward the eastern Delta. We were traveling by van through one of the villages when I heard Muhammad cry out, "Shut the blinds! Shut the blinds!" We scrambled to shut the blinds.

After a few minutes I asked, "Muhammad, is it okay that we go there?"

He said, "No problem, no problem."

"We do have permission, correct?"

He put his hands up and said, "Yes, of course. No problem, no problem. You can open the blinds now."

Ten minutes later he suddenly yelled again, "Shut the blinds and get down! Lay down on the floor."

This little exercise went on several more times, and each time Muhammad assured us, "No problem, no problem. Everything is fine. No problem."

Below:

Excavations at Tell el-Dab'a in the eastern Nile Delta.

We finally arrived at Bietak's dig site and were greeted by several soldiers who acted as security for the site. Their outpost consisted of folding chairs under the shade of a group of palm trees next to the road. The actual dig site was about a 100 yards farther off in a bright green field of waist-high grain. Next to the site was a square tent with a peaked roof, just what you might have seen in a Tarzan movie from the 1950s. On each side of the digging area were large piles of dirt. As we walked closer, I saw a long line of workers trudging up the slope of the pile, carrying baskets of dirt, some on their heads and some on their shoulders. There was an older Egyptian man who had the bearing of authority. He wore a long, dark blue robe and a white scarf wrapped around a gray cap. He carried a long, thin wooden stick. I took him to be the foreman.

Gray pipes ran along the large hole that was being systematically excavated. These pipes seemed to be attached to some type of water pump. Not too far off in the distance, a gas engine could be heard beating out a continuous *tat, tat, tat, tat, tat, tat, tat!*

At the center of the site were seven or eight archaeologists and students. Some sat on stools drawing, others were next to workers digging, and one was on her knees measuring an uncovered artifact and recording the measurements in a notebook.

It was then that I saw Professor Bietak coming out of the main tent. He looked very serious as he approached us, but I couldn't hide the huge smile on my face. "Professor Bietak. Professor Bietak," I called out over the sounds of the distant water pump. "I can't believe I finally found you."

I could tell our arrival had caught him by surprise because the closer he got, the more unhappy he looked. "You can't just come here without the appropriate permissions," he said, with an Austrian accent. "We are on a very limited time schedule at this dig site. We have only weeks until it will return to the farmer, and we can't have any distractions." In his voice I could hear impatience and frustration with the uninvited film crew that had just descended on his dig site.

"I'm sorry. We didn't mean to cause any problems." I knew I had to do something fast or Bietak would ask us all to leave. I wasn't willing to let that happen after coming so far. I turned to Muhammad. "Everyone needs to leave right now. Do you understand? Right now!"

He understood and yelled, "Everyone, back to the vehicles!"

As they left, I could see Bietak relax. I needed this moment alone with him. In a very sincere voice I said, "I can't believe I've finally met you." I think he could see my genuine excitement. It was as if I had found Livingstone in Africa.

He looked from the dig site to me and said, "You have to set up these interviews in advance. You just can't come unannounced."

I said, "Yes, I agree. And I have been sending you messages with no response for weeks."

"You must have been communicating with my office in Austria."

"Yes, we did."

"I haven't been in Austria. I've been occupied with the dig here in Egypt."

"I didn't know," I said. We were both silent. Now it was my turn to look off into the dig site. It had taken an awful lot to get there. All I could do was simply plead my case and trust that he would be reasonable. "Since I was here in Egypt I thought I would try to find you."

Bietak repeated, "These type of things need to be arranged."

Professor Manfred Bietak, Director of the Austrian Archaeological Institute in Cairo, at Tell el-Dab'a.

"Yes, I understand." I didn't say anything after that. I just looked around the site. There they all were – the archaeologists, the workers, the pottery shards piled in baskets, and the outlines of a dwelling emerging with each scrape of the trowel. I couldn't leave now. I looked up at Bietak and said, "Well, now that I am here and have come from such a far place, could I at least ask you a few questions on film about what you have found?"

He paused, thinking for a moment. Then he said, "Yes, I suppose that would be fine. But only for a few minutes."

"Thank you, Professor Bietak. We'll respect your time."

I knew that this interview was terribly important to the investigation because Bietak and his Austrian team have been digging for over 30 years in Egypt's Nile Delta at the site of Avaris, which lies directly beneath the southern sector of the city of Ramesses.

Muhammad was nearby, and I signaled him. "Get the crew back here. He will do the interview, but make it fast. We only have a limited amount of time."

In ten minutes we were set. My mind was calm as I prepared a short list of questions concerning this connection between the evidence at Avaris and the early Israelites. We were standing near the center of the dig site. The midday sun was high in the sky. Bietak was dressed in cream-colored slacks and a long-sleeved, white linen shirt, pressed to per-fection. On top of that he wore a green gentleman's vest. Around his neck was a white and yellow ascot, and on his head was a white and black head scarf. He was fit and trim, in his early 60s. There was seriousness in his demeanor that spoke of a man who had given much of his life to understanding this narrow strip of land around us.

"What have you found at this site?"

Bietak said, "We uncovered the remains of a huge town of 250 hectares with a population of approximately 25,000-30,000 individuals. These were people who have originated from Canaan, Syria-Palestine. Originally they may have come here as subjects of the Egyptian crown or with the blessing of the Egyptian crown. Obviously, this town enjoyed something like a special status, like a free zone, something like that."

I would learn that this city of foreigners had had a long history in the midst of Egyp-tian territory, with no walls or defenses. These facts indicate that it had been allowed to develop by the authorities. What Bietak said sounded exactly like the Bible. The Bible says that the pharaoh gave his blessing by allowing the early Israelites to settle freely in the best part of Egypt. Once there, they and their flocks prospered and multiplied greatly. [5] This was just what I was looking for.

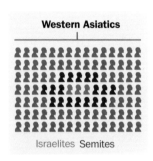

Western Asiatics

Israelites Semites

Semites and Israelites

The Egyptians used the general term "Asiatics" to identify all their neighbors to their north and east. This covered a diverse number of groups and nations in western Asia. One prominent cultural group among these was the Semites. The Israelites were one branch of these Semitic peoples. Therefore, finding archaeological remains of Semites would be the first step in locating the Israelites.

So I asked him, "Could these foreigners be the early Israelites?"

He was careful as he replied, "We have some evidence of shepherds. We find again and again in this area pits with goats and sheep. So we know shepherds, probably Bedouins, with huge herds roamed around this. But to connect this with the proto-Israelites is a very weak affair."

CONQUEST OF CANAAN 1210 BC

RAMESSES EXODUS 1250 BC

SSIVE SEMITIC POPULATION

1800s BC 1700s BC 1600s BC 1500s BC 1400s BC 1300s BC 1200s BC 1100s BC

I was stunned when Bietak said it was a weak affair. This was not what I had expected to hear from him. A weak affair? I thought this was a new discovery, a new connection to the story in the Bible. The *tat, tat, tat, tat* of the water pump seemed to grow louder as my mind tried to comprehend what I had just heard. My attention was brought back by a flock of startled birds rising from the adjoining field. Bietak was waiting for my next question.

"Why couldn't these be the Israelites when they match the Bible's story so well?"

The period of massive Semitic settlement that Bietak sees at Avaris ended hundreds of years before the Ramesses Exodus date.

"According to my opinion, the settlement of the proto-Israelites in Canaan only happened from the 12th century BC onwards."

What Manfred Bietak was saying was that the physical evidence of these people at Avaris was centuries too early to be connected to the events of the Exodus. He believes that the earliest settlement of the Israelites in the land of Canaan didn't happen until after the time of Ramesses II.

The Size of Avaris

A hectare is 10,000 square meters or just under 2.5 acres. So 250 hectares would equate to about 618 acres or just under a square mile. This makes Avaris one of the largest cities of the ancient world.

Proto-Israelites

Proto-Israelites refers to the earliest members of the Israelite culture. This would include the patriarchs and the 12 tribes of the children of Israel in Egypt that would coalesce into a unified body under Moses during the Exodus.

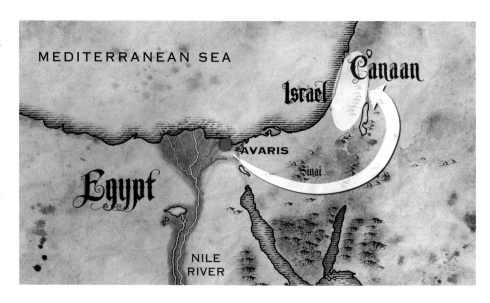

The Bible states that the Israelites' Conquest of Canaan took place 40 years after the Exodus, and Bietak be-lieves the first sign of new Israelite occupation in Canaan occurs in the 12th century (1100s) BC.

I thanked him for his interview and then directed the cameraman to film some of the activities of the dig site. While I walked back through the tall grass to the van, I didn't know then how those five minutes with Bietak would impact my life for years to come.

We rode back to Cairo with the countryside projecting its images against the window. The sun had set, and blurred reflections of palm trees, fields, and canals escorted our journey home. Now I had done it. I had gone to the very location where the events of the Exodus were said to have happened and stood before one of a handful of men in the world who could tell me if there was any evidence for the Israelites in Egypt, and he'd basically told me there wasn't any. The implications were profound, because no Israelites in Egypt means no Exodus. And no Exodus means that the foundational story of Judaism is based on a myth.

For Christians, if the Exodus never happened, it means that Jesus Christ and the writers of the New Testament also got it wrong, since they all accepted the historical reality of Moses and the Exodus and built their teachings on them. [6]

For months after I returned home from Egypt I replayed the interview with Bietak in my thoughts. I wanted to be open-minded, but as the reality of what he'd said set in, a cold chill came over me. All my life I had believed the Bible's stories to be true. I know that some people say you don't need any evidence. They say just have faith. But if there's no hard evidence for any of it, had I believed in a lie all this time? What about my kids and grandkids – what should they put their faith in? Whether you believe these stories or not, isn't it important to know what's really true?

As usual, it was a cold winter in Minnesota. The constant snowfall meant I would be getting plenty of exercise this evening clearing off the 60 yards of our driveway. My home is on a hill overlooking a valley. On a clear day I can see the ski hill five miles away. Tonight I could see the lights of the ski jump. They reminded me of my high school days as a ski jumper. I put the snow blower away. I was hungry and looked with anticipation at the warm glow of the dining room light reflecting on the snow outside the window.

After dinner I decided to play some music. If you ask musicians, most will tell you that playing music allows them to think, and I had plenty to think about. For me, the best thinking happens when I'm playing folk instruments. I go through musical phases. One year I'll be interested in the fiddle. Another year it's the banjo. Lately it's been the Dobro that's been my thinking partner. It has a resonator, and it's played on the lap with a bar and picks. When I tune it in a minor key, it's haunting.

I was haunted as I thought about the complexity of the Exodus and the lack of evidence surrounding it. Bietak had not seen any connection between the biblical Israelites and the city of Avaris. Was this the truth? I looked out the window at the night sky. Because the air is much thinner in the cold of winter, distant objects appear much clearer, and that was the case tonight. This evening the stars shone crisply even though they were light years away. And that was comforting because at this time I needed things to appear clearer. It was late and time for bed. As I laid my head on the pillow I felt very tired, but it wasn't just my body that was tired. My mind was tired, too. I hoped that I would have more clarity tomorrow.

I was a teen the first time I ever ski jumped. I'll always remember the snow coming down on that day. Not the tiny flakes but the big, fat ones that float gently to earth in

Had I believed in a lie all this time?

Thinking over the issues of the Exodus while playing the Dobro.

silence. Those kinds are my favorite. It was after school, and the ski tracks of the wooden jump were lit with faint light bulbs protected from the elements by green metal sconces. These were attached to posts every 15 feet along the path of the jump. The flakes passed from the darkness through these pools of light and gently onto the two ski tracks. This was the first time our ski team had ever jumped, and it was now my turn. I was excited but still afraid of crashing. While I stood with my skis in the tracks at the top of the jump, I felt as if I could almost see the world. The jump stood above the trees, on a high hill overlooking the city. What jumpers can't see is the part of the hill they're going to land on. It's hidden by the steepness of the slope. That's why all I saw was the end of the jump and then the bottom of the hill 160 yards further in the distance. I wouldn't be able to see where I would land until I flew off the jump. Why would anyone do this? you ask. Because it's quite amazing to be 17 years old and fly almost 80-90 feet at the height of tree tops. I made that first jump without falling, and I loved it.

My mother would come to the meets and smile. I think she was proud. She didn't seem too nervous, which surprised some of my other relatives. At least I wasn't out getting into trouble. We continued to jump through the season, going for more distance, trying to qualify for the state meet in Cloquet, Minnesota. Late in the season it didn't snow for weeks. As the hill grew hard and icy, jumping became much more difficult and dangerous. It was like landing on a steep cement parking lot of ice at 40 miles an hour.

One day I jumped unevenly. My ski tip went down, and I caught the top of the hill with it. That sent me head first down the steep slope. It wasn't hitting the hill that hurt as much as the sudden stop at the point where the slope leveled off at the bottom. My face and arms were cut from the ice, but I had no broken bones. I had crashed before, but this was one of the most dramatic and drew a good crowd.

"Mahoney, are you okay? Are you hurt?" yelled my ski coach as he came sliding down the hill with his clipboard and 1960s stocking cap.

"I'm all right. I just cut up my arms on the ice," I said, trying to untangle myself from the seven-foot jumping skis.

"Well, it looks like you cut your face, too."

"Hey, Mahoney," yelled one of my teammates. "That was the coolest crash, man. I thought you were gonna break your neck."

"Well, if it wasn't for my arms breaking the fall, I might have come close to breaking my neck." I got off the hill, and the coach came back over to me.

Bietak's Reasoning

In Bietak's view, the evidence for the Semitic occupation he's uncovered at Avaris runs from about 1850 - 1550 BC. Since the Conquest of Canaan happened shortly after the Exodus, this makes the Avaris evidence too old to be connected with the Ramesses Exodus Theory date around 1250 BC.

"Do you know what happened?"

"I think I dropped the tip of my ski when I jumped."

"Do you want to take a break?"

"No."

"Yeah, if you don't go back up the hill and climb that ski jump, it will just get harder to do in the future." I knew he was right, so I grabbed my skies, threw them on my shoulder, and started the long hike back up the hill.

The next morning, as I stood in my driveway and glimpsed the ski jump in the distance, I was reminded of the lessons from those high school days. The more I thought about it, the more I could see that the same principles were true with this investigation. I shouldn't give up. Despite the great odds against finding any evidence, I couldn't stop now, no matter how hard it would be. Something was drawing me back. Just like a ski jumper, I would have to climb that old wooden jump and have another go at it. ♆

IV: ADOPTING A NEW APPROACH

Professor Kent Weeks with his wife, Susan, inspecting canopic jars in KV 5 – the tomb complex containing several sons of Ramesses II.

I. Who Was the Pharaoh of the Exodus?

It was clear that in order to continue the investigation our team had to return to Egypt. We needed to explore other possible connections to the story of the Exodus and learn more about Pharaoh Ramesses II, who many believe was the pharaoh that Moses confronted. I contacted the Press Office of the Embassy of Egypt to discuss the requirements for the filming. They were incredibly helpful, providing all the necessary permits, press personnel, and security to assist at all the locations.

I arranged to meet with one of America's leading Egyptologists, Professor Kent Weeks, who rediscovered KV5, the tomb of the sons of Ramesses II in the Valley of the Kings. This tomb had been partially excavated in the 1800s but was thought to be insignificant. After it had been forgotten and buried by the sands of the desert, Weeks and the Theban Mapping Project reopened the site in 1987. Over time they were able to dig further and ended up uncovering over 110 underground chambers with corridors stretching deep into the hillside. This tomb is one of the largest and most important ever found.

I met Professor Weeks at the Ramesseum, the mortuary temple of Ramesses II on the west bank of the Nile just outside the city of Luxor. We walked together in the cool shade of the temple's overarching beams. In another setting, you might think he was going off to play golf or maybe do a little fishing. He wore one of those classic fly fishing hats that look relaxed and comfortable because they are. The only things missing from it were several lures or flies tucked above the brim. Weeks had a great smile that made you feel good, like he was really listening and cared about what you were saying. Not far from

Mahoney and Professor Weeks in the mortuary temple of Ramesses II, the Ramesseum.

us was a colossal statue of Ramesses II. In some distant century it had fallen during an earthquake and broken in several large pieces. We came to an area of the temple where the pillars had large bases, each with a ledge where we could sit and talk.

When I interview someone like Professor Kent Weeks, I'm always interested in how they've arrived at their positions in life. So I asked, "Why did you become an Egyptologist?"

Weeks smiled. "Well, I was lucky in one way. I was eight years old. I had gone through the wanting to be a paleontologist phase, and then I went through the being a garbage collector phase and settled on Egyptology, got fascinated by it, and by luck of the draw had numerous teachers in elementary school who convinced me that this was not as weird a thing as one might think, that there was a career potential at the end of the line, and they encouraged my interest in ancient Egypt. I knew at the age of eight that's what I was going to do and, fortunately, I never wavered."

"Where did you grow up?"

"Just outside of Seattle, actually Everett, Washington."

"Well, it's pretty wet there, isn't it?"

He laughed. "Well, yes. I think that's one of the other reasons for choosing Egyptology, to get away from the bad weather."

"How did you get involved with the Valley of the Kings?"

"One of my first jobs was as Director of the University of Chicago's archaeological headquarters here in Luxor. I thought, frankly, something has to be done to protect these monuments or they're going to disappear in our lifetime. And I decided the first and most basic step in protecting them was to make a map to where they are located and inventory what we had to worry about. The Valley of the Kings was a nice, well-defined area to do that in. So I decided to make an archaeological survey. Well, 20 years later we finally finished an atlas of the Valley of the Kings and have since also done archaeological master plans to protect it from incursions of tourists and to ensure that its monuments will be around for a while."

I asked, "There's a very important tomb that you have been working on. Why do you call it KV5?"

"King's Valley, Tomb Number 5," he answered. "The fifth tomb in from the entrance to the Valley of the Kings. KV5 was not something we set out to explore, but as we were mapping tombs in the Valley of the Kings we thought, well, as long as we are doing

Statue of Ramesses II in Karnak Temple, Luxor, Egypt.

it, what about all of those tombs that were mentioned in 19th century travelers' reports that have gone missing for whatever reason and are not visible today? Why don't we see if we can't relocate them and put at least their entrance on our tomb plans?"

"What does it mean to relocate?"

"The tomb had gone missing. It had been seen in 1825 by an early British traveler, but he determined or decided the tomb had no interest whatever and so he abandoned it, walked off and ignored it. A hundred years later Howard Carter came along and he, too, was convinced that the tomb had no value, and so he used the entrance as a dumping ground for the debris he excavated while searching for the tomb of Tutankhamun – buried it under another three meters of silt. We relocated the tomb entrance under Carter's debris and decided it might be more worth exploring than Carter thought it was."

"Okay." Now I was getting very interested. I loved these kinds of stories.

He continued, "And we did that and then walked – well, didn't walk, crawled between the ceiling of the tomb and the debris, the flood debris that filled it, as far into the tomb as we could go, which was only a few meters. And we agreed with Howard Carter's assessment and that of a 19th century traveler: the tomb seemed to be unimportant, undecorated, uninteresting. But by the luck of the draw, as we were crawling out, thinking that we were going to abandon work here and move on, we happened to kick a few stones away from the wall near the tomb entrance and found inscriptions on the wall."

"Really?"

"The next season, when we came back, we did a bit more clearing of the first chamber of KV5 and discovered that there were inscriptions that in fact gave us the names and titles of several sons of Ramesses II."

"A very important pharaoh," I said.

Weeks nodded, "Well, a very important pharaoh and obviously very interesting to have a tomb in which one of his sons was buried. But to have several sons buried in one tomb is almost unique in Egyptian history, and the tomb therefore took on considerable importance to us."

I asked, "Can you tell me who Ramesses II was?"

He leaned back. "That's a question that has perplexed Egyptologists for a long time, and there are several reasons for this. Partly because Ramesses II lived into his 80s at a time when the average life expectancy of an Egyptian was in the mid-30s, he ruled Egypt for 67 years. That means that probably two generations of Egyptians had never known

Cameraman Jack Tankard filming at the Valley of the Kings.

another pharaoh."

I didn't know this ruler thought to be the pharaoh of the Exodus had lived and reigned for such a long time.

Weeks went on, "During his lifetime, Ramesses managed to do a lot of things that certainly justify his being called Ramesses the Great. He was a military leader, conducted numerous battles, extended and maintained the borders of Egypt well beyond the Nile Valley."

"Ramesses had an empire, is that what you are saying?"

"Indeed he did, and it was one of the economic mainstays of the country. During his lifetime Egypt was remarkably well off economically, and that meant among other things Ramesses could engage in elaborate building programs. I doubt there's a monument that was standing in his reign that he didn't add to or usurp. And there are certainly numerous other monuments that he built from scratch. We're sitting in one, the Ramesseum, his mortuary – a memorial temple."

I then asked, "Could Ramesses II potentially have been the pharaoh of the Exodus story?"

He became more serious. "This is a real can of worms, this question of who was the pharaoh of the Exodus, and there have probably been as many suggestions put forth as there are Egyptologists and ancient historians to suggest them. And the reason for the confusion, or the lack of agreement I should say, is because there is simply so little evidence to go on. There's no mention of this in ancient Egyptian sources, and you might say, well, why would there be? Why would the Egyptians carve on their temple walls for all eternity a note saying, 'Yes, there were big problems in town. We suffered a great loss or we lost a battle'? These are not the things you want to inscribe in perpetuity."

This was exactly what Professor Kitchen and Mansour Boraik had told me.

Weeks then raised a question that would become immensely important for me. I caught myself leaning forward as he spoke.

"But Ramesses II is the pharaoh of the Exodus? How can we prove that? Chronology doesn't really help. The chronology of Egypt is still a bit ambiguous. Correlations between Egyptian chronology and that of other cultures in the ancient Near East is even more confusing. We don't know precisely when the Exodus happened. Some people say it was Ramesses II. It makes nice theater because he was a great, powerful ruler. Everybody knows his name. He built fantastic monuments. Everything really is appealing to have him be the one to choose."

"Because he'd be a very large opponent, wouldn't he?"

"He would be indeed."

"And he had declared himself a god," I added.

"Exactly right again. So, yeah, pick Ramesses II as the pharaoh of the Exodus, but other Egyptologists, other ancient historians disagree. Any pharaoh reigning during that time could be the pharaoh of the Exodus, if we can prove there even was an Exodus, which we cannot. And there are many Egyptologists, biblical scholars, ancient historians who argue that the Exodus has as much historical veracity as, say, the legend of Camelot. It's a great story, it lends a certain degree of unity and historical tradition to a culture, but there's no way we can prove that the Exodus even happened. So, we're stuck with an event that may or may not have occurred, whose principal character may or may not have been a 19th Dynasty ruler, but it's all conjecture."

The cartouche (name ring) of Ramesses II.

Weeks seemed to be pretty negative about the pursuit of hard answers for the Exodus. I had noticed the tendency among many scholars to think that this story is unsolvable and possibly mythological. So they discourage the exercise of trying to look for evidence. I didn't know anything about "proving" the story. I just wanted to ask the same kinds of questions I would in any other historical investigation and see where they might lead. After all, this is one of the biggest mysteries in the history of the world.

Later I was sitting in the dark of the edit suite with a hot cup of tea, sweetened with honey, something I'd grown fond of during the cold winter months. As I reviewed the interview a second time, I appreciated more the issue Weeks had brought up. In fact, it would become pivotal to the entire investigation.

If Ramesses II might not be the pharaoh of the Exodus, then who was? Looking for the Exodus in a different time or reign in Egypt's history could be the solution since searching in the wrong time period wouldn't produce any evidence. But could I really question a viewpoint that was held so strongly by so many experts?

I remembered my conversation with Mansour Boraik at Karnak, as we stood in the side corridor of the Temple of Khonsu. I replayed the scene of our interview in my mind. When Boraik had talked, he didn't dictate what he thought the truth was. That openness shouldn't have surprised me, but it did.

Egyptologist Mansour Boraik challenges Mahoney to think scientifically.

I could see Boraik pointing to his head. "Scientifically, you have to open your mind to all the opinions and read it by yourself." His eyes were wide with passion. He continued, "Don't let anybody affect what you believe. But also, on the other hand, you have to accept the other opinions. Your opinions are not always the right opinions. You have to accept other opinions and debate with me, discuss. You can convince me, or shall I convince you? Leave it to the public to judge. We have a myth. We have a story. It's in the holy books. Who knows? And then you will come with a conclusion. And this conclusion will be in front of the public; the public can judge."

I could understand what Boraik meant by "accepting" other opinions. I was to be open to new ideas and to talk about them with others. I wanted to do this, and his words confirmed what I was sensing: I would need to continue a dialogue with participants from all sides in this debate, and then let the audience decide for themselves whether the Exodus was a real event. It was also clear that I needed a new approach, what might even be considered a scientific approach, which began by taking a closer look at the details of the biblical story, and then went on to investigate whether these key events could be found in the archaeology of Egypt.

But so many people don't think the Bible is meant to be taken literally. Could you really take the information that was written so long ago and test it word by word, phrase by phrase?

II. Looking at the Text Objectively

One wintry morning Steve Law, my writing partner and researcher, came into my office, which he only did when something was on his mind. Normally he stayed in the writing/ research room surrounded by archaeological books, maps, and piles of paper.

Steve was an athlete. Like me, he had been a skier, which led him into coaching cross-country skiing. In his research and writing, just as in cross-country skiing, he had the endurance to keep going farther and deeper when many others would have quit, fatigued by the staggering effort. For Steve, yes, this investigation was difficult, but the challenge actually energized him to seek out hidden information that might help solve one of the biggest mysteries in history.

"I found a place in the Bible that gives a complete overview of the events of the Exodus that will be a useful guide in our investigation," he said.

I challenged him. "Is that approach really scientific? Aren't we just assuming the credibility of the biblical text?"

Steve responded, "Not at all. Here's the central question of our investigation: Did the events of the Exodus really happen? In other words, is the Bible a credible historical document or not? In order to test that question objectively, we need to know what the text is actually claiming. Only then can we go out to see whether there is hard evidence that strongly supports it or not."

"Yes, I get it. Otherwise we won't be testing the Bible," I said seriously. "We'll just be testing a theory that may or may not have anything to do with the Bible's claims. Then we won't be looking for the right things."

This is a problem we've noticed in our research. Most scholars, whether they are very skeptical of the Exodus or they highly regard its historical credibility, have disagreements over almost every aspect of the biblical text. And the tendency is to alter the details of that account to accommodate a new theory.

Steve sat down on the chair next to my desk. "Take, for example, ideas about the tenth plague, the death of the firstborn, or the size of the Israelite population when they left Egypt, or the sea that was said to be split in two. There are lots of clever theories that downplay the text and replace it with opinions. Well, when people looked for evidence for these creative theories and found nothing, was it really the Bible's account that was found to be faulty, or the scholars' theories?"

I stared out the window. I could hear the sound of distant tires pushing through the slush on the road. The sun's glare reflected off melting snowbanks. The car drove past. It cautiously turned the corner and disappeared.

I looked back at Steve. "We need to avoid this at all costs or else we will end up just like so many others who have attempted to explore this story – getting nowhere!"

III. Abraham: The Six Steps of the Biblical Sequence

The oldest accounts of the Exodus events were written in Hebrew, the ancient language of the Israelites. Today we find the story in the second of the first five books of the Bible, known to Jewish people as the Torah. In order to test the Exodus fairly, I wanted to know what this story was actually claiming. The challenge I faced as a filmmaker was not only understanding the details of these events myself but more importantly trying to communicate them to an audience who often didn't know the stories, much less the details. It was clear that the film needed a biblical storyteller, someone who could elaborate where needed and at other times condense the narrative of the Exodus.

As my storyteller I chose Rabbi Manis Friedman, a member of Judaism's Orthodox branch. Rabbi Friedman teaches around the world but lives in Saint Paul, across the Mississippi River from my home in Minneapolis. When I first talked with him about this project, he was curious, and we met at my studio to discuss how he might narrate the biblical story. We spoke for several hours, and I could see he was perfect for the role since he had a natural simplicity, a calm sense of authority, and a gift for dry humor.

It was late when we finally finished our conversation. We walked out into a perfect summer night, one of those pleasant times that keep us living in this harsh northern climate. The streetlight cast a warm glow down the sidewalk and over the front steps of the building. I asked him, "So what do you think?"

With a twinkle in his eye that I would come to enjoy, he said, "Why not, let's do it."

"So you're in?" I was relieved. "That's great."

He smiled. "This is a very important story. So yes, I'm in."

Just as we were about to leave, he turned and said, "You know, I've always felt that someday I would be in a movie."

Months later we met at a Jewish retreat center. Both Rabbi Friedman and I had decided that it was the best place to film him recounting the stories from the Torah. This location housed a particularly beautiful handwritten copy of these sacred scrolls that would be a part of many of his storytelling scenes.

The Torah

The Hebrew word *Torah* means teaching or instruction. It is used to designate the five books ascribed to Moses' authorship: Genesis, Exodus, Leviticus, Numbers, and Deuteronomy. The books of the Torah, the first five books of the Bible, are considered the holiest writings in Judaism, and ornate scrolls for use in Jewish services are painstakingly copied by hand onto animal skin using the ancient Hebrew script. The Torah is one of the three main divisions of the Hebrew Bible, called the Tanakh by Jewish people and the Old Testament by Christians. Christian scholars usually call the five books of Moses the Pentateuch.

Rabbi Manis Friedman telling the story of the Exodus from the ancient scrolls of the Torah.

I was sitting across from him. The camera was just behind my shoulder. In the front of the room, behind Rabbi Friedman, was a platform with railings along the sides. Across the back was a tall wooden cabinet known as an ark, where the scrolls were kept when not in use. On either side, curtains of deep purple and blue hung from the ceiling to the floor. As usual, my hometown field producer Kim Dulas had seen to it that everything was set up just right. In front of the platform was a large, four-legged lectern on which the three-foot long Torah scrolls could be carefully laid down, unrolled, and read. Looking up from my notes, I could see everyone was ready.

"Roll camera," I said quietly.

I waited a few moments, and then nodded for the rabbi to begin. He started to speak with the confidence of someone who knew this story very well. Just what I needed. It confirmed how right a choice he really was.

"The story of the Exodus begins before the Israelites leave Egypt. It begins with Abraham, when God brings him to the land of Canaan and makes a Covenant with him, and in that Covenant he spells out the entire Exodus. [7]

"The Lord said to Abraham, 'All this land you see I will give to you and your off-spring forever. Go walk through the length and breadth of this land, for I am giving it to you.' On that day, the Lord made a Covenant, a formal promise to Abraham. He said, 'To your descendants, I give this land.'

"God led Abraham outside and he said, 'Look up to heaven and count the stars if you can.'

"And God said, 'So numerous will your offspring be. Your descendants will be foreigners in a country not their own, and they will be enslaved and oppressed. But I will judge the nation they serve as slaves, and afterward they will come out with great possessions and return here.'"

The Bible states that Abraham was given a series of promises that spelled out the events of the Exodus. He was promised that his descendants would become as numerous as the stars.

According to this text, the events of the Exodus were not a historical accident. They were directed by the God of Abraham every step of the way.

As Steve Law and I looked more closely at this account, we could see that these biblical events formed a sequence – a sequence that could guide my entire investigation.

I imagined the Wall of Time with the six steps of the biblical sequence – the major events of the Exodus story – running parallel to Egyptian history, starting with:

- The **Arrival** of Abraham's descendants in Egypt,
- Their tremendous **Multiplication**,
- Their descent into **Slavery**,
- The **Judgment** of the nation that enslaved them,
- Their deliverance and **Exodus** out of Egypt,
- And finally, in Canaan, their **Conquest** of the Promised Land.

Below: The six major steps of the biblical sequence depicted on the Wall of Time when tied to the Ramesses Exodus date around 1250 BC.

If the Exodus really happened, there are elements in the story that are so distinctly prominent that you'd expect some remnants would have been left behind, somewhere in Egypt's past.

In my office Steve and I talked further. It was evident he was excited by this new approach. "By breaking down the big questions into these six primary steps, we now have a much more precise tool to test the evidence."

"I agree, and for an Exodus theory to match the Bible, it would need to fulfill all the criteria."

As we continued to discuss the matter, it was clear to us that this was a breakthrough. Any theory on the Exodus would have to contain these three criteria:

1. Have evidence that fits this sequence,

2. Have evidence in the correct time spans,

3. Have evidence for all six of the steps.

We knew science solves problems by looking for patterns of evidence, and a truly objective approach looks for those patterns no matter where they exist. I set out to see whether a pattern of evidence matching these steps could be found somewhere in ancient history, starting with the first step – the **Arrival** of the Israelites in Egypt.

V: STEP ONE:
EVIDENCE OF ARRIVAL?

The account of Abraham and his descendants is found in the pages of Genesis, the Bible's first book. Rabbi Friedman resumed the story.

"The book of Genesis tells us that the first descendant of Abraham to arrive in Egypt was his great-grandson Joseph, one of the 12 sons of Jacob. Joseph's brothers had sold him as a slave to a caravan of traders who brought him down to Egypt.

According to the Bible, the special Covenant passed from Abraham through Isaac to Jacob (Israel) and his 12 sons including Joseph. Moses came from the line of Levi.

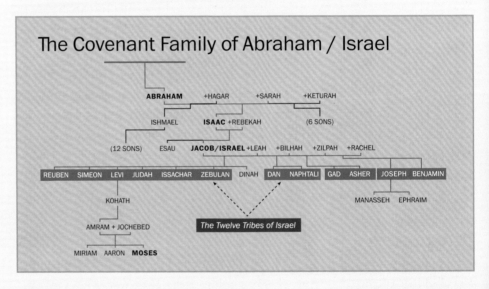

"Then, in an amazing turn of events, he rises to become the highest official in Egypt. He saves the country from a terrible famine and enables his father Jacob and his entire family to settle in the best part of Egypt's Delta, a place called Goshen." [8]

My objective was to see if archaeologists had uncovered any specific evidence of this Semitic family group arriving in Egypt as the Bible says. So far I had none. As I sat in the edit suite and reviewed the footage from my previous interview with Manfred Bietak, all I had were doubts. When I had asked Bietak if he had found any evidence of the early Israelites at his dig site, he had said, "So far not. We only know we have some evidence of shepherds." But according to the Bible, this was one of the primary locations where the Israelites lived while in Egypt.

I was stuck.

I replayed this clip again and again, and each time the words of Manfred Bietak echoed, "So far not. So far not."

I stared at the editing screen, my thoughts filling with uncertainty and apprehension. Then, suddenly, something was telling me to go to my library and search out a book I had never taken the time to read. It had been given to me the year before by a musician friend who thought it might be helpful.

Paging through the book, I was startled. The author, a well-known English Egyptologist, had written about Avaris, the same site that Manfred Bietak had been excavating. Was this a coincidence? I returned to the edit suite with the book, *Pharaohs and Kings: A Biblical Quest*. I saw pictures and graphics supporting a totally different interpretation of Bietak's finds.

I would soon learn that David Rohl had shaken the world of archaeology when he saw what he believed were major problems with the way Egyptologists had reconstructed history. His solution proposed new dates for events in ancient Egypt that challenged the standard view. While most scholars think that the events of the Exodus happened in the New Kingdom, Rohl places the Exodus in an entirely different period: the earlier Middle Kingdom, where he claims evidence for the Exodus can be seen. And that is remarkable because he is an agnostic and remains unconvinced of the existence of God. Yet he clearly sees archaeological evidence for the biblical Joseph, Jacob, and the early Hebrews in the Nile Delta region of Egypt.

For the first time I had a lead to a new way of interpreting the evidence at Avaris, and I recalled that interpretation plays a big role in how archaeology works. Ze'ev Herzog, the Israeli archaeologist, had said, "Archaeology is about 10 percent data and 90 percent interpretation."

I knew I had to meet David Rohl, who at the time lived in Kent in southern England. We arranged a date to film in the study of his home, and I traveled by myself with camera and lights. When I arrived, his lovely wife, Ditas, was concerned that I hadn't eaten and prepared a late lunch for us. Just like Kent Weeks and other scholars, Rohl's interest in Egypt began as a child when his mother, a college professor, took him up the Nile on King Farouk's paddle-steamer to visit the temples and tombs of the great pharaohs. From that point on, he was changed. He went on to spend his life exploring the Middle East and studying the mysterious inscriptions and hieroglyphs of the pharaohs and what they might reveal about ancient history.

Rohl was surprised that I had come alone to his home. Like most people I have interviewed, he was expecting an entire camera crew. But I have found that a camera team can be very distracting to an interviewee, and it's more expensive. So I've enjoyed those times when it is just me, the camera, and the scholar, as was now the case.

"Who is David Rohl?" I asked.

"David Rohl is an Egyptologist and a historian who studied these subjects at university. He's also a little bit of a rock and roll star as he has been a musician for many years."

"Were you a composer?"

"Yes. A composer, a musician, and a recording engineer."

"We have a lot in common then. I have done all those things as well."

Surprised, Rohl said, "And I also was a photographer."

"Really?"

"Yes. I was once kidnapped by the Moody Blues."

"What?"

"It's a long story. I was at art college doing a project to photograph their concert when someone asked me to go to the train station and pick up some people. So I went with my "Mini Moke." It's like a 1960s version of a dune buggy jeep, which I had covered in hieroglyphics. I went to the train station and brought back some of the members of the band with their instruments all crammed into my little car."

"That is hilarious."

"The concert was great, and I sent them my photographs. The next time they came back from Manchester on their UK tour, I photographed them again. At the end of the concert they said, "You're not going home. You're coming with us on tour.""

I laughed. "So that's how they kidnapped you?"

"Dead right. I wasn't even allowed to go home for a change of clothes. It was a great experience traveling all over the north of England in two shiny black limousines, talking about pretty much everything in the universe. As Moody Blues fans will know, these guys

Egyptologist David Rohl believes evidence for the Exodus exists in a period earlier than normally considered.

spent much of their lives searching for answers to the great questions of human existence, which is reflected in their music."

"So you weren't really kidnapped, you were adopted."

"Yes. I was a 19-year-old student, and they made me a part of their family. They are amazing and kind people."

"How did you get into the studio business?"

"I was always in bands and recording. Eventually, I became Chief Engineer at Strawberry Studios, and with the royalties gained from producing bands and solo artists, I had enough funds to retire from the music business and go back to college and to my love of Egyptology."

"So you were older when you went to study Egyptology formally?"

"I came to university as a mature student and actually took the rock and roll attitude with me. So I never really sat at the foot of a professor and observed everything without asking questions. I wanted to know why things were being said to me. Why was it that my tutors were telling me certain things? What was their evidence? And this challenge, if you like, to their teaching was very interesting to them as well. I came with a lot of ideas which I had developed over the years and brought them to the professors, and they responded in a very positive way."

Rohl stopped for a second, considering his next words. "The problem then arises when people, who don't know you as an individual and don't have that interaction, tend to think of you as a rebel because you are questioning things that are already well established."

"Why do these ideas threaten the established thinking?" I asked.

"Because they raise important questions about how we date history."

"Are historians unwilling to consider new ideas about the ancient past?"

"Well, it is undeniable that there are huge problems raised by the latest archaeological evidence, especially concerning biblical archaeology, a term that has become an embarrassment to scholarship these days. Nobody wants to call themselves a biblical archaeologist anymore. But the issues I and others have identified lie in how we have dated the ancient world, not in the biblical text. And the historical credibility of the Bible is what has suffered as a result.

"And the joke, if you like, is that I have no biblical axe to grind here because I'm an agnostic. I don't need these stories to be true. But the reality is, although archaeologists have been looking in all the right places for the biblical stories, they have been looking in entirely the wrong time."

"Well, if it's so obvious, why is there so much resistance to this simple new idea?"

"Although the idea is simple, in other words, look for the Bible stories in a different time period, the actual process of restructuring the chronology of Egypt and the ancient world is very complex. And most Egyptologists steer clear of it. They rely on a small group of experts to do the number crunching and when somebody like me comes along and says, 'Hey, there are major chronological anomalies here, there's something wrong with your timeline,' they see it as rocking the boat."

"So you're questioning decades of scholarship with what you're proposing?"

"The simple truth is many scholars don't understand what I am proposing. I'm in a situation now where I'm fighting for a new idea and I'm getting huge resistance from academia because I am a revolutionary, because I am trying to change things in a dramatic way. I'm not just simply, you know, pushing the envelope slightly. I want to go beyond the envelope and take us to a completely new way of thinking."

I was looking forward to hearing him present his case, and this would happen on several occasions in England, Egypt, and Minnesota. That very first interview with Rohl was shot in an older video format. Several years later, when high definition video became popular, I needed to replace the earlier footage, and he agreed to meet in the States for another interview. I've often wondered why so many experts I've had the privilege of filming were willing to participate in a project like this. So I asked him, "Why did you trust me enough to come and be filmed?"

"You asked the best questions," he said.

I. Avaris: The City Beneath Ramesses

For my second interview with Rohl, I chose the historic James J. Hill Library, built in Saint Paul in 1917. Hill was a wealthy railroad baron who financed this magnificent structure with its marble floors, fine wood paneling, and grand columns flanking the great central hall. The backdrop was stunning and richly set the tone for our dialogue. That morning the weather had turned cold earlier than expected. The snow was falling heavily outside, but inside the great hall it was warm. I could see that Rohl was eager to get started, and I was worried that we might not finish the interview before the library opened at noon.

Just as we were about to film, Rohl turned to me and said, "I don't want to be interviewed."

I looked up. "What?"

"Don't interview me in the standard way. That's boring. Let's just talk, you and me, back and forth."

This would be a change from almost everything I had previously done, but at that moment I could see he was right. A bit of sparring would be more entertaining and energetic. I knew time was slipping by. In a split second I went for it and called out, "Quiet! Roll cameras." After a pause I opened with a broad question. "Considering all your work with the ancient world, what do you think is significant about the Bible?"

"Well, people dismiss the Bible as a work of fiction. But what happens if it's not? What happens if it's a real history, a history of a people we call the Israelites? Then it would become the first history book in the world. It predates Herodotus, if you like, by 1,000 years. Herodotus is supposed to be the first historian, but in fact I think Moses is. And it spans about 4,000 years of time as well." [9]

David Rohl being interviewed at the James J. Hill Library.

It surprised me that Rohl, who doesn't have faith and is undecided about the existence of God, had such respect for the Bible.

His enthusiasm continued. "It's an amazing story of one people from their beginnings to their exile."

"What biblical events are you referring to?"

"From the beginning when Abraham comes into the land in Genesis all the way through to the time of the Israelites' exile and diaspora when they are scattered to all parts of the world. So it's a book that is extraordinarily valuable if it's true. But if it's a work of fiction, if it's a fairy story, if it's been invented, then it becomes a complete nothing."

"Nothing?"

"It's not better than a Harry Potter novel, for instance. So the question is, is it a real history book? And the only way to determine that is to look into the archaeology – what's in the ground – and find evidence."

Professor Manfred Bietak uncovering the ancient city of Avaris.

Then I brought up the topic I'd wanted to ask about for over a year: why had Rohl and Manfred Bietak reached such different conclusions about Joseph and the early Israelites?

"Tell me, who is Manfred Bietak?"

"Manfred Bietak is probably one of the greatest archaeologists alive today. And he's dug up one of the most important sites in the eastern Delta, a city called Avaris, which is in the land of Goshen, as the Bible calls it. And I believe this is the place where Joseph and his brethren lived."[10]

Of course, I knew from talking with Bietak that he had a different interpretation. And most Egyptologists believe there's no evidence of the early Israelites in the city of Ramesses.

I challenged him. "I went to see Manfred Bietak, and that's not what he said. He's saying there's no evidence of this in the time of Ramesses."

Rohl said, "Exactly right. Most scholars will say if you look at the city of Ramesses, there are no Asiatics there. There are no Semites. There are no western Asiatics living at that particular city. But dig down a little bit deeper and you do find a city full of Asiatics."

I was surprised and wanted him to clarify what he was saying. "Yeah, but the Bible says it happened at the time of Ramesses. What are you saying?"

"I'm saying that this particular mention of the city of Ramesses – the building of Ramesses – is what we call an anachronism. It's something that's been added into the text later by an editor. So what the editor is basically saying is, 'This is the place where the Israelites built the store city, and we know it today as Ramesses.'"

I was starting to understand the point Rohl was making. Here the Bible's use of the word *Ramesses* might not be connected to a specific date but only to a place. "Okay, so the people would know the area, the region, and they would know what it's called today."

"The people of the Bible would've known where Ramesses was and where therefore their ancestors actually built the city. In the ancient times it was called Avaris," he said.

"Do you have any other examples of that?"

"Yes, there are plenty of examples throughout history. In our British history, for instance, we have the Roman legion, the sixth legion, that built a garrison town at a place called York. We all know York today. But it wasn't called York at the time the Romans were there. It was called Eboracum. It was only later when the Vikings came and called it Jorvik that it got the name York. So there's a typical example of an anachronism."

"So this has happened throughout history?"

"Yes."

"And in this case, people today know it as York because that's the name that has become common in their time?"

Rohl nodded. "Yes, they'd identify it as York, just like the people of the Bible would've known where Ramesses was, and where therefore their ancestors actually built the city."

Asiatics

This term is not being used here to describe East Asians. The broad term "Asiatics" identified for the Egyptians their close neighbors to their north and east. Western Asiatics or Semites were the broad cultural group of which the Israelites were a part.

Anachronism

The act of attributing a name, a custom, or an event to a time in which it does not belong.

Ramesses in Genesis

The name "Ramesses" is not only used in Exodus 1:11 for the store city built by the Israelites during their slavery; it is also used back in Genesis 47:11 during the time that Jacob's family moved to Egypt. In Genesis it seems to have the same meaning as the name "Goshen" (compare to Gen 47:6).

Then Joseph settled his father and brothers in the land of Egypt and gave them property in the best part of the land, the land of Rameses, as Pharaoh had commanded.

(Gen 47:11)

I saw what he meant. We were sitting in the middle of Saint Paul, the capital city of my own state. It was given that name by a Catholic priest who had established a log chapel, which later developed into the Cathedral of Saint Paul. But the settlement on the Mississippi landing had originally been called Pig's Eye, after a popular tavern established by a French-Canadian fur trapper, Pierre "Pig's Eye" Parrant. The priest made it known that now the settlement should no longer be called Pig's Eye but only Saint Paul. Visitors today would never recognize the original name.

Significantly, in Genesis, the first book of the Bible, the word *Ramesses* was also used to describe the land where Joseph's family settled. This reference seemed to be another anachronism using Ramesses as a geographical location. It's an anachronism because, according to the timeline laid out in the biblical story, the settlement of Joseph's family took place at least 100 years before the building of the city of Ramesses mentioned in Exodus 1:11. [11]

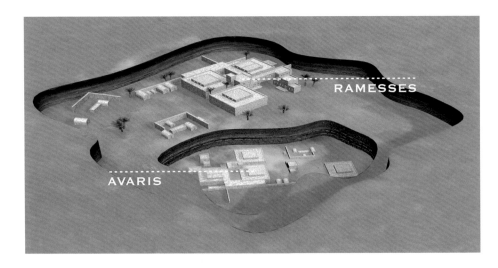

The remains of the older city of Avaris lie underneath the southern sector of the city of Ramesses.

If the name Ramesses in Genesis does not refer to the time of Pharaoh Ramesses II, then why should the mention of Ramesses in the book of Exodus be any different? If this is the case, then the Bible would not actually be saying that the Exodus took place in the time of Pharaoh Ramesses at all. That would just be a mistaken interpretation made by scholars. And if both of these biblical references to the name Ramesses are anachronisms, then the Exodus could have happened in a completely different time than the era of Pharaoh Ramesses II. [12]

Sitting in the expansive hall of the library, I glanced over Rohl's shoulder and down the row of pillars to a set of tall arched windows. As I thought about this question I watched the snow fall gently outside the library in large, soft flakes. I remembered that, according to the Bible, Joseph's father and brothers were allowed by Pharaoh to settle in the area referred to by two different names, Goshen and Ramesses, thought to be located in the eastern Delta. This family tended livestock. Over the next generations they would multiply into a large population before being enslaved and forced to build a city the Bible calls Ramesses.

Rohl's next words about this location were profound yet so simple. "Now, this Avaris is the city which lies under the biblical Ramesses. Ramesses of the New Kingdom – Avaris of the Middle Kingdom, the 13th Dynasty. It lies underneath the city that's mentioned in the Bible. So when Bietak digs up a huge population of Semitic speaking peoples with Semitic culture, living in this city of Avaris for several hundred years, and then at the end of the period these Semites all leave – depart with their belongings and abandon the city – whatever Manfred says, that to me sounds awfully like the Israelites."

After all the negative conclusions I'd gathered from other scholars, to finally hear of this potential connection between Joseph's family and the archaeological evidence was fascinating to me, and Rohl's confidence made me want to know more. Could Avaris really be the place where the Israelites had lived? It seemed to be a possibility because it lies underneath the ruins of the city of Ramesses and would therefore be older. But why was Bietak's interpretation so different from Rohl's?

I challenged Rohl again. "Well, what Bietak told me was that there was no connection."

"Well, look at the evidence of what you've got here. Right at the beginning, in the heart of this tiny community of Avaris at the end of the 12th Dynasty, we see a Syrian house appear. The Austrians call them *Mittelsaal* houses," he said.

"This type of house is found in north Syria, the area where Abraham came from. It's exactly the same style of house you'd expect Jacob to build for himself in Egypt. And we know that the Israelites sought their brides from Haran in that region. They all went back to get their brides from there. [13]

"So, the culture that turns up in Egypt at the end of the 12th Dynasty seems to have come from north Syria originally."

This means that the culture seen at Avaris matches that of the early Israelites.

Syrian Mittelsaal House

This reconstruction of the structure unearthed by the Austrian excavators of Avaris was classified as a "Mittelsaalhaus" or "middle room house." Common in north Syria during the Middle Bronze Age, this design featured rooms arranged around a central hall or courtyard. The Mittelsaalhaus at Tell el-Dab'a was the first dwelling built on a low southern hill within the area that would become the city of Avaris.

The culture of the earliest residents of Avaris matches that of north Syria around the area of Haran where Abraham came from and where his grandson Jacob spent 20 years of his life.

Egypt's Dynasties

The conventional dates for Egypt's ruling dynasties can be seen above. In times of power and stability, dynasties would rule one after another. In times of weakness and fragmentation, competing dynasties sometimes ruled simultaneously from different parts of Egypt. Most scholars would place the Exodus in the 19th Dynasty, during or after the reign of Ramesses II. Some scholars argue for the 18th Dynasty. However, David Rohl believes evidence in Egypt matching the events related to the Exodus can be found entirely in the 12th and 13th Dynasties of the earlier Middle Kingdom.

II. Joseph: The Search for a Semitic High Ruler

"So is there a connection with Joseph at Avaris?" I asked.

Rohl said, "Well, after this house of Jacob – if we can call it that – is built, eventually it's flattened, and on top of it an Egyptian palace is constructed. The palace is classic Egyptian architecture this time, but the occupant was not Egyptian.

"The palace had courtyards, colonnades, audience chambers. There was even a robing room. It obviously belonged to some high official of state who was very, very important to that state. Because when somebody gets a palace like this given to them, it means they've been honored for what they've done for the state."

The Egyptian-styled palace at Avaris.

120

I recalled that the biblical story has Joseph becoming second in command over all Egypt as a reward for interpreting Pharaoh's dreams. Joseph was also given the daughter of a high priest in marriage, as well as fine garments, a gold necklace, and a signet ring, which signified his new position. [14]

Rohl had a glint in his eye as he relayed the next piece of the story. "Now in the garden behind the palace, the archaeologists found 12 main graves with memorial chapels on top of them."

"You have 12 graves?"

"We have 12 graves."

"And why would that be significant?"

"Well, think about it. How many sons did Jacob have?" he asked.

"He had 12."

"How many tribes were there?"

"Twelve tribes."

"Exactly. And what's also amazing is the palace had a façade, a portico with 12 pillars, just like these," Rohl said, pointing to the grand columns standing in the hall behind us. "So you've got 12 sons, 12 tribes, 12 pillars, and 12 tombs." [15]

Behind the palace at Avaris, 12 special graves had memorial chapels built above them.

The 12 pillars of the palace.

"Interesting," I said, contemplating the possible connection.

"Yes. Is that all a coincidence?" He paused and smiled, knowing there was more to come. "Now, one of these 12 graves was very special because it was a pyramid tomb. This in itself is extraordinary because only pharaohs and queens had pyramid tombs at this time. Yet the person buried in this tomb was not a king. Even so, he was honored with a king's burial.

A reconstruction of the pyramid tomb and chapel found behind the palace.

"And inside the chapel of the tomb was a statue. What we know from the statue is that this man had red hair; he had pale yellow skin, which is how Egyptians depicted northerners. He had a throw stick across his shoulder, a unique symbol of office made

Above: Re-creation of the Semitic official's statue that sat in the memorial chapel of the pyramid tomb.

At left: The head of the statue recovered from the pyramid tomb's chapel.

Statue with face broken off.

3D rendering of full statue.

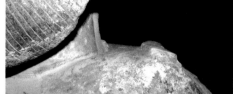

Statue's shoulder shows paint fragments.

Highlights show the pattern of paint fragments.

for this Asiatic official living in the land of Goshen. And on the back of his shoulder we see the faintest remains of paint – of colored stripes from a multicolored coat. And that matches exactly with the story of Joseph in the Bible. The multicolored coat is a gift, which shows that he was the favorite of the father. And it almost becomes his insignia, this coat. It's the thing we remember about him most of all." [16]

"Yes, I remember as a child hearing the story of Joseph and his coat of many colors."

He nodded. "And not only that but the statue is of superb workmanship."

"How can you tell?" I asked.

"I attended a conference at the British Museum where one of the speakers was Dorothea Arnold – a renowned art historian from the Metropolitan Museum – and she devoted an entire lecture to the subject of this statue. She was able to determine that the quality of the carving was so sophisticated that it was undoubtedly made in the royal workshops at Hawara where the famous Labyrinth and the pyramid of Amenemhat III stood, and where many of King Amenemhat's statues were carved. So the man buried in this pyramid tomb at Avaris had a colossal cult statute made for him by royal decree!"

"Do you know of any other statues of a Semite of this kind in Egypt?"

Rohl became serious and slightly shook his head. "No. There is nothing else like this in the whole of Egyptian history. Nothing at all."

The evidence was so powerful that I wanted to get a second opinion concerning this pyramid tomb and its Semitic occupant that Bietak had uncovered at the location of Avaris.

I went to interview Professor Charles Aling, an Egyptologist who has also investigated the events of the Exodus in Egypt. I did not have to travel far for this interview because the University of Northwestern, Saint Paul, where Professor Aling teaches ancient history, is just across the river from my hometown. He is known as one of the favorite professors among the students there.

It was a frigid winter morning with wind chills well below zero the day we arrived on campus. At the entrance the security guard waved us through as he stayed warm in his little hut. Our car squeaked as it traveled down the long winding drive through a miniature valley formed by the snowbanks piled high on either side. I was hoping we were early enough to find a parking space close to the loading zone. Fortunately there was one. We got out and opened the frozen back door of the truck. It groaned. When it's really cold like this, sound is different. The sky is bluer, and the air is thinner. I could

Egyptologist Charles Aling sees a connection between the statue and the account of Joseph.

see wisps of smoke escaping from the chimneys on the red brick buildings. On days like these you stay out of the wind because it cuts like a knife.

Inside the old Jesuit building, the wood floors had sounds of their own. The creak of footsteps preceded me as I walked down the hall to find Professor Aling's office. I enjoyed the ambiance of the old building with its high ceilings and woodwork. At his door I poked my head in and saw a heavy wood desk piled with papers, and a large bookcase sagging under the weight of hundreds of books. I set down the tripod and decided that the main source of light should come from the multi-paned windows.

"Hello, Tim," I heard a voice say behind me.

I turned. "Hello, Professor Aling. It's good to meet you again." He had just finished teaching his class and was now free. I decided to do the interview right at his desk. I'm sure there was an organization to this desk, but its charming disarray made it look like a set piece from *Indiana Jones*. I positioned him in front of it, sitting in a courtroom-style chair.

"Many scholars claim there's no evidence for the Exodus or for the early Israelites in Egypt. What do you think about that?"

Aling leaned back. "I heard Professor Bietak say once that they have been excavating for 60 seasons at Tell el-Dab'a, but after all that time, they have only uncovered about three percent of the total site. A season lasts about two or three months. They do two seasons a year usually."

"So for about 30 years they've been excavating there?"

"Yep, and they have excavated approximately three percent."

I was surprised. The figure seemed so small to me. They had barely scratched the surface.

Aling went on, "So when people say, 'Oh, there's nothing that's been found to verify the Bible' and so on, they're basing it on awfully slim evidence."

I wanted to hear what he would say about the important tomb that Rohl had connected with Joseph, so I asked him, "Would it be unusual for a tomb to have a statue?"

"No, no, it's not unusual. It's unusual to have one this large. This statue would be probably twice the size of a normal human being."

"What does that tell you when the statue is larger?"

"That it's a very important person," he explained. "Now, of course, this is not a pharaoh's tomb or palace, but the man who lived there, archaeologists can identify his

The colossal statue at the pyramid tomb was about twice life-size.

nationality by looking at the fragments of the statue. The fragments reveal three things: the hairstyle he has, which we often call the mushroom hairstyle; secondly, his weapon, a throw stick that he carries over his shoulder, which we would associate with an Australian boomerang; and then the coloration of the skin. The skin is yellow. All those things indicate that this would have been a Syro-Palestinian."

I asked Dr. Aling point-blank. "Do you think this is Joseph?"

"Either it is Joseph, or it's somebody who had a career remarkably the same as Joseph did. It's just an incredible thing to find this at this time period."

This certainly supported what Rohl had also concluded. Would there be any more evidence that fit this growing pattern?

III. Pharaoh's Dreams and Joseph's Famine Policy

In the ancient world people believed that dreams were significant because they foretold the future. The Bible records many instances when dreams predicted or warned of coming events. The book of Genesis records that Joseph as a young boy had dreams of his brothers and parents bowing down to him. His older brothers were greatly offended because these dreams were implying that Joseph would rule over them. They plotted to kill him but instead sold him as a slave for 20 shekels of silver. [17]

When I talked with Egyptologist James Hoffmeier, he told me he sees credibility in the details of the Joseph story. He explained, "There are a number of little details in the narratives that specialists in Ancient Near Eastern studies have noticed. For instance, the slave price of Joseph. He was sold for 20 shekels of silver, which sounds like a bargain price because later on in history we know that the price of slaves had moved up to 30 shekels of silver by the middle and later part of the second millennium BC."

"Did the slave price remain at 30 shekels?" I asked.

"When we get to the first millennium, it moves up to 50 shekels. And in the first millennium during the Persian period, the price goes way up off the charts. So 20 shekels fits the price of slaves from ancient documents from the early part of the second millennium BC."

"Why is this significant?"

"That's the kind of detail in the story that is not only authentic, but hardly one that a later writer a thousand years later could have dreamt up and got it right, knowing the economic considerations of the day."

Hoffmeier was arguing against Israel Finkelstein's claims that these early events in the Bible were compiled from myths and stories many centuries after the lives of Joseph and Moses. He was saying the slave price given in the account matches the specified time period too accurately to have been invented.

I asked Professor Hoffmeier about another aspect of the story, Joseph's interpretation of Pharaoh's dreams. "How important were dreams in the ancient Egyptian world?"

"We have these wonderful stories of Joseph interpreting dreams in the book of Genesis. Most people in the ancient world believed that dreams were a way in which a deity would communicate with a human directly. And so dreams were taken very seriously. We know this, thanks to a papyrus in the British Museum, the Chester Beatty papyrus. There were dream interpretation manuals in Egypt, which apparently would have been held by priests at temples."

"How did they use these manuals?"

"Apparently you could go on your way to work in the morning, swing by the temple and check with a priest and say, 'Look, I dreamt so and so last night. What does it mean?' And he could go through the scroll and find something similar. These dreams are arranged in two categories: those that have good outcomes and those with bad outcomes."

"That relates very specifically to the story of Joseph," I added.

Hoffmeier nodded in agreement. "It seems as if Joseph is presented as a wise man who can interpret dreams without the benefit of the dream interpretation manual. So that very nicely fits into an Egyptian setting."

The important details of the biblical story were proving to help us in the investigation. Now it would be necessary to look for details in the next events of the Genesis narrative that Rabbi Friedman continued to unfold, Joseph's rise from slavery to rule in Egypt.

"The Bible tells us that Joseph, with God's help, interpreted the dreams of Pharaoh. These dreams were about cattle coming out of the water of the Nile. In the first dream seven fat cows came out of the Nile, and in the second dream seven lean cows came out of the Nile and devoured the seven fat cows. Joseph was able to save Egypt by warning Pharaoh of a coming calamity: seven years of plenty would be followed by seven years of

Fishermen on the banks of the Nile River.

terrible famine. Pharaoh was so impressed by Joseph's ability to explain the dreams that he put Joseph in charge of preparing for the famine, and made him second in command over the entire country. " [18] [19]

In my interview with David Rohl he also expanded on the Bible's account of Joseph's interpretation of the dreams. "It's an extraordinary story, but the clue here is that these cows are coming out of the Nile. It's the Nile itself, which is the cause of both the plenty and the famine."

I echoed his thoughts. "So there's some type of connection to the Nile."

Rohl continued, "Yes. Now, what mechanism could have caused that? People often imagine that a low Nile, low inundations, or when the fields are not flooded, can cause famine. Well, they probably could, but it's not going to stop you from planting your crops if the water doesn't flow over the land for a couple of months of the year. What matters is the other way around, when there's so much water coming in that the land is flooded for too long and you can't plant your crops in the ground and then you don't get any harvest. Now if that happens for seven years on the trot, you're going to get a really major famine. I think that's what happened."

It reminded me of where I live. When the spring rains come after a heavy snow season, the river valleys can flood the fields for such a long time that the farmers can't plant. I added, "And then the other thing that happens is all the rain goes into one area of the country like the Midwestern United States, but it doesn't go in another area like California and the Southwest. They are in a drought."

"Yes, that's very similar to what's transpired in the biblical story," he replied. "Something's happened further upstream in the river. The river Nile has its sources up in central Africa and the Ethiopian Highlands, for instance. And normally in spring, it rains a lot in that area, and that water flows down the river and floods the Nile. So what happens if this rainfall was four or five times the normal amount?"

"The river would flood," I said.

"Exactly. To four or five times the normal level. It would take so long to disappear. I think that's what happened. Now what mechanism could have caused that? I think it's possible we've got a shift of the climatic zones."

"So do you think there was no rain where Joseph's family was up in Canaan, but it was raining somewhere else?"

Rohl said, "What has happened is the tropical zone around the equator has shifted northwards, causing rain to fall far more heavily on the Ethiopian Highlands. And what that does is push the dry Saharan climate into the land of Israel, into the area where Jacob and his family were living. So they were suffering drought while the Egyptians were suffering high floods at the same time. So you end up with a situation of high floods in Egypt, which is causing famine because they can't plant their crops, and Jacob is in a parched landscape, desperate to bring his people into Egypt, which of course is what happens when Joseph saves Egypt from the famine. Pharaoh invites the rest of his family to come down to settle in the land of Goshen."

That was an interesting theory, so I asked, "Do you see anything in Egyptian history that shows this kind of flooding happening?"

He smiled. "We have something quite remarkable. When we look for these high Niles, if you go right down to the southern border of Egypt, at a place where the water comes through a gorge, we find inscriptions on the cliff face marking the heights of the Nile during the inundation, during the flood, and they're four times higher than they normally are in this period. So there's a massive amount of water entering Egypt at the time, and it takes so long to dissipate out to the Mediterranean."

"So the high flooding causes serious problems."

"They can't plant their crops, and therefore they don't get a harvest, and therefore you get famine."

"So, this record shows that it happened over a series of years?"

"Yes," he said, "consecutive years, right in the time of this king Amenemhat III. That for me is Joseph's famine. The reign of this pharaoh was in the Middle Kingdom, conventionally dated around 1850 BC." [20]

"Has anything else been found that connects Joseph to this flooding in Egypt?"

"There's a canal, or a waterway, which flows parallel to the Nile and enters into a large lake area called the Fayum. The Fayum was like an oasis basin to the west. It's in the Sahara Desert. This canal has the name Bahr Yusef, which means the waterway of Joseph. And this goes back thousands of years as far as we can tell."

"Interesting," I said. "So there's actually a canal that has the very name of Joseph. Why do you think the canal has that name?"

"Because I think he made it," Rohl replied. "I think it was under his instructions as vizier of Egypt that that canal was cut. It's a brilliant idea. It diverts 50 percent of the water to the Fayum Basin and saves the rest of Egypt from flooding."

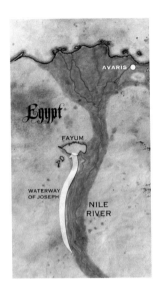

The Bahr Yusef, or waterway of Joseph, was originally constructed in the 12th Dynasty of the Middle Kingdom.

I was intrigued by the concept that flooding could cause a famine just as easily as drought. "So what you're suggesting is that Joseph anticipated these floods that could wipe out the cropland, and he prepared for them by creating a canal to siphon off the water?"

"Exactly. Reduce the water by half and you get back to the land of plenty again – back to the situation where the water levels are just right for growing crops."

"Can you still see the canal today?"

"Yes, absolutely. It's nearly the size of the Nile itself. It's a huge waterway. What's interesting about the construction of this water diversion system is that it is known to have been developed in the same period as the early settlement at Avaris in the Middle Kingdom."

The Joeseph Canal as it looks today.

"Fascinating. Does the name go all the way back to the time of Joseph?"

"The name Bahr Yusef is Arabic, and scholars don't know what it was called before the Arabic period, which began in 639 AD. I think the name was not simply invented at that time but instead was based on an ancient tradition, which held that Joseph was the builder of the canal. But the one thing we do know is that the waterway itself was actually made around the time of Pharaoh Amenemhat III, which coincides with the early development of Avaris."

Whether David Rohl's theory is correct or not, it seems plausible that this water diversion system would have been helpful in drought as well as in high flooding. In low-flood years the meager amounts of water could have been conserved in the basin and channeled into smaller canals surrounding the Fayum in the following months.

When I had first interviewed Israeli President Peres, he talked at length about the stories of the Bible. I wanted to find out his perspective on the destiny of Joseph and his rise from slavery to a position of second in command in Pharaoh's court. "If you look at the way the story is written," I said, "God chose Joseph for a mission to save his family, Egypt, and the surrounding nations."

Peres was thoughtful. "I read somewhere that Tolstoy said that this is the greatest story ever published in human literature – the story of Joseph and his brothers, and his going to Egypt. Joseph was the first Jewish advisor on the Earth. And he advised the most powerful empire in the vicinity. He conquered the heart of everybody he saw, men and women. It's really a fascinating story. So a child that has imagination could get enough food for the rest of his life in Joseph and the Passover."[21]

IV. The Rise of Pharaoh's Power

Rabbi Friedman went on to tell the biblical story of Egypt's preparations for the coming famine. "Joseph gathers up all the grain during the seven years of plenty in Egypt. He gathered as much as the sand of the sea, and then the famine comes to the entire region, and only Egypt has bread. So everyone comes to Joseph for what they need for survival.

"When their money runs out, they sold their animals. When that ran out, they sold their land, and eventually they sold themselves. So Pharaoh by the end of the seven years owns everything in Egypt." [22]

Archaeologist Bryant Wood at his home in Pennsylvania.

I flew alone to Pennsylvania to see Dr. Bryant Wood, an archaeologist who has spent many years studying the Exodus and the Conquest. It was my understanding that he had insights into Egypt's history and its possible connection to the story of Joseph. I hoped the rental car I was getting at the airport had good windshield wipers. With the heavy rain coming down that evening, I would need them. I drove for almost an hour down the Interstate before I reached my hotel around midnight. But that was okay. Now I was only a few miles from the Woods' home.

When I woke up the next morning, there were slivers of light outlining the window in my dark room. I got up and peeked through the drapes. The rain had passed, and the morning was turning into one of those beautiful summer days after a storm has cleared the air. Driving down the highway through the Pennsylvania farmland, I took notice of how nice it was for the Woods to live in such a peaceful setting. I turned past a cornfield and down a tar road where milking cows were lazily chewing grass in the meadow. The road then turned and led me into a newer development of homes.

It was Dr. Wood's wife, Faith, who met me at the door.

"Come in, come in," she said with a big smile.

"Thank you."

"Bryant will be down in a minute. Just make yourself at home."

When I arrive at a new location I always try to figure out the best setting for the interview. The Woods had a large living room that extended into their dining room. The warm reflection of the morning sun was coming in from the east through two patio doors. For a while this would work as a fill light for the filming, so I set the gear up in the living room and was almost ready when I heard him coming down the stairs.

"Hello, you must be Tim Mahoney."

"Yes, I am."

"Glad to meet you. Did you have any trouble finding us?"

"None at all," I said. "Your directions were very clear."

I would guess he was in his early 70s. He wore glasses, his hair was neatly combed, and when he smiled, it was genuine because he smiled with his eyes. The maroon shirt he had on bore the logo for the *Associates for Biblical Research*, an organization for which he was the research director.

"I was just printing off some information about my work that I thought you might like to have for your project," he said as he sat down in the chair in front of the camera. Sitting opposite him, I made some last minute adjustments to the camera's focus.

"Excellent. We're creating quite a library now," I admitted.

Curious, he asked, "Who have you interviewed so far?"

"Well, quite a few. Professor Ken Kitchen, Jim Phillips, Jodi Magness, Israel Finkelstein, Norma Franklin, Manfred Bietak, Charles Aling, David Rohl, Prime Minister Benjamin Netanyahu, and Shimon Peres to name a few."

"Well, that's quite a collection, I must say."

"Yes, it is." I was a bit distracted. There was something buzzing in my headphones, something in the background. Where was it coming from? Oh, there it was. It always happens around kitchens.

I smiled. "Would you mind if I unplugged your refrigerator for the interview? I can hear it humming through your microphone."

"Oh, yes, certainly."

"I promise to remember to plug it back in, but just to be sure let's tell Faith. We know she'll remember." It's always good manners to remember to plug things back in when finished, especially refrigerators. There have been a few times when I forgot.

Finally we were ready. I leaned over, started the camera, and said, "Tell me about your background."

Wood gave me a charming grin. "I had 13 years with GE, dealing with nuclear reactors, and was involved most of the time with testing the nuclear reactor, gathering data relative to those tests, analyzing the data, and then publishing the results. So, when I got into archaeology I discovered that this background was very, very helpful because I'm doing pretty much the same thing with regard to ancient questions, biblical questions."

"Could you elaborate on some of these similarities?"

"Archaeology is gathering data, pottery, architecture, and so on, things we dig out of the ground. And by analyzing the data, then we can reach conclusions." He paused for a moment. "I find that others in this field do not have this approach. They do not have technical backgrounds, scientific backgrounds. Many times they will say, 'Well, such and such archaeologists believe this, so we should all follow that esteemed authority figure' or 'Most scholars believe this.'"

"Why is that a problem?" I challenged.

"Well, that's not the scientific approach. The scientific approach is to analyze the data, reach conclusions based on that data, and then publish the results, and that's the approach that I take in the field of archaeology."

I think Wood was trying to impress on me that just because a view has the support of the majority of scholars doesn't mean that it's always right.

I remembered the biblical story of the famine and wondered if there ever was a time in Egyptian history when a dramatic shift of wealth and power occurred between the people of Egypt and the pharaoh. When I asked Wood about this idea, he told me something surprising.

"Well, if you examine Joseph's famine policy, you'll see he was very astute. He didn't simply give the grain away, as some kind of giant welfare program. He sold the grain, and so the people had to buy the grain. So over those seven years all the wealth of Egypt came into Joseph, which meant that it came to Pharaoh, because Joseph was sort of the chief steward, you might say, for Pharaoh."

"Do you see anything similar in Egyptian history?"

Throughout much of the Middle Kingdom's 12th Dynasty, the regional governors (or nomarchs) had tremendous wealth and power. At one point the influential status of the nomarchs suddenly ended as all the wealth and power shifted to the pharaoh.

"We find something very significant happening at this exact time. Egypt was divided up into areas called nomes, kind of like districts, all over the country. Prior to the time of Joseph, the leaders of these nomes – nomarchs they were called – had tremendous wealth and tremendous power. [23]

"We get to a point in Egyptian history when suddenly that all changes and all the wealth is concentrated with the pharaoh. What on earth happened here? If you read the Egyptian history books, there is no explanation for it."

"None at all?"

"They don't know what happened or how it happened. I mean this was a tremendous socioeconomic change in Egypt, a very conservative country, which does not change easily, but suddenly the whole thing is turned upside down. Instead of the nomarchs having all this power and authority and wealth, it's all concentrated with the pharaoh."

"So what do you think happened?"

"Well, we have the answer in the Bible, and it's Joseph's famine policy, and he brings the wealth into Pharaoh. And it fits exactly with Egyptian history."

Was this just a coincidence?

The interesting thing is that David Rohl had mentioned another detail that matched the occurrence of famine and central control at this time in Egypt. While we were talking at the great library in Saint Paul, he told me, "We have this new administration that sets up in Egypt, an agency called the Department of the People's Giving, where the people grow their crops and bring them to government storehouses where they're kept and then, apparently, in times of crisis, the food's then redistributed back to the people. This Department of the People's Giving exactly fits the Joseph story."

Hearing all of this from Aling, Wood, and Rohl was making me step back and think to myself, *It's not very likely all of this could be a coincidence.*

RISE OF AVARIS

SENUSRET III 1878-1839

AMENEMHAT III 1860-1814

1900s BC   1800s BC   1700s BC

00s
BC

Rohl believes the time of the famine occurred during the overlapping reigns of two important Middle Kingdom pharaohs.

Rohl told me he believes that this upheaval occurred around 1850 BC, during the overlapping reigns of two important Middle Kingdom pharaohs, Senusret III and his son Amenemhat III. Rohl identified features on both their statues that suggest some kind of hardship was in the land at that time.

"That sounds interesting," I said. "Tell me more about those features."

"Amenemhat is depicted with worry lines. His ears are turned out so that he can listen to the concerns of the people. He's got a frown on his face. He looks like a very concerned pharaoh, a very human pharaoh. He's not depicted in the usual bland way that you see on all the other statues of past and future pharaohs," explained Rohl.

"What do you conclude from this?"

"I think that this indicates there are serious problems in the land. The people are struggling to survive, and he is showing you sympathy for that struggle in his face. So I think that's an important sign that this is the era of famine. And guess what – he builds his pyramid right next to Bahr Yusef, the Waterway of Joseph."

In our research we came across another interesting example in the archaeology of Egypt that demonstrates the tremendous growth in the pharaoh's wealth and power during this Middle Kingdom period. Archaeologists uncovered a series of Egyptian super-forts built on Egypt's southern Nile border with Nubia. The discovery of these forts baffled archaeologists because their advanced architecture appeared to be thousands of years ahead of their time and the size of these forts was far larger than any military need.

These fortresses resembled great medieval castles with walls about 33 feet high and 16 feet thick. They contained moats, drawbridges, bastions, buttresses, ramparts, and even catapults. The largest of these super-forts covered 40,000 square meters (an area equivalent to almost seven American football fields, including the end zones). Some of these forts were started by earlier pharaohs, but their later funding and development to super-size were done by Senusret III, who reigned concurrently with Amenemhat III and built 11 forts in all. Sadly, all of these forts were covered by Lake Nasser when the Aswan Dam became operational in 1970. [24]

Again, the biblical story states that all the wealth and power came into the pharaoh during this time of famine. Did this fuel the tremendous building activity of these super-forts in southern Egypt?

The statues of Amenemhat III (seen at top) were depicted in a more serious and realistic way than typical pharaohs (as seen below).

V. The Egyptian Tomb of Joseph?

David Rohl and I had been talking for almost an hour, yet the time had swept by so fast I hardly noticed. I had just heard a number of amazing similarities in Egypt that supported the story of Joseph's rise to power and the policies he may have instituted during the time of a great famine. But Rohl wasn't finished. He had one more amazing connection based on the evidence at the pyramid tomb of Avaris.

By now I knew him well enough to tell that his next point would be really dramatic. "The crucial clue for me, which says that this man with the multicolored coat is Joseph, is found in the story of Exodus. When Joseph is on his deathbed, he tells his brethren that when they leave they must take his body with them to the Promised Land. But what matches the story even more incredibly is that that pyramid tomb was empty when the archaeologists found it. There was nothing in it at all apart from a few fragments of this smashed statue. There were no bones; there were no mummy beads, no coffin wood, nothing. It was cleaned out."

"Was it a grave robber?"

"No! What grave robber is going to take the bones? Bones are intrinsically of no value whatsoever. Nobody takes the bones. Only people who are treating the body with reverence take the bones. The body was taken out, and all the grave goods were taken out."

"So what do you think happened?"

"I think this is the tomb of Joseph – the pyramid tomb of Joseph – honored by Pharaoh with a colossal statue. When Moses decided to take the people out of Egypt, he made sure he fulfilled that promise to Joseph, to take the body out of the tomb and take it to Shechem and bury him in the Promised Land." [25]

Joseph tells his family that they must take his bones with them when they leave Egypt.

VI. Shechem: A Place of Conflict and Promise

The Bible claims Joseph's bones were buried in a town known as Shechem. When Abraham first came into the land of Canaan, God spoke to him at Shechem and promised him and his descendants the land. Perhaps this is why Joseph asked his descendants to take his bones with them to the Promised Land to rebury them there. He didn't want his remains to be left behind in Egypt. [26]

Shechem is where many believe Joseph's bones were finally laid to rest. The shrine of Joseph there has been considered a holy site for centuries and throughout the ages has been venerated by many Jews, Samaritans, Christians, and Muslims. Today Shechem is known as Nablus on the West Bank, a city populated by well over 100,000 people. [27]

In the year 2000, just hours after the Palestinians gained control of the West Bank, the shrine of Joseph in Nablus was attacked and damaged by a mob during the Second Intifada demonstrations. Since that time, the tomb has been repaired, but this is still a politically sensitive area.

The stories from the Bible tap into deep emotions and unresolved conflicts that go back for centuries on all sides. This was one reason I was reluctant to investigate these ancient events. But I also experienced a positive side to this complex story when I filmed in Israel with both Israelis and Palestinians. We became a great production team, working together as friends. In Egypt as well, our crew was from different religious and political backgrounds. They were all good people, and without them, I couldn't have done it. Going to the Middle East taught me that most people around the world want very much the same things: food, shelter, a way to make a living, and of course a future for their families.

One day while in Minnesota, I went to my co-producer, Pete Windahl, and asked, "Can you find out if Biblical Productions can get us to a location in the West Bank?"

"Where?"

"To Nablus. It's the place where Joseph's bones were said to have been buried, and I would really like to see it."

"It could be tricky."

"See what you can do," I said. As usual, Sharon Schaveet came through.

Weeks later, our crew was traveling up a steep road to the ruins of a Byzantine church and castle situated on top of Mount Gerizim. It overlooked the city of Nablus. We had gotten permission to go to the mountain but not to the shrine of Joseph in the city just below.

When we arrived, the wind was blowing low clouds through the ancient ruins. The view over the valley was spectacular. I yelled to the cameraman, "Follow me! We've got to hurry before the sun burns these clouds off."

"Where are we going?"

"To the edge."

The mountain was several thousand feet above sea level, and there we were, standing in clouds as they passed through us. It was a gift I didn't want to miss. I walked along the edge of a stone wall above a drop-off as my cameraman filmed me. The backdrop was the valley below and, beyond that, more mountains. For a moment I envisioned what this land might have looked like thousands of years ago – shepherds with their flocks grazing peacefully beneath the shelter of the mountains. Directly below me I noticed more ancient ruins. The Bible records that Shechem was a place of much blessing and promise, but it had also seen much conflict and tragedy throughout its history.

The Shrine of Joseph photographed in the 1800s.

The view overlooking the modern city of Nablus (ancient Shechem).

"They're gone," I shouted to the cameraman. The last of the clouds faded away. "Did you get the shot?"

He put up his thumb and nodded yes.

It was from this vantage point that we zoomed in on the shrine of Joseph. This was as close as I could get for now. It was just too risky to call attention to ourselves by setting up a film crew down there.

After we returned from that trip, I wasn't very satisfied with the results. "Pete, that just wasn't enough."

"I'll see if we can get something better."

Pete talked with Sharon Schaveet, and she hired a local cameraman who filmed the shrine and the nearby archaeological site more extensively. When the new footage came, it was very exciting to finally see what we were dealing with. In time, I would come to realize how significant the ancient area of Shechem is, and how well the archaeology fits the stories of the Bible. But a fuller look at those connections will have to wait for now.

Central Park in New York City, several blocks from Jackie Mason's home.

VII. A Lesson From the Life of Joseph

What can we learn about conflict and forgiveness from the story of Joseph, whose life began with great tragedy? I discovered one answer to this question in an interview with comedian Jackie Mason. I got the idea to interview Mason after talking with Michael Medved, who was in town hosting a "Night at the Oscar's" at the Saint Paul Hotel. As we sat in the hotel restaurant for coffee the next morning, I talked to Michael about the intrinsic Jewish nature of the Exodus story. I asked if he knew of any noteworthy Jewish people that I could interview. He paused to think. Then a smile came over his face, and he reluctantly said, "Well, what about Jackie Mason?"

"The comedian?" I laughed, which is what comedians want you to do.

"Yes. Don't laugh. When Jackie was a young man, he was ordained as a rabbi, and I think he comes from a long line of rabbis."

I thought for a moment about the few times I had seen him do his act. He certainly was a unique personality, and I grinned. "Well, that certainly would be an interesting interview."

I contacted Mason's agent, and we went back and forth for a while. Just when I thought we were done talking, the agent would call back. It seemed that Mason was intrigued. We finally reached an agreement, and I flew to New York City. When we met at his apartment just a few blocks from Central Park, Mason started to give me the tough guy routine, which is a little humorous in itself since I'm about twice his size. He stood in front of his dining room table and gave me a serious look. "Okay, what's this all about anyway? Why are you making a film about the Exodus? What kind of thing is this? What are you – a part of a religious cult or something?"

I didn't say anything for a moment. I was thinking, *Hey, I just flew here to film you. I thought you wanted to be interviewed.* Then the idea came to me to tell him about my childhood. I told him about my dad roughing me up as a kid and my parents' divorce. Jackie listened intently as I shared how my mother tucked me in at night and said bedtime prayers. She was the one who told me the stories from the Bible, and now I just wanted to know if they were true or not. I could tell my story connected with him.

Jackie Mason being interviewed at his home in New York.

When I finished talking, he was done questioning me and kindly showed me into his living room. "No problem. You can set up your gear right over here. Where's the rest of the crew?"

"I am the crew."

He left for a few minutes so I could set up. The big challenge was Jackie's living room. It was full of mirrors and windows. Every background reflected the camera and lights. I did manage to find one wall where Mason could not see his own reflection.

I got him settled and opened the interview with a little humor. "So you're Jewish?"

"Well, I came from a family of rabbis, and it was considered my destiny to become a rabbi, and I felt that I owed it to my father and everything that he lived for and everything that was his most guiding principles in life. That's why I went into it. Then I became a rabbi and I realized that I was much more interested in jokes. And jokes to me create happiness, and it won't help me exactly fulfill all of his mission, but at least I'll fulfill part of his mission."

"So what kind of jokes are we talking about?"

"The joke that gets the biggest laugh in my act is when I talk about the Lord saying to Moses, 'Come forth.' We all know what happened. Moses came fifth, and the Lord lost two dollars."

I smiled. "What else you got?"

"I go to a temple that's so reformed that the rabbi is a Gentile. And they have a big sign in the front that says 'No Jews Allowed.' There is one temple that's so reformed that it's closed on Jewish holidays."

That one made me laugh out loud.

He told another one. "Then I imitate the Reform rabbi speaking, 'I walketh, I talketh, I seeth, I goeth,' and the Lord said to Moses, 'Where?' and Moses said, 'What are you talking about?' And the Lord said to Moses, 'Take me back to my people – where are my people?' and Moses said, 'What do you want from me? They're in Miami Beach.'"

Mason continued using humor, but after a while both of us knew it was time to get serious. Then I asked him a question that brought forth a response I didn't expect to hear from a comedian. "Jackie, why is Joseph such an important character in the Torah?"

"We learn so much about life from Joseph. We learn the principle of forgiveness, for instance, how he forgave his brothers for all their transgressions."

I knew what he was talking about. The Bible states that early in his life Joseph was betrayed by his jealous brothers who tossed him into a pit and planned to kill him, but then they changed their minds and sold him as a slave to traders on their way to Egypt.

He became more passionate. "When somebody treats you like that, for you to forgive them is totally inconceivable to people."

"You're right."

"The easiest thing is retribution because hate comes naturally whenever somebody commits any kind of crime against you – or perception of a crime."

The Bible says that after Jacob died, Joseph's brothers feared he would kill them in revenge, but he didn't. Instead he assured them that though they had meant their deed for evil, God had meant it for good. [28]

"The principle of forgiveness should be the greatest principle, and it's the most desecrated and neglected of all the great humanitarian principles of life," he said.

"Do you think the story of Joseph and his brothers was a true story?"

Mason was adamant. "I think Joseph was positively a literal story. It positively had to be a true story because there are too many events that happened that strike anybody who studies the Bible as a simple reality. This cannot be contrived. This cannot be introduced as some kind of fable."

"Why not?"

"Because a fable can never reach us in those terms and strike the hearts of people the way that did."

After the interview I looked directly at Mason and said, "Your father the Rabbi would be very proud of you."

VIII. Arrival Summary and Timeline

The amount of archaeological evidence matching the first step of **Arrival** in the biblical sequence seemed overwhelming to me:

- The Syrian-styled house that appeared in the Delta along with a palace fit for royalty whose occupant was a high Semitic official from the Canaan area, who wore a multicolored coat,
- The Waterway of Joseph, contemporary with the rise of Avaris,
- The end of influence and wealth for the regional governors as the power of Pharaoh reached new heights,

The 400-year distance between the new Semitic settlement at Avaris and where Arrival evidence would be expected in the Ramesses Exodus Theory.

143

- Yet, this event happened at a time in the Middle Kingdom when the statues of the pharaohs were depicted in a uniquely careworn way – the tell-tale signs of a kingdom in distress,
- And the empty tomb of the Semitic Ruler.

As we sat in the great hall of the library in Saint Paul, I asked David Rohl a nagging question. "Why haven't Professor Manfred Bietak and others considered the possibility of a connection here?"

"Because in the scheme that's used by scholars to date all these events, they're way too early. They're much too early to be Israelites."

For a moment I thought back to the interview with Bietak. "You're right. Bietak said that to connect the people he found at Avaris with the proto-Israelites was 'a very weak affair.'"

Rohl leaned back in his chair. "Well, that's a great way out of this situation, isn't it?"

Come to think about it, I had noticed that many scholars do not like to use the term *Israelite*. Looking at Rohl, I said, "Yes, he used the word *proto-Israelite*."

Rohl nodded his head as if he had heard this all before. "Right. And many scholars do. What they're basically saying is, 'We're quite happy for you to use these events and these personalities, these people from earlier times, and make them the basis of the biblical story, but that doesn't make them the real people of the Bible.' I'm basically saying, 'Well, why not call a spade a spade?'"

Our time in the great library was over, and we walked out into the city of Saint Paul. I was coming to a deeper realization of the controversy surrounding the Exodus on so many levels – religious, political, and archaeological. It is religiously controversial because it raises questions about the historical credibility of Judaism and Christianity. It is politically controversial because it implies a piece of land was given by God to Abraham and his descendants, the children of Israel. And it is archaeologically controversial for anyone to suggest that this specific evidence at Avaris matches the story of Joseph and the early Israelites' arrival in Egypt. This is because the Avaris evidence is much earlier than the time the Israelites were supposed to be in Egypt according to conventional thinking. But at this stage I had to remind myself to be open-minded. I needed to stick with one of the main guidelines of the investigation and look for a pattern of evidence wherever it might exist. ♱

VI: Steps Two and Three: Evidence of Multiplication and Slavery?

I. Multiplication: Semitic Growth at Avaris

It was time for Rabbi Friedman to explain the next part of the story, which is covered in Exodus, the second book of the Bible. I asked him to move closer to the ark that held the Torah scrolls and adjusted the camera accordingly. Behind him was a deep blue tapestry that overlaid the front of the ark. On this tapestry were embroidered ornate images of the ancient scrolls.

It was very easy working with Rabbi Friedman. He had told these stories for decades, and it showed in his relaxed manner. "There is another clue we must look for," I said. "What does the Bible say happened next?"

The Rabbi's tone was serious. "The biblical account tells us that Joseph dies, as well as his brothers and their entire generation. But the Israelites are exceedingly fruitful until they fill the land." [29]

As I moved forward with my new approach, I needed to know if archaeologists had found any evidence that matches this second step of the six-step pattern – what the Bible calls "exceedingly great" **Multiplication.**

The city of Saint Paul, as I have mentioned earlier, had a meager beginning, and it also experienced a great multiplication. Along the east bank of the Mississippi River, the population around the original trading post grew into the settlement of Pig's Eye. Upon his arrival a Catholic priest, Father Lucien Galtier, immediately built a small chapel in the area in 1841. Whether the words were his or just folklore, Galtier reportedly proclaimed, "Pig's Eye, converted thou shalt be, like Saul; arise, and be, henceforth, Saint Paul!" [30]

Rabbi Manis Friedman explains the next step of the Exodus story – the Multiplication of the Israelites.

The mansion built by James J. Hill, which overlooks the city of Saint Paul.

Below: Donkey burials at Avaris in the tradition of Semitic cultures.

A Semitic-styled burial with unique body position and grave goods.

From that time the city has been known by that name, and it grew over the years to become the capital of Minnesota.

It was on the bluffs, above the site of this early settlement in the city of Saint Paul, that David Rohl and I now walked through the melting snow to our next filming location. It was a mansion built by railroad baron James J. Hill, who had also built the library where we had just come from. Overlooking the Mississippi River, surrounded by wall and fence, it was an estate that peered over the growing populace. Outside its arched gates and across the street is Saint Paul Cathedral. For over a century, the bells from its high towers have been heard throughout the streets of the city.

We walked inside the mansion, through a large atrium and past two massive doors into the main hallway. I had chosen this setting as the primary background for the next part of Rohl's interview. It displayed a historic elegance with its main fireplace and wood paneling of rich, deep brown tones. Behind us was a gigantic staircase with intricately hand-carved woodworking, an art form from the 19th century that now seems to be lost. We sat down and began to talk.

"David, what happened next in the Delta that matches the biblical story?"

Rohl told me about the remarkable Semitic expansion at Avaris. "At first there is a virgin land with no population at all. And suddenly there is a small group of Semitic people settled there."

"How many are we talking about?"

"There's probably a dozen or 15 houses – let's say about 70 or 100 people all told. And over a period of maybe three or four generations it becomes a very large city, one of the largest cities in the ancient world."

"What's unique about it?"

"This city is a city of foreigners in the Egyptian Delta. And it's been allowed by the Egyptian state. At this stage these people are not slaves. These Semitic peoples have migrated here, bringing their flocks with them, and are living here and surviving in such a way that they become quite rich and wealthy."

In Chicago I also asked Professor James Hoffmeier about these people who arrived at Avaris. "What does the archaeology say about the area Joseph's family is said to have settled?"

Hoffmeier said, "We do know that there was a large Semitic speaking population, which probably came in from Syria, Canaan, sometime in the early part of the second millennium BC. Their remains have been found at a number of sites. We have tombs that are clearly those of foreigners, Semites; we can tell this by the pottery, by the kind of weapons. These are not Egyptian-type axes and daggers. In some cases, they have donkeys buried with them."

Avaris quickly expanded into one of the largest cities of the ancient world. Image based on dig-site data.

"Is that unusual?" I asked.

"This was not an Egyptian practice. So the types of tombs, the types of architecture, are not Egyptian. These are clearly foreigners who have moved into Egypt and have lived there long enough to establish mudbrick homes and some sort of permanent dwellings."

I wondered if it was possible that these people were the early Israelites. "So these people, according to the archaeology, were not Egyptians?"

Semitic weapons, including daggers and axes found at Avaris.

He shook his head. "These were non-Egyptians; they were clearly from the Semitic-speaking world. The material culture of these people fits with the southern Levant, the southern part of Canaan. We can't say for sure that any of these were Hebrews, but we probably couldn't distinguish a Hebrew from a Canaanite in Egypt culturally speaking anyway. They would have looked very much alike. They would have spoken a very similar dialect. So archaeologically it would be hard to tell a Hebrew from a Canaanite in the archaeological record in Egypt."

Then Hoffmeier started to tell me about a magnificent tomb built by a regional governor at the site of Beni Hasan in central Egypt. On its walls there are paintings depicting a caravan of Semitic traders coming down to Egypt with their families.

Beni Hasan Traders

This tomb painting from Beni Hasan was made by the powerful nomarch Khnumhotep II. He served the Middle Kingdom's Pharaoh Senusret II (conventionally reigning from about 1897-1878 BC) who immediately preceded Senusret III, thought by some to be Joseph's pharaoh. It includes an inscription saying that the party of 37 under the leadership of a man named Ibsha (or Abishai) were trading eye paint used for makeup. The yellow skin, facial hair, and colorful clothing distinguish the Semitic group from the Egyptian men in the row below. Could a similar group from this period have brought Joseph down to Egypt to sell him as a slave?

"The famous painting in the tomb of Khnumhotep of Beni Hasan shows a group of 37 Semitic-speaking foreigners who've come to Egypt," said Hoffmeier.

"What are they doing?"

"They are probably engaged in trade. There are pictures of their bellows for their stoking up the fires for their smelting work and so on. So we do know that foreigners were coming into Egypt at different periods of time. And so the idea of a family like Jacob, an extended family moving into Egypt for hardship or economic reasons, is not unparalleled. These sort of things did happen."

I learned that the tomb of Khnumhotep II at Beni Hasan is one of the last examples of the extravagant wealth and power held by the regional nomarchs before their sudden decline and the rise of pharaohs Senusret III and his son Amenemhat III. Hoffmeier believes these types of inscriptions give general support for the idea of Semites coming to Egypt, just as Jacob's family came to Egypt in the Bible story. But he also stresses that there are limitations to what we can expect from the archaeological record.

"Is there any parallel here with Jacob's family and the early Israelites coming to Egypt?"

"We probably will never find an inscription that says that Jacob slept here. We'll probably never find a similar document that says Abraham rode a camel or rode a donkey on this road. This is an unrealistic expectation of what archaeology can and cannot do. What archaeology can do is provide some of the background information. We have no direct archaeological evidence to confirm the reality of these individuals or the events the Bible talks about," explained Hoffmeier. "There is, however, a large segment of what I call contextual or background information which enables the story to come across as very realistic and authentic."

Israelites (Hebrews) and Canaanites

Jacob's family, all the way back to Abraham, had been living in the region of Canaan and North Syria. This would have been a period of over 200 years. At the time they entered Egypt, they would have had a Semitic culture indistinguishable from their Canaanite neighbors.

II. Music in the Mix

During the early production of this film, I worked with screenwriter and creative consultant Bart Gavigan for over a year, including several weeks in England. Bart and his lovely wife Patricia were living west of London near Hurst, where they've converted a carriage house into production offices and an edit suite. There during the mornings and afternoons I would work alone; then at the end of each day I would discuss the edits with Bart.

Screenwriter Bart Gavigan suggests taking the film to the next level with music.

The editing bay must have been a large horse stall at one time. On pleasant days I would open wide the old wooden door with its metal hinges, hoping the sun would warm the brick room from the chill of the previous night. It was enjoyable listening to the wind blowing leaves across the stone driveway. Holding a cup of hot tea would help me to think through all the storytelling options. Late one afternoon I heard a familiar voice.

"Timothy, how is it going today?" It was Bart. He walked in through the open door and sat down next to me at the editing console. He was so good at making people feel accepted, and it was his and Patricia's generosity that let me stay over for a while. He wore one of those long scarves that wrapped around his neck and flowed past him as he walked. What I enjoyed about our friendship was his gift for storytelling. To be honest, it was his idea that I get out from behind the camera and tell the story in front of it as well.

"Well, I need more music," I said. "I like what I am cutting, but it won't be enough without more music."

"Yes, you do need more music but you need real music with a live orchestra. I have a feeling what you are doing here in this film is very, very significant. You need to get a composer and have the film musically scored. Once that happens, we should go to

Budapest and record the soundtrack with a full orchestra and possibly a choir. I have done this in the past and I know just the right people to help pull it off."

It was another twist in the long road, but one that I would not regret.

III. Multiplication: Semitic Expansion in the Nile Delta

If the Israelites had multiplied exceedingly as the Bible describes, they would have expanded beyond the city of Avaris until they had filled the land. To explore if there was further evidence of Semitic expansion in Egypt's history, I needed to know what the Bible says, so I could test it against the archaeology and see if there was support for it or not. Just how many Israelites would have lived in Egypt at this time?

According to the Bible, there were over 600,000 Israelite men by the time of the Exodus, which suggests a total population of over two million with women and children. Many scholars dispute these figures and claim the Bible has been misunderstood on this point. Some suggest the number is around 20,000 Israelites. I needed to determine what number the Bible actually portrays since it would affect how large a group of people we should be looking for. Is it a massive group of two million or a relatively small group of 20,000? Some of the debate over this topic and an examination of the validity of the 600,000 number is included at the back of the book in Bonus Chapter C.

During the course of the investigation, I heard about John Bimson, a biblical scholar in Bristol, England. He has written extensively about archaeology and the accounts of Exodus and the Conquest. I was hopeful he would have information about this expansion in the Delta area of Egypt. I sent him an introductory message.

....

Hello Professor Bimson,

I would like to interview you for a feature film I am working on concerning the Exodus and the Conquest. My researcher thinks you would be a great addition to our project. I will be coming to England to film April 30 - May 1. Would we be able to connect during this time?

Tim Mahoney, Director

....

The challenge again was contacting Professor Bimson. He wasn't returning my email, and I was very concerned we wouldn't connect on my layover in England on the way to my final visit to Egypt for this project. I am a compulsive email checker. And when I have emails out like fishing lines to different people, I check for "bites" from the moment I wake up until the time I go to bed. And sometimes, I confess, I check my phone on the nightstand in the middle of the night.

Finally, several weeks before leaving I received the long anticipated email from Professor Bimson.

....

Dear Tim,

I'm sorry to be slow replying to your emails. I've been away and not picking up emails until yesterday.

Thank you for the invitation to take part in your project, which sounds very interesting and worthwhile. Unfortunately, I'm not available April 30 - May 1, as I'm already fully committed, teaching in Bristol for the whole of that week. I hope your other filming in the UK goes well.

John
Dr John J. Bimson
Tutor in Biblical Studies

....

Hello John,

How can I say this, but I think you are one of the most important voices for the Conquest and I can't see making a film about this subject without your participation. Would it be possible to do an interview if I come straight from the airport April 30th, Sunday? I would love to meet you if we could work this out.

Sincerely,
Tim Mahoney
Director Exodus film (working title)

....

Dear Tim,

Thank you for your kind words.

I'm slightly confused by your email which speaks of April 30th as Sunday when in fact it's Monday. If in fact you mean Sunday, I fear my complicated lifestyle will be a problem for this plan. On the other hand, if you mean Monday, I could be free roughly 5.00-6.00 pm.

Best wishes,
John

....

Hello John,

I did mean Monday, April 30th, and I will plan to interview you between 5PM and 8PM.

Tim

This was excellent. Persistence had helped again to reel in another interview, and a very important one at that. Since I knew it would take more time, I extended it by two hours. I can't believe how close this interview came to not happening.

The following week David Wessner and I landed in London on a Sunday and took the train from the airport terminal to Bristol two hours away. We met up with Malcolm Turner, a producer, and Crawford Teller, a former BBC cameraman and one of the funniest Scotsmen you'll ever meet. They would be my crew for the interview.

On the southwest side of England, the city of Bristol is a seaport flowing out to the Atlantic Ocean. It has existed for nearly 1,000 years and has a history known for its sea merchants and its trade in commodities. Since then, it has grown into a modern metropolis involved with education, arts, and media.

The next morning was one of those English days that starts out raining. Crawford filmed me both in Bristol and along the River Avon, getting a number of location shots, which we would use in the film. Fortunately, the weather cleared up in the afternoon, just in time for the shoot at Trinity College.

Professor John Bimson speaking to Mahoney on the grounds of Trinity College in Bristol, England

Professor Bimson was fit and in his 60s. Immediately I liked him. His manner was a little reserved, but he smiled easily. When he spoke, his voice was soft and thoughtful as he chose just the right words. He wore blue jeans, loafers, and sported a green shirt with a button-down collar. He had just come from a full day of teaching. Since it was late in the day and getting cooler, he suggested we bring our jackets and take a walk on the campus grounds.

I asked, "Who is John Bimson?"

"I am an author and professor of the Old Testament. I'm also interested in environmental issues and in developing a biblical perspective on the care of creation."

"As you know, I'm a filmmaker investigating the Exodus story and its connection at Avaris."

"Yes, I've heard."

"And you have some special interest in this topic?"

"Yes. I've been very interested in the tools of history and archaeology to better understand the events of the Old Testament."

"What connections have you identified between the biblical account and the growth of the Semitic site of Avaris in the Nile Delta?"

"Well, did you know," he asked as he smiled, "there are more sites than just Avaris with a Semitic population?"

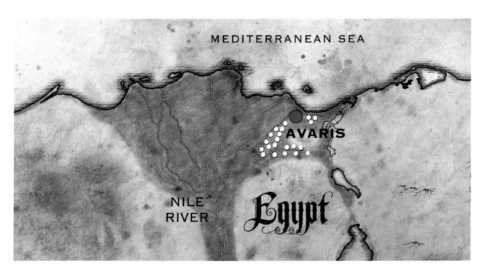

Semitic settlements in the Delta during the Middle Kingdom/Middle Bronze Age.

"Really? How many sites would there have been?"

"If we go back to the 18th and 19th centuries BC, you've got a good many settlements, 20 or more, which would fit the land of Goshen where the Bible says the Israelites were settled. Many of these settlements have not been fully excavated yet."

"How do they compare to Avaris?"

"We don't know whether they're as big as the Avaris site until people start digging there. The Avaris site, of course, no one knew how big that was until excavation began. So there could be a lot of stuff in the ground waiting to be discovered and to throw a lot more light on this period of Asiatic settlement."

"Do you think these sites could possibly represent the early Israelites' population growth in the Delta?"

Bimson was matter of fact. "Until we have more excavations of more of these sites, we can't say exactly when or why they arrived or exactly why or when they left. But there's certainly plenty of evidence for Asiatic, that is, Semitic, settlement in that area in Egypt at a time that would fit the biblical accounts of Joseph and the arrival of the tribes leading up to the Exodus. If they all turn out to be as big as Tell el-Dab'a, then it would take hundreds of years to fully investigate." [31]

"In your opinion, does the archaeology in the Delta reflect what the Bible says happened?"

He responded affirmatively. "It fits the archaeology if you look for the archaeological evidence in the right time period. The Egyptians would've called them Asiatics. There's certainly plenty of evidence for Asiatic or Semitic settlements in that area of Egypt at this time. It would fit the biblical accounts of Joseph and the arrival of the tribes leading up to the Exodus."

Many Egyptologists will disagree with Bimson's interpretation and state that these Semitic settlements are too early to be linked to the Israelites. However, in the period most scholars assume the Exodus happened (which is the New Kingdom and the time of Ramesses), there is no evidence for a very large population of Asiatic or Semitic people. This is strikingly different from the earlier period around the Middle Kingdom, which is the only time the archaeology shows massive numbers of Semites living in ancient Egypt.

The archaeological record only shows massive numbers of Semites in Egypt during the Middle Kingdom and the following dark period.

IV. Slavery: Mudbricks and Tomb Inscriptions

It was now time to ask a new question. Is there any time in Egypt's history that contains evidence for the next step of the biblical sequence – **Slavery?**

To lay out the next details to be investigated, Rabbi Friedman picked up the biblical narration. "A new pharaoh arises, and he doesn't remember Joseph. He enslaves the people because they're growing too numerous and becoming a threat. So he puts them to work and embitters their lives by making them build the store cities of Pithom and Ramesses with bricks they had made of mud and straw." [32]

Cecil B. DeMille portrayed this slavery in two of his famous films about the Exodus, both called *The Ten Commandments*. I was able to discuss the project with the DeMille family, and they graciously granted me permission to license footage from the earlier version. The scale of DeMille's vision, his large cast, and his elaborate sets were stunning, especially for 1923. Although DeMille's Hollywood version of slavery focuses on the Israelites moving large blocks of stone, the Bible never mentions this.

It was intriguing for me to see mudbrick construction in numerous parts of Egypt. These bricks had been made from mud and straw, just as recorded in the Bible, and were used as a form of retaining and structural support to many stone building projects. I often found myself asking if any of these ancient bricks had been molded by the hands of Israelite slaves. However, in my interview with Egyptologist Mansour Boraik, he had been quick to remind me that these types of mudbricks are present throughout Egypt's history and don't prove any direct relationship to the Israelites.

Others say that these mudbricks provide general background evidence for the authenticity of the biblical story. They argue that if Exodus was not written by an eyewitness, as the Bible claims, how would someone without firsthand experience accurately describe the details of this type of brick construction?

Professor Hoffmeier also sees evidence of Semitic slavery in Egypt. "We have the depiction in the tomb of Rekhmire. And there we can see POWs, Semites from both Canaan and Syria, working alongside prisoners of war from Nubia, black Africans. And there they are making bricks, overseen by Egyptian taskmasters with sticks. Exodus 1:14

Cecil B. DeMille, one of the great directors of America's early film industry.

In the biblical account the Egyptians enslaved the Israelites and forced them to make bricks of mud and straw.

actually says they worked in brick and mortar and agriculture. We have agricultural scenes, especially work in vineyards, where the workers again are Semites, Nubians, and so on. So interestingly, the very two areas the Bible says the Israelites were forced to work in, agriculture and construction work, are the very two places we see this sort of work going on in private tombs in Egypt in the 15th century BC."

Construction with mudbricks and straw is found throughout Egypt.

This tomb painting from an 18th Dynasty official named Rekhmire shows Egyptian prisoners of war making mudbricks.

Hoffmeier sees these scenes as providing more background information that supports the biblical account. But the fact that the scene depicts POWs does not fit the specifics of the Exodus story because the children of Israel entered Egypt freely and were never said to be prisoners of war. I wondered if there was any evidence for slavery that more exactly matched the story of the Exodus.

V. Slavery Clues at Avaris?

I asked David Rohl if the Middle Kingdom had any evidence of slavery at Avaris, the older city beneath Ramesses that has shown such promise. "Tell me, what happened at Avaris?"

He said, "We've got a situation of prosperity followed by a lack of prosperity and a shortage of life. We begin to see in the graves of these people Harris Lines in the bones, which indicate shortage of food and nutrients. These people suddenly have become impoverished, and they are dying at an age typically between 32 and 34 years."

"What would explain this dramatic change?"

Rohl became very serious. "The obvious answer is slavery."

This hardship and early death that Rohl sees in the archaeology at Avaris reminded me of the conversation I had had with Israeli leader, Shimon Peres. When he talked about these stories from the Bible, he gave me insight into how slavery would have affected the early Israelites. I was keenly aware that Peres had witnessed the beginning of his nation as many Jewish people emerged from the ashes of the Holocaust.

"What do you think of the slavery in the story of the Exodus?" I asked.

"Well, the story has several chapters with the ideas of slavery and freedom. The descriptions of slavery were so horrible, downhearted – to take a whole people and make of them an inhumane group of men, working so hard. They wanted to free themselves. It would have taken a long time to be relieved from slavery and to become free."

I believe Peres was suggesting that their recovery from slavery would have taken many years, especially after they had been living under oppression for generations. The mindset of being a slave – the injustice and fears that accompanied slavery – would have become ingrained in their bodies and souls. Even after they left Egypt, they would need time to heal in every way – physically, emotionally, mentally, and spiritually.

Rabbi David Hartman in Jerusalem.

While I was in Jerusalem, my Israeli producer arranged for me to interview Rabbi David Hartman, a philosopher, author, and founder of the Shalom Hartman Institute. I met with Rabbi Hartman twice in Jerusalem. The first time was to film him at his Institute, which resided in a large stone building of yellow Jerusalem limestone, a material that has been used since ancient times. Surrounding the Institute were beautiful gardens with flowering trees, paths, and a very large courtyard where people could gather.

Rabbi Hartman was older, in his late 70s. He wore a gray sweater over a button-down shirt. On the back of his head was a kippah, the small skullcap that Jewish men wear for religious reasons. His hair was gray, but his eyebrows were still dark. What I liked were his eyes. They were sharp and alert. His voice was that of a man who knew pain and loss and yet was not overcome by them. It was a voice of hope.

The second time I met Rabbi Hartman was more than a year later. I had come to show him an early version of the film and the way I had cut his interview into the story. I was interested in what he thought. He watched the section that included his interview, and I reached to shut off the television.

"No, don't," he said. "I would like to keep watching."

We sat for almost a half hour to the end of the film. I turned off the TV. We were quiet, and I didn't know what to expect. He turned to me. "Normally, when I see footage taken of myself for these types of projects, I am not that impressed. But I must say I'm very impressed." He then offered to help me in any way he could and invited us to return for a showing at the Institute. Sadly, it took me longer to finish the film, and we never spoke again before his death.

In our first meeting Rabbi Hartman had talked about the freeing of the Israelite slaves. I asked him, "Why is the Exodus a significant event in history?"

He had much to say. "Well, the significance of the Exodus is that you can't bring a people to Sinai and ask them to be holy if their bodies are enslaved. In other words, exploitation has to be overcome before you can give people a spiritual message. So freedom is a condition for listening to the Ten Commandments because the crucial event in Jewish history is the Sinai moment – that's when God elects Israel as a Covenantal people and that's a very fundamental idea, and in some way that is only possible after they have been able to find some modicum of freedom.

"So in a sense the idea of the Exodus is a liberation story, a story which in some way reveals that the condition for spirituality is freedom and liberation. And only if the social conditions provide the opportunity for freedom and the expansion of the self, is spirituality possible. If you ignore the body, then you can't speak to the soul."

I could see the truth in what he was saying, yet later I recalled that the Bible does contain several stories of people who lost their freedom yet maintained their spirituality, just as Joseph did when he was a slave in prison. I am sure Rabbi Hartman and I would have had a good conversation about this topic. I only wish we could have had more time together.

The big question that had started this research and film project still remained uppermost in my mind. Did any part of this story really happen? Almost all archaeologists, including some of the most respected, such as Israel Finkelstein, Mansour Boraik, and Kent Weeks, say there is no evidence for these biblical stories. But have they overlooked any possibilities? Could some of their basic assumptions be wrong? Then again, how could anything have been missed when so many experts have looked into these stories and found nothing?

Exodus chapter 2 tells of the Egyptian princess discovering baby Moses near the shore of the Nile River.

Rabbi Friedman carried on with the story of slavery in the Exodus account. "The Bible then tells us that the more the Hebrews were enslaved and oppressed, the more they multiplied and the more they spread throughout the land of Egypt.

"Pharaoh gives the order for the Egyptians to throw into the river all the Hebrew baby boys. It was during this time that Moses is born. And in fear for his life, his mother hides him in a basket and floats it among the reeds of the Nile.

"But God is watching over baby Moses. When Pharaoh's daughter comes down to bathe in the Nile, she finds him, adopts him, and names him Moses, which means 'drawn from the water.'" [33]

I asked Rohl, "Is there anything in the archaeology at Avaris that might reflect the death of Israelite infants from this part of the slavery story?"

"At this particular point," he said, "we start to see an increase in the number of infant burials at the site. Now normally in a typical Middle Bronze Age cemetery we'll get something like 25 percent of burials of infants. In this particular case, it jumps up to an extraordinary figure."

Rohl then directed me to information in the dig reports from Avaris, to what Bietak's team called "an extremely high mortality rate of newborns." According to the report, when all the children's graves aged ten and younger were identified, it was found that nearly 50 percent died in the first three months of life.

I had to consider that perhaps this was just an epidemic that hit the newborns especially hard. But when the graves of those who made it to adulthood were examined, it was seen that there were 60 percent females to 40 percent males. The reduction appears to have been in the male side of the population. So could this massive increase in infant burials at Avaris be evidence for the killing of male Israelite children?

Wherever I travel and see children playing, I know it's good and something that is almost sacred, because real play happens when you're a child and lasts for only a short time. Then you grow up, and life becomes too serious and difficult for play. And for some children this happens way too early.

While in Egypt on my second trip we decided to sail on the Nile one evening and film along the shore until sunset. Off in the distance I could see young teens standing knee-deep in the river, throwing fishing nets into the shallows. There were children taking their evening bath, running and splashing. Their mothers sat talking in small groups along the bank. Further up was a field where an extended family was playing soccer. I

Children's Graves

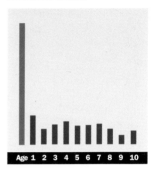

Remaining Adult Graves

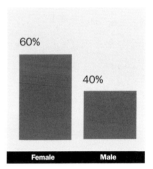

The spike in infant mortality and the skew toward adult women in Middle Bronze Age Avaris.

could see they were having a lot of fun. I was once a soccer player myself and had coached all my kids. We stopped the boat, and I went up to them. "Hello, hello," I yelled, waving my hands over my head.

They stopped playing and the father came over to me. He was curious.

"Would you mind if I join you? I played soccer."

He didn't understand the word *soccer.*

I pointed at the ball. "I mean football. I played."

"You played?" he said with a big smile. He yelled something in Arabic to the rest, then turned to me. "Yes, yes. We play!" We picked teams among the seven or eight children, the father and I on opposing teams. We ran up and down that field, raising dust and scoring goals. It was fun playing with kids again. One of them reminded me of my boyhood friend Mooser, a Native American who lived down the alley from me. I was playing again, just as I had years ago with Mooser, running and laughing, caught up in the game. Then one of the littler ones ran in front of me. *Be careful,* I told myself.

My biggest fear was that I might step on someone's bare foot with my hard shoes and all the fun would end. Thankfully I didn't. After the game and a number of high fives and fist pumps with the Egyptian lad who reminded me of Mooser, I returned to the sailboat. It was getting dark. The wind had died down, and our Egyptian producer Ramy had called for a motorboat to tow us back to the other side of the river to our hotel. The low, steady sound of its motor was lulling as night fell over the Nile.

I reflected on the intriguing evidence of the infant burials at Avaris. It all followed the biblical story quite well. But it made me sad to think of what it could have meant — the murder of thousands of innocent boys. Whether you believe this story or not, you can imagine each family's dread during pregnancy as they waited to see if the child was a boy or a girl.

What I found fascinating about the story of Moses' birth was that his parents saw something beautiful in this child, and they knew that they couldn't let him go. And when he could be hidden no longer, his mother found a creative solution that technically conformed to Pharaoh's commands. She did place their baby son in the Nile as Pharaoh had commanded. She just placed him in a basket coated in pitch before floating it along the reedy shore. I think it's this tenacity for life, and the simple determination not to conform to injustice, that gives us courage in our lives.

For generations the Exodus has given hope to people around the world in their quest for liberation. And that is still true today. This great story of the freeing of slaves from the most powerful nation on Earth has inspired millions. But what are people really putting their hopes and dreams in if this story is merely based on a myth?

Professor James Hoffmeier brought up a compelling point that he believes lends authenticity to the Exodus story. "Who would invent a story about 'our ancestors were slaves'? I can see people saying, 'Our ancestors were princes, our ancestors were great merchants, our ancestors were,' you know, something wonderful and glorious and noble but 'we were slaves'? Why? I mean, if you are going to dream up a story, surely you would come up with a better one than that."

VI. Israelite Slaves on an Egyptian Papyrus?

There is another piece of evidence, maybe the most significant of all, that relates to the third biblical step of slavery. I had learned about an Egyptian document that was stored in the Brooklyn Museum in New York. Commonly called the Brooklyn Papyrus, it's a Middle Kingdom Egyptian papyrus with a list of slave names that seem to come right out of the pages of the Bible. We contacted the museum, and they suggested we purchase their book on it, which contained a translation and commentary of the papyrus.

I asked David Rohl, "What can you tell me about the Brooklyn Papyrus?"

"This particular document is quite amazing. It's actually a list – maybe up to a hundred people – of domestic servants from one estate in the south of Egypt. You can imagine that if such a document existed from the north in the Delta, it would be even more spectacular. [34] When we look at these names, 70 percent of them are Semitic names. And some of these names actually occur in the Bible: Menahem; Issachar and Asher, the names of two of the tribes of Israel; Shiphrah, one of the Hebrew midwives in the Exodus story. All these names appear in this list of slaves."

Rohl was making the point that these were not just typical Semitic names; some of them are clearly in the same forms as Israelite names found in the Bible. He wasn't saying they were the exact people mentioned in the Bible but that these names were commonly used by the Israelites. It's similar today. We have common names that become very popular – male names like John, Robert, and Michael, or female names like Sophia, Emma, and Olivia.

I. THE "a" ENTRIES

Taking, then, only the righthand, or "a", column of each successive section of the list we read in order:

(Plate VIII)
1. The king's servant, the son of Renessonbe (*Rn·s-snb*), *Ankhu (*nḫw*)
2. The female servant, the daughter of Iy (*'Iy*), Satgemini (*Stt-Gmn(·i)*)
3. Her daughter, Rensonbe (*Rn-snb*)
4. The king's servant, the son of Yûsni (*'Iw·s-n·i*), *Asha (*ʿŜ*)
5. (The king's servant),[332] the son of Iy, Ibu (*'Ibw*)
6. The Asiatic, Senebressonbe (*Snb-Rs-snb*)
7. The female Asiatic, Reḥwy (*Rḥ-wy*)
8. Her son, the son of Nefu (*Nfw*), Ressonbe (*Rs-snb*)
9. The Asia[tic *A]pra-Rašpu (*[ʿ]p-r-Ršpw*)
10. 10 The female Asiatic, Hay'immi (?) (*Ḥḭimmi*)
11. The female Asiatic, Munaḥḥima (*Mnḥm*)
12. The Asiatic, Su . . . i (*Sw . . . i*)
13. The female Asiatic, Sakratu (*Sk-r-tw*)
14. " " " 'Immiṣukru (*'Imtmṣk-rw*)
15. " " " 'Aduttu (*'Idwtw*)
16. " " " Sakratu

332. By indenting Line 5 the scribe has indicated that the title *ḥm-nsw* of Line 4 is to be understood here also. The same device is employed in Lines 13-16.

(Plate IX)
17. The female Asiatic, 'Aḫâti-mil(katu)(?) (*ʿḫ-t-m-r*)
18. The Asiatic, *Dôdi-ḫu'at(u) (*Tw-t-wit*)
19. The Asiatic, Qu'a . . . (*Kwi . . .*)
20. [2]0 The king's servant, [the son of] Iywy (*'Il-wy, ...*)
21. The female Asiatic, Šiprah(?) (*Šp-r*)
22. The female Asiatic, *Sukrap(a)ti (*Sk-r-wp[w]ty*)
23. The female Asiatic, *Aŝra(?) (*Iŝr*)
24. Her daughter, Šenebtisy (*Snb·tisy*)
25. The female Asiatic, *'An[at]'a(?) (*ʿn-[t-]i*)
26. The female Asiatic, Šamaŝtu(?) (*Šmŝ-tw*)
27. The Asiatic, Irṣibtu (*'Iṣibtw*)
28. The female servant, the daughter of Wewi (*Wwi*), Ir(y)et (*'Ir(y)t*)
29. The [female] Asia[tic], .ʔ.'a'hu'atu (*.ʔ.Iȝ-hltw*)
30. 30 Her daughter, Ded(eti?)mût(?) . . . (*Dd(iʔ)-Mwt(?) . . .*)
31. Her son, *Ankhseneb (*ʿnḫ-snb*)
32. The [female] Asiatic, *Aḫâ[ti] . . . (*ʿḫ-[t] . . .*)

Even in the museum's book, the commentary by the author, William C. Hayes, associates these Hebrew names with their biblical counterparts. For example, on page 95 he writes about the different forms of the name Issachar: "All these names are feminine and cannot be separated from the biblical Hebrew names."

Rohl continued, "These are Hebrew, Israelite slaves, and they're in a papyrus from the 13th Dynasty. Not from the 19th Dynasty, not from the time of Ramesses II in the New Kingdom, but from the 13th Dynasty, the Middle Kingdom."

I asked him, "What does this mean to you? What does this say?"

"This is real evidence for the time when the Israelites were in Egypt as slaves. It's when you get a text, suddenly you've got history. Archaeology you have to interpret. When you have a text, this is something very different," insisted Rohl.

This slave list from the Brooklyn Papyrus reveals two other significant things. First, the slaves from this single estate were predominantly female, which matches the grave evidence from Avaris, and the story of the reduction of male children in the Bible. Secondly, if these were Israelite slaves in the south, the slave list supports the Bible's account that the Israelite population multiplied and spread throughout the land of Egypt. [35]

Rabbi Friedman added his interpretation of the biblical account of slavery. "The fact that the Hebrews continued to multiply despite the oppression, despite the slavery, despite the boys being killed – it just shows that there was a divine plan here at work and that this whole event was miraculous."

As I thought about how closely the Brooklyn Papyrus supported the biblical story and documented a Hebrew presence in Egypt, I was puzzled. I asked Rohl, "Why do so many Egyptologists disregard, even ignore, the Brooklyn Papyrus?"

He nodded. "Although everybody recognizes that this is a list of Semitic slaves, and everybody recognizes the names appearing in the list are also Israelite names, these can't be the Israelites, because it's the wrong time period. The Israelites are much later in history. So these people we're seeing here in this Brooklyn Papyrus cannot be the Israelites."

I was beginning to understand. "So that's why they disregard it?"

Frustrated by this state of affairs, Rohl explained, "So scholars put the text to one side and say it's another coincidence."

Sections of the Brooklyn Papyrus with the Hebrew names highlighted along with their corresponding entries.

Israelite Names in the Bible

Examples of Israelite names in the Bible that match names found in the Brooklyn Papyrus:

In the thirty-ninth year of Judah's King Azariah, **Menahem** *son of Gadi became king over Israel and reigned 10 years in Samaria.*
(2 Kings 15:17)

These are the names of the sons of Israel who came to Egypt with Jacob; each came with his family: Reuben, Simeon, Levi, and Judah, **Issachar**, *Zebulun, and Benjamin; Dan and Naphtali; Gad and* **Asher.**
(Exodus 1:1-4)

Then the king of Egypt said to the Hebrew midwives, one of whom was named **Shiphrah** *and the other Puah,*
(Exodus 1:15)

The forms of the first three of these names found on the papyrus are the female equivalents to the male forms found in the Bible.

Images at left from "A Papyrus of the Late Middle Kingdom", 1955, the Brooklyn Museum (edited by William C. Hayes).

VII. Multiplication and Slavery Summary and Timeline

As I looked back at the investigation of **Multiplication** and **Slavery,** there appeared to be strong evidence matching these steps of the biblical sequence:

- Evidence indicates a rapid expansion of the Semitic population at Avaris as well as the presence of many other western Asiatic settlements. This is the only time in Egyptian history that Semites dominate the Delta like this.
- At first these Semites are free, powerful, and prosperous but then they succumb to impoverishment, malnutrition, and early death.
- There is a sharp rise in the number of infant burials, "with a greater percentage of females surviving to adulthood."
- And near the end of this period comes a list of slaves from an estate in southern Egypt, many with Hebrew names.

And all of this occurs 400 years earlier than would be expected with a Ramesses Exodus Theory. Most scholars think that if an Exodus actually happened, evidence for these steps would need to appear in the centuries immediately before the time of Ramesses. Therefore, they consider all these finds to be just a coincidence. But now I am questioning whether all this evidence in the Middle Kingdom is really a coincidence. What if the Exodus actually did happen much earlier than the reign of Ramesses? But how could that be? How could the dating of these historical events be off by centuries? Maybe they aren't and this is just a fluke. But, from a rational point of view, there seemed to be a strong pattern pointing in a new direction that I had to follow. Besides, if this is one of the greatest stories ever told, how could I not keep on trying to solve this mystery? ⸰

At right above: Some of the evidence matching the Multiplication and Slavery steps of the biblical sequence. At right below: The Brooklyn Papyrus joins the pattern of evidence that matches the first three biblical steps existing about 400 years earlier than expected with a Ramesses Exodus date.

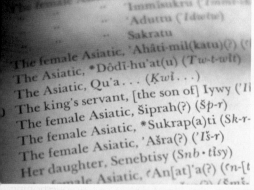

The female Asiatic, Sakratu (...)
"   "   Immisukru (...)
"   "   'Aduttu (...)
"   "   Sakratu
The female Asiatic, 'Ahâti-mil(katu)(?) (...)
The Asiatic, *Dôdî-hu'at(u) (Tw-t-wît)
The Asiatic, Qu'a . . . (Kwi . . .)
The king's servant, [the son of] Iywy ('Ii...
The female Asiatic, Šiprah(?) (šp-r)
The female Asiatic, *Sukrap(a)ti (Sk-r-...
The female Asiatic, 'Ašra(?) ('Iš-r)
Her daughter, Senebtisy (Snb·tîsy)
...male Asiatic, 'An[at]'a(?) (ʿn-[t...

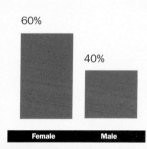

60%

40%

Female   Male

BROOKLYN PAPYRUS
SEMITIC SLAVE LIST

400 YEARS

2000s BC   1900s BC   1800s BC   1700s BC   1600s BC   1500s BC   1400s BC   1300s BC   1200s BC   1100s BC   1000s BC

VII: STEP FOUR:
EVIDENCE OF JUDGMENT?

At this point the evidence matching the first three steps of the pattern – **Arrival, Multi-plication,** and **Slavery** – was so compelling that an alternative to the popular Ramesses Exodus Theory seemed possible. I was very eager to investigate whether more evidence could be found in the Middle Kingdom. To determine if that was the case, I needed to look more closely at the details of the biblical story concerning the next steps of the sequence: the **Judgment** of Egypt and the deliverance of the Israelites from bondage.

The Bible records that Moses fled to the land of Midian. There he met a man named Jethro and married one of his daughters. After 40 years of living as a shepherd, Moses first encountered God. [36]

*Moses' flight to Midian
at age 40.*

Rabbi Friedman elaborated on this supernatural meeting. "Moses sees a bush from the distance, and it's on fire but it's not being consumed. So, curious, he approaches to see what's going on, and God says, 'Don't come any closer. Remove your shoes, for this place is a holy place.'

"God says to Moses, 'I have surely seen the oppression of my people who are in Egypt, and I have heard their cry.' Like a shepherd rescuing his sheep, God commands Moses to go back to Egypt and tell Pharaoh, 'Let my people go, so that they may serve me.' And Moses asked, 'Who shall I say has sent me?' God gave Moses a most unusual reply, 'Tell them I AM has sent you.'" [37]

The comedian Jackie Mason also talked about this encounter. I was sitting across from him in the living room of his home. "Jackie, in the Torah it states that Moses met God in the desert. What do you think happened?"

His voice suddenly became serious. "Moses comes across the burning bush. He gets a message from God and he hears the message saying 'I AM.'"

At that moment it seemed that Mason realized the cosmic dimension of this encounter. He became more passionate with every word.

"And, that gives him the message that God is the universal leader and the universal God of his people, that God's word and God's deed and God's rule is the almighty power that rules this whole universe. The words *I AM* mean that I am before and now and after and always, of all times and in all ways and in every direction. God hovers over this universe and controls the fate of every human being on this Earth."

When he had finished, we sat for a moment in silence because I think we were both surprised by what he had just said. Once again, I just didn't expect this kind of insight from a comedian, but I guess comedians have a lot of insight since they see things that most of us miss.

Moses at the burning bush encounters God (Exodus chapters 3-4).

I. The Ten Plagues

The Bible records that God gave Moses three miraculous signs to convince the elders of the Israelites and Pharaoh that he came from God. These three signs were turning his staff into a serpent, pouring water that turned into blood on the ground, and making his hand leprous and then healing it immediately. Then Moses returned to Egypt.

Rabbi Friedman explained the confrontation Moses faced next. "Moses comes to Pharaoh. Pharaoh does not listen; he refuses to let the people go. And God sends the first of a series of spectacular plagues against the land of Egypt."

According to the text, the ten plagues were set in motion at the Nile. Moses waited

Rabbi Friedman reading the account of the ten plagues in the Torah.

The Ten Plagues on Egypt

The Bible records that ten plagues were brought against Pharaoh and the Egyptians, each one building upon the other over a period of time:

1. Waters of Egypt turned to blood
    Exodus 7:14-25

2. Infestation of frogs
    Exodus 8:1-15

3. Swarms of bugs/gnats/ mosquitoes/lice
    Exodus 8:16-19

4. Wild beasts (Jewish tradition) or flies
    Exodus 8:20-32

5. Death of the livestock
    Exodus 9:1-7

6. Boils on man and livestock
    Exodus 9:8-12

7. Storms of fire/lightning and hail
    Exodus 9:13-35

8. Locusts
    Exodus 10:1-20

9. Darkness
    Exodus 10:21-29

10. Death of the firstborn of man and beast
    Exodus 11:1-12:33

for Pharaoh to come down to the river. It was there in the presence of Pharaoh that Moses' brother Aaron raised his staff over the waters of Egypt and they turned to blood and became unfit for drinking. But Pharaoh's wise men were also able to turn water into blood with their dark magic. So Pharaoh's heart was hardened, and he would not listen to Moses nor would he release the Israelites.

"They say he hardened Pharaoh's heart because Pharaoh believed in his own power and his own godliness." Jackie Mason was looking straight at me.

I nodded. "That's what the text says."

"He thought that he was god. He believed in himself as the almighty power, and his own almighty power is being challenged by another force that he didn't believe exists in those terms, that could actually overcome the level of his power. He thought that he was the ultimate power. It was like a fight that he had to win."

"What do you mean?"

"It was like a fighter jumping into the ring with you and you believed that you are the best fighter in the world and somehow this guy thinks he can beat you and you had to prove the point because nobody could ever beat you before. That it's even possible for somebody to do it – Pharaoh didn't know such a power exists. He refused to believe it." Again, Mason's early rabbinical training was coming back to him.

Egyptologist James Hoffmeier also talked about the dramatic struggle between the God of the Israelites and Pharaoh. "In Exodus chapter five the God of Israel says, 'Let my people go.' Pharaoh says, 'Who is the Lord? Who is Jehovah? Who is Yahweh that I should listen to him?' And so we have setting up there this contest. Who really is the god to be obeyed? Who is the one in control of things? And in the Egyptian view of things, Pharaoh was the god of the Egyptian state. He was responsible for cosmic order. He was responsible for the proper flow of the Nile, the rising of the sun, the fertility of the fields, and so on."

"So there's a big challenge to Pharaoh's authority going on here?"

He nodded. "Now we have the God of Israel, the God of creation, of the Bible, who's saying, 'Wait a minute. That's not what you do. I'm the one who controls all these things.' So God begins with the Nile and ends in the ninth plague with the sun. And these two things that Pharaoh is said to control are completely outside of his control." [38]

Jackie Mason expanded on the reaction of the Egyptians to the plagues. "They thought between one plague and the other that somehow it will end, that this is the last plague. They couldn't believe in the power of God to do this much damage to them and hurt them this much and create this much pain and agony and misery. They thought that his power might be limited in some way. They couldn't imagine that God had this kind of power because they didn't believe in him in the first place."

Rabbi Friedman continued to tell the biblical story. "God protected the children of Israel from these plagues, while the rest of the land was being devastated by them to such an extent that Pharaoh's servants themselves pleaded with him, saying that this was the finger of God and that Egypt was being ruined. But Pharaoh would still not relent. He knew that Egypt depended on the work of these foreign slaves." [39]

Hoffmeier summed up the freeing of the Israelites. "The story of the Exodus is about the God of the Exodus. It's not about the pharaoh. The pharaoh is a minor character. It's really about the God, because that's going to be the foundation for what happens next, when the Israelites go to the mountain and enter into that Covenant relationship with God. God will look back and say, 'I am the LORD your God who brought you out of Egypt; out of the house of slavery.' That is the basis for the Covenant relationship. God rescued the Hebrews; therefore, they are his people and he is their God." [40]

II. Visualizing the Ancient Story

There was a problem I now faced as a director. The depth of the drama was growing while the biblical story unfolded. We had always wanted the depiction of all the archaeological sites to be accurate and realistic, and the intensity of the story only increased our desire to do that. What the audience would need to fully understand these biblical events were very sophisticated visual effects, and a complete recreation of two ancient cities: Avaris and Jericho, the city that was destroyed later in the Conquest. After numerous attempts and false starts, Pete Windahl finally solved the problem when he found two talented animators from Utah, Dorian Vanergrift and Clarence (C.J.) Olson.

We started to Skype daily.

"Dorian, what we need to do is recreate a city called Avaris. I want it to authentically represent what it looked like during the era of the Exodus."

"Oh, this is going to be fun!" Dorian's excitement was apparent.

"So you're not intimidated by the scale of building an entire city?"

The first plague: the Nile turning to blood.

The fifth plague: death of livestock.

The seventh plague: storms of hail.

"This is what we love doing. What C.J. and I will need, though, is all the survey specs for the size of the city, its buildings, temples, and where the palace compound would have resided."

The re-creation of Avaris, one of the largest cities in the ancient world.

After months of incredibly long hours, Dorian and C.J. built the city to the exact archaeological proportions. We then started to move the camera around the site and to look at a variety of angles at different times of day. It was stunning to think that we might be capturing for the first time on film the re-creation of a city that hasn't been seen for over 3,500 years – the ancient city of Avaris.

Another critical visual aid were the maps. I was very concerned about them because I knew it was necessary to explain where these biblical events might have occurred. I also had the idea to combine dramatic recreations from the biblical story with their locations on the maps. I discussed this with Chad Greene, my editor, and we decided to scan in elements from hand-drawn maps of Egypt and Palestine dating back to the 16th and 17th century. Peter Wagner, a talented animator and graphic artist, then took these scans and developed two very beautiful maps from which all the rest could be generated.

My cinematographer John Burch and I spent a full day filming the exact sections of the Torah that Rabbi Friedman would be speaking about. I then suggested that we could overlay scenes of Abraham, Joseph, and Moses into the very text. The results were powerful.

All these visual ideas, along with the Wall of Time, tended to come at odd moments. Sometimes early in the morning a creative thought would appear like dew. As I leapt out of bed, my wife would startle.

"What's wrong?"

"Oh, nothing. I've just had an idea about using ancient maps to open the film."

"What time is it?"

"It's 6:15."

"It's Saturday morning. Can you give it a break?"

"No, I'm just going over to the office for a while. I promise I'll cut the grass this afternoon."

"Well, it's starting to look like a field."

"I know. This afternoon."

It took an entire week to film the map sequence for the opening credits. On a large table we spread out about 20 ancient maps, along with books from the 19th century and a beautiful dagger and compass from the times of Lawrence of Arabia, which Lennart Möller had contributed. We did have one accident when some candle wax dripped on the edge of a map. Thanks to a talented conservation and restoration specialist, things were made as good as new.

Egypt's pharaohs had great power and some considered themselves to be gods.

It was midmorning when I began another Skype call to the animators.

"Dorian, there's a very dramatic scene that will happen over the city of Avaris."

"What are we talking about?" he asked with his usual eagerness.

"It's the tenth and final plague. I want a wide shot of the city at night. And I want a billowing cloud to come out of the heavens and head straight towards the city. Have you ever done anything like this before?"

"No, but we'll figure it out."

III. Death of the Firstborn

The biblical text then says that God sent the tenth and final plague – the death of the firstborn of man and beast – to force Pharaoh's hand. But for the children of Israel God gave instructions for a Passover feast to be held that night. He told each household of the Israelites to slaughter a lamb and mark the doorposts with its blood. And on that horrible

The tenth plague: the death of the firstborn males – man and beast.

In the first Passover described in Exodus chapters 11-12, death passed over the houses marked with the blood of a lamb, but everywhere else the firstborn son of each family died.

night, death went through the land and wherever there was blood on the doorposts, it passed over that dwelling, sparing all the firstborn males in that household. But in every home that was not marked with the blood, all firstborn males died. There was crying and wailing in every Egyptian home because each family had lost someone. [41]

Rabbi Friedman shared how this final, climactic plague impacted all of Egypt. "The tenth plague, the death of the firstborn, affected everybody. Even Pharaoh's firstborn died that night. And the will of the people, the Egyptians, was completely shattered. The tenth plague also broke Pharaoh's defiance of God, and he finally let Moses and the people go. In fact, out of fear the Egyptians urged the Israelites to leave, and Moses told the Israelites to ask the Egyptians for silver and gold jewelry, and for fine clothing. And the Lord gave the people favor in the sight of the Egyptians, so that they let them have what they asked. Thus, they plundered Egypt.

"After the final plague Moses led them out of Egypt into the wilderness to worship God. But then Pharaoh changes his mind, pursues the Israelites with his army and all his chariots, trapping Moses and the children of Israel at the sea. God then miraculously parts the waters so that the Israelites can escape. And as Pharaoh's army and chariots pursue them into the sea, they are destroyed as the parted waters collapse upon them, while Moses and the Israelites are saved on the opposite shore of the sea." [42]

IV. Celebrating Passover

Every year Jewish families from around the world celebrate the deliverance of Israel from Egypt during the feast called Passover. Records confirm that Passover has been observed for thousands of years. Many believe it is difficult to explain the origin of Passover if there was no real event on which it was based. [43]

In Jerusalem I asked Rabbi Hartman, "Can you explain why Passover is so significant to Jewish families?"

"Each year we celebrate the Exodus as if we were there. We were slaves to Pharaoh in Egypt and we dramatically celebrate the Passover Seder as if we were participants. So, there is always a renewal, always a renewed giving and a new spirit into the Passover Exodus story. And the Exodus story was also a story of hope because in remembering the Exodus, we remember that in the dark conditions of history God, the Lord, had in some way made possible through Moses our liberation. So there is always a faith that the Covenant always says that God will not abandon Israel and that we are a people with whom God has a special relationship."

But what about those who think the Exodus never happened?

When I interviewed Israel Finkelstein, he argued that the Exodus did not happen in the manner described in the Bible. I asked him, "Do you believe in celebrating Passover."

He replied with conviction, "Sure, celebrating the Passover? Definitely. I think that I make a distinction in my private life, in my life as a scholar, in my life as part of a family. I make a very clear distinction between scholarship and tradition. When I sit at a Passover meal and we read the Haggadah with the family, that evening, it's all history, from A to Z. Perfect history. Because history is not only about the time of Moses, let's say. History is also about all those many generations of my forefathers who were sitting to the same table at Passover at the same time and reciting the Haggadah. This is also history, which means that I am part of something bigger – which goes on and on for many generations, and this is important for me. So, yes, the answer is that there is a clear distinction between the two."

I thought for a moment. "What would you say to those people who are concerned with the idea that these stories didn't happen as they were written?"

"I would tell them that this is not important. Whether the stories, whether things happened exactly in that way is not important. I think that it is more important to understand the meaning of Exodus, the moral of Exodus, for our civilization, for humanity, for mankind, for understanding the biblical text and the authors. This, in my opinion, is more important."

As I have mentioned before, Finkelstein's work and ideas greatly influenced Rabbi Wolpe to write his controversial Passover sermon, in which he suggested that the Exodus didn't happen as written in the Scriptures, and that statement shook many people. In his interview with Wolpe, Medved leaned forward and asked about this sermon. "I know that a lot of people who heard your sermon all of those years ago, questioning the historical reliability of the Exodus, felt as if they had been hit right in the guts."

"I know."

Medved continued, "What did you want people to feel, not to think, but to feel about the Exodus?"

Professor Israel Finkelstein talks with Mahoney about celebrating the Passover.

The Passover has been celebrated for thousands of years (reenactment).

Rabbi Wolpe speaking about the relationship between historical reality and faith.

History and the Ten Commandments

The preamble to the Ten Commandments clearly shows the connection between God's mighty acts in history and his moral commands:

Then God spoke all these words: I am the LORD your God, who brought you out of the land of Egypt, out of the place of slavery. Do not have other gods besides Me. . . . (Ex 20:1-3)

This passage assumes that God actually brought the Israelites out of Egypt, and it makes that reality the basis of his commandments.

"I wanted them – not about the Exodus, but about their faith – I wanted them to feel that their faith was unshakable, that it didn't matter what the conclusions were of archaeologists, scientists, and historians."

Medved questioned, "If it turns out that there is better archaeological, scientific, and historical evidence of the actuality of the Exodus, of the accuracy in its core of the biblical account that can be shown scientifically to be reliable – does that change your theology?"

Wolpe smiled. "I'll dance in the streets! But no, it doesn't change my theology. But I'd be very pleased because at least the controversy would be over. Look, if there is historical evidence, I think it's wonderful and I'd be thrilled, and that's great. But that's not what my faith is based on. It just isn't."

"Okay," said Medved. "Let's take the Passover for instance. In every single generation the whole heart of the Haggadah, the Passover service, the Passover liturgy that every Jewish home goes through –"

Wolpe nodded. "Right."

"What does that mean if we weren't delivered from Egypt?"

Wolpe paused. "Whether or not people were delivered then, does that affect my ability to empathize with what slavery is like now? I don't think so. This year, for example, I gave a sermon to my congregation and said, 'You're the Egyptians. The people who are working for you in your house, they're the Israelites. How do you treat them? Do you treat them well? Do you make them stay late and pay them almost nothing? Do you speak badly to them?' That's a powerful lesson no matter what happened in Egypt."

In Bristol, England, the sun was moving behind the clouds as Professor Bimson and I were walking the lawn of Trinity College. The time had come to move inside the main building. He led me down a hall to a wood-paneled room. At one time, it might have been a small chapel or a room for reflection. There was a seating area on the far end of the room. I would call it a small cubby. It was projecting out from the main room by several feet. It had a wooden ceiling and leaded glass windows that overlooked a courtyard. I joined Professor Bimson at a small wooden table next to the windows. The chairs felt very comfortable, as if they had been hand carved for their guests.

I asked Bimson, "Can you have a belief in the Bible if there is no historical basis for its events?"

He held a view very different than Rabbi Wolpe's. "If you took away the historical basis, then you've really deprived it of a lot of its theological truth. So much of what the

Old Testament says about the character of God and his purposes in calling Israel are intertwined with this story of this people coming out of Egypt and entering the Promised Land. So history and theology are tightly intertwined in the Bible."

After more than a decade of searching, it comes down to this question: Is the Bible's account true history, or is it simply the traditions of a devout people?

V. To Budapest With Love

On August 7, 2005, we landed in Budapest and headed over to the official Hungarian public radio station, Magyar Radio. The building I would guess was built sometime in the last century. In 1956 the station had witnessed the Hungarian Revolution against the Soviet-controlled government. Bullet marks around the entrance called to mind the sober, not too distant past.

The Budapest Film Orchestra recording one of the main themes for Patterns of Evidence: The Exodus.

Our group walked down a long corridor and past a maze of studios and engineering rooms. I seem to remember all the walls were paneled with a light-colored wood. Only the outline of a door, its handle, and a small plaque with the studio number indicated a room behind the vertical paneling. We continued down the hall. Our recording would be done in Studio 22.

Jonathan David Neal was one of our composers. He was a perfect choice. Jonathan had a degree in intercultural anthropology with a minor in composition. After attending UCLA to study film scoring, he went on to record at Capitol Records and Abbey Road, as well as at studios in Nashville. He had worked at Magyar Radio with Bart in the past, so a level of comfort and trust with the engineering staff was already established.

We opened the eight-inch thick door and walked into Studio 22. The room was very large and beautiful, much of it covered in wood up to its high ceilings. The Hungarian engineering team was already setting up chairs, music stands, and the mics for the 75-piece orchestra that would be coming in the next day. I had once built a recording studio in my home and had a natural love for such things. It was exciting to finally be here, and I could hardly wait for the sessions to begin.

Jonathan turned to me. He was carrying a satchel filled with new film scores, some of which he had written while on the plane. Among them were 30 full-length pieces of never-before-heard compositions – *Ancient Secrets*, *Joseph's Palace*, and *Desert Highway*, to name a few.

He set his satchel on a chair near the conductor's podium. "Well, just so you know, I've completed most of the big scores for the large orchestra we'll record tomorrow. But I still have my ethnic instruments to write for. I'll just set my alarm and get up around four and finish them by Thursday."

"I'm sorry you've had to work so hard to prepare for this."

He smiled. "Don't be sorry. We'll get it done, and it's going to sound amazing."

The next several days we recorded with the Budapest Film Orchestra. Some of the finest players had been handpicked from the three major orchestras in Budapest. We also recorded choral compositions with a 60-person choir. The language barrier was solved by our translator Csilla, a wonderful woman who spoke seven languages.

Composer Jonathan David Neal reviewing the film's music score in Budapest.

Our recording engineer from Los Angeles was Tim Jaquette. He had engineered for Babyface Edmonds, Paula Abdul, and Melissa Manchester, among other celebrities, and had worked with a number of major studio orchestras for other movies. The mission he had to accomplish in the next four days was to record in 5.1 Surround Sound almost two hours of new music.

One of the most enjoyable parts of the experience was recording the ethnic music that would bring the audience into the ancient story of the Exodus. Jonathan had arrived a week earlier to interview and select musicians that would be used to create this Middle Eastern sound palette. These musicians and the singer had to know the authentic improvisation styles of Middle Eastern music, but they also had to know Western music so they could blend with the Budapest orchestra. Jonathan's anthropological background was just what he needed to research, write, and record the ethnic music required for the film.

Bea Palya, one of Hungary's most well-known singers, adds the wailing voices for the recording.

The morning of the ethnic session I asked him, "How did you decide which instruments should play?"

"Well, next we're going to be recording the *Burning Bush*. For this piece I chose the gadulka because it has a haunting and mysterious sound. It's a stringed instrument played with a bow like a cello. I felt it was perfect for the story of Moses in the desert tending his sheep before encountering the Burning Bush."

The vocalist Jonathan had selected was Bea Palya, one of Hungary's most well-known singers. Half Hungarian and half Gypsy, she has studied the improvisational techniques of Middle Eastern and Indian music in Paris. Bea had a tremendous ability to capture the emotional and cultural aspects of the story as well as the haunting cries of the Egyptian women mourning the death of the firstborn.

The session in Budapest provided the musical foundation that the story of the Exodus deserved. It brought about the emotional underscore that I as a director had hoped for.

But as the investigation moved forward, new elements were always being uncovered and added to the film, which meant there was a continual need for new music. Sometimes it would take months to find the best emotional support for the story. Once while I was working on the Passover sequence, I couldn't find the right piece to fit this profound event celebrated by so many Jewish families. I called another friend, Minneapolis composer Rob Barrett. Rob had contributed a number of pieces to the film and had a great gift for creating stunning melodies with deep emotional impact.

The recording included many talented musicians playing ethnic instruments, such as Kálmán Balogh on the cimbalom.

"Rob, I'm stuck. I need some help creating a piece for the Passover scene."

As usual he was very positive. "Send me a clip. I'd love to help."

A few days later we talked.

"I've got a melody in my head and I think you'll like it," he said.

He recorded the piece with real strings, and I didn't like it. I loved it, so much so that I decided to use *Passover* as one of the two music themes for the closing credits, both composed by Rob. I was very fortunate to have such talented people supporting my vision for the project.

Another musical thread I wanted in the film was folk music from my own world and my own heritage. I would often sit in my den at night playing the Dobro or banjo, thinking about the story and scenes that these folk instruments might well represent. During those thinking times I took the stringed instruments and started composing themes and songs that supported my questions. I knew that folk music, though different from orchestra, choral, and ethnic Middle Eastern music, had a place in the film's multiple dimensions.

András Dés plays the gadulka.

It was during my second interview with David Rohl, when we had a discussion about his own musical compositions.

"So you have scored for films and television?" I asked.

"Oh, yes, extensively."

"I am looking for an international feeling because of all the travel that takes place during the investigation. And I would like to create more atmospheres for some of the existing musical pieces."

"I understand. Let me send you something in a few days and see if it might work for you."

That was the beginning, as David succeeded in developing a number of pieces through layering musical atmospheres and secondary themes over the top of some of Jonathan's music. These new sounds became part of a collaborative hybrid. David also created other original compositions – *The Journey Man, Timothy with Ambience*, and *I AM Who I AM*. Each scene would require some new type of emotion, yet maintain and repeat themes that all three composers had created for the project.

All of the music in the film turned out wonderfully, and for the first time I learned the value of a subwoofer. There is nothing more frightening than a mysterious cloud coming out of the sky as the sound of death approaches in such a low rumble that your stomach feels queasy. Welcome to David Rohl's *The EXODUS Plagues.*

VI. Aftermath of the Plagues: Egypt's Devastation

If the Judgment of Egypt happened as described in the Bible, Egyptian society would have collapsed. It could not have withstood such devastation:

- The loss of their agriculture and livestock with the first nine plagues,
- The loss of their firstborn sons in the tenth plague during the night of Passover,
- The loss of precious items such as gold and silver jewelry and clothing,
- The loss of their slave force with the exodus of the Semitic population,
- The loss of their army in the Red Sea.
- In fact, Moses recorded that Egypt was still suffering from defeat 40 years after the Exodus. [44]

This devastation provides another clue to look for. Was there a time in Egypt's history when such a breakdown occurred? Critics are quick to point out that there is no such record of supernatural judgment and devastation in Egypt. But might this be because they are restricting their search to the New Kingdom only? Others believe there is a document written by an Egyptian scribe from earlier in Egypt's history that actually gives an eyewitness account of the plagues and chaos surrounding the Exodus.

VII. The *Admonitions of an Egyptian Sage*: The Ipuwer Papyrus

I traveled to Holland and the Leiden Museum, which houses a copy of this document, often called the *Admonitions of an Egyptian Sage*. This significant papyrus appears to have been written by a scribe named Ipuwer. It was raining lightly as we drove through the idyllic towns and villages of the Netherlands. The serenity of the countryside contrasted with the occasional cement fortifications from WWII, now overgrown with vegetation. Fortunately, there was also the friendly sight of windmills, one of the trademarks of Dutch culture that fascinated me so much as a child.

Most cities in the world are built near water, but Leiden is built in such a way that the rivers and canals really become part of the life of the city. Bicycle riders passed as I walked over a canal bridge and down the cobblestone street to the museum entrance. I thought how privileged I was to pursue this investigation in the beauty and charm of this old European setting. The museum faced the canal. It was a tall brown brick building, and a light stone trimmed the windows and the two large black doors at the entrance. The sign read "Leiden Museum."

I met Egyptologist Maarten Raven in the expansive museum lobby. There must have been a field trip from a local school happening because there were children everywhere. I left the camera gear with my wife, Jill, and went to look for an interview location among the artifacts of the museum. As we walked down the corridor, I wanted to break the ice with Raven. I've learned it's always important to get people to relax before filming. "We'll have some fun here. It's a beautiful museum," I said.

"Thank you. It is."

"Why did you choose this occupation?"

He smiled. "I became an Egyptologist because, as so many people, at a very young age I became fascinated by ancient Egypt, and this happened already at primary school."

"This was your childhood dream then?"

He nodded. "I still feel this fascination, and it's great to have been able to make my hobby into my profession."

"I know what you mean. Filming for me is the same. It was my hobby and now my career. I love doing this, traveling and meeting people like you from around the world,

Maarten Raven, the curator of the Department of Egyptology at the Dutch National Museum of Antiquities in Leiden.

179

talking about fascinating things."

I could see Raven was beginning to relax. We had something in common. We both were able to do what we love for our living. He took me down a long hall and into a room that housed the carved forms of several members of Egyptian royalty. It was a great location.

"I know why you have come," Raven said.

"What do you mean?"

"Because you used the name Ipuwer, I know why you have come."

"Why is that?"

"Because only people who are interested in connecting this document to the biblical story use that name. Normally they would call it the *Admonitions*."

"Is that all right?"

"Yes, I have no problem with you asking questions. It's fine. People can think and ask as they like. It's fine."

I went back to get the lights and camera. As I worked I thought more about it. Yes, I had come to Leiden to learn about this Egyptian document that some say echoes the story of the biblical plagues. Was there a connection? Or was I just being foolish? I'd first have to know who would be capable of writing something like this.

I positioned Raven in front of the grand statues on their thrones. Standing next to the camera, I opened our conversation. "Let's talk about scribes. What was the role of an Egyptian scribe?"

"If you became a scribe, that meant that you belonged to the elite, to the one percent of the population that could read and write, and by that faculty you became somebody with power. You became useful to the government, to the pharaoh, and in fact you could fulfill all other professions. You could become an army officer; you could become a physician, a magician, a priest, anywhere where they needed literate people."

"How did one become a scribe in ancient Egypt?"

"One became a scribe because one belonged to a family of scribes. That assured that you could get access to the proper school system and you became more and more specialized as time went on. But the whole education could take up to ten years."

I found that interesting. "What was the primary language they were writing in? Was it just hieroglyphics, or were there different periods of time when that language changed?"

"Of course everybody knows about the Egyptian writing system, the hieroglyphs," said Raven. "But hieroglyphs were something from monumental art. They were carved by sculptors, whereas a scribe would make his notes on a sheet of papyrus. He needed a quick writing system, something cursive, and that was hieratic. Hieratic is just stylized hieroglyphics."

It was time for me to get more specific. "Now I want to ask you about the Ipuwer Papyrus, or the *Admonitions of an Egyptian Sage* as you would call it, because you have that document at this museum. What is it?"

"The so-called papyrus of the *Admonitions of an Egyptian Sage* was given that name by the first editor, Sir Alan Gardiner, in 1909. He made the first scientific edition of the papyrus, which is unique. It's one of a kind. There is only one copy of this specific text and that is here. This is the most important document in the Leiden Museum."

"Why is it so important?"

"The importance of the text is that it is a book of wisdom, a political treatise, which shows what happens if order falls away and chaos comes – and we don't want that. It's a very, very vivid report, or would-be report, of what happens to Egypt when the central power falls away."

Raven told me that his estimate for the date of the original composition of the *Admonitions* is around 1800 BC. He continued, "The copy we have was made almost 600 years later – from the Ramesside Period – by a school boy who used it as a school exercise to practice his hieratics."

I knew the original composition was attributed to a person known as Ipuwer, so I asked, "Who is Ipuwer? Do you have any idea?"

"We don't know who Ipuwer was, but he was obviously somebody in a position to address his majesty, the king. At the end of the text we suddenly read, 'These are the words that Ipuwer answered to the king.' So far his name hasn't been mentioned. But the beginning of the papyrus is lost and so is the end, so just before the end, we suddenly hear his name. Does this mean that he is in fact the speaker of all the preceding words?"

"What do you think?" I asked.

"We don't know, but this is the general interpretation by Egyptologists; that these are his words and this is the instruction of Ipuwer, who is addressing the king."

I then turned my questioning to the subject of the biblical Exodus. "Is the Exodus a historical reality?"

Raven responded somewhat skeptically, "The story of the Exodus is described in the

A section of the Admonitions of an Egyptian Sage housed in the Leiden Museum.

The scribe Ipuwer as depicted in the film.

Old Testament. It's part of the national history of the Jewish people, or so they say. We have no independent evidence that this is a real historical event. We can believe it because we believe in the Bible?" He shrugged. "There are no Egyptian sources that describe it. There are no other documents. There are no archaeological sources that could prove this took place as a mass exodus."

Again, Raven's position is the same as most Egyptologists today. But there are some scholars who suggest that descriptions found in the *Admonitions of an Egyptian Sage* bear a remarkable resemblance to the plagues of the Bible, only from an Egyptian point of view. This document poetically describes a series of calamities and the chaos that followed them.

As outlined in section four of this chapter, a collapse of Egypt's power is exactly what would have been seen, if the plagues and catastrophic events that followed really happened as described in the Bible. And as I compared the book of Exodus to the writings of Ipuwer, I was intrigued. There are different word choices that can be made when translating these texts into other languages, but as I looked at the basic meaning of each line, I saw that the general chaos described in this papyrus matched the devastated Egypt of Exodus, and the similarities between some of the specific events were stunning.

I will juxtapose portions of the two accounts, first the words from the biblical text, then Ipuwer's words.

The Bible says [God speaking to Moses]:
"*Take some **water from the Nile and pour it on the dry ground**. The water you take from the Nile will become blood on the ground.*" EXODUS 4:9"

Ipuwer writes:
"Behold, Egypt is fallen to the pouring of water. And **he who poured water on the ground** seizes the mighty in misery." IPUWER 7:5

The Bible says:
"*And all the water in the **Nile was turned to blood**. The fish in the Nile died, and the river smelled so bad the Egyptians **could not drink water from it**.*" EXODUS 7:20-21

Ipuwer writes:

"**The River is blood**. If you drink of it, you lose your humanity, and **thirst for water**." IPUWER 2:10

The Bible says:

"*All the Egyptian livestock died . . . . Lightning struck the earth, and the LORD **rained hail on the land of Egypt. . . . The flax and the barley were destroyed.**" EXODUS 9:6, 9:23, 9:31

Ipuwer writes:

"**Gone is the barley** of abundance . . . . Food supplies are running short. The nobles hunger and suffer . . . . Those who had shelter are in the **dark of the storm**." IPUWER 6:3, 3:3, 7:13

The Bible says:

"*[The locusts] covered the surface of the whole land so that the land was black, and they consumed all the plants on the ground and all the fruit on the trees that the hail had left. . . . Pharaoh's officials asked him, 'How long must this man be a snare to us? Let the men go, so that they may worship Yahweh their God. Don't you realize yet that **Egypt is devastated**?'" EXODUS 10:15, 10:7

Ipuwer writes:

"What shall we do about it? **All is ruin!**" IPUWER 3:13

The Bible says:

"*Now at midnight the LORD **struck every firstborn male** in the land of Egypt, from the firstborn of Pharaoh who sat on his throne to the firstborn of the prisoner who was in the dungeon, and every firstborn of livestock.*" EXODUS 12:29

Ipuwer writes:

"Behold, plague sweeps the land, blood is everywhere, with **no shortage of the dead** . . . . He who buries his **brother** in the ground is everywhere . . . . Woe is me for the grief of this time." IPUWER 2:5 6, 13, 4:3

The Bible says:

"*And there was a **loud wailing throughout Egypt** because there wasn't a house without someone dead.*" EXODUS 12:30

Ipuwer writes:

"**Wailing is throughout the land**, mingled with lamentations." IPUWER 3:14

VIII. Objections to an Ipuwer - Exodus Connection

"All the time we have to convince ourselves that this person can't have seen all this," Raven said with passion. "He imagined it, or he had received this information from other similar propagandistic literature."

"Because it's so fantastic?"

He nodded. "Yes, it's very fantastic. But he hasn't seen it. He just imagined it."

At first I wondered if it is really being objective to assume that Ipuwer just imagined the scenarios? How can we know that? Why must we dismiss the historical nature of these two documents just because they are fantastic? Besides, other than the Nile turning to blood and the death of the firstborn, most of the events described seemed to be more chaotic than fantastic.

"Many people see striking similarities between these stories," I suggested.

Raven was adamant. "I see no connection between the papyrus of Ipuwer and the stories of the plagues of Egypt. It is in a way, in a very indirect way, an eyewitness report of a historical period. It *pretends* to be such a report, but in fact it isn't."

He went on, "Don't confuse this with the message of the Bible, the ten plagues. That's a quite different story. Whether this happened or not is irrelevant. It's a beautiful literary document, and again, yes, God was angry and punished the Egyptians. But this is a literary cliché that went maybe from one culture to the other. Maybe the composers of the biblical books knew about these Egyptian stories – maybe they have been influenced. But don't forget there's a lapse of many, many centuries in between. But this is just a literary cliché."

"Could you explain what you mean?"

"These writings are rather propagandistic. They are not just very sad about what happened, but there is a lesson in this: don't let this happen again."

"So they are warnings?" I asked.

"They are warnings, certainly. 'Don't let this happen, ever.'"

"And that's what the *Admonitions* are?"

"Yes. And in a way that's also why this papyrus is so important, because this was the lesson that Egyptian scribes learned at school. They were taught by copying the great literature of the past. And as in a lot of this kind of literature, 'These are our Egyptian traditions – better stick to them.' And that's how this culture lasted for 3,000 years."

Did Egypt's literature influence the Bible? Or could it be that Ipuwer was an eyewitness of the Exodus and then wrote a firsthand report of the events as warnings to future generations of Egyptians?

When I returned from Holland I talked with my writing partner, Steve, about Maarten Raven's response. "It didn't seem that Raven was open to seeing any connection between the *Admonitions* document and the Bible. He dismissed that idea out of hand."

Steve thought for a moment. "On the surface, it seems we have two ancient documents describing very similar incidents. And if we have a source outside the Bible that is agreeing with it, why isn't that support for the idea that the Exodus really occurred?"

I challenged Steve. "Or is Raven right that these events are just too fantastic to have happened? What are other Egyptologists saying about this?"

"Well, I know what Miriam Lichtheim said."

"Who is she?"

"She was an influential Egyptologist who specialized in the writings of ancient Egypt. She ruled out the possibility that the *Admonitions* papyrus referred to a real national calamity because it was written in the form of a poem."

"She discounted it because it was poetic in nature?"

"That's right. She asserted that since it was a poem, it couldn't also be true history."

Steve handed me her book *Ancient Egyptian Literature*. "Read this paragraph that talks about why she thinks Ipuwer cannot be real history."

I read Lichtheim's words. "I submit that there is a strong inherent reason why this cannot be so. If the *Admonitions* is the 'direct response to a real calamity,' then it cannot also be a 'historical romance.' The two are mutually exclusive."[45]

I asked David Rohl about Lichtheim's view of the *Admonitions* and the Egyptian scribe. He had a different interpretation. "Most Egyptologists would say that this story is a didactic story. It's a story of morals, telling about how Egypt can collapse if Pharaoh isn't in control."

"It's a form of poetry, isn't it?"

Rohl said, "Yes. It's a type of literature they call pessimistic literature, which we have in the ancient world, which basically says, when all collapses into chaos, it's because the king is not taking responsibility for his duties. But it's usually based on events and realities. You don't write stories like that, and didactic tales like that, in a situation where you

David Rohl talking about the Admonitions of an Egyptian Sage.

have no real historical events to back it up. It's from experience. And why not the story of Exodus?"

The *Iliad*, the famous ancient Greek epic poem attributed to Homer, was an account of the Trojan War. For centuries many considered the entire war and the existence of a place called Troy as merely a poetic invention – until the city of Troy was discovered in 1871. Haven't people always passed on their life experiences in the form of poetry and songs? And isn't my own national anthem a form of poetry? Will historians a thousand years from now dismiss the historical events portrayed in "The Star Spangled Banner" just because it's a poetic song?

Miriam Lichtheim gave another reason why she felt that Ipuwer could not be referring to real events. Agreeing with other scholars, she stated the following: "The description of chaos in the *Admonitions* is inherently contradictory, hence historically impossible: On the one hand, the land is said to suffer from total want; on the other hand, the poor are described as having become rich, of wearing fine clothes, and generally of disposing of all that once belonged to their masters."[46]

However, when you read the biblical account, it becomes clear how this apparent contradiction could have happened. The scene described by Ipuwer actually echoes the biblical account in a most amazing way.

The Bible says:

*"The Israelites acted on Moses' word and asked the Egyptians for **silver and gold jewelry** and for **clothing**. And the LORD gave the people such favor in the Egyptians' sight that they gave them what they requested. In this way they plundered the Egyptians."* EXODUS 12:35-36

Several months after the Exodus when the Israelites were at Mount Sinai, the book of Exodus talks about the precious stones used in the priest's breastplate. This makes clear that the Israelite slaves had also acquired many other precious gems.

The Bible says:

*"Place a setting of **gemstones** on it, four rows of stones: The first row should be a row of **carnelian**, topaz, and **emerald**; the second row, a **turquoise**, a sapphire, and a diamond; the third row, a jacinth, an agate, and an **amethyst**; and the fourth row, a beryl, an onyx, and a jasper. They should be adorned with **gold filigree** in their settings."* EXODUS 28:17-20

Now look what happens when you compare the actions and materials listed in the Bible passage to Ipuwer's account. The similarities are remarkable.

Ipuwer writes:
"People are stripped of clothes . . . . *The slave takes* what he finds . . . . Behold, *gold*, lapis lazuli, *silver* and *turquoise, carnelian, amethysts*, emeralds and *all precious stones* are *strung on the necks of female slaves*." IPUWER 6:3, 2:4-5, 3:2-3

The point that Miriam Lichtheim viewed as "contradictory," and therefore "historically impossible," is the very detail that most specifically matches the biblical text.

The composition of the Admonitions late in the Middle Kingdom fits the other steps of the earlier pattern but appears to be about 400 years before the Ramesses Exodus date.

But Maarten Raven remained unconvinced, and he revealed to me the main reason why. "It's out of the question that this can refer to one and the same event. Conventional chronology has it that the Exodus took place somewhere during the Ramesside Period in Egypt, maybe around 1200 BC. Whereas our papyrus, when you look at the grammar and literary figures, and so forth, there's no question that it was composed in the Middle Kingdom and it is six, seven, eight hundred years earlier."[47]

However, I realized that the *Admonitions* of Ipuwer, along with all the other evidence I had looked at, was actually converging in the Middle Kingdom, not the time of Ramesses.

I remembered how David Rohl had challenged me. "Is it just another coincidence that this document was originally composed in the only period when Egypt's Delta was dominated by large numbers of Semites?" ♆

VIII:
CHALLENGING THE RAMESSES EXODUS THEORY

I had now seen evidence that fits every one of the first four steps of the biblical sequence – **Arrival, Multiplication, Slavery,** and **Judgment** – but this evidence is not recognized by most scholars because it's from the Middle Kingdom, centuries before the time of Ramesses II. Finding the Exodus is all about chronology. During what time period does the Bible actually place this event?

Over the years I've had friends ask me, "What difference does it really make whether Ramesses was the pharaoh of the Exodus?" It was one day while driving to work that I finally could see how crucial questioning the Ramesses view is to this whole endeavor. First of all, the Ramesses Exodus Theory is a giant in this debate. It is held by the vast majority of scholars, whether they accept the historical credibility of the Exodus or not. Secondly, the reigns of the pharaohs are what Egyptologists have used in constructing the timeline of the ancient world. They have worked from the known back to the unknown, adding up the reign lengths as they go. Consequently, if you choose the wrong pharaoh for the Exodus, you will end up with the wrong time period and won't find any evidence.

It might be like a team of archaeologists thousands of years from now looking in the 21st century for evidence of America's George Washington and the Revolutionary War, when those events actually happened in the 18th century. As they talked about their findings over dinner each night, they would eventually conclude that the war and its great hero must be only a legend with no basis in real history.

But what if somehow they discovered that their assumed date for the search was wrong? Then they'd be free to look for patterns of evidence elsewhere. When the 1700s were examined, the supporting evidence for the events would suddenly emerge, shedding new light on the birth of a nation.

Opposite: A statue of Ramesses II in the Cairo Museum.

Could the Ramesses Exodus Theory be blinding archaeologists from seeing real evidence for the biblical events, and leading many scholars to conclude that the Exodus and the story of the birth of ancient Israel is only a myth? It may seem unlikely since these are really bright people standing on the shoulders of the great scholars of the past. But what if their original assumption was wrong? What if somewhere along the line they got off track and everyone is now standing on the shoulders of a flawed premise? Is it okay to ask these kinds of questions? I think we have to.

Was Ramesses really the pharaoh of the Exodus?

In order to investigate this question, I would need to determine if the reign of Ramesses II showed any signs of major problems, such as a sudden collapse of power, that would match the biblical **Judgment** of Egypt.

I. Devastating Judgment at the Time of Ramesses?

The entrance to the Ramesseum, the mortuary temple of Ramesses II in Luxor.

They were headless, the four giant stone sentinels on each side of the large courtyard at the mortuary temple of Ramesses. Every one of them. When I asked why they cut the heads and noses off these magnificent statues, I was told that those who violated statues believed their actions harmed the person in the afterlife.

Next to these sentinels was an enormous fallen bust of Ramesses, lying on its face near the edge of the ancient plaza, shaken from its glory by an earthquake. As we walked, Professor Kent Weeks and I passed a smaller granite statue of Ramesses' head that for millennia has watched visitors climb up the ramp to the temple.

It was cool in the shade of the Ramesseum. Both of us were sitting on the bases of ancient pillars as we discussed the pharaoh who might be the greatest in Egypt's history.

"Some suggest that you look for the Exodus in a time when Egypt collapsed as a nation, when they were on their knees. Are there time periods in Egypt when this has happened?" I asked.

Weeks nodded. "There are time periods when Egypt fell on hard times. You've got the First Intermediate Period, the Second Intermediate Period. You've got the coming of the Hyksos. Some people would argue that those events were conflated in historical tradition to help create the myth of the Exodus. They would say it never occurred at any

The Hyksos

The Hyksos were foreigners who swept down from western Asia to dominate much of Egypt for more than a century during the Second Intermediate Period. They came in late in the 13th Dynasty and remained until being driven out by the first pharaoh of the New Kingdom's 18th Dynasty.

specific period of time but it's a story woven from the thread of historical traditions that go back over 1,000 years."

I rephrased the question. "Well, if Egypt lost their army, their crops, their leader, and their slave force, is there a time period in Egyptian history when this loss would have been seen?"

"I don't see any evidence that during the reign of Ramesses II there was a significant decline in the strength of the army, in the economic well being of the country, in the maintenance of trade relations with foreign lands, in the agricultural productivity of the Nile Valley," he admitted. "I don't see anything in the succeeding reign of Merneptah either that would allow this. And interestingly enough, we do have some fairly good economic records from the Ramesside Period in Egypt – good enough that we've been able to explore the economic situation in Egypt in the 19th and 20th Dynasties in some detail. And I don't know of any evidence that would say, okay, this is where the plagues had to have occurred and these are the results that we can see from Egyptian texts of there having been a major problem."

Not far from where we were sitting, I could see the fallen colossal statue of Ramesses. It's difficult to imagine how it was created and hauled from the quarry to this temple. On its shoulder was a bold inscription: "King of Kings." [48]

Weeks continued, "One of the reasons that Ramesses II has been called Ramesses the Great is in part because of his great building activity and in part because of the empire he had managed to maintain and enlarge. Now, the building activity is a direct result of the economic well being of the country. Without a strong economy, this kind of architectural and engineering undertaking simply couldn't have been done. The fact that Ramesses had an empire, enlarged an empire and maintained it, is in part due to the military control that Egypt exercised."

"So Ramesses' success was based on good economic conditions?"

"It meant that there was access to a lot of raw materials that could be brought into the country. It meant that Egypt didn't have to worry about launching major military campaigns in order to maintain a safe country within its own borders. But there was more to Egypt's well being than that, and a lot of things had to come together in a very unpredictable way for Egypt to have had that kind of a socioeconomic environment that would allow the Ramesside period, particularly the reign of Ramesses II, to be as successful as it was."

Professor Weeks discussing the strength and stability experienced by Egypt during the reign of Ramesses II.

191

I was beginning to understand. "So you are saying there was some type of stability that was formed?"

Weeks summarized, "There was a great deal of stability during this period. Had to have been for a lot of these things to have occurred. That is only partly due to military activity. Equally important would have been the economic situation at home."

II. Conquest of Canaan at the Time of Ramesses?

If Ramesses' great empire also covered the area of Canaan, which the Israelites are said to have conquered after they left Egypt, was there any evidence of the Israelite Conquest in the 13th century BC?

Israel Finkelstein has been surveying and digging in Israel for many years. After our first interview, he invited me to come back the following season and join him at his primary dig site of Megiddo in the northern part of Israel. For the next year I looked forward to participating in the excavations, but had to decline when I joyfully learned that my son and his fiancée were getting married around the same time. I explained the situation to Finkelstein and took a rain check. Then I decided to send our film team with a list of questions.

The dig site at Megiddo in northern Israel, which Professor Finkelstein directs.

The site of Megiddo is on a mound known as a tell, where over the centuries ancient cities have been built upon each other, one after another like a giant layer cake. As the film crew approached the hillside, they could see Professor Finkelstein surrounded by 20 to 30 students who were busy unearthing one of Israel's most important and ancient archaeological sites. There were several excavation pits that revealed stone walls, floors, and passageways that had lain hidden below the surface of the earth for thousands of years.

Our Israeli producer Sharon Schaveet and crew set up under one of the canopies that provided shade for the workers. Finkelstein joined her. With the sounds of picks, brushes, and dirt shoveled into buckets in the background, she asked, "Do you see any instability during the time of Ramesses that might demonstrate a biblical Conquest of the land?"

Finkelstein explained, "Ramesses II had a very strong force in Canaan. Canaan in his time, the 13th century BC, was an Egyptian province, ruled by Egyptians. Which means that there were Egyptian centers – garrison cities in Gaza, in Jaffa, in Beit She'an not too far from us today to the east, and there were military forces here. There were administrators here, and every small problem that evolved between the city-states was brought in front of the Egyptian legislators, and then letters were sent to Egypt and so on. Egypt was then in the peak of its force as an empire in the Levant, in the ancient Near East. I suppose that all the way from Syria to Egypt nobody could make an extra move without the Egyptian administration knowing about it. So in a situation like this, I don't think that the Egyptians would allow a large group of people to come from outside, from the desert, invade Canaan and start destroying cities and lands and agricultural output and things like that. This I think is impossible, not in the time of Ramesses II."

Both Weeks and Finkelstein agree that there was no major weakness during the reign of Ramesses in Egypt or its provinces in Canaan. Strong evidence for an uninterrupted period of prosperous and stable conditions at this time is completely opposite of what would be expected from the Judgment described in the Bible. I would learn another striking detail about the major Conquest site of Jericho, along with some of the other cities mentioned in the Conquest narrative. The archaeology shows that these cities were abandoned ruins throughout the era of Ramesses – in his time there were no high-walled fortresses in these places for the Israelites to defeat.

So the case against the Bible in the time of Ramesses goes far, far beyond the absence of archaeological evidence.

III. A Defense of the Ramesses Date

With so many factors opposing the Ramesses Exodus Theory, I needed to raise the obvious question again: What if the Exodus really did happen earlier than the time of Ramesses II? However, Professor Hoffmeier resists this idea and maintains he has found more evidence in the Bible, besides the building of the store city of Ramesses, for the Ramesses Exodus Theory. Much of this evidence concerns the names of locations mentioned in the Bible's account of God leading the Israelites out of Egypt and eventually to the crossing of the Red Sea, which in Hebrew is called *Yam Suph*.

During the Exodus from Egypt, Moses and the children of Israel are said to have crossed a sea on a path of dry ground miraculously opened up by God.

I wanted James Hoffmeier to tell me about this additional evidence. "You mentioned that during the time of Ramesses, there are more place names in Egypt fitting the biblical account than any other period."

He explained, "I happen to favor the 13th-century date because in the book of Exodus we have geographical terms or what we call toponyms (place names) that are mentioned in connection with the Exodus. First of all, we have the cities that the Israelites are said to have helped to make bricks for, Ramesses and Pithom. We also have the reference to Migdol, in Exodus 14:2."

"What does Migdol mean?"

"Migdol means tower or fort. And we do know from Egyptian texts in the 13th century that there was such a fort on Egypt's northeastern frontier, called the Migdol of Seti I. The name Migdol was given in the Bible as one of the locations where the Israelites camped on their flight from Egypt."

Hoffmeier also pointed out there are other names from Egyptian records in the 13th century that match the biblical text. These are names of key locations tracing the Israelites' journey after they left Egypt.

"Can you give some of these examples?" I asked.

"Exodus 14 has the names of Pi-hahiroth, Migdol, and Baal-zephon all in connection with the sea, which is also called the Sea of Reeds, Yam Suph. And so this collocation of Migdol and Yam Suph, Ramesses, Pithom, also known from 13th century Ramesside Period papyri – these all suggest to me that these names are authentic and fit very nicely into the 13th century BC. To this we can add Succoth. This was the Egyptian term *Tjeku*. This place was fortified. We know it from texts, including the famous Anastasi

Papyri. So all of these fit very nicely into the 13th century BC."

Hoffmeier's point seemed valid. But if some of the biblical names do connect best to documents from the time of Ramesses, might there be other explanations for these connections? Could these names in the Bible be anachronisms, just as the name of Ramesses appears to be an anachronism for Avaris, as I had discussed with David Rohl? If so, these names may not be implying a Ramesses date for the Exodus events themselves, but rather implying a Ramesses date for when the text was updated – especially since there are many places in the text that point to such an updating. [49]

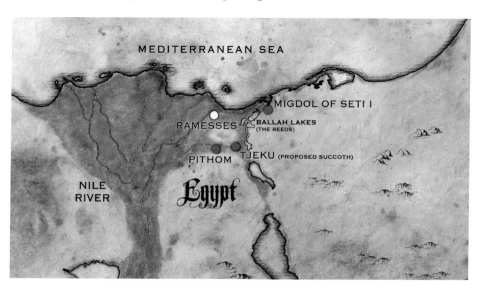

The locations of several places mentioned in the Bible as proposed by James Hoffmeier. The Hebrew Bible uses the name Yam Suph for the sea that was crossed by the Israelites, which Hoffmeier interprets as the Sea of Reeds. He places the crossing in an area that was known as "the reeds" on Egypt's border.

IV. Discovering a Second Exodus Date

I respect Professor Hoffmeier greatly. However, there is another major hurdle that the Ramesses Exodus Theory needs to clear in order for Ramesses II to keep his title of Pharaoh of the Exodus. It was brought to my attention that the Bible itself contains a passage that indicates the Exodus occurred hundreds of years before Pharaoh Ramesses ruled. But this historical clue has been largely ignored or discounted today.

So He led the people around toward the Red Sea [Yam Suph] along the road of the wilderness. And the Israelites left the land of Egypt in battle formation. Moses took the bones of Joseph with him, because Joseph had made the Israelites swear a solemn oath, saying, "God will certainly come to your aid; then you must take my bones with you from this place." They set out from Succoth and camped at Etham on the edge of the wilderness. The LORD went ahead of them in a pillar of cloud to lead them on their way during the day and in a pillar of fire to give them light at night, so that they could travel day or night.
(Exodus 13:18-21)

Then the LORD spoke to Moses: "Tell the Israelites to turn back and camp in front of Pi-hahiroth, between Migdol and the sea; you must camp in front of Baal-zephon, facing it by the sea."
(Exodus 14:1-2)

The Bible in 1 Kings 6:1 states that King Solomon, one of the most famous kings of Israel, built a temple to the God Yahweh. The text clearly says it was 480 years from the building of Solomon's temple back to the time of the Exodus out of Egypt. Many scholars believe the reign of Solomon began in 970 BC. So if the accepted dates for Solomon are correct, then 480 years before this date would place the Exodus around 1450 BC, which is 200 years before the Ramesses date. [50]

The Exodus date based on 1 Kings 6:1 compared to the Ramesses Exodus Theory.

What I found striking about this passage is that it is such a clear and direct chronological statement. I wondered how proponents of the Ramesses Exodus Theory, such as James Hoffmeier, dealt with it.

So I asked him, "When do you think the Exodus actually happened?"

Hoffmeier replied, "Well, there are two important sources of information about the dating of the Exodus. And the problem is that you can't take both of them literally. First Kings 6:1 refers to the 480 years from the beginning of Solomon's Temple back to the Exodus. However, in Exodus 1:11 we also have a very important datum, and that comes with the reference to the building of the city of Ramesses."

"How do you solve this problem?" I asked.

He continued, "So, the historian has to deal with one of two problems. You either take the 1 Kings 6:1 reference literally, and say you are in the 15th century, or you take the reference in Exodus 1:11 literally, which forces you into the 13th century. And either way you have to interpret one verse literally, and one you have to find some other accommodation. But you can't take both of them literally."

As I thought about it, there was another possibility. What if Exodus 1:11 was an anachronism, used as a geographical marker for the location of Avaris under the city of Ramesses? Then 1 Kings 6:1 could be read as a plain chronological reference, which the style of writing seems to support. If this was the case, there would be no contradiction.

Since Weeks and Finkelstein had stated that there was no evidence of a collapse in Egypt at the time of Ramesses, I decided to press Professor Hoffmeier on the lack of any sign of a major judgment of Egypt. "This time is one of the greatest times in Egyptian history, and there's no evidence of a great collapse of the Egyptian culture, as an Exodus would have produced."

Hoffmeier responded, "Right. Well, the reality is we have no evidence of a great collapse for either period. We must remember that the Egyptians were not inclined to write about failures and setbacks. Only in the most discreet ways would such a thing have happened. So, I'm not surprised as a historian to find no direct reference to this military or economic or environmental collapse, or series of disasters, which came upon Egypt."

What Hoffmeier is saying is that both dates commonly used for the Exodus have a problem. There are no references to a collapse during the time of Ramesses or at the earlier Exodus date of 1450 BC. And as I learned from Weeks and Finkelstein, there is no archaeological evidence for a collapse either. The mystery, then, is why Ipuwer describes chaos and plagues matching the Bible's story of **Judgment** in the Middle Kingdom. And why does evidence for all the earlier steps of **Arrival, Multiplication,** and **Slavery** appear there as well?

The Bible's Older Exodus Date

Solomon began to build the temple for the LORD in the four hundred eightieth year after the Israelites came out of the land of Egypt, in the fourth year of his reign over Israel, in the second month, in the month of Ziv. (1 Kings 6:1)

V. The Case Against Ramesses Builds

It was turning fall again. Another summer had passed. The leaves were beginning to take on their autumn reds, yellows, and browns. This is one of my favorite times of the year.

Yet there is a sadness in the autumn because it means the end of a season of life, warmth, and things that once grew flowers and fruit. The acorns from the 200-year-old oak trees that surrounded my home were abundant this year. Over the past few days they had fallen hard like hail from a storm, and this morning they carpeted my walk and driveway.

At the studio I brought up something I had been contemplating. "Steve, I've been thinking about this investigation. From the beginning we decided to test the Bible for what it says."

"That's correct."

"Well, why is it that scholars tend to ignore certain details in the biblical text?"

"This seems to happen when those points don't fit their theory."

"So if we test the story of the Exodus as it is actually written in the Bible, does it create any other problems for the Ramesses Exodus Theory?"

"It does. For example, when the Bible mentions the building of the city of Ramesses, it has this happening around the time that Moses was born. It then says that the pharaoh who had sought Moses' life died before the Exodus out of Egypt occurred, while Moses was spending 40 years in the land of Midian. So how could Ramesses II have been both the pharaoh who built the store city and the pharaoh of the Exodus as well?" [51]

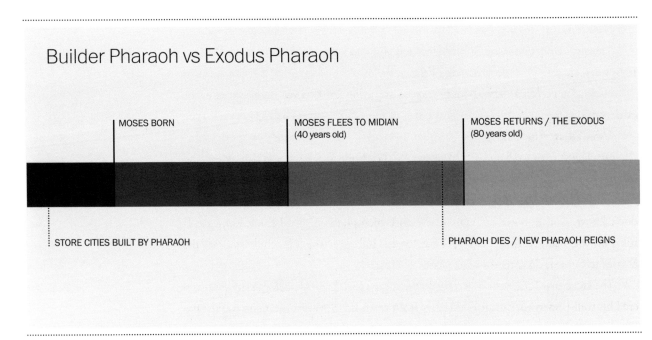

Builder Pharaoh vs Exodus Pharaoh

MOSES BORN

MOSES FLEES TO MIDIAN
(40 years old)

MOSES RETURNS / THE EXODUS
(80 years old)

STORE CITIES BUILT BY PHARAOH

PHARAOH DIES / NEW PHARAOH REIGNS

"I see. It's not possible for him to be both."

"Another problem for Ramesses has to do with Pharaoh dying at the Red Sea crossing."

"What kind of problem would that be?"

"If Pharaoh died at the sea crossing, then whoever was the pharaoh of the Exodus must have reigned less than 40 years. That's also because the pharaoh who sought Moses' life ended up dying during Moses' 40-year stay in Midian."

"I get it. So there would be a new pharaoh starting his reign sometime during that 40-year period and then he was killed in the sea crossing in the same year that Moses returned to confront him."

"And a reign of less than 40 years does not fit Ramesses II because he is known to have reigned more than 60 years. If the pharaoh of the Exodus drowned in the sea, then Ramesses could not have been that pharaoh."

"That's right! How do scholars get around that?"

"It's simple. Some scholars argue that the Bible does not clearly state that Pharaoh died in the sea crossing. But again, according to the details in the text, Pharaoh personally led his army to the sea in pursuit of the fleeing Israelites. It then explicitly says that the entire army went into the sea, and that all who went into the sea were destroyed." [52]

"Is it right to consider the details?"

"That's the big question. But remember if you don't test the details, then all you are testing is someone's invented version of the story."

"Yes, and a missed detail here or there could take you to a place where there's no evidence."

"Absolutely. That's the point!"

While in Luxor I talked with Mansour Boraik about Ramesses' age. Boraik gave his insight. "According to the stories of the holy books, we know that the pharaoh followed them until he sank in the Red Sea with the army. That's the story. Which pharaoh, we don't know. And nobody can tell you exactly which pharaoh. But I think Ramesses II ruled 67 years and he lived until 97. And for this old age, I think he could not ride the chariot to fight or do something like this."

The facts, that Ramesses II lived to a ripe old age and that archaeologists have uncovered his well-preserved, mummified body from its coffin, are also arguments against the idea that he was the pharaoh spoken of in the Exodus account. [53]

VI. Was Ramesses' Son the Pharaoh of the Exodus?

As I was considering the evidence I had just seen, I was becoming more doubtful that Ramesses was the pharaoh of the Exodus:

- The lack of a collapse during his reign,
- The archaeology that shows Jericho and other Conquest cities were empty ruins during the time of Ramesses,
- The date derived from 1 Kings 6:1 that puts the date of the Exodus 200 years before Ramesses,
- The mention in the Bible that the pharaoh who built the city of Ramesses died before the Exodus of the Israelites out of Egypt,
- His exceptionally long reign that does not fit the 40-year limit for the pharaoh of the Exodus,
- And his old age and well-preserved mummy.

The last three bullet points on this list lead some scholars to suggest that Ramesses' son was actually the pharaoh of the Exodus. His name was Merneptah and he had to wait until Ramesses died in his 90s before ascending the throne. I wanted to be sure to test the Merneptah option proposed by scholars before eliminating Ramesses' family as possible pharaohs. That would require more filming. But since the film needed additional footage anyway, this would just be another item to add to the list.

One of the harder decisions I had to make was whether or not I should go back to Egypt in the middle of its revolution during 2012. But that is what happened. The film project had been going on now for ten years. I had often struggled to work on the film and yet not neglect my regular job of running a studio that produced TV commercials and web videos. There were stretches of time when I wasn't able to touch the film at all. I knew everyone on the team, including myself, wanted the project to be finished.

I awoke to the first light of dawn. This morning would be different from others. I looked up at the ceiling and just knew I had to return to Egypt. If I didn't go back, I wouldn't be able to finish the film. Of all times to be planning a trip, 2012 seemed a bit crazy. But I felt peaceful about the idea of returning. I called David Wessner.

"We can't make the kind of film we need to make without going back to Egypt," I said. "I don't have the footage to finish it."

"What would be the exact purpose of this trip?" he asked as he had on so many previous occasions.

"I'd ask David Rohl to come and take me to key locations where he sees connections to the Exodus story."

"Okay."

"We need to interview some more viewpoints from other Egyptologists and get answers about a new aspect of the debate we've uncovered. We need an Egyptian perspective as well."

"Anything else?"

"Our early footage was not shot in high definition, so we need updated temple shots, tombs, and some more recreations to tell the story."

The other end of the line was quiet again. Then he spoke. "I've never been a part of a project that seemed to be so hard to control."

"I know it keeps getting bigger. But I think we are closing in on some big answers."

"I think you're right. You should go back to Egypt."

David at various times could see that what we were doing was visionary. And I believed that as well. We both felt we were uncovering something profound. I kept pushing for excellence in every aspect, and we had to follow every important lead. Thankfully, David had the courage and vision to back me up.

That didn't mean we didn't have a budget. We did. We just kept adjusting it to accommodate the ongoing investigation. This required our business manager, Diane Walker, to have as much patience as David did. She often needed to adjust and track all the changes on the business end of things, even when it seemed that there was no way to make it work. But good things always came out of this dogged determination. For ten years now we had been digging into this subject that was just poking through the surface. We couldn't have imagined at the start that what we saw then was only the tip of the iceberg. Underneath, hidden from all, was a mountain of revelation and intrigue.

Our role was simply to go to the scholars, hear what they had to say, and turn their views into a visual presentation that took complex ideas and made them understandable for everyone. This discipline took time, money, and a lot of creative energy. We all invested in one way or another.

I was still on the phone with David. "Well, as I've been thinking about it, I don't want to go alone. I think you should come with me."

There was a slight pause again. I knew he was thinking and I hoped he would agree. "Yes. Why not? I'd like to come. I've never been to Egypt."

"Great, you can be my soundman."

I contacted the embassy and worked for several weeks clarifying all the details. With all the unrest, there were not a lot of tourists traveling at this time, so I was a little nervous the day we landed in Luxor. As David and I rode from the airport through a crowded square, I sensed that something had happened. Something was wrong. Later we learned that protests had begun again in Cairo. People had died that day.

The hotel where we were staying was almost empty. After a quiet dinner that evening David asked, "Are you okay?" I guess I looked worried.

"Well, I have been around some difficult situations in the past, and yes, I am concerned whether we should have come at this time."

"Well, don't worry. It will be fine," he said with a reassuring look.

"You're right. See you in the morning. We've got a big day tomorrow." I opened the door to my room.

David Wessner (Executive Producer) working as a soundman in Egypt.

The next morning David came down to breakfast looking awful. "What happened?" I asked.

"I woke up around three this morning in a panic about what you said. I couldn't get back to sleep."

We both laughed and ordered coffee and breakfast.

As it turned out, this trip was very valuable to the project. I was able to film David Rohl, Mansour Boraik, and Kent Weeks during this time. We also got many of the scenes of me wandering around temples and tombs. The only little shocker came late in the week when I was awakened by gunfire from automatic weapons. I found out later it was only fireworks from a wedding party being held at the hotel.

After several days, David Rohl joined Kent Weeks and me at the Ramesseum. We walked to an area of the temple to look at a massive wall inscription depicting all the royal sons of Ramesses II.

Rohl pointed to the inscription. "What amazes me about this is the way that the princes are all listed in a row. Then we get the guy who succeeds – he's number 13. All of these princes here have died before you get to Merneptah."

Weeks agreed. "Exactly right, and that's relatively sure because we have numerous scenes like this in various temples in which the sons of Ramesses are shown standing in processions. The number of sons differs depending on when in Ramesses' reign the scene was carved. But invariably, the order of the sons is consistent, regardless of what period you are talking about."

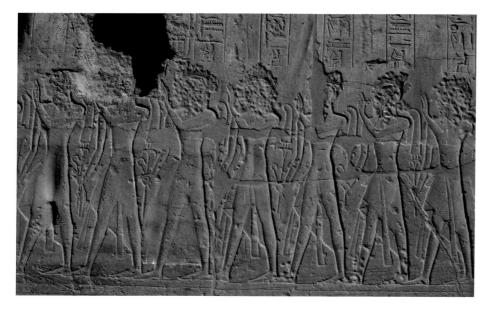

David Rohl, Kent Weeks, and Timothy Mahoney investigating the question of whether Ramesses was the pharaoh of the Exodus.

An inscription depicting the sons of Ramesses II at the Ramesseum.

"So the hierarchy works all the way through," Rohl added.

"Exactly," Weeks replied. "Amun-her-Khepeshef is number one. If you have Merneptah, he's always number 13."

Rohl asked Weeks, "So number 13 here, Merneptah, what sort of age would he have been when he succeeded?"

"I don't know exactly, but he certainly would have been middle-aged, I think," Weeks said.

Rohl nodded. "Right."

Weeks continued, "So these fellows all died, predeceased Merneptah, predeceased their father and were themselves middle-aged or even older. Amun-her-Khepeshef, for example, may have been as old as 50, 53, or so when he died. Some of the others in their 30s and 40s. None of these died in infancy or early youth."

"So these are all of the sons of Ramesses II?" I asked.

Weeks replied, "Well, they are all the sons of Ramesses born to wives of stature, principal wives. He undoubtedly had many other children born of concubines or secondary or tertiary wives. These are the ones who, I think, could in order have been considered heirs apparent to the throne." [54]

Merneptah, the 13th son of Ramesses, became the next pharaoh to reign after Ramesses II. He would become significant in our investigation to determine if someone in Ramesses' family could have been the pharaoh of the Exodus.

VII. Merneptah Stele: The First Mention of Israel in Egypt

The Merneptah Stele is thought to be the oldest and only mention of Israel in ancient Egypt. It was found in the ancient city of Thebes on the west bank of the Nile. It commemorates Egypt's victories over its enemies and was erected by Pharaoh Merneptah (1213-1203 BC) in his 5th year. He was the 13th son of Ramesses II and was the next pharaoh to follow him on the throne.

Merneptah is best known for erecting a stone monument, or stele, that mentions the nation of Israel. Commonly called the Merneptah Stele, it was uncovered in 1896 by an English pioneer in Egyptology, Sir Flinders Petrie, who considered it his most important discovery because of its connection to the Bible. The stele was found in King Merneptah's funerary chapel in Thebes, the ancient Egyptian capital on the west bank of the Nile. On the opposite bank is the Temple of Karnak. The original stele stood here for thousands of years before it was taken to the Egyptian Museum in Cairo. I have filmed at both locations.

Merneptah erected this monument just a few years after his father's death. Rohl and many others believe that the victory poem on this stele demonstrates that neither Ramesses II nor his son Merneptah could be the pharaoh of the Exodus. I was anxious to know why.

It was 117 degrees Fahrenheit the day Rohl took me to see the Merneptah Stele. I knew it was hot when the Egyptians were looking for shade, but there was no shade as we approached the stele in the open courtyard. In one corner stood the stone artifact with its back against the wall that surrounded the courtyard. Rohl surveyed the ten-foot-high slab. "So this is the famous Merneptah Stele, or what we call the Israel Stele, and it actually belongs to the king, Merneptah. Up there at the top you can see him facing the god Amun."

"What does it say?" I asked.

"It's like a summary of the achievements of the dynasty, and he lists here, in a poetic form, all the different conquered nations, the nations that are at peace. But right at the bottom, you have three crucial lines, because this is where we find a link to the Bible."

"So that's why you brought me here?"

Rohl knelt and pointed to the lower portion of the monument. "I brought you here to see this. In particular, one name. You have the two reeds. That's the sound "e" or "ee", okay? Then the bolt of cloth, which is "s", then an "r", an "a" and an "l". Is-ra-el.

"Israel." I was fascinated. After all I had heard about the lack of biblical evidence, here in the middle of Egypt was an inscription with the name that came from the Bible, Israel.

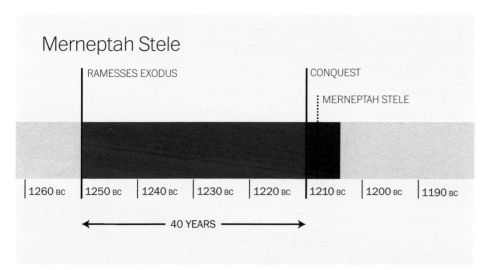

The Merneptah Stele was made in Merneptah's 5th year. If the Israelites had left Egypt around 1250 BC, the stele would have been carved during the second year of the Conquest, which matches neither Israel's establishment as a nation nor the idea of a major conflict between Israel and Egypt before this time.

The name Israel graphically enhanced on the Merneptah Stele followed by the people or nation determinative (read right to left).

Sir Flinders Petrie in 1903. Petrie was a pioneer of early Egyptology and discovered the Merneptah Stele.

"Israel," Rohl echoed. "This is the only time that we see this name on an Egyptian monument."

"This is very significant, isn't it?"

"It's hugely significant." Rohl then directed me to focus on the hieroglyphs next to the name Israel. "After the name Israel are these two seated figures of a woman and a man, and three strokes underneath."

"What does that mean?"

Rohl explained, "These three strokes mean plural. So it means the people or nation of Israel. And then this is the interesting bit. It says *Fekty bin peret f.* That means 'Israel is laid waste, his seed is no more.'"

"Does it mean that they were literally no more?"

"No. It's a sort of poetical way of saying they'd been overcome, defeated."

"Or pacified?" I asked.

"Yes. All these phrases are like that; it's a poetical phrase effectively."

The four major nations along with the four cities of Merneptah's poem.

Rohl continued his argument by directing me to look more closely at the pattern of the "victory poem" on this monument. "What we have are two introductory lines, then we have two major entities, the Libyans and the Hittites, then we have four towns, then we have two more major entities, Israel and Syria. And we finish off with two more lines to close the poem.

"The way the pattern of the poem works tells us that Israel was a major entity at the time. So it's effectively the nation of Israel, and it's out there in the northern part of the world outside Egypt. They seem to be a political entity."

The reflection of the Egyptian sun off the stele was blinding. Its heat was like a furnace. I could feel sweat trickling down my face. But none of that mattered at this moment. What Rohl had just revealed I knew was very important to this question of whether Ramesses is the pharaoh mentioned in the Bible. "How significant is this then to the story of the Exodus?"

Rohl drew himself up beside the stele and looked at me. "Well, for me it's very important, because if we're talking about Ramesses II or Merneptah being at the time of the Exodus with Moses and Joshua, this just doesn't fit the pattern. It makes no sense at all."

I could see that this poses a problem for the Ramesses Exodus Theory. The Bible states that the Israelites didn't even begin to conquer Canaan until 40 years after they left Egypt. So how could Merneptah be the pharaoh of the Exodus if Israel was already established in the land of Canaan by the fifth year of his reign? According to the biblical information, it's just not possible.[55]

Egyptologist David Rohl and Mahoney at the Merneptah Stele replica.

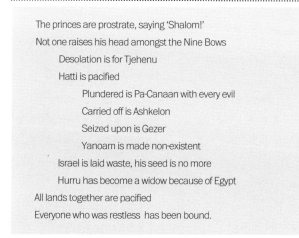

The princes are prostrate, saying 'Shalom!'
Not one raises his head amongst the Nine Bows
Desolation is for Tjehenu
Hatti is pacified
Plundered is Pa-Canaan with every evil
Carried off is Ashkelon
Seized upon is Gezer
Yanoam is made non-existent
Israel is laid waste, his seed is no more
Hurru has become a widow because of Egypt
All lands together are pacified
Everyone who was restless has been bound.

Merneptah's Poem

According to David Rohl, the pattern of the victory poem written at the bottom of the Merneptah Stele shows that Egypt considered Israel to be established as one of the great powers of the day – just like Libya (Tjehenu), the Hittite kingdom (Hatti), and Syria (Hurru). "Shalom" is the Hebrew word for peace, and the "Nine Bows" were Egypt's traditional enemies.

VIII. Berlin Pedestal: An Even Earlier Mention of Israel?

For more than a century, the Merneptah Stele contained the oldest known mention of Israel in all of the world. But then I heard about another inscription that names Israel.

Discovered on an Egyptian statue pedestal and now residing in the Berlin Museum in Germany, this inscription might prove to be an even older reference to Israel.

I wished I had heard about this find earlier, so I could have gone there to conduct interviews. But like so many times during the research for this project, I didn't know what I didn't know. It has always been a process to uncover new leads. So it wasn't until later in Minnesota, when talking with Egyptologist Charles Aling, that it was brought to my attention.

Aling walked me down the hall to another wing of the university where we entered a darkened lecture room, lit only by the glow of a projector. There were rows of tables where students could sit side by side. The screen displayed a broken Egyptian artifact. Historian Clyde Billington glanced up over his reading glasses from behind the lectern as we entered. He looked to be in his 60s and wore a suit and tie. His dark hair was combed back and graying on the sides. He impressed me as a kindly person, approachable, the type who welcomed students after class.

Aling introduced me. "Professor Billington, I'd like you to meet Timothy Mahoney, the filmmaker investigating the story of the Exodus."

"It's good to meet you."

"Likewise. I understand you have some interesting information about a new discovery?"

"Yes, it's relatively new and relatively unknown." Billington turned to the image projected on the screen beside him. He was enthusiastic. "Besides the Merneptah Stele, there's another reference to Israel. It's called the Berlin Pedestal. It's in the state museum in Berlin, Germany, and this is something that's just now being studied and discussed by scholars."[56]

As I looked at the statue base, Billington showed me a row of name rings. Each of these name rings depicted a city or nation defeated by the pharaoh in the area of Canaan. This was the region where ancient Israel would have been located.

He explained, "This hieroglyph – this is called an enemy name ring. You have an image of the enemy being bound, and you have a ring, and the name of the enemy within it."

I noted, "What's interesting is that I can see their arms are behind them. I haven't seen that before."

"Yes," he said, "they actually have their arms bound behind them. That's rather

Professor Clyde Billington of the University of Northwestern, Saint Paul, believes the Berlin Pedestal is a significant find demonstrating that the Exodus happened much earlier than the time of Ramesses.

The Berlin Pedestal showing the enemy name ring of Israel on the far right.

traditional for pharaohs, to have enemy name rings."

"So would these have been captured people?"

"Realize that pharaohs exaggerated all the time, to say the very least," Billington replied.

"So he is bragging?"

He smiled. "He's bragging. He's saying, 'I've conquered these people. I control these people.'" Billington told me that the names represented on the enemy name rings were grouped in the same geographical area, which also supports the conclusion for the end ring being Israel. "This is the name Ashkelon. This is the name Canaan."

"What about the third inscription, the one on the end?" I asked.

"This is the one that's caused all of the excitement because, again, you have a bound enemy, so it's telling you that these people are enemies of the Egyptians. And the name down here, while it's partially broken away, has been reconstructed, and it's the name *Israel*."

Aling agreed. "This is very crucial evidence that we see here."

I asked, "So this is a relatively recent find?"

"Yes," Billington answered, "the actual article that everybody is looking at now was actually published in 2010, although the original work probably dates back as much as

The reconstructed name ring on the Berlin Pedestal containing the word Israel.

20 years. The person who first discovered it was named Manfred Gorg, a German, and he sent a copy of it to an Israeli Egyptologist named Raphael Giveon, and Raphael Giveon actually looked at it and said it's the name Israel. Now, he didn't publish. Manfred Gorg eventually published and then he got some criticism, and he got a couple of other German Egyptologists, and they published this article, arguing that this name is Israel, and I'm absolutely convinced that they're right."

The three name rings on the Berlin Pedestal all represent locations in the same geographic region.

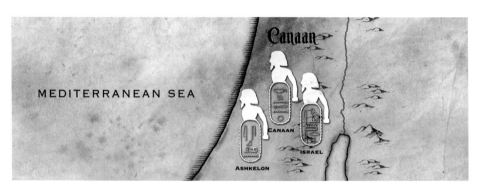

I asked, "What is the date of this artifact?"

"Now, there are various arguments about when exactly this should be dated, but one thing is for certain: it dates a lot earlier than a lot of people anticipated. I would probably place it in the reign of Amenhotep III, probably somewhere around the year 1360 BC. In other words, that makes the late-date theory of the Exodus at 1260 BC an impossibility. This is 100 years earlier."

"Professor Aling, why don't other Egyptologists see this and connect that idea?" I asked.

"Well, I think many Egyptologists do see it. They don't want to make the connection. That's one of the problems."

"Are there other problems?"

"Well, with all of this being German, and much of the original publication in German, the ordinary biblical scholar doesn't necessarily have the language skills or know the source material well enough to appreciate it."

I had just learned that the Merneptah Stele was evidence that Ramesses or his son could not have been the pharaoh of the Exodus. However, the fact that the Berlin Pedestal names Israel as a nation in the area of Canaan 100 years earlier than Ramesses II was an even stronger indication of that improbability.

IX. The Shepherds of God

The ruins of the ancient temple of Soleb.

But there was one more piece of evidence, which again points to the Exodus happening much earlier than the time of Ramesses. Aling and Billington have co-authored an article about a little known discovery of Egyptian hieroglyphs that also involve enemy name rings. These hieroglyphs contain the same word that was used in the biblical account of Moses at the burning bush. When Moses asked what name for God he should give to the Israelites when they asked who sent him, this is how God responded: *"Say this to the Israelites: Yahweh, the God of your fathers, the God of Abraham, the God of Isaac, and the God of Jacob, has sent me to you. This is My name forever; this is how I am to be remembered in every generation."* (Exodus 3:15)

The clue in this passage relates to the personal name of God – Yahweh. This name is considered so sacred that most Jewish people won't even pronounce it. The word *Yahweh* is key to the next piece of evidence because the Bible claims that this name wasn't revealed until the time of the Exodus.

Billington changed the slide to reveal the ancient ruins of an Egyptian temple. I looked from the screen over to Aling and asked, "What was found that you wrote about in your article?"

I could see his excitement. "There's a temple down in the land of what the Egyptians would have called Nubia, known today as Sudan. It's called the Temple of Soleb."

"What time period does it come from?"

"It had been constructed by Pharaoh Amenhotep III, so it's conventionally dated to about 1390 BC."

"So it's before the time of Ramesses?"

Aling responded, "Yes, it's way before Ramesses II. And this temple has the only known mention of Yahweh in all of Egyptian hieroglyphic texts. It's on a list of places."

I asked, "Could you clarify who is Yahweh?"

"Yahweh is the God of Israel, the God of the Bible."

Billington added, "Jehovah sometimes."

"Jehovah sometimes in English," said Aling. "Yahweh is the God of the Old Testament who delivers Israel from Egypt and who was not known in Egypt at the time of the Exodus."

The location of the Temple of Soleb in ancient Nubia.

The Shasu of Yahweh inscription was found on a pillar base such as this one at Soleb.

A reconstruction of the pillar base containing the inscription, Ta Shasu Yahweh ("The land of the Bedouin of Yahweh").

"So you're saying that at this location there's an inscription that relates to that. Can I see the inscription?"

"Yes." Aling then changed the picture on the screen. I could see a photo from the base of one of the temple pillars.

"Okay, what is that?"

"A cartouche. The ring is called a cartouche. But it's not for a king. In this case it's for a Bedouin, an enemy group." Just as on the Berlin Pedestal, on the base of the remains of this pillar were carved a set of enemy name rings, each depicting a different nomadic or Bedouin group.

"So what is the connection to Yahweh?"

"What they normally do is say 'the land of the Bedouin of' and then give you a place name. But right in the midst of all these comes 'the land of the Bedouin of Yahweh.' Obviously not a place name."

As I looked at the image, I asked, "Could you repeat that?"

Aling smiled. "It's called the Shasu of Yahweh inscription. It says 'Ta Shasu,' the land of the Shasu (the land of the Bedouin), of 'Yahweh.'"

"How big of a discovery is this?"

"Tremendous, a mention of the God of the Bible! The only mention of Yahweh in all of Egyptian texts. One of the most astounding discoveries that's been made in recent centuries in Egypt. This is an account, a naming of Bedouin peoples who are worshippers of Yahweh. Yahweh is not a place name. You wouldn't find any example of that."

Billington continued, "Now if you know the story that you have there in Exodus, Moses appears before Pharaoh, tells him that Yahweh says we need to leave and go worship him, and remember what Pharaoh says is 'I've never heard of this God Yahweh!'"

"So what you're saying is that Moses introduced the name of this God, Yahweh, to the Egyptians?" I asked.

"The very name of it, yes. When Moses appears for the first time before Pharaoh, Pharaoh says, 'Who is this god?' He doesn't do that the next time, by the way, when Moses appears."

The Bible claims that the name Yahweh was first revealed at the time of the Exodus, and the Shasu of Yahweh inscription uses the name Yahweh. Therefore, it seems to follow that this inscription must have been made after the Exodus.

Aling then gave a personal insight as he speculated about how this might have connected with Egyptian history. "Now, it's also interesting because of the way Yahweh is treated. You'll find that Egyptians have dozens of foreign gods from Nubia, from

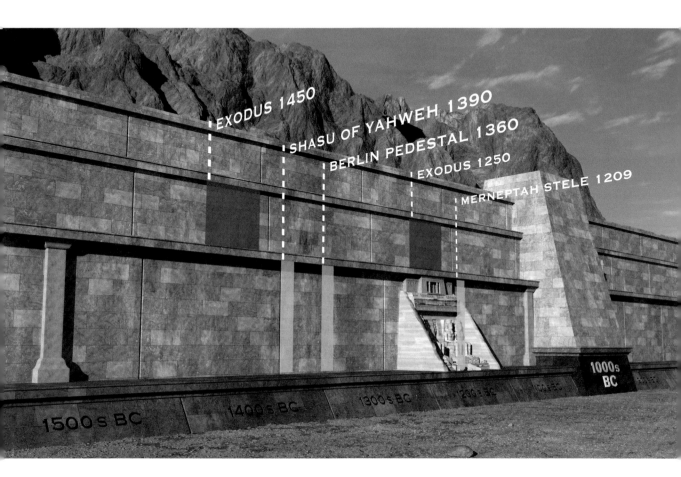

Canaan, from the Libyan area. And normally they will build temples to them, they will worship them, they will equate them sometimes with Egyptian deities."

I didn't quite understand. "Okay, what's different about this?"

Aling went on, "Yahweh is never used in any of those contexts, which means I believe, that they disliked him, because of the events of the plagues, and the Exodus, and the deaths of the firstborn – all those judgments that God brought down against Egypt."

His reasoning made sense. If the Exodus really happened, the Egyptians would not have wanted anything to do with the God of the Israelites. I also thought back to Ipuwer's

These three Egyptian inscriptions all point to the Exodus happening before the Ramesses Exodus date.

descriptions in the *Admonitions of an Egyptian Sage.* Weren't those writings passed on through the centuries to warn Egyptians never again to allow these foreigners to fill their land? And wouldn't this also apply to their God?

I asked Aling to clarify. "Your interpretation is that this God known as Yahweh was not liked in Egypt?"

Aling agreed. "That's right. Absolutely. Not liked and not venerated."

I could see what this could mean for the validity of the Ramesses Exodus Theory. "Professor Billington, is this Egyptian inscription, the Shasu of Yahweh, significant for the dating of the Exodus?"

He raised his eyebrows. "Well, I think it's highly significant, first of all, because it's so early, dating around 1390 BC. We know from the Old Testament that the name Yahweh only comes into use in the days of Moses. Yet here you have a pharaoh in 1390, and he's heard of Yahweh. So obviously, then, the Exodus has to take place before this." He smiled. "In other words, the Exodus has to be before 1390 BC."

Aling chimed in, "Yes, absolutely. Long before Ramesses II lived." [57]

X. Moving Beyond the Ramesses Exodus Theory

These inscriptions, along with the other evidence I had looked at, all demonstrate that if the Exodus ever happened, it wasn't in the time of Ramesses II or his son Merneptah. Many indicators point to an Exodus occurring much earlier:

- No sign of devastating **Judgment** at the time of Ramesses,
- Evidence contrary to a **Conquest** in Canaan at the time of Ramesses,
- 1 Kings 6:1 giving an **Exodus** date 480 years before the Temple of Solomon, centuries before Ramesses II,
- The pharaoh responsible for building the city of Ramesses is said to have died before the **Exodus**,
- The Merneptah Stele, Berlin Pedestal, and Shasu of Yahweh inscriptions all indicating that Israel was already in the land of Canaan long before the time of Ramesses' reign.

Bedouin

Bedouin, whom the Egyptians called "Shasu," were tribes of people who did not usually settle permanently in large cities but rather lived in tents. These nomadic groups often roamed their home territory in a regular circuit looking for good grazing land for their flocks and herds. This label fits the condition of the Israelites during their 40 years in the wilderness as well as the lifestyle of much of their population in Canaan during the Judges Period (Judges 7:8, 1 Samuel 13:2, 2 Chronicles 25:22).

Yet for many decades university professors, scholars, and archaeologists have based their conclusions about the myth of the Exodus mainly on one issue. This issue is chronology – the dates assumed for the Exodus, and the lack of evidence at the time of Ramesses II. Their ideas have been transmitted into the classroom and beyond through popular culture in magazines, books, movies, and television programs. They are good scholars, standing on the broad shoulders of the important historians of the past, but now I'm beginning to think they have all been standing upon a giant, false assumption.

Ramesses just does not fit the descriptions and the narrative of the Exodus from the Bible. This means that these scholars and archaeologists are wrong. Wrong about their primary supposition of Ramesses being the pharaoh of the Exodus, and perhaps wrong about the Exodus never happening.

It was late in my interview with Professor Bimson. The sun was no longer shining as brightly outside the windows of the small side chamber at Trinity College. I raised the issue of why scholars have clung to the Ramesses date for an Exodus. "If they've picked the century that doesn't actually match the biblical narrative, then they'll have no archaeological evidence."

"No! No!" Bimson was adamant. "And I think there's a deep irony here because one of the original reasons why people focused on the 13th century BC is the reference in Exodus 1:11, where it says the Israelites built for the pharaoh the cities Pithom and Ramesses. And that name Ramesses has led people to look at the reign of Ramesses II. So the original reason for focusing on the 13th century BC goes back to a piece of information in the Bible, which the current generation of scholars largely rejects, and yet even though they've rejected it, their focus remains on the 13th century BC."

I shook my head at the logic of it. "So they've rejected the idea but they've retained the time period?"

Bimson nodded. "Yes, exactly."

"And would you say that's the bottom line for why they don't find any evidence for the Bible?"

Bimson continued with a smile. "I would, and I find it deeply ironic. It's a date that is based on very flimsy indicators. But this is where the majority of scholars look, almost out of habit really. Earlier periods have just dropped off their radar."

Is the popular identification of Ramesses II as the pharaoh of the Exodus a giant standing in the way of finding biblical events?

XI. Reestablishing the Bible's Timeline

The Israelite Sojourn in Egypt

Some may notice an apparent problem with the length of the Israelites' stay in Egypt on the Wall of Time. This is because there are actually two main schools of thought on how long the Israelites were in Egypt before the Exodus took place. This discussion is covered in Bonus Chapter D at the end of the book.

So Finkelstein and many others are right when they claim that the case for a Ramesses Exodus around 1250 BC is very weak. But instead of jumping to the conclusion that the Exodus never happened, why not consider the possibility that the Ramesses reference was simply a geographical locator and not meant for chronological purposes? If this word *Ramesses* is an anachronism, then it can't be used to date the original events of the Exodus. However, the reference in 1 Kings 6:1, that the Exodus happened exactly 480 years before the building of the Temple, is clearly a chronological reference. And the fact that it's a time marker is very significant. It means that the biblical date of the Exodus would move to a position about 200 years earlier than Ramesses, to a time around 1450 BC.

However, despite this major breakthrough, my challenge wasn't over because this biblical date is still about 200 years away from the pattern of evidence that has been found in the archaeology of Egypt. I was determined to see if I could find more answers to this mystery. To do so, I needed to look beyond the Ramesses Exodus Theory to other time periods, including the Middle Kingdom where the evidence has been so strong. ♛

The six steps of the biblical sequence shifted 200 years back from the time of Ramesses to align with 1450 BC, the new biblical date for the Exodus.

Before

EXODUS 1250 BC

2000s
BC
1900s BC   1800s BC   1700s BC   1600s BC   1500s BC   1400s BC   1300s BC   1200s BC   1100s BC
MIDDLE KINGDOM
NEW KINGDOM
1000s
BC
900

After

EXODUS 1450 BC

2000s
BC
1900s BC   1800s BC   1700s BC   1600s BC   1500s BC   1400s BC   1300s BC   1200s BC   1100s BC
MIDDLE KINGDOM
NEW KINGDOM
1000s
BC
900

217

IX: Step Five: Evidence of the Exodus?

I. Abandonment at Avaris

I had now seen compelling evidence, all happening in the Middle Kingdom, for each of the first four steps of the biblical sequence. This led me to ask David Rohl if he knew of any finds in Egypt's history for the next step of that sequence: a massive and sudden **Exodus** of Semites following the death of the firstborn. [58]

"What does the archaeological record show?"

Rohl told me about what was unearthed at Avaris. "We find an extraordinary thing happens. The archaeologists who've been digging this area suddenly find lots of pits in the ground. And in these pits are bodies, and they've been tossed into these pits. They're not buried formally. They have no grave goods or anything like that. These bodies are tossed on top of each other. They're lying strewn; you have hands and legs crossing over."

A plague pit at Avaris.

Another plague pit at Avaris with bodies tossed upon each other.

"What was going on? What does Professor Bietak think this was?" I asked.

"Bietak thinks it's actually some sort of plague that's happened. A dramatic event where suddenly they have to bury people very quickly because of contamination of the living population. So it's an emergency burial essentially."

Rohl was directly connecting this evidence to the Exodus. This evidence was at the end of a layer known as stratum G/1 in Tell el-Dab'a, which means it equates to the late 13th Dynasty near the end of the Middle Kingdom. My understanding was that Bietak didn't make the connection because in his thinking these pits were far too early to fit into the accepted dating of the Exodus.

"What happened next?" I asked.

Rohl leaned forward. "All of a sudden, the site is abandoned. These Semitic people who were living there suddenly get up, they pack their bags and they leave, and the whole mound is abandoned. And we don't know for how long. And it just falls to ruin."

"What do you think was going on here?"

He raised his eyebrows. "Well, isn't that just like the story of Exodus?"

It did match the story. This one location mentioned in the biblical text encompassed an arrival, multiplication, slavery, and now the abandonment of its Semitic population. I considered if there could be some other explanation. Perhaps scholars could think of many that were unrelated to the Exodus, but the pattern was striking. [59]

II. Another Abandonment: Kahun

One day my researcher and writing partner, Steve Law, entered my office with a book. "I got something you should know about," he said, with about as much excitement as a glass of milk. But that's just Steve. I have learned over the course of seven years to pay attention when he brings things up. And this was one of those times.

"What's going on?" I asked.

"There's another abandonment that fits the pattern," said Steve.

"You're kidding. Where?"

"About 120 miles to the south of Avaris, at a place called Kahun, which began as a pyramid builders' compound."

"When was it uncovered?"

"Around 1890 by Egyptologist Sir Flinders Petrie, who also discovered the Merneptah Stele. He found a walled and guarded settlement that supported a large Semitic population."

"Really? And no one's connected any dots?"

"Almost no one's looking in the Middle Kingdom."

I listened as Steve showed me the book he was reading, *The Pyramid Builders of Ancient Egypt*, written by Rosalie David, an Egyptologist from the University of Man-

The location of Kahun.

chester who reported on Petrie's digs. She stated that the site was conceived and built to a predetermined plan:

"It was enclosed by a thick brick wall, designed to confine the workmen and their families in a certain area. It is evident that the sites, all on the desert edge, were chosen because they were near to the worksite, but also because, isolated and surrounded by hills, they could be guarded. . . . It is noteworthy that even the proximity of a good water supply was not considered essential to these town sites, the requirements of isolation and security being greater." [60]

"This looks like it could have been a slave community," I said.

Steve nodded. "As a matter of fact they found documentation of slavery at the compound there. If you remember, the biblical text states that the children of Israel multiplied so greatly that they spread throughout the land. A group of what the Bible calls an 'ethnically diverse crowd' are also said to have left with the Israelites. Many of these were probably Semitic Asiatics as well."

"Could these enslaved Semitic people at Kahun be a part of that story?"

"Well, there's some mystery here. These inhabitants seemed to have disappeared overnight. Like Avaris, the evidence at Kahun points to its abandonment occurring late in the 13th Dynasty, at the very end of Egypt's Middle Kingdom." [61]

According to Professor David, Kahun's abandonment was sudden, and their goods

Egyptologist Rosalie David.

A reconstruction of the pyramid-builders compound of Kahun.

were found in the streets and houses of Kahun exactly where they were left, before being buried by the sands of the desert so long ago. She wrote:

"Domestic wares, the workmen's tools, the agricultural equipment, weaving equipment, children's toys, the make-up and jewelry of the women, and the articles associated with their daily religious observances have all been discovered, lying as they were left, some 4,000 years ago, in the streets and rooms of the houses. . . . The quantity, range and type of articles of everyday use which were left behind in the houses may indeed suggest that the departure was sudden and unpremeditated." [62]

Again, according to the biblical narrative, the children of Israel left in haste after Passover night. The first century Jewish historian Josephus wrote that Moses gathered together all the Israelites before the final night of the plagues. [63]

Professor David observed that the town of Kahun "seems to have been deserted by its inhabitants in such a hurry that some kind of disaster may have occurred, though this can hardly be plague, which has been suggested, since no bodies except the baby-burials were found. Whatever happened, the paucity [lack] of cloth is unusual – if sandals and precious needles were left behind, why not unwanted clothes?" [64]

Steve was still standing in the doorway. I motioned for him to sit down. "Besides the abandonment, what else connects Kahun to the Exodus story?" I asked.

"First, Moses told the Israelites to ask for clothing from the Egyptians as they left. And Professor David found the absence of clothing at Kahun to be very puzzling."

"But it actually fits the Exodus account very well, doesn't it?"

"Exactly!" Steve went on, "And secondly, although a plague has been ruled out because of a lack of bodies, remember in the Exodus story that the death of the firstborn only occurred among those who didn't follow the instructions of Moses to put a lamb's blood over the door."

"If this compound had complied to that command, according to the text, then there wouldn't have been any dead bodies," I added.

"Right, and thirdly, David also mentions the numerous baby burials that were found under the houses of the compound."

"Now that's curious," I said. "Could that be related to the command to throw the baby boys into the Nile?"

Steve shrugged. "Well, there's no way to prove it."

He continued to make his fourth point. "Then David writes about two intriguing

Egyptian letters found in the area of Kahun that give the impression of an angry exchange between the writers. The second ends with the words, "May you be plague-stricken!" but then follows with a postscript, "Come that I may see you. Behold, we are passing an evil hour." [65]

A reconstruction of the streets of Kahun after abandonment.

"Fascinating!" I thought for a moment and then recalled, "That's consistent with Ipuwer the Egyptian sage writing 'Plague sweeps the land. Death is everywhere. Woe is me for the grief of this time.'"

"It certainly does. Finally, here's what Professor David wrote about one other curious discovery made there." Reading from the book, Steve carefully quoted the section:

"Perhaps the strangest find at Kahun is what the famous pioneering Egyptologist Sir Flinders Petrie describes as 'a set of tent-pegs,' with ends of rush fiber rope still knotted round one of them. [66] Made of wood and measuring about 12.5 cm, each one is cut with a large, round head and a deep groove for rope. . . . Petrie does imply that they were together when discovered. We cannot know on such slender evidence whether the Kahun townsfolk had any dealings with tented people, but it remains an intriguing possibility." [67]

"So why do you think there were tent pegs in the compound area?" I asked.

Steve had a possible explanation. "Well, according to the biblical text the Israelites had been a tented people, and after the Exodus they would once again become a tented people during their wanderings in the wilderness."

"Could those pegs have been preparation for their upcoming journey?"

"Maybe. It's a good thing somebody forgot them. If they hadn't, we wouldn't be able to ask these types of questions."

David Rohl claims there is evidence for the collapse of Egypt.

III. The Only Collapse of Egyptian Power in 1,000 Years

Further down the Nile from Kahun is the location of another unsolved mystery from this time. Near the border of Egypt, just inside Nubia, were the southern super-forts that Pharaoh Senusret III had built with his wealth and power during the height of Egypt's Middle Kingdom. Later, around the end of the Middle Kingdom, evidence shows that these supremely powerful forts suddenly fell into the hands of Kushites from the south, with no sign of major conflict. Amazingly, monuments from the time record the Egyptian commanders of the forts proudly declaring allegiance to the new Kushite king. Scholars have not been able to provide an answer to the mystery of how and why this happened. [68]

David Rohl was beginning to give more evidence from the end of the Middle Kingdom. "What happened to the nation of Egypt at this time?" I asked.

"One of the great moments in Egyptian history," said Rohl, "is the collapse of Egyptian civilization. When these foreigners invade – we call these the Hyksos rulers. When the Hyksos come in and destroy the land, the Egyptian native rule is completely suppressed. Egypt is on its knees. That's what we see in the archaeological evidence of this period. And it only happens once in 1,000 years of Egyptian history."

"Is there anything else that might connect this time to the biblical narrative?"

"Perhaps we can link this to a very famous tradition told to us by an Egyptian priest called Manetho, who wrote a history of Egypt in the third century BC. And what we end up with is a story like this: In the reign of a king called Dudimose, one of the last kings of the 13th Dynasty – in his reign, 'God smote the Egyptians.' And *God* here is singular. You would expect to see 'and the gods smote the Egyptians,' but you don't. You see 'God smote the Egyptians.'" [69]

This description of a smiting from God really was beginning to sound very similar to God judging Egypt during the Exodus when he took the Israelites out. I asked Rohl,

"What happened next in Manetho's story?"

"Then, because of this smiting, whatever the smiting is, foreigners – 'people of obscure race' – invade Egypt from the north. And they conquer the land – 'without striking a blow' is the term used. Now why? Because God smote the Egyptians."

"So what you're saying is that prior to this smiting, Egypt was a mighty power?"

"Egypt was a great power in the Middle Kingdom," he said.

"Did something else happen in the history of Egypt that opened them up to being taken over by northern armies so easily?"

"During the 13th Dynasty there was a slow decline, but not a decline sufficient to prevent them from repelling an attack from foreigners. We're talking about foreign hordes here. We're not talking about sophisticated warfare. Something else must have happened which changed things in Egypt dramatically. And Manetho tells us what it is. He says, 'God smote the Egyptians.'"

I could see the importance of this account. Here was an independent source, outside the Bible, stating that a powerful god had smitten Egypt, leading to an invasion by for-

Egypt experienced only one major collapse in 1,000 years of history – near the end of the Middle Kingdom's 13th Dynasty.

eigners. If Egypt was devastated by the plagues, the destruction of their army, and other calamities, then there would have been a tremendous weakening that allowed enemies to take advantage of the situation by invading Egypt. "So there was a power vacuum there?" I asked.

Rohl went on, "Something had happened to devastate Egypt, which made them unable to defend themselves. And these marauding hordes took over the country. And we call this the Hyksos Period. And they enslaved the Egyptians. But the point is they could have defended themselves. They had a mighty army – except for the fact that 'God' had smitten the Egyptians."

I wanted Rohl to be more specific. "How do you interpret this?"

"You look for a collapse in Egyptian civilization, and that's where you'll find Moses and the Exodus."

I had to remind myself that Rohl is an agnostic, someone who is not sure about God and his existence, yet he still sees evidence that supports the biblical story. It made sense that this singular collapse points to the most likely time to look for the Exodus out of Egypt. This kind of collapse does not occur at the time of Ramesses around 1250 BC. And Hoffmeier had said that there was no sign of collapse at the 1450 BC Exodus date either. However, once again, the fact that this collapse happened two centuries earlier than 1450 BC is consistent with the previous four steps of the pattern I had been discovering from Rohl and others.

According to the Bible, God judged the nation of Egypt.

Rohl concluded, "In that period must be the time of the Exodus of the Israelites. And why don't we put those things together then? We have the story of the ten plagues, the destruction of Egypt, the collapse of Egyptian civilization, the Israelites leaving Egypt, and Egypt itself is on its knees for several hundred years. That's what we see in the archaeological evidence of this period. That to me all fits together into a single story."

This story from Manetho was more evidence matching the Exodus account but because it's considered to be from the wrong time, mainstream scholarship sees no connection between it and the Exodus.

IV. Judgment and Exodus Summary and Timeline

The earlier pattern of evidence for the **Judgment** and **Exodus** steps in the earlier Middle Kingdom includes:

- An Egyptian text from the Middle Kingdom, written by Ipuwer, that describes events remarkably similar to the biblical plagues,
- Grave pits filled with bodies, hastily buried, followed by abandonment at Avaris,
- Abandonment at other Semitic sites in Egypt's Nile Delta,
- Evidence of sudden evacuation of a Semitic slave population at Kahun,
- An Egyptian account by Manetho, that states a powerful god acted in Egypt's history and delivered a deadly blow, which led to an invasion by foreigners,
- And all this coinciding with the only collapse of Egyptian society in 1,000 years of its history.

It all seemed to fit together so exactly. Was it just a coincidence? This was why I couldn't stop investigating this material even though it's so controversial.

Why is this pattern controversial?

Remember that in the eyes of most scholars the pattern of evidence I've found is still occurring 200 years before 1450 BC. Therefore, tying this evidence to the Exodus is unthinkable to many.

Even scholars who accept the biblical account of the Exodus do not agree on an Exodus date, and many would not recognize the validity of the Judgment and Exodus evidence I've just been examining:

The Hyksos in Egypt

The 13th Dynasty would witness the first time since the establishment of the Old Kingdom that Egypt experienced domination by foreigners. Scholars disagree about whether the Hyksos invaded in a scenario such as described by Manetho or if it was more of a gradual process of infiltration. Regardless, the archaeology confirms that the native Egyptians lost most of their power and the Hyksos ruled over much of the country for more than a century before being forced out by the rise of the New Kingdom with the 18th Dynasty.

- Hoffmeier and Kitchen claim that the Exodus happened late in the New Kingdom at the 1250 BC Ramesside date.
- Wood and Aling see the Exodus happening early in the New Kingdom.
- Bimson believes that the Exodus happened at the *end* of the Middle Bronze Age, roughly equivalent to the end of the Middle Kingdom.
- Rohl suggests the Exodus happened a little earlier than the end of the Middle Bronze Age.
- And many more Exodus dates have been proposed, including some others earlier in the Middle Kingdom.

These are a wide range of views. But could the dates that have been assigned to the Egyptian periods be the problem, not the Exodus date? All these scholars, except Hoffmeier and Kitchen, endorse the 1450 BC biblical date for the Exodus, but some think that this date happens in a different period of Egypt's history. And that's the controversial part.

However, when I'd looked at theories outside of the Middle Kingdom, the evidence was fragmented. These theories only contained a few of the steps in the biblical sequence. And most importantly, they didn't have a distinct collapse of Egypt.

On the other hand, the pattern I'd seen in the Middle Kingdom was beginning to fit like the grooves of a key that opens a lock. However, this key would only fit and successfully unlock the mystery of the Exodus if it matched every step of the biblical story. And so far, five of the six steps had matched incredibly well. ♆

At right: Four views among pro-Exodus scholars featured in this investigation.

James Hoffmeier supports the conventional dating for Egypt with the Exodus happening at a Ramesses date around 1250BC, and an Israelite stay in Egypt around 400 - 430 years.

Bryant Wood and Charles Aling also support the conventional dating for Egypt but with the Exodus occurring around 1450 BC and an Israelite stay in Egypt of about 430 years.

John Bimson places the Exodus around 1450 BC and the Conquest near the end of the Middle Bronze Age. He believes the dating of Egypt and Canaan are incorrect and need to shift forward in time. He goes with a shorter stay for the Israelites in Egypt of a little more than 200 years.

David Rohl also believes the dating of Egypt and Canaan are incorrect and need to shift forward in time. He places the Exodus around 1450 BC but puts the Conquest more than a century before the end of the Middle Bronze Age. This produces a greater shift than John Bimson's view. He goes with a shorter stay for the Israelites in Egypt of a little more than 200 years.

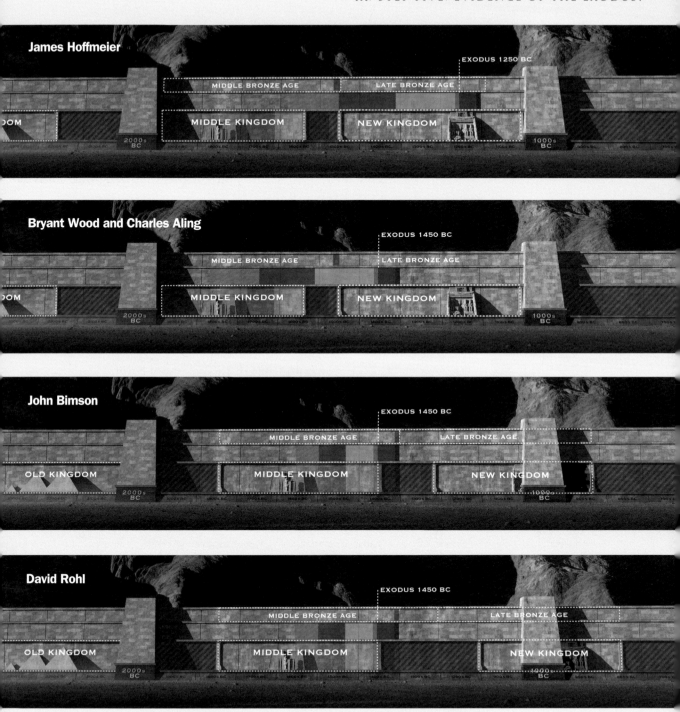

X: Step Six: Evidence of the Conquest?

Israeli archaeologist Norma Franklin sees no evidence for Joshua and the Conquest.

Ancient biblical cities in the region of Canaan.

What about the final step of the biblical sequence – the Israelites' **Conquest** of Canaan, the land that had been promised to Abraham and his descendants? Would the earlier pattern of evidence continue there as well?

For his telling of this closing step of the Exodus story, I directed Rabbi Friedman to stand in front of a large wooden podium used for unrolling the scrolls before reading the Torah. For thousands of years scrolls like these have been copied by hand and passed on through the generations. The meticulous preservation of this story in a scroll like this is how we have come to know about these biblical events today.

Rabbi Friedman recounted the biblical narrative. "The children of Israel left Egypt and traveled to Mount Sinai where they received God's law and made a Covenant to be his people. Then after 40 years of wandering in the wilderness, Moses transferred his authority to Joshua and ascended the heights of Mount Nebo, where he died. The Israelites had been waiting centuries for the promise to be fulfilled. And now it was Joshua who would lead them in their Conquest of Canaan." [70]

In the early days my investigation primarily explored where the Israelites may have gone on their journey to the sea crossing and Mount Sinai. But telling about that search would have to wait until later. For now, I was focused on finding out more about the final step of the sequence. If we could find evidence for the Conquest, then our team would be closer to answering the question of whether the Exodus happened in the first place.

I. Why Do Many Archaeologists Reject the Conquest?

It was during the Conquest that the Israelites were said to have overcome the fortified cities of the Promised Land. The land of Canaan was very different from Egypt. It was a

230

land ruled by many independent city-states with names like Hazor, Jericho, Hebron, and Arad. The history of these cities has been divided into two major time periods: the Middle Bronze Age and the Late Bronze Age. During the Middle Bronze Age, which approximately matches Egypt's Middle Kingdom, these city-states were thriving and fortified by high walls. Then a sudden destruction and burning came upon the land, leaving most of these cities in ruins and bringing in the period known as the Late Bronze Age, which matches the time of Egypt's New Kingdom.

Israeli archaeologist Norma Franklin is among a large group of scholars who sees no evidence for a biblical Conquest of the Promised Land in the 13th or 12th century BC. Back in the hill country of Israel, I asked her about this issue. "Let's talk about the Conquest and Joshua. What do you think happened with the story of Joshua?"

Franklin was forthright. "As an archaeologist, I hate to disappoint people, but we have no evidence for a single mass migration of people from one country, wandering over a period of 40 years, and then coming into another country."

"What is the archaeology telling you about cities being destroyed?"

"There is destruction, amazing destructions. None of them actually fits any other. The great problem is, we now know they were not destroyed all at the same time. They all happened within a hundred years but not overnight. Not what you'd expect in the Conquest. You know, Joshua didn't live that long, if he existed, okay? So we're not look-

The Middle and Late Bronze Ages in Canaan as conventionally dated.

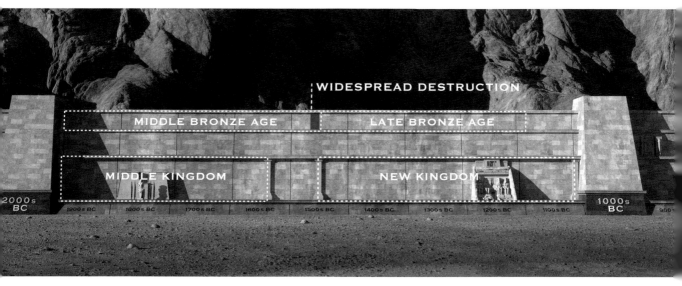

WIDESPREAD DESTRUCTION

MIDDLE BRONZE AGE · LATE BRONZE AGE

MIDDLE KINGDOM · NEW KINGDOM

2000s BC · 1900s BC · 1800s BC · 1700s BC · 1600s BC · 1500s BC · 1400s BC · 1300s BC · 1200s BC · 1100s BC · 1000s BC · 900s

231

ing at an event of Joshua – one man coming in with the children of Israel and doing this incredible campaign. That we don't see."

"What is your explanation of these destructions?"

Franklin shrugged. "Perhaps earthquake, perhaps local bands fighting one another, local rulers who saw themselves as kings of city-states. You know, this is my city. My city is my kingdom. I'm fighting the other guy. There's nothing, there is no inscription saying, 'Joshua did this.'"

"But can the time period when Joshua was supposed to have lived match the destruction of cities like Jericho?"

"No, Joshua and Jericho don't go together. We also have other sites such as Ai, which the name tells us a lot. It's called Ai in the biblical narrative. It's called et-Tell by the Arabs in Arabic. Both names mean 'the ruin.'

"Let's talk about that destruction."

"Now in the destruction of Ai by Joshua, it says he destroyed somewhere that's called 'the ruin.' So think about it. If you go to a site and you're taking your child there, your grandson, and the kid is saying, 'Daddy, why is this all destroyed?' And you don't really know but you know that you have the narrative, your history, your tradition that your great-great-great-grandfather came in and did these wonderful things. And of course you'd tell him, 'Joshua did this.' But in the story, the name of the site in the Bible means 'the ruin.'"

"Are you suggesting this is how the Bible stories came to be?"

"This is how many of the stories, perhaps, came together into the Bible. They were narratives that explained to the people what happened. It doesn't mean it didn't happen, but not as one act."

As we walked together down the gentle slope to the vehicles, I remembered something several of my archaeologist friends had said. They were interpreting evidence to create a backstory for history, trying to fill in the pieces about what actually had happened. Was Norma Franklin's interpretation of Joshua and the Conquest correct? Did these events not happen as described in the Bible?

Franklin's colleague at Megiddo, Israel Finkelstein, expanded on the problem. "First and foremost, many places which are mentioned in Joshua in the Conquest story, specifically mentioned as major places in Canaan, were excavated, and no evidence for a city in the Late Bronze Age has ever been found. And I'm speaking about major excavations.

Professor Israel Finkelstein pointing out that, in the 13th century BC, the evidence does not fit the biblical Conquest.

The City of Ai

Ai was the second city said to be destroyed in the Conquest of Canaan (Joshua chapters 7 and 8). Issues related to this city are covered in Bonus Chapter E.

And we are speaking about many sites. It's systemic; it's not only a single site. Take the example of Jericho. In Jericho there is no big city in the 13th century BC, okay, any way you look at it."

From his surveys of the hill country of Israel, Finkelstein could see that many of the Conquest cities mentioned in the Bible were not even populated in the 13th century BC, at the time the Conquest was supposed to have occurred. This has affected Finkelstein's view of the origin of the people of Israel.

I asked Professor Finkelstein about these surveys. "What did you learn about the people of Israel that was different from what you originally thought?"

"We are not dealing with groups that came from without, from outside of the country. We are dealing with a local start, with the local population, which went through shifts from sedentary life to nomadic and back, influenced by political, economic, social transformations along many centuries."

In other words, Finkelstein was saying there was no Conquest. The Israelites just gradually developed from the local population.

The following year when I couldn't join Finkelstein at his dig site, I sent my crew to Megiddo for a second interview. Surrounded by workers unearthing the site, our Israeli producer Sharon Schaveet asked Finkelstein about this controversial aspect of his theory. She pressed him. "In your book you have said that the Israelites were Canaanites. Can you explain this conclusion?"

Professor Israel Finkelstein directing his team at the Megiddo dig site.

Finkelstein replied, "We can sum up and say that the Israelites came from the local stock of the population of Canaan in the second millennium BC. So from this point of view they were Canaanites."

Now I understood why Finkelstein had told me he believes the Israelites formulated their own history from ancient memories and traditions. I could see that the biblical understanding of Israel's origins was at stake in this Conquest issue. Were they a distinct people who came out of Egypt to conquer the Promised Land? Or were they a group of Canaanites who crafted a mythical history to legitimize their control of the population and the land?

The lack of evidence creates problems for anyone trying to propose a biblical type of Conquest in the 13th century BC, around the time of Ramesses, when most think it occurred. However, it is also a serious issue for my search of an earlier Conquest. According to mainstream scholarship, what Finkelstein says about the lack of matching evidence also pertains to the entire Late Bronze Age, which would even include a Conquest happening 40 years after the 1450 BC Exodus date. But just as I had seen with the other steps in Egypt, what if this last step also happened in the *earlier* Middle Bronze Age? It seemed only logical to begin by looking at the key site of Jericho, the first city the Israelites are said to have encountered in their Conquest of the Promised Land. And archaeologists know exactly where that is.

II. Jericho: Did the Walls Come Tumbling Down?

The Bible states that Jericho was the first city encountered in the Conquest of Canaan. Its high walls were said to have been miraculously brought down and the city burned by the invading Israelites. Major archaeological excavations at this site were initiated in the early 1900s with a German team led by Ernst Sellin. This was followed by a British team headed by John Garstang in the 1930s. At the time of their digs, both Sellin and Garstang believed they had uncovered a layer of destruction that matched the biblical story.

The ancient site of Jericho as it looks today.

German archaeologist Ernst Sellin (seated center with tall hat) with his excavation team at Jericho.

However, things took a dramatic turn when Kathleen Kenyon dug at Jericho in the 1950s. She demonstrated that there was no evidence for a destruction of Jericho matching the biblical account because she dated the demise of the city much earlier, to around 1580 BC. A wave of skepticism swept across the field of archaeology. It appeared that Kenyon's discoveries at Jericho had undermined the entire Exodus story. [71]

At Trinity College in Bristol, England, I asked Professor Bimson, "So the issue of *time* is really crucial as to whether evidence can be connected to the biblical events or not?"

"Yes," he said. "Jericho, of course, is significant because it's one of those cities on which the Bible devotes quite a lot of narrative. It's not just a brief mention; it's a long account of how this city came to be conquered. Kenyon was expecting that if there was any evidence there at all, it would be in what we call the Late Bronze Age – and it simply isn't there. If the Israelites had arrived in the 13th century, they would have found almost nobody there, no walls to collapse. It just wouldn't have fitted the biblical narrative at all."

"So let me understand this. Kenyon and a lot of other people thought that the Exodus happened in the 13th century, is that correct?"

"That's been the prevailing view since about the middle of the 20th century, yes."

"Okay," I said. "So the problem was, when Kenyon excavated Jericho, she found nothing at that level."

"That's right, yes."

"Okay, so what ended up happening was the Bible was considered false because Kenyon found there was no Jericho to be destroyed at that time?"

"Basically, yes, that's true," Bimson said. "Her excavations helped to compound this very negative view that was developing not just from Jericho but from other sites as well."

Kenyon was fully aware of both possible Exodus dates, 1450 BC and 1250 BC. But clearly, neither the early or late Exodus dates would fit the final destruction seen at Jericho if that destruction occurred around 1580 BC.

I wanted to look more broadly for possible Conquest dates, so I asked Israel Finkelstein, "Is there a time when Jericho was destroyed, where walls fell down or it was burned?"

Finkelstein was negative. "I don't think so. I don't think we have evidence, this kind of evidence, in the case of Jericho and I don't think that we can really look for this evidence. We are very much past this phase of archaeological research."

But David Rohl sees things differently. When speaking to him on this topic of Jericho, I said, "You seem to be suggesting that we need to look at these problems of history in a different way. Could you explain that?"

Rohl replied, "If people are telling us there is no Jericho at the time Joshua conquered the Promised Land, and therefore Joshua is a piece of fiction, and therefore the

British archaeologist John Garstang at Jericho.

The findings of archaeologist Kathleen Kenyon at Jericho dramatically impacted the credibility of the biblical account.

Conquest is a piece of fiction, and then probably Exodus is a piece of fiction as well, if that's the case, why don't we ask the simple question, 'Well, when was Jericho around, when was Jericho destroyed,' and start from that point of view?"

Rabbi Friedman went on with the biblical account. "The Conquest began with the Israelites crossing the Jordan River. Joshua sent men to spy out the massively walled city of Jericho. And there they met a harlot named Rahab, who reported that all in the land had heard what God had done for the Israelites and they were terrified. Rahab hid the spies and aided their escape to the mountains." [72]

Re-creation of Jericho, the first city encountered by the Israelites in their conquest of the Promised Land.

One of the main reasons I had come to Bryant Wood's home in Pennsylvania was to question him about an article he had written on his findings at Jericho. The late morning sun was moving to the south. I could feel its rays on my shoulder as I sat across from him in his living room. "What evidence do you see matching the Conquest at Jericho?"

Wood turned slightly. "First of all, we're told that Jericho was fortified. It speaks of the gate when the spies went there. And we have the story of them hiding in Rahab's house, and they had shut the gate so that they couldn't leave the city. So obviously, we would expect Jericho to have a gate and a fortification system, and that's exactly what the archaeologists found, that Jericho was very heavily fortified." [73]

"Could you explain more about the fortifications that were found there?"

Wood nodded. "When the archaeologists dug the city, particularly Kathleen Kenyon when she did her work in the '50s, they discovered that the tell, which the city's built on, was surrounded by a great earthen rampart."

Excavators found that Jericho was protected by a brilliant defensive system. At its base, there was a stone retaining wall more than 15 feet high with a defensive extension wall of mudbricks rising still higher. Beyond this, there was the rampart, a steep slope covered with a slick surface of white plaster, where attackers would have been exposed to arrows and sling stones from above. At the top of this rampart was the main city wall, also made of mudbricks. This main city wall was more than 25 feet high and 10 feet thick.

The Bible states that God told Joshua to march around the city of Jericho with armed men, priests carrying the Ark of the Covenant, and seven priests blowing trumpets of rams' horns for seven consecutive days.

"Imagine the dread and the desperate panic of the people of Jericho," related Rabbi Friedman. "Day after day for six days the people of Israel are walking around their city with the Ark of the Covenant and the sounding of rams' horns. [74] Then on the seventh day they encircle the city seven times, and the priests give a long blast on their horns. The people let loose with a mighty shout, and the walls come tumbling down, allowing the Israelites to climb up into the city, taking it and commencing the conquering of the land of Israel." [75]

I asked Wood, "What else did Kenyon find at Jericho?"

"Well, when the city met its end, these mudbrick walls collapsed and they actually fell down to the base of the stone retaining wall. Kenyon excavated that material and other archaeologists have as well, but Kenyon describes it very clearly and in detail in her excavation report, and she says the mudbricks at the base of the retaining wall came from the city wall."

"Do you see a connection here to the Bible?"

"Yes, we have a number of points that are verified by the archaeological findings in Jericho, and we see even in the Hebrew words that were used in the account a very precise description. For example, the word that is used to describe the falling of the walls is the Hebrew word *tahteyha*. Now this is always translated 'flat.' The walls fell flat. But the Hebrew word has a richer, more descriptive meaning. It actually means 'the walls fell beneath themselves.'"

Early excavations at Jericho revealed strong fortifications that matched the biblical account.

Wood expanded on Kenyon's conclusion about the destruction. "For Kenyon, it had no connection with the Bible because she dated the destruction of the city to 150 years before Joshua. But there is dramatic evidence for the wall of Jericho falling just as the Bible says, and that Hebrew word describes it perfectly. They fell beneath themselves because they had to fall and then slide down that rampart and were deposited at the base of that stone retaining wall. So even in the Hebrew words that are used, we see evidence that this is not some account that was written hundreds of years later by somebody in the Exile Period, you know, some later time period. This was written down by somebody who actually saw it and was describing what they saw."

"What happened next?"

The mudbrick walls at Jericho fell and slid down to the base of the stone retaining wall at the bottom of the tell.

"We're told the Israelites set the city on fire. And that's exactly what we find; Jericho was massively destroyed by fire. Kenyon said it was very clear that within the city, the walls of the buildings had fallen as well. And she says that the walls fell before the fire. And so we have the sequence that we read in the Bible: first the fallen walls, and then the city being set on fire by the Israelites."

Excavations at the site uncovered clear evidence for a massive destruction by fire with a very thick burn layer of extremely high temperatures. This caused Kenyon to attribute the burning to an enemy attack and not to fires that would result solely from an earthquake. [76]

Wood leaned back in his chair. "Kenyon claimed that the city was destroyed around 1550 BC by the Egyptians. Well, there's absolutely no evidence that the Egyptians were ever in the Jordan Valley at this time period. But nevertheless, that's her theory and that's the dating she came up with, and her dating has been accepted by archaeologists and followed to this very day." [77]

"What is your explanation?"

"I've done a lot of research on Jericho. I've analyzed the pottery from all of the expeditions starting with Garstang in the 1930s, who by the way dated the destruction to 1400 BC, and did a very fine job in my opinion of analyzing his pottery and coming up with that date, but that was overturned by Kenyon in the 1950s. So, I've studied her pottery, and all of this pottery, when you study it in detail, it gives you the dating of 1400 BC. It's Late Bronze 1; there's no question about it. It's Late Bronze 1, around 1400 BC."

"Who determined that?" I questioned.

"The dating of Late Bronze 1 pottery?"

"Yes. The pottery there."

"Well, the dating of the pottery is based on my analysis. Kenyon herself never did an analysis of the pottery she excavated. She only made some off-the-cuff statements in various articles she wrote about Jericho, about the dating. And in her final excavation reports, there is no analysis of that material unfortunately. And so I have analyzed it, and I need to publish that obviously, so that other scholars can look at it and realize that the site was not destroyed in 1550 BC, but it continued down to about 1400. It's very clear."

I knew that Wood accepted the conventional chronology for Egypt and the Bronze Ages. But he was unconventional in his attempt to redate the pottery of Jericho from 1550 BC to 1400 BC. This idea was challenged by many other archaeologists including

Revetment walls found at Jericho.

The evidence points to an intentional burning of Jericho after the walls fell down.

Finkelstein and Franklin who claim there is no evidence for a Conquest during the Late Bronze period. I encouraged Wood. "If you have data, then you need to publish it. It's been over 20 years."

"Yes, I need to do that."

All I wanted were answers to the question of whether or not Jericho was destroyed at the time and in the manner described in the Bible. Many believe the Bible's credibility depends on those answers.

In England, I asked Professor Bimson about Jericho. "What is your interpretation of what Kenyon and the others found?"

He said, "We do have a major city at Jericho. It covered about ten acres possibly. It was very heavily fortified, probably a double fortification wall around it; it certainly had big enough fortifications to have made the Israelites feel there was no way to conquer this place, and yet it was destroyed. The outer mudbrick city wall was built on top of a stone revetment wall that would have supported the slope going higher up; and that wall certainly seems – judging from where the mudbricks are distributed – seems to have fallen outwards. Now if that had fallen outwards, it would have provided a very convenient ramp actually for any attackers to have charged up the slope and into the main part of the city."

"Did Kenyon find anything else?"

"Kenyon found a very thick burn layer which showed that the city had been burned, so that also fits with what the Bible says happened at Jericho."

So both Wood and Bimson could see that Kenyon's report on Jericho mirrored the biblical description of the city's fall, but because she dated its destruction more than 150 years before the earliest time the Israelites were supposed to be there, she didn't connect the archaeology with the Bible's account. But once again, this date fit the earlier-than-expected pattern I'd been seeing.

The thick burn layer found at Jericho.

III. Further Intrigue at Jericho

Then Wood brought up another compelling find at Jericho. "Within the city a very unique discovery was made. Both Garstang and Kenyon found in the houses that they excavated many storage jars full of grain."

Bimson also discussed this detail. "The store jars in the city were pretty full. That suggests the harvest had only recently been gathered in. And the details in the biblical account point to an event that happened sometime in the spring. And down there in the Jordan Valley, spring is when the harvest is gathered in – the grain harvest."

Wood agreed. "When the Israelites crossed the Jordan, the first thing they did was celebrate Passover. Well, when is Passover? Again, the spring of the year."

The full jars also indicated that if this was a siege, it was very short, which would be unusual for a strongly fortified city such as Jericho. [78]

Wood explained, "That matches the biblical account because in its story the siege was only seven days. Otherwise, the people inside would have consumed a lot of that grain if it dragged out for months."

"Was this grain found all over the city?"

"Yes. In every house that was excavated they found jars of grain."

"Is this unique?"

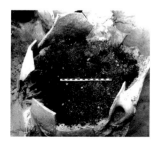

Storage jars with burnt grain found throughout the city.

He nodded. "This is unique because when a city was conquered, the conqueror would go in and plunder the city, including the grain because grain was valuable not only for food, but you could use it for bartering. It was like money." [79]

"If this grain was so valuable, why do you think it was left in Jericho?"

"Well," Wood replied, "the answer is in Joshua chapter 6, where we read that God commanded the Israelites not to plunder Jericho. It was to be offered up as an offering to the Lord, the first fruits of the Promised Land." [80]

I could see Wood's point. This was a very specific parallel with the Bible. If the Egyptians had destroyed the city as Kenyon suggested, what reason would they have had to leave the grain?

There was one other intriguing detail in the evidence at Jericho that fit the Bible remarkably well. It had to do with a promise made to Rahab. "She actually lived in the city wall," Rabbi Friedman explained. "After hiding the spies, she was promised that her family would be protected when Joshua and the Israelites attacked the city. And they kept their promise. She had marked her home with a scarlet cord, which she hung out the window." [81]

It had always puzzled me that if Rahab's house was built into the city wall, how could she and her family have survived when the walls fell?

I came across the actual archaeological report that the German excavator of Jericho,

Ernst Sellin, had published in 1913. It was a rare find, which our research team purchased from a bookseller in Jerusalem. But it took years before I realized that this scholar was the same person who had led the German excavation team in Jericho.

Mahoney examining Ernst Sellin's detailed drawings and photographs.

Sellin was the first to conduct a major excavation of the site, and I could see that his work was impressive but now seemed to have been long forgotten, overshadowed by the findings of Kenyon. The book had detailed plans and photographs of the Jericho site, including a part that echoed the Rahab story in an unexpected way.

Wood got quiet for a moment as one does when telling someone something very important. It was as if he'd been saving the best for last. "The Germans [led by Sellin] found that, in this one short stretch on the north side of the city, there were houses built on the rampart between the lower city wall and the upper city wall. And some of those houses were built right up against the lower city wall. They found that the city wall did not fall in this area. So that provides an explanation for how the spies could have saved Rahab and her family. Because God brought the wall down everywhere else except where her house was, and we have archaeological evidence to back that up."

This seemed to match the Bible's story almost too closely. Could Wood be trying too hard? I knew he was the head of an organization called Associates for Biblical Research, so I challenged him. "What if people say, 'You're biased'?"

He was forthright. "I think everybody in the field is biased one way or another. I admit my bias. However, I cannot make up the evidence. I cannot plant it in the ground. And I have analyzed it and compared it to the Bible and I see, wow, it matches exactly. That's science. Look at your evidence and come to a conclusion based on the evidence."

According to the biblical account, Jericho would not be rebuilt for hundreds of years after the Conquest. The archaeology shows that after the destruction, the city of Jericho was indeed abandoned for centuries. [82]

But of course, this all happens in the wrong time in the view of most scholars.

Bryant Wood believes that Kenyon misdated the pottery at Jericho, resulting in a wrong destruction date. He along with Charles Aling believes that a case can be made for the Exodus occurring in the mid-1400s BC using the conventional timelines for Egypt and Canaan.

However, David Rohl and John Bimson have a different idea. They propose that Kenyon came to a wrong destruction date at Jericho because the dates assigned to the Middle Bronze Age are not correct and need a major adjustment. Nevertheless, all these scholars agree that this Jericho was destroyed in a manner that matches the story of Joshua and the Israelites.

IV. Hazor: Another City Burned

However, there was more to the Conquest than just Jericho. Spies had reported that Canaan was a beautiful land, flowing with milk and honey. But it was filled with great, fortified cities that had walls reaching up to heaven. One by one, they would fall to Joshua. [83]

Rabbi Friedman continued, "Then Joshua turned north and headed for the city of Hazor. Jabin, king of Hazor, gathered all the kings of the region against Israel. Hazor formerly was the head of all those kingdoms. Joshua captured Hazor and struck its king with the sword. And Joshua destroyed Hazor by fire."

The Bible records that the city of Hazor was defeated twice by the Israelites, first during the Conquest and then again in the days of the judge Deborah. Archaeological

Alternative Views

For more information on this debate, read Bonus Chapter E at the back of the book. Because of the pattern of evidence Mahoney saw developing in the earlier period, he decided to focus his investigation there.

The Bible is silent as to whether these conquered cities in the south of Canaan were burned or not. However, the archaeological remains of the cities near the end of the Middle Bronze Age show destructions by fire.

remains at the site show that it was indeed destroyed and burned twice. Unlike Jericho, Hazor was rebuilt after the earlier destruction, only to be destroyed again several centuries later. [84]

Aerial view of the ancient city of Hazor.

Israeli archaeologists at Hazor found that the massive burn layer from its earlier defeat matched the date of Jericho's destruction. They also found something else.

At the old mansion in Saint Paul, David Rohl and I had been talking for hours. It was now time to turn our conversation to the topic of the Conquest. "Can you see any evidence beyond Jericho that suggests that Joshua and the Israelites went into the Promised Land known as Canaan?"

Leaning in, Rohl revealed, "If you place the story in the Middle Bronze Age and not the Late Bronze Age, we have much more than just Jericho. First of all, Hazor, the greatest of all the kingdoms, as the Bible says. We found tablets in the Middle Bronze Age palace belonging to a king called Jabin. And that's the name of the king that Joshua actually stuck his sword into in the story."

Surprised, I asked, "So you have a connection between the Bible story and these tablets?"

"We have a name. It's identical. We have a tablet coming out of the ground with the name Jabin on it, and in the story of Joshua, Joshua killed King Jabin of Hazor."

I asked Bimson, "Do you see a connection between this early destruction at Hazor and Jericho."

Bimson replied, "Hazor fits very well when you put that alongside Jericho. At Hazor you have a Canaanite city that's burned but very quickly revives as a Canaanite center and, interestingly, in the book of Judges we encounter Hazor once again as the center of Canaanite power under a king called Jabin. Let's call him Jabin II. So both in the Bible and in the archaeology at Hazor you have a major city that's destroyed but revives again quite quickly. And at the same time Jericho is destroyed and doesn't revive. So when you put those cities side by side, the biblical account and the archaeology match extremely well."

V. Joshua and the Missing Conquest Evidence

Once again, archaeologists have not connected this evidence at Jericho and Hazor with the Conquest because they date the destructions to a time far earlier than when they assume the Conquest occurred, which is the 13th century BC. [85]

At their home in Pennsylvania, Wood's wife, Faith, told us it was time to come out onto their sun porch for the noon meal. She had made a farmhouse chicken dinner with fresh potato salad, several types of vegetables, homemade rolls, and dessert. As we sat down at the table, I kidded Wood, "How can you keep so trim with meals this good?"

His wife told me his secret. "Bryant is a walker. He's been walking several miles every day for years."

He smiled. "It's good therapy. Let me give thanks for this food." I found out later that Wood had been an outstanding athlete, even setting the school record for the mile run while attending Syracuse University.

As we were enjoying our meal, I asked, "Tell me, why should we be concerned about these scholarly, academic arguments and discussions? Who cares, you know, whether Jericho was destroyed at this date or that date?"

He became serious. "Well, it is important because the scholars conclude by their interpretation of the archaeological evidence that the Bible is not historically correct with regard to Jericho and with regard to Ai. And so that has undermined the whole Conquest narrative, and scholars now say there never was a Conquest."

"Yes, I've observed that as well," I said.

"And it's a domino effect, because they say, 'Well, obviously, if there never was a

The tablet containing the name of Jabin in cuneiform writing found in the remains of the Middle Bronze Age palace at Hazor.

Conquest, the Israelites didn't come in from outside and conquer the land,' and they make up this theory about they were always living there, they were indigenous people. Well, then there were obviously no wilderness wanderings if they always lived in Canaan, which means they were never in Egypt."

"So that would mean there was no Exodus."

He affirmed, "There was no Exodus, and so because of two archaeological problems, Jericho and Ai, it has led scholars to conclude that Genesis, Exodus, Leviticus, Numbers, Deuteronomy, and Joshua – and probably most of Judges – are not historically true. Seven books of the Bible down the tubes because of incorrect interpretations of archaeological data at two sites in Israel."

"So that's the bottom line."

"That's why it's important that we correct the record, set the record straight, and get the facts right, because the facts agree with the Bible, and will show that it is historically true and accurate. It's not a folk story. It's not mythology. It's not etiology. It's not made up stories. It's not a construct. It's real history."

Over the course of our investigation, our team has learned that the problems surrounding the Conquest are broader than just two cities. They center on two main points that cause scholars like Finkelstein, Franklin, and Herzog to dismiss the Bible's account:

1) There is no sign of the culture suddenly transitioning to a new people group in Canaan.

2) There is no evidence of simultaneous, widespread city destructions.

These scholars are primarily looking for a Conquest to have happened around 1200 BC, after the time of Ramesses II. However, the problem is that they can't find a new culture or widespread city destructions at the time of Ramesses or throughout the entire Late Bronze Age, which would include both the early and late Exodus dates.

I began by exploring the first of these two reasons for dismissal: the lack of a new culture suddenly appearing in Canaan. I knew that Finkelstein's surveys had shown many new settlements popping up in the hill country after 1200 BC. However, these settlements had the same culture as the preceding century, which led to his view that the Israelites developed from the surrounding Canaanite population instead of coming in from the outside.

After lunch, I was curious to hear Wood's thoughts about Finkelstein's views. When

Bryant Wood believes there is evidence for a Conquest around the conventional dates of 1410-1400 BC. He argues that there are good reasons why there is so little evidence for Israelite culture entering Canaan.

Etiology

An etiology is a mythical story crafted for the purpose of explaining the origins of something.

we returned to his living room for the second part of the interview, I asked, "There are a number of scholars who are suggesting that there is no evidence of a new Israelite culture coming in, which would be expected if a Conquest had occurred."

Wood thought for a moment before he responded. "Many scholars claim that there's no evidence for the presence of Israel as early as, say, 1400 BC. Well, let's again deal with the realities of the situation. The Israelites had wandered in the desert for 40 years. They were nomads basically. The Israelites who had left Egypt were the ones who had skills. They knew how to build; they knew how to make pottery. Probably there were metal workers, weavers, carpenters, all kinds of skilled people."

"What happened to them?"

"They all died in the wilderness. It was only the young children under age 20 that continued on for 40 years, and those of course who were born in the wilderness, that entered the Promised Land. That earlier generation, except for Caleb and Joshua, all died in the wilderness. So you're talking about a rag-tag group of nomadic wanderers who had no material culture. So they come into the Promised Land, and how are they going to live? Well, they're going to live as they did in the wilderness initially. They're going to be living in tents. They're going to be pastoralists, and they're not going to be building cities. They're not going to be making pottery. They're not going to have a material culture."

I could see where he was going with this. "So what you're saying is that the people who came in during the Conquest, they didn't have the materials or types of skills to actually make a footprint?"

Wood nodded. "That's exactly right. From an archaeological point of view, we can say they were archaeologically invisible. Now, one of the interesting things we find in this time period, which we call the Late Bronze period in archaeological terminology, is that we find many burials and cemeteries that are not associated with any sort of a settlement. They're kind of isolated cemeteries. Well, these would be good candidates for Israelite burials, because they lived in tents, they didn't build cities, and when you excavate those burials, what do you find? You find Canaanite pottery, Canaanite weapons, Canaanite tools. And so people conclude, "Oh, these are Canaanites." Well, are they? Where did the Israelites get their pottery from, or their weapons from, or their tools from? They bought it from the Canaanites. They went to the market, and they would probably barter. And so you cannot distinguish Israelites from Canaanites in this early period."

I wanted Wood to comment directly on Finkelstein's statements so I said, "When I

Pastoralists

Pastoralists are herdsmen, and the remains of pastoralists – tents and animal skins – tend to decay within a few years. Therefore, these people leave few enduring physical remains compared to city dwellers, and those remnants would likely not be found thousands of years later.

talked with Israel Finkelstein, he said that there's no evidence of people coming in at the time and manner that the Bible states. What do you have to say to that?"

Wood candidly replied, "I agree with Finkelstein and these other scholars in their interpretation of the data from the 13th century and 12th century. They're saying this is the first evidence we have for the appearance of the Israelites. The first evidence of the Israelites building a village. But that doesn't say they weren't in the land before that, living in tents and leaving no archaeological footprint. And so it depends on your perspective and your preconceived notions as to how you analyze this data."

I was beginning to get it. When the Israelites came into Canaan they lived in tents and didn't have much of a hard material culture. When they needed things like tools and pottery, they got them from the Canaanites. So in the eyes of today's archaeologists, there would be no sign that a large nomadic group of people had just moved into the land.

I asked Wood, "Do you think archaeologists like Finkelstein are ignoring this?"

"Many of these scholars believe in the concept that the Israelites were Canaanites and were indigenous to the land, and suddenly became a separate people somehow or another; they don't really explain that very well. But that's based on this data basically from the 12th century BC and the small agricultural villages that sprang up suddenly during that time period, which are attributed to the Israelites. I believe, yes, they're exactly right – they're Israelite villages, and they appear to have been in the land because the pottery is a continuation of the previous centuries. The tools, the weapons are Canaanite in nature. That's because the Israelites lived in the land prior to the 12th century, and they learned their material culture from the Canaanites."

John Bimson agreed with Wood's assessment. I asked Bimson, "If they came into the land, did they basically absorb the culture that was there until they started to create their own?"

"Well, yes," he said, "I think that's plausible. I think also a good many of them might have continued to live a fairly nomadic existence within the land." [86]

"So they were shepherds and weren't leaving many remains?"

"Yes, and settling down over quite a long period. They came in as people who had been wanderers for 40 years according to the biblical tradition, so they wouldn't have had a distinctive material culture. They wouldn't have been carrying pottery around, for example, for 40 years. You don't do that. And the Bible, you remember, does give a very mixed picture of how the Conquest happened. If you only read chapters 1-11 of Joshua you might get the impression this was an all-out victory right across the land. Then you read Judges 1, and there you find stories of the Israelites in various pockets of the country settling among the Canaanites, living side by side with the Canaanites. So the biblical tradition itself, I think, leads us to expect that there would be a borrowing or absorbing of the culture that was already there. I don't think that we should expect to see the sudden arrival of a new culture that we could point to and say, 'Here are the Israelites.' That doesn't happen for quite a long time."

I was really surprised by the number of biblical references to the Israelites living among the Canaanites because they couldn't drive them out. [87]

At my studio one morning I was going for a cup of tea when I passed Steve's office and noticed a piece of paper lying on his desk. The writing on it was so small that only Steve could decipher it. He could put more information on one sheet of paper than most people could fit on ten pages.

He looked at me. "I've been researching what the Bible says about the Israelites coming into the land of Canaan."

"What did you find?"

"Something really interesting in Deuteronomy 6:10-12." He glanced down at his piece of paper. "It says:

'When the LORD your God brings you into the land He swore to your fathers Abraham, Isaac, and Jacob that He would give you – a land with large and beautiful cities that you did not build, houses full of every good thing that you did not fill them with, wells dug that you did not dig, and vineyards and olive groves that you did not plant – and when you eat and are satisfied, be careful not to forget the LORD who brought you out of the land of Egypt, out of the place of slavery.' (Deuteronomy 6:10-12)

If this is what the Bible itself is saying, then why are archaeologists assuming that the Israelites would have brought in a completely new material culture?"

"This is amazing." I said. "The Bible is saying something completely different."

Steve smiled. "If the Israelites took over Canaanite culture, there would be no way to tell an Israelite from a Canaanite."

"You're right. This passage clearly explains why they wouldn't find a big change in the culture," I said.

For a second opinion I asked Professor Bimson. "A sudden change in the culture in

Canaan isn't really what the Bible says happened, is it?"

Bimson agreed. "It doesn't give us any reason to expect that. So it would be a mistake to look for that kind of material cultural change in the archaeological evidence."

As I reflected on what Bimson and Wood had told me, it made me wonder why scholars ignore the details of the biblical story. They use the lack of cultural change as one of their main reasons for dismissing the Conquest when the details of the Bible's narrative paint quite a different picture. Once again, theories that didn't match the Bible were being used to discount the Bible.

However, if one focused on testing what the Bible actually claimed, I could see there were answers to be found.

VI. The Forgotten Story of the Conquest

Now I needed to take a closer look at the second major reason that scholars dismiss the Conquest, which centers on the lack of evidence for simultaneous, widespread city destructions. When I interviewed scholars in Israel, England, and the United States about this, I learned that there are two widely divergent ideas regarding the amount of destruction that should be expected in the archaeology from the Conquest.

On one hand, some think that a Conquest requires very widespread destructions. Yet the verse in Deuteronomy 6:10, considered in the previous section, shows that many cities were not destroyed in the Conquest but remained intact for the Israelites to occupy. So it may be that archaeologists are expecting more devastation than the Bible actually describes. [88]

In my interview with James Hoffmeier I asked, "Can we talk about the fact that the Bible doesn't say that all the cities were destroyed completely and burned to the ground?"

Hoffmeier seemed very familiar with this issue. "The Conquest as portrayed in the book of Joshua, if you read the text carefully, is not making the claim that dozens and dozens of cities were destroyed. People seem to think that Joshua had this scorched earth policy of going in, burning, destroying, leveling, et cetera. Now we must remember that the purpose of the Israelites taking the land is finding a place to live. You don't scorch the land you intend to live on. So the whole expectation that archaeology is going to reveal all these burned and destroyed cities is just not realistic."

Hoffmeier believed that it was important to look more closely at what cities had been burned in the account. He went on, "So, what we need to do is look at the Bible carefully. And it only presents three cities as having been destroyed and burned with fire: Jericho, Ai, and Hazor."

What Hoffmeier said highlighted the two opposing views on how much Conquest destruction we should expect to find. One camp (including Finkelstein and Franklin) expected to find a lot. The other camp (including Hoffmeier and Wood) expected to find very little. But focusing only on the cities that are explicitly said to have burned did not tell the whole story of the Conquest. I would discover that there was a third way to look at this.

VII. Nine Cities Destroyed in the Conquest

Just how many cities does the Bible claim were destroyed? The biblical account specifically names nine cities that it appears to portray as experiencing destruction at the hands of the Israelites, with possibly as many as 19 named cities in this category for the Conquest as well as in the decades that followed. [89] The text claims that at the time of the Conquest, these cities generally contained high-walled fortifications. Is there a pattern of evidence anywhere in the archaeology that matches this? [90]

Professor John Bimson argues that the archaeological evidence from Canaan near the end of the Middle Bronze Age fits the biblical Conquest remarkably well.

Finkelstein had brought up the serious challenge that many of the defeated cities of the Conquest did not exist during the entire Late Bronze Age. No high walls. No massive destructions. Only a series of burnt-out and empty ruins. This is perhaps the biggest factor contributing to the current skepticism regarding the biblical account of the Conquest.

John Bimson specialized in this area and confirmed Finkelstein's point. He dealt extensively with this issue in his pioneering book, *Redating the Exodus and Conquest*.

I asked Bimson, "Does what happened according to the Bible fit the archaeology?"

He clarified, "It fits the archaeology if you look for the archaeological evidence in the right time period."

"What do you mean?"

"There was a major collapse of urban civilization at the end of what's called the Middle Bronze Age."

According to Bimson, near the end of the Middle Bronze Age the cities mentioned

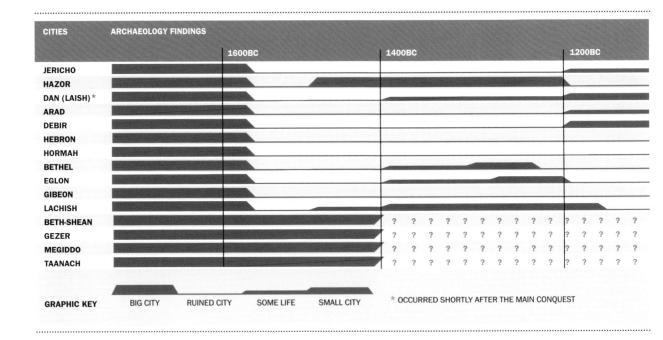

CITIES	ARCHAEOLOGY FINDINGS		
	1600BC	1400BC	1200BC
JERICHO			
HAZOR			
DAN (LAISH) *			
ARAD			
DEBIR			
HEBRON			
HORMAH			
BETHEL			
EGLON			
GIBEON			
LACHISH			
BETH-SHEAN		? ? ? ? ? ? ? ? ? ?	? ? ? ? ?
GEZER		? ? ? ? ? ? ? ? ? ?	? ? ? ? ?
MEGIDDO		? ? ? ? ? ? ? ? ? ?	? ? ? ? ?
TAANACH		? ? ? ? ? ? ? ? ? ?	? ? ? ? ?

GRAPHIC KEY	BIG CITY	RUINED CITY	SOME LIFE	SMALL CITY	* OCCURRED SHORTLY AFTER THE MAIN CONQUEST

The archaeological condition of major cities in Canaan. Some cities were destroyed around 1200 BC, but these destructions were spread out over a century or more, causing the skepticism of many scholars. There is only one time that appears to fit the biblical account well – near the end of the earlier Middle Bronze Age (1550 BC under conventional dating).

in the Bible's Conquest story were all occupied and were guarded by high walls. And amazingly, the archaeology shows that most of these cities suffered major destructions, including burning, in the same short time period. The Bible states that these cities were destroyed or defeated but is silent as to whether they were burned or not. So these archaeological remains pointed out by Bimson could fit within the descriptions found in the Bible.

"Are there other cities that were destroyed that make you think the Conquest actually happened?" I asked.

"Well, all together we have about 30 sites which were either destroyed or abandoned at the end of the Middle Bronze Age. I wouldn't say the Israelites attacked every one of those because that would go way beyond what the Bible describes. But then I wouldn't expect the Bible to be telling us every detail of what was happening. I think there were lots of factors feeding into the collapse of these cities," replied Bimson.

"What do you think was causing the collapse then?"

"It does seem to have been a time when there was a lot of internal conflict between cities, and cities turning against their rulers perhaps. And this would fit very well what we read in the Bible because we have Rahab at Jericho who helps the Israelites to get in and

Cities of the Conquest
A COMPARISON OF THE BIBLICAL RECORD

CITIES	DEFEATED	DESTROYED	BURNED	AFTER THE MAIN CONQUEST
JERICHO	●	●	●	
AI	●	●	●	
JERUSALEM	●	●	●	
HAZOR	●	●	●	
DAN (LAISH)*	●	●	●	●
ANAB	●	●	?	
ARAD	●	●	?	
DEBIR	●	●	?	
HEBRON	●	●	?	
HORMAH	●	●	?	
ASHKELON*	●	?	?	●
BETHEL	●	?	?	
EGLON	●	?	?	
EKRON*	●	?	?	●
GAZA*	●	?	?	●
GIBEON	●	?	?	
LACHISH	●	?	?	
LIBNAH	●	?	?	
MAKKEDAH	●	?	?	
BETH-SHEAN	NO	NO	NO	
GEZER	NO	NO	NO	
MEGIDDO	NO	NO	NO	
TAANACH	NO	NO	NO	

Bible Conquest Cities

The four cities at the top of the list are explicitly said in the Bible to have experienced burning during the Conquest. Dan/Laish is said to have been destroyed and burned in the period following the Conquest, perhaps a few decades later. The second group lists defeated cities that appear to have been destroyed and included in the idea of "the curse of destruction." The Bible does not mention whether these cities were burned or not. Nine other major cities were said to be defeated, but there is no mention of whether they were destroyed and burned, except for the city of Gibeon, which seems to have been largely abandoned according to the account (Joshua chapter 9). Of all the cities on this list, about half appear to have been generally unoccupied or empty throughout the entire Late Bronze Age, which causes problems for any proposal that places the Conquest of high-walled cities in that period. [91]

conquer the city. We have a man of Bethel, according to Judges chapter one, who helps them to overthrow Bethel. The Gibeonites make a treaty with them. So it does seem as though you have a time of widespread disturbance, realignments, breaking of the bonds of society basically, which I think would provide a very good background of the arrival of the Israelites and their Conquest of selected cities."

"And this all happened around the end of the time that archaeologists call the Middle Bronze Age?"

Bimson nodded. "We know that cities like Jericho and Hazor were major cities at that time, and in both of those cases, those cities were destroyed by fire, as the Bible describes. So if we go to this earlier date, we have a very good fit, with a whole list of sites, a good fit between the biblical narrative and the archaeological evidence." [92]

I could see why the evidence from the earlier Middle Bronze Age is so significant. It matches the Conquest story very well, whereas the archaeology from the Late Bronze Age does not. Once again, dating is the key to this skepticism, because dating is the main reason why the archaeology does not match the early history recorded in the Bible. And it also matches the pattern I had seen in Egypt for the first five steps of the biblical sequence.

"What is the archaeology telling you?"

He chose his words carefully. "Well, let me put it this way. I would never claim the archaeological evidence proved that there was a Conquest. I don't think archaeology can prove things except in some very rare cases. What it can do is to tip the balance of probabilities."

I wanted Bimson to give his conclusion. "Do you think that there is a pattern of evidence that exists in Palestine that shows a Conquest happened?"

"When we look at the right period, I think we have enough destroyed and abandoned cities to say this fits the sequence of events the Bible is describing in the book of Joshua and the book of Judges. There's a high probability that we're looking here at Joshua's Conquest."

If scholars have been looking at the wrong time for the Conquest, it is understandable that they don't find any evidence. I said to Bimson, "So in many ways, Finkelstein and Norma Franklin are correct in what they are saying about the 13th century BC."

"They are correct about the 13th century,' he said. "Where they go wrong is to deduce from that there was never any Exodus or Conquest. I think those events happened much earlier. I mean, if you take the Bible's own clues seriously, it puts these events about two centuries earlier."

The problem is that the end of the Middle Bronze Age is currently thought to be four centuries earlier than the 13th century BC, not two centuries earlier. However, this fits the pattern of evidence I had been seeing that matched all the other biblical steps. I would need to find out soon what was at the bottom of this mystery.

It seems clear, according to the biblical account:

- Joshua did not destroy and burn most of the cities of Canaan. The vast majority of cities were left intact for use by the Israelites.
- The Israelites are said to have destroyed more than the three cities that are often mentioned as being burned.
- A change to a new material culture in Canaan is not to be expected according to the biblical account.
- Scholars who are looking for the previous three criteria as evidence of Joshua's Conquest are looking for the wrong thing.
- Those cities that the text designates as being defeated and destroyed do in fact show archaeological signs of the destruction of high-walled fortresses near the end of the Middle Bronze Age.

VIII. Shechem: A Center of Biblical History

It had been a long day of filming in Saint Paul. That morning it had snowed half a foot and then turned bitterly cold and windy. Now it was evening. For hours Rabbi Friedman had recounted the ancient stories of the Bible. I appreciated his effort. I knew he had taken time out of his busy teaching schedule to help me and I felt that his storytelling was the best way to communicate what the biblical account was actually claiming.

Rabbi Friedman preparing to finish telling the Conquest step of the biblical story – the account of the Covenant renewal after the Israelites had returned from Egypt to the land promised to Abraham.

As we prepared for the final scene that would conclude the six steps of the biblical sequence, I had a thought. Here I was, filming a rabbi on a wintry evening, talking about events that were said to have happened 3,500 years ago in a desert on the other side of the world. The contrasts were striking. The story had started with the promises to Abraham, went on to the time in Egypt and the Exodus, and now was finishing with Joshua and the Israelites who had returned to the Promised Land to conquer it. What was it about this story that has given it such an enduring and profound legacy and yet has made it the root of so much controversy? I nodded for the camera to roll, looked at the rabbi and said, "Tell me what the Bible says happened at the end of the Conquest."

He drew a breath and began. "It was to Shechem, all those years ago, that Abraham first came when he entered Canaan, and God promised that land to his descendants. It was in Shechem that Abraham built an altar to God, and so it was to this location that Joshua called the Israelites to gather after conquering the land of Canaan. And Joshua kept the promise made to Joseph and buried Joseph's bones in Israel." [93]

Many scholars see the connection at Shechem with Joseph and these biblical characters as mythical. They suggest monuments like Joseph's shrine in Nablus were built many centuries after the supposed events in order to support the beliefs and folklore of the culture. But once again, I was struck by the pattern of evidence that would converge at this site. [94]

The first time I visited there I hadn't realized how important this location was in biblical history. But now I could see that this ancient site had connections with Abraham, Jacob, Joseph, and Joshua. It was here at Shechem that both the biblical story and the investigation would now come full circle.

Rabbi Friedman continued to unfold the details of the story. "The elders of the tribes of Israel assembled in front of the temple there, and Joshua recounted all that God had done in bringing them out of slavery in Egypt, giving them the land, and fulfilling the promises that God had made to Abraham."

Just 200 yards from the shrine of Joseph's tomb, lies the remains of an ancient fortress temple. It was discovered by Ernst Sellin, the German explorer who co-authored the book about the first major digs at Jericho. As he excavated the ancient site of Shechem in 1913, he started to uncover the huge stones of a fortification wall. In it he found a gateway leading to a broad, terraced platform upon which a massive two-towered temple had been erected.

These archaeological discoveries by Sellin matched what the Bible would later call "the tower of Shechem," the temple where Joshua and the Israelites gathered after the Conquest. It was also associated with the "House of the Millo." The word *millo* simply means "filling" or "terrace." [95]

Centuries later, the Bible relates that the main temple would be the scene of a terrible massacre when a ruthless leader set it on fire along with a thousand people trapped inside. It was destroyed and the city abandoned. Sellin again found that the archaeology of this temple, originally built in the Middle Bronze Age, would later show a violent destruction by fire followed by abandonment. He believed he had uncovered the biblical fortress temple of Shechem also known as Baal-Berith.

Other excavations have found older and smaller courtyards that suggested this was

The gateway and fortification wall surrounding the temple complex at Shechem can be seen in the foreground in front of the vehicles..

The archaeological site at Shechem/Nablus.

The archaeological site at Shechem/Nablus with a re-creation of the fortress temple.

a holy site centuries before the main temple was built. Interestingly, David Rohl points out that these older structures fit the idea of the outdoor worship that the Bible indicates was practiced by Abraham and Jacob at this very location.

"Rabbi Friedman, tell me, how does the story of the Conquest end?"

He looked at me and spoke in a solemn tone. "In the presence of the elders of the tribes of Israel, Joshua set up a great stone under an oak by the sanctuary of the Lord to renew the Covenant that God had made with Israel at Mount Sinai. He challenges the Israelites saying, 'Choose this day whom you will serve, the Lord or other gods. But as for me and my house, we will serve the Lord.'

"And the people responded by saying, 'We will serve the Lord'. And Joshua said to the people, 'Behold, this stone shall be a witness against us, for it has heard all the words of the Lord that he spoke to us. It will be a witness against you lest you deny your God.' After the renewal of the Covenant, Joshua sent the people home, every man to his inheritance." [96]

The Bible states that Joshua initiated a Covenant renewal ceremony in front of the temple at Shechem.

One last find at Shechem fits this part of the story in an amazing way. David Rohl related that in the open courtyard in front of the temple, Sellin discovered a great white stone that was carefully carved and fitted into a base. It measured more than seven feet high. We don't know if Sellin identified this as Joshua's stone, but he did believe it was the main religious symbol of the temple. To Rohl, the conclusion seemed obvious: this was the covenant stone of Joshua.

"That standing stone is still there today in the ground. You can go and see it for yourself."

"Oh, really? So this stone wouldn't be there naturally?" I asked.

"No. It's a white stone that's been erected in front of the temple, like a pillar almost. And it's a covenant stone. It's the sort of the thing that people did in the ancient world. They would erect a standing stone and they would get people to swear some sort of oath in front of that stone."

"So this standing stone is near the temple?"

"It's right in front of it."

"Really? And they were associated with each other in biblical times?"

"Yes, absolutely," said Rohl, who then paused with a growing smile as he could see the wheels turning in my mind. "History's coming alive here. Can you not see that? Look at how the archaeology and the history work together."

It almost seemed hard to believe that it could fit the story this well, so I challenged him. "How do you know for sure that that's the standing stone of Joshua?"

"Well, we don't, but it fits the story again. Why is it not the standing stone of Joshua in the conventional thinking? Because it's in the wrong time period."

The standing stone was found by Ernst Sellin on a raised terrace in front of the remains of the temple.

German archaeologist Ernst Sellin (center) was fired for suggesting that the fortress was also a temple and the standing stone an important religious symbol.

Sellin's conclusions that the structure was a temple and that the standing stone was a religious symbol were rejected, and he was fired by the dig sponsors. The director who followed believed the stone was a fake and accused Sellin of fraudulently setting it up and staging the whole episode of its discovery. He was so furious with Sellin's ideas that he dislodged the standing stone from its base, throwing it down the slope of a dump, breaking it in the process. [97]

Over time other archaeologists, including Harvard's Ernest Wright, who dug at Shechem in the 1960s, verified that Sellin was right all along. The structure was in fact a temple, and the stone in front of it an authentic religious symbol, central to the site. Wright took the one piece of the stone that could be found and re-erected it in its original position. However, scholars still do not associate these finds with the biblical Conquest. After all, they are considered to be far too early for any link to be made.

The remains of the standing stone at Shechem that David Rohl suggests is the covenant stone of Joshua.

When investigating Sellin's work at Shechem, we discovered that all of Sellin's field records and his final report were destroyed in bombing raids on Berlin during World War II. It was disappointing to learn this. I suppose this contributed to his findings being neglected and largely ignored by the world. Perhaps if we had been able to read Sellin's reports, we would have found out if he connected the site with the story of the Conquest.

What happens when you look at an old problem with a fresh perspective? You are able to see possibilities in a whole new light. That is what I found happening throughout the investigation. And this was definitely the method I saw David Rohl using. It was this approach that allowed Rohl to make new connections between the Bible and the archaeological evidence.

Rohl was the first person to connect Bietak's evidence at Avaris with Joseph, and now he was the first in this century to see a connection between Sellin's archaeological reports and the story of Joshua and the Conquest.

IX. Conquest Summary

Archaeologists working in Canaan have uncovered:

- The remains of a city at Jericho with high fortification walls that fell down,
- Evidence that the city was intentionally burned after the collapse,
- Storage jars filled with charred grain, evidence of a short siege in springtime,
- A section of houses within the wall at Jericho surprisingly preserved, fitting the story of Rahab,
- The remains of major destruction and fire at Hazor from the same period,
- A tablet from Hazor containing the name Jabin, the king mentioned in the Bible,
- A pattern of cities mentioned in the biblical Conquest account that show archaeological evidence of high walls and destructions at the same time as Jericho and Hazor (near the end of the Middle Bronze Age),
- A Middle Bronze fortress temple at Shechem that matches the Bible's mention of the temple where Joshua and the Israelites renewed the Covenant,
- Smaller, older shrines at Shechem that fit the idea of outdoor worship previously practiced by Abraham and Jacob at the site,

- An ancient shrine said to be the tomb of Joseph, lying only 200 yards from the temple,
- And a standing stone at Shechem that matches the story of Joshua setting up a large stone as a witness to the renewal of the Covenant.

These finds join all the other details of the six steps that I had been examining, details that fit the biblical story in an uncanny way. Yet all of this is discounted because it exists centuries earlier than even the early Exodus date around 1450 BC. Sitting across from David Rohl, I felt as if I had to ask one more question. I was somewhat reluctant, because I knew what his answer would be. I knew it would challenge the foundations of history and Egyptology. "David, the events that you're suggesting in Egypt and Canaan, are they in the right sequence?"

Rohl became very serious as he leaned forward and moved his hands across the surface of the table as though he was marking off each event on a timeline. "The whole thing – from the beginning of the sojourn in Egypt, the slavery, Moses and the Exodus, the Conquest of the Promised Land – is all there in one nice neat line, but it's way too early."

It was now time to address this problem. ♱

XI: A Pattern Among the Rags and Tatters

Early morning in Karnak Temple.

I. A Question of Time

Why does so much evidence matching the Bible appear in the archaeological record earlier than expected? I could think of only four possible explanations for this situation. First of all, the pattern we were seeing in the Middle Kingdom could be merely a coincidence. That is, in fact, what many archaeologist today do say, because usually they only consider one or two isolated pieces of the pattern. To my knowledge, most have never been made aware of the larger sequence. But it was the strength of this sequential pattern that motivated our team to look beyond the idea that it was just a coincidence.

Secondly, it is possible that our understanding of the biblical date is off and Egypt's dating is correct. In other words, the Exodus actually happened long before 1450 BC. Since that possibility contains a number of problems, we set it aside as a less convincing interpretation. [98]

Then there is a third way of understanding this situation. Some scholars accept the evidence found in the Middle Kingdom for the first three steps only. According to them, the pattern found in the last three steps is not related to the Exodus. These are historians who hold to the conventional chronology for Egypt. For them, the Exodus occurred in 1450 BC, squarely in the New Kingdom, not the Middle Kingdom. They can incorporate the first three steps because they hold to a longer, 430-year stay for the Israelites in Egypt (see Bonus Chapter D).

However, we were particularly intrigued by a fourth possibility, one that is more dramatic. Rohl, Bimson, and others have proposed that the standard timeline for ancient Egypt contains a flaw. That is why the evidence is not matching up with the story in the Bible. They boldly suggest that the founders of Egyptology developed their chronology incorrectly. Over the years, historians built upon this faulty framework, and our legacy today is a timeline that is not correct. To rectify the chronology, scholars like Rohl and Bimson are urging that the history of Egypt be reevaluated and that a portion of the Egyptian timeline be shifted forward by centuries.

Rohl, Bimson, and other scholars suggest that a portion of the Egyptian timeline is inaccurate and needs to be adjusted forward several centuries.

For a 1450 BC biblical Exodus date to fit the six steps of the sequence, such an adjustment would be required.

I asked Rohl, "So what are you proposing?"

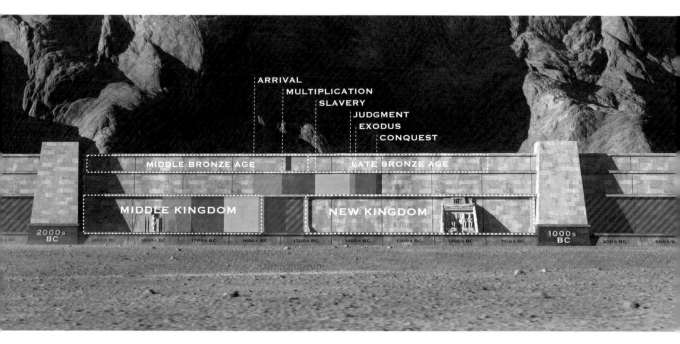

ARRIVAL
MULTIPLICATION
SLAVERY
JUDGMENT
EXODUS
CONQUEST

MIDDLE BRONZE AGE · LATE BRONZE AGE

MIDDLE KINGDOM · NEW KINGDOM

2000s BC · 1900s BC · 1800s BC · 1700s BC · 1600s BC · 1500s BC · 1400s BC · 1300s BC · 1200s BC · 1100s BC · 1000s BC · 900s BC · 800s BC

With a look that invited me to open my mind, he said, "Let's just suggest for a moment that we've got the timeline wrong, and what we should be doing is revising that timeline. Shorten it by, say, about three centuries, something like that, and all of a sudden these things that are too early become contemporary with the events in the Old Testament. They sync up again. Everything links together."

I was excited and intrigued to hear of this possibility. It would explain why all the evidence has been consistently earlier. But at the same time I wanted to be objective.

Could the history that scholars had created for Egypt really be off by centuries? Egyptologist James Hoffmeier didn't think so when I returned to Chicago for a more in-depth interview with him. As we sat in the lower level of the lecture hall, I asked about the problems with Egypt's dating. "Could we talk about Egyptologists like David Rohl who suggests the chronology is off? Do you see any possibilities with this approach?"

Hoffmeier shook his head. "I'm very much against chronological revisionism. Very good, very competent historians have been working for decades and decades on Egyptian chronology and Near Eastern chronology. There's still more work to be done, but I don't see the possibility of moving things centuries. A few years here, a few years there, maybe a decade here, a decade there, but I think we're locked in by some pretty significant anchoring points."

In Israel at the University of Tel Aviv's archaeology department, Professor Finkelstein was equally resistant to changing the chronology of Egypt. We were coming to the end of our interview in the pottery room. I had waited to the end to bring up this controversial topic. "There are some people who say the Israelites are really from the Middle Bronze Age. They think a better Egyptian chronology would solve the problem."

Finkelstein was dismissive. "I don't think so. I think this is another attempt to harmonize archaeology. What's behind it is the idea, 'Well, we don't have a Conquest in the 13th century so let's look for a Conquest sometime earlier and harmonize it with the archaeology in the Bible.' I'm not into this business at all. And I think that we know enough to say that we know we may be wrong, ten years here, and ten years there, but there's no way to shift centuries. I mean, forget it. Look, I don't need to go this direction. I think that we are on solid ground. So, there's no need to look for different centuries."

What was I supposed to do now? Hoffmeier and Finkelstein represent mainstream opinion, and I couldn't just ignore it. I was also warned by scholars close to me not to question Egypt's chronology. "The topic is too controversial," they said. "You'll regret it." But I was trying to keep an open mind just as Mansour Boraik had advised me. At the beginning of this investigation I had set out to find a pattern of evidence no matter where it led me. I had found a clear pattern, but it was all pointing to the earlier period.

The fact remains that the majority of scholars, even scholars who are believers in the Bible, won't allow the evidence I've seen to be connected to the Exodus. It's just too early. This was the biggest giant of all, standing in the way of finding answers for the mystery of the Exodus. But the biblical pattern was so strong I just couldn't let it go.

II. A Collection of Rags and Tatters

Every year my wife, Jill, makes a trip over to England where she serves on a board of a trust. I usually tag along if I can, enjoying the countryside or trips to museums, or a day in London. A week before we were to leave, Steve came up to me.

"How close will you be to Oxford?"

"I don't know. Why?"

"Have you heard of Sir Alan Gardiner?"

I nodded. "Of course, he's one of the greatest Egyptologists of the 20th century."

"Well, I've been digging around and found something he wrote that I think gives another side of the story. It might help you counter the pushback you've received from the scholars about Egypt's chronology."

As it turned out, I was only 40 minutes by train from Oxford University. I came

Photograph of Sir Alan Gardiner's portrait located in the archival room of the Griffith Institute.

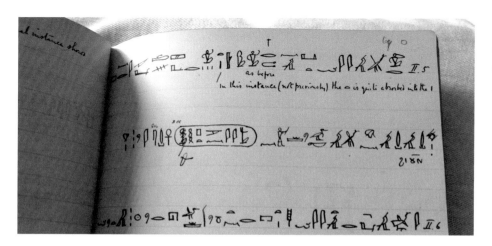

Sir Alan Gardiner's personal notes preserved at the Griffith Institute.

with a small camera and tripod to St. John Street and the Griffith Institute, one of the greatest storehouses of Egyptological documents in the world. The late Sir Alan Gardiner was perhaps the 20th century's greatest specialist in reading hieroglyphs. He had a great hand in uncovering what we know today but still he implied our knowledge of ancient Egypt was greatly lacking.

Two librarians led me down the stairs of a narrow hallway and into a small archive. Large metal shelves lined one side of the room that housed the original manuscripts, documents, and notebooks of some of the most renowned scholars in the world. On the other side of the room were tall windows divided by two large portraits, one of Sir Alan Gardiner and the other of Howard Carter, who had discovered King Tut's tomb.

They seated me at a wood table. One librarian called out from a closet. "You'll need to put these on first." She returned with a pair of clean, white gloves. I think they were made of cotton.

"Of course, certainly."

It was exciting. This is what I had come for. They carefully arranged Sir Gardiner's notebooks in front of me. I was moved as I looked through his personal notes. In some ways I was following a path that he had helped clear.

After a lifetime of searching, Gardiner wrote something that directly impacted the question I was dealing with: "It must never be forgotten that we are dealing with a civilization thousands of years old and one of which only tiny remnants have survived. What is proudly advertised as Egyptian history is merely a collection of rags and tatters."

If all we have is rags and tatters, how sure can we be about the dates?

At the mortuary temple of Ramesses II in Luxor, I was able to ask Kent Weeks about what Gardiner had written. "Is it still true today that what we have is 'rags and tatters,' or do you think that's changed?"

Weeks said, "No, I think that basically is true. What's interesting about the source material from ancient Egypt, though, is that those rags and tatters are more numerous and of a more varied kind than almost any other civilization on the face of the Earth. The remarkable preservative nature of the Egyptian climate has ensured that we have things here that classical archaeologists in Greece or Rome or western Asiatic archaeologists could only dream of. I mean who can imagine – costume, cloth, stone, wood, papyrus, you name it. Every kind of material imaginable has come down to us, not complete, but tantalizing rags and tatters from practically every period over 5,000 years and for practically every part of the country from the Mediterranean south to the First Cataract."

Looking through the columns of the temple into the desert hills, I said, "This climate in some ways is almost the perfect museum, isn't it?"

"Well, it is a perfect museum," he said, "and it's a wonderful thing to have all of this material. But it's also extremely frustrating because it means there's that much more room for argument and doubt."

I wondered what other mysteries might still lie beneath the surface of the land of Egypt, waiting to be found. Would they shed light on the great questions of history such as the Exodus? I probed Weeks. "How much do you think has been uncovered so far? Do you have any guesses?"

Weeks smiled. "I can't even hazard a guess. I know that there is enough material, new material, in Egypt that archaeologists will be kept busy digging for centuries. By the same token, I think there is a lot of material in museums that has not yet been translated, and a lot of material that needs reinterpretation. No, graduate students have nothing to worry about. There are PhD theses galore waiting to be written. We're not going to run out of discussions, arguments, and reexamination of the facts."

Mahoney questions Egyptologist Kent Weeks: "How much do we really know about Egypt's past?"

III. Questioning Egypt's Timeline

Kent Weeks made no indication that he'd be in favor of anything as major as shifting Egypt's history by centuries. But the reality is, any shift of Egypt's timeline would affect more than just Egypt, because the archaeological dates for Canaan and the surrounding region are all dependent on Egypt's history.

Weeks went on, "There are many problems with Egyptian chronology and I think we will all agree that those problems magnify the further back in time we go, but even in more recent periods, late periods of history, there are still some problems. That said, the chronology of Egypt is still a lot better founded than the chronology of most other parts of the ancient Near East, which means, when all is said and done, it's the Egyptian chronology that underpins everything else that's being done throughout the rest of the known world. It's a big responsibility, and it's one of the reasons that people look at it so closely because in terms of reconstructing ancient history, a lot hinges on the answers."

So if Egypt's historical dates are not that certain and possibly need adjusting, then

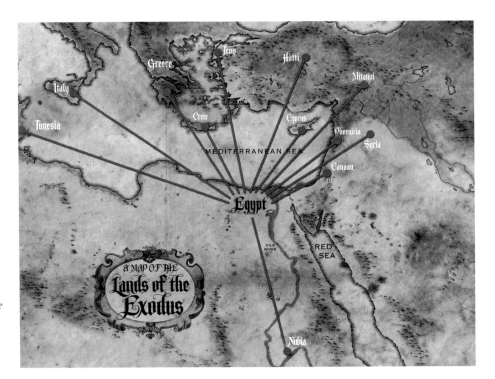

The dates assigned to artifacts in the regions surrounding Egypt are all tied to the Egyptian timeline.

Canaan's history would also require the same kind of shift, because the histories of Egypt and Canaan are connected.

I challenged John Bimson about shifting Egypt's timeline. "A lot of people don't want to do that."

Bimson agreed with me. "Oh no, no, because Egyptian chronology has been assumed to be fixed now for a very long period of time. So the whole idea of taking it apart and starting again is an anathema to most Egyptologists."

I smiled. "Because it would undo a lot of their books, wouldn't it?"

Bimson laughed. "Well, it certainly would, yes."

"Is it just the Bible, or are there other problems with the current reconstruction of Egyptian history?"

Bimson nodded. "There's a whole host of reasons for being skeptical about the current Egyptian chronology. Some of them have to do with Egypt itself, but a lot of them arise from outside Egypt, which a number of people are beginning to look at."

Other good scholars insist that we don't need to change Egypt's timeline in order to see evidence for the Exodus. But if this pattern I'd been seeing really is the Exodus and not just a coincidence, then it would require some kind of major change. Either the Exodus happened long before 1450 BC, or the dates for Egypt's timeline are off.

For an entire year we'd been editing the film around a solid working script. Our editor, Chad Greene, had skillfully organized over a thousand hours of footage, from interviews to scenes of temples and dig sites. His work was a marathon.

In the spring my wife, Jill, and I traveled back to England for her annual board meeting. During the afternoon one of the board members, a longtime friend Kevin O'Neill, and I went for a walk over the fields to the local pub to get some lunch. The sun had just come out as we sat on the patio watching a half-dozen couples, all dressed in white, bowling on the beautifully manicured lawn. I started to share with Kevin how the film was going.

Kevin O'Neill,
Creative Director

"I think we're close to being finished," I said.

"Really! That's fantastic!"

"What we need now is some good branding and a poster."

"Well, you know I would love to help you in any way I can."

I was hoping he would say that. Kevin is a world-class creative director and was always very interested in what I was doing. I had looked forward to perhaps working together someday.

"How would we get started?" I asked.

"I can take your whole group through a creative development process."

"Let me talk with David Wessner, but I think it's something we should do."

As it turned out, Kevin would join our team and develop all the branding-related aspects for *Patterns of Evidence*, including the design and layout of this book.

In August we had a series of test showings to a wide variety of audiences. The film was scoring really high marks across the board. Not just Christians and Jewish people but even agnostics and atheists liked the movie. In one survey 9 out of 10 gave the film a good to excellent rating and would recommend it to their friends. This is what I wanted – a film that could reach a broad audience and have a dialogue with the world.

Most nights I come home from work tired. Sometimes it's the good kind of tired, and sometimes it's the bad kind. This was one of the bad tired nights. On top of the film editing and the showing success, I had been working for nine months writing this book. That evening when I came in the door of our home, my wife of the last 36 years read me like a book.

"What's wrong?"

"I got a phone call from a scholar who's challenging some of the ideas in the film. He wants me to be more careful about the problem with the chronology of Egypt's timeline."

"Really? But you're done with the film. It's made. It's finished!"

"Yes, I told him that, but he believes I should add more material concerning other viewpoints."

"Well, this isn't *his* journey. This is *your* journey, and you have to go where the pattern is strongest. You have to be true to where this investigation has led you."

I nodded as I set my briefcase down and sat on the sofa.

"And how many more viewpoints can you add?"

"I know, but he thinks we're opening ourselves up to attack."

"Everyone you talk to will have a different opinion, and you are not going to be able to please everybody."

She walked over and looked me in the eyes. "You have to be true to the truth of your journey and how it's played out."

"You're right. I don't want to diminish what I believe is a strong pattern."

Jill suggested we take a walk around one of the lakes near our home. It was good just to get some fresh air. As we followed the path along Lake of the Isles, she continued to encourage me.

"You've built this material solidly, so don't worry about it being attacked. Besides, what you're really doing is asking questions. Really good questions."

"You're right, honey. Can I ask you a really good question?"

"Yes."

"How would you like to go out for dinner?"

IV. Shifting Egypt's Timeline

We were not the only ones questioning the chronology of ancient Egypt. In fact, as we looked into this matter, we saw that the debate over the dates of ancient history was growing. While the conclusions of those who supported major adjustments differed in the details, they all agreed that these things were worth investigating, and that chronology wasn't fixed and final. Even when I talked with archaeologists who didn't agree with the need for a major change, they did acknowledge there are problems with the dating. [99]

Researchers like Rohl and Bimson believe the main problem lies in the lesser-known dark periods of Egypt's past. They think scholars have miscalculated their lengths, causing distortions in the dates for everything before them.

The most troublesome part of the timeline is this very long Third Intermediate Period. New information suggests that this dark period has been over-inflated by centuries. If it were shortened, all of Egypt's history before about 700 BC would need to move forward in time.

The Third Intermediate Period (dark period) is seen on the far right. At bottom, Bimson and others assert that the cultures surrounding Egypt have been forced to insert extended dark ages into their histories, in order to align with Egypt's dates.

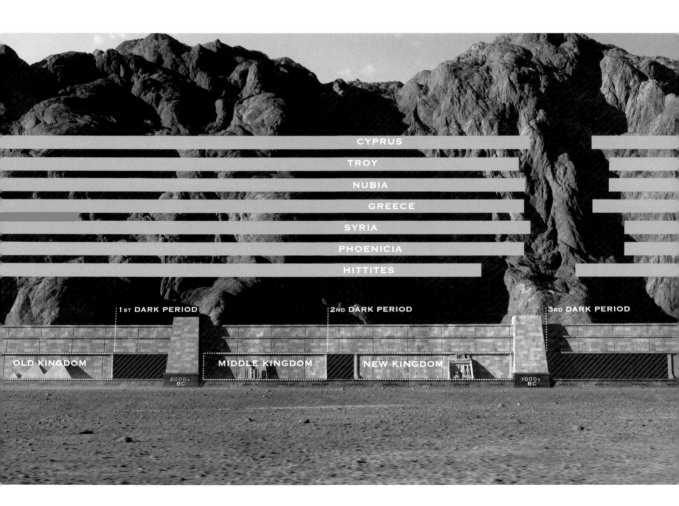

271

Professor John Bimson suggesting there is a serious problem with Egypt's dating system that prevents linking the archaeology of Egypt and Palestine with the events recorded in the Bible.

For many years the giant of Egypt's dating intimidated me. But what made me take a second look was when I learned that it's been necessary to artificially insert dark periods into the timelines of all the surrounding civilizations, so that they match the dates of Egypt's Third Intermediate Period. Yet some scholars maintain that the archaeology of these cultures does not seem to support such dark periods. They believe something is wrong.

This seemed crucial to me, and I asked Bimson about it. "You mean the other civilizations around Egypt, they have been given dark ages as well? Why?"

Bimson nodded. "Those dark ages only exist because of the current reconstruction of the Third Intermediate Period in Egypt. It's the source of a whole host of archaeological conundrums."

"So everything is built upon itself, is that what you are saying?"

"Yes. I guess you could imagine it as a tower of blocks and if some of those blocks at the bottom are out of position, it affects everything on top of them. The 18th, 19th, and 20th Dynasties are dated too early because the Third Intermediate Period is too long."

I thought a moment and then asked, "If the timeline was shifted, would that impact how people see the biblical evidence?"

Gesturing with his hands as if addressing a room of students, Bimson explained, "It would open up a whole new set of possibilities for correlating biblical history with Egyptian history and also with archaeological periods."

"Why is that?"

"Because the archaeological periods in Palestine, in what's called the Late Bronze Age, have the dates they do because of links with Egypt. If you start moving Egyptian history, you start moving Palestine's archaeological history as well."

"So that could bring the Conquest evidence forward in time and allow it to line up with the biblical dates."

"It's opening up a whole new set of possibilities, which a number of people are beginning to look at, and I think this is a very exciting new phase that we're entering for looking afresh at the archaeology and the biblical narrative."

I wondered what Egypt's history might look like if the dark periods were adjusted in a way that some scholars believe the evidence demands. According to Rohl and Bimson, the biggest change would occur in the Third Intermediate Period, a time when Egypt was divided into competing kingdoms that ruled simultaneously. Rohl and Bimson have

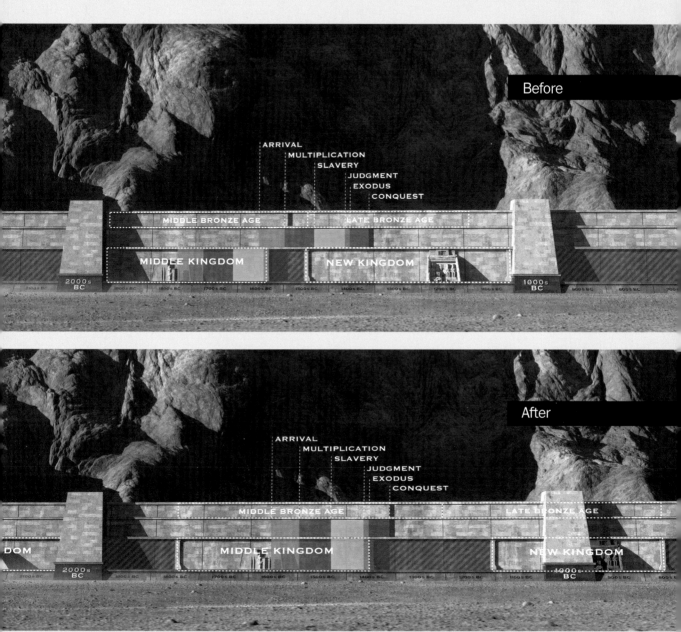

Before: The pattern of evidence in the Middle Kingdom compared to the biblical sequence of a 1450 BC Exodus, before any corrections to Egypt's standard chronology.

After: When Egypt and Canaan's timelines are shifted relative to the Bible's timeline, the biblical sequence comes into alignment with all six steps of the pattern of evidence.

found evidence indicating that these Egyptian dynasties were not sequential but overlapped each other to a much greater extent than previously believed.

If this was the case, the Third Intermediate Period would need to be radically shortened. This adjustment would pull the oldest part of Egypt's timeline – including the Old, Middle, and New Kingdoms – forward in time. It would also shrink the timelines of all the surrounding cultures, including Canaan, because their dating systems are all connected to Egypt.

David Rohl was animated when I talked to him about this time shift. "It's like a domino effect. If one period on the timeline changes, then everything further back in time has to change as well. But what doesn't change, interestingly enough, is the Bible timeline, because that's not affected by it. So if you're changing the Egyptian timeline, you're moving it against the Bible timeline. So all of a sudden, things that were not in the right time period between the two – between the Old Testament and the Egyptian record – are suddenly lining up in a different way. And that's the exciting bit, because that's when we suddenly start to find evidence for the biblical story."

I could see how shrinking this huge dark age pulled everything forward in time, aligning the pattern of evidence found in both Egypt and Canaan with all six steps of the biblical sequence.

I had to remind myself that Rohl was an agnostic. He wasn't telling me this because he was defending his faith. He was excited about the historical evidence for what he believes to be a great document – the oldest account of history in existence.

I asked Rohl one final question. "David, what I've been looking for is a pattern of evidence. How important is the consistency of this pattern?"

Leaning back in his chair, Rohl lifted both of his hands as if he were holding all of time in his grasp. "History is all about patterns of evidence. If you have one piece of evidence in isolation, it's not history. If you can string together a whole sequence of things that are happening that match a story, then you can say that story is no longer a story. It suddenly becomes history."

V. Six-Step Summary and Timeline

It's startling to think how significant this could be, since chronology (the dates assigned to these events) is the thing being used to convince the world that the Bible is just a fairy tale. Throughout this investigation, a pattern of evidence has been uncovered for each step of the story:

- Evidence matching Joseph and the early Israelites' **Arrival** in Egypt,
- Their tremendous **Multiplication**,
- Their descent into **Slavery**,
- The **Judgment** and collapse of Egypt,
- The deliverance and **Exodus** of the Semitic population,
- And finally, in Canaan, evidence matching the **Conquest** of the Promised Land.

I know there's a lot of disagreement over the dating, but what strikes me is that if we put all the dates to the side for a moment, what emerges from the archaeology is this pattern that matches the Bible every step of the way. And doesn't that deserve to be taken seriously?

I'm not sure if shifting Egypt's timeline is the solution, but it certainly is intriguing. However, for now, many who hold to the established chronology of Egyptian history will dismiss these ideas for change. This means the Egyptian and Canaan timelines will have to return to their previous positions on the Wall of Time, and the conventional view will continue to prevent any connection between this amazing pattern of evidence and the biblical Exodus. ⵠ

This depiction of the conventional view recognizes there were overlapping dynasties in the Third Intermediate Period. However, David Rohl and others suggest there is evidence that supports the idea that the overlapping is much greater than is typically believed.

XII: How Did the Problem Get Started?

I. A Curious Problem

In the beginning of this quest I set out to see if a pattern of evidence matching the Bible could be found no matter where it existed. Now a strong pattern has been discovered, and from what I know, it is the only complete pattern there is. It's not fragmented but whole.

The problem is that this pattern is discounted by most scholars because of their commitment to Egypt's conventional timeline. Perhaps of all the ideas to account for the earlier pattern of Exodus evidence, the simplest and best explanation is that the current construction of Egypt's timeline is faulty and needs to be significantly shifted. However, it's hard to change ideas once they've become established. The traditional views of scholarship are strong. Too many people have vested interests in maintaining what has been set up.

But how did these ideas originate in the first place?

To investigate this question, I needed to go back to the beginnings of modern Egyptology, when the chronology of ancient Egypt was first determined by scholars. What I would learn next would only deepen my doubts about the accuracy of Egypt's dating.

The Father of Egyptology Jean-François Champollion was gifted in languages, mastering a dozen by the age of 16.

II. The Early Days of Egyptology

The origins of Egypt's timeline go back to the father of Egyptology, Jean-François Champollion. In 1822, he broke the code of Egyptian hieroglyphics by deciphering the famous Rosetta Stone. This discovery would unlock the mysteries of ancient Egypt, where he traveled to test his new knowledge.

As I remember it, the fall sky was intensely blue the day I went to the Chicago Field Museum. Walking up the front steps from the plaza, I enjoyed seeing the warm sun shining on the tall stone pillars of the museum's entrance. I entered the lobby and made my way to Sue, a giant Tyrannosaurus rex skeleton, the largest and most complete ever found. It was here where Professor Jim Phillips suggested we meet. And who could miss such a rendezvous location as Sue? He led me up the stairs off the main hall to his workroom on the second floor. I wanted to know about the early days of Egyptology, so I asked him, "How did Egyptology begin in the first place?"

Phillips responded, "Egyptology as an academic discipline began certainly in the late 19th century. All of this, of course, was based on the translation by Champollion of a stele or a large black slab found by Napoleon's troops in Egypt near Rosetta in the Nile Delta in the late 18th century – 1799."

"I understand there were three different texts or languages on the stone. And deciphering it was a breakthrough in understanding the secrets of ancient hieroglyphs."

"Yes," he said, as he leaned forward. "The Rosetta Stone was written in Greek, in hieroglyphs, and in Demotic, which is a cursive script of the Egyptian Pharaonic language."

"So Champollion opened the door to the development of Egyptology by deciphering this code of the hieroglyphs?"

"The actual science or academic discipline of Egyptology was based originally on looking at the hieroglyphs and trying to understand the hieroglyphic writing found in the tombs of the Egyptian pharaohs and their wives and their children, such as the tomb of Ramesses II at Luxor. Now, the people who actually began working on this in the late 19th century were, generally speaking, clergymen."

"So they were churchmen?" I asked.

"Many of the original Egyptologists were specifically clergy people who didn't have parishes, actually, but went into academia because they were interested in both Egyptian religion and the study of the writing of language – the study of the graphics of language, the study of why languages were written down the way they are, and more specifically the study of hieroglyphs."

"So were these people the founders of Egyptology?"

"They became professors at major institutions. Many of the people who founded the study of Egyptology were from American universities and western European universities. As time went on in the 20th century, they became interested in pharaonic history – not

The Rosetta Stone was a breakthrough in deciphering ancient Egyptian hieroglyphs.

Rosetta Stone close-up.

necessarily interested in trying to look at the Old Testament, which of course is the basis of Judaism, Christianity, and Islam, and trying to read some of the stories and relationships that mention Egypt and see if there's any reality to those stories. I don't see that happening in Egypt today."

III. The Origins of Egypt's Timeline

I wanted to know more about Jean-François Champollion. It was my understanding that soon after he had decoded the Rosetta Stone he embarked on an expedition to Egypt, eager to read the hieroglyphics on the temples, tombs, and monuments there. One of the things he was searching for was a link between Egypt and the events recorded in the Bible.

At a temple wall in Karnak, Champollion made a discovery that would literally shape history. It happened while he was in the process of examining a relief that recorded the military campaign of a pharaoh called Shoshenq I, who marched an army into the Holy Land. Here, the Frenchman identified the name-rings of cities and places defeated by Shoshenq, many of which seemed to leap off the pages of the Bible.

Egyptologist Salah el-Masekh with Mahoney and David Rohl at Shoshenq I's campaign wall in Karnak.

I had come to Karnak now with David Rohl. The Egyptian Egyptologist Salah el-Masekh was excavating in Karnak at this time. He had discovered some fantastic Roman-style baths from the Ptolemaic Period. Rohl and I met up with el-Masekh and walked to the wall reliefs of the temple. We were standing exactly where Champollion would have stood nearly 200 years earlier. There was a mystery here, and I hoped we could solve it. I turned to the two Egyptologists. "So this wall is a record of the victories of this pharaoh?"

"Yes." said el-Masekh. He pointed to images of enemy name rings. "We can see here the victims and the enemies in the front of the main god, or the king of the gods, Amun."

Rohl agreed. "If you look at the fists of Amun, he's dragging by rope these figures, which are representing the different cities and locations in the North."

"What is the story being told here?" I asked.

"The captives are being brought for the smiting scene here, where the individuals are being clubbed to death by the pharaoh. So basically, these names here are all the names of the cities and places in the north where this pharaoh went on his victorious campaign."

"So what made Champollion so interested in this inscription?"

Rohl looked from the wall to me. "Well, Champollion believed he had found the major link between Egypt and the Bible that he had been searching for."

"How did he make that connection?"

"Champollion remembered that, long after the Exodus, the biblical books of Kings and Chronicles record that following the death of King Solomon there was much strife in the nation of Israel."

"Yes, didn't the nation split?"

"It did. The land was divided in two – the northern kingdom of Israel and the southern kingdom of Judah, with its capital at Jerusalem. Judah fortified 15 strongholds in anticipation of an attack. That attack came from the Egyptian pharaoh Shishak at the head of a mighty army."

A closer look at this account in the Bible revealed a dramatic story. During the reign of King Solomon of Israel an official named Jeroboam rebelled against the king and was forced to flee for his life to Egypt where a pharaoh named Shishak gave him safe refuge. After the death of Solomon, Jeroboam returned to Israel, and there was strife between Solomon's son Rehoboam and the northern tribes of Israel. When the kingdom split in two, Rehoboam was left with the two tribes to rule in the southern kingdom of Judah, whose capital was Jerusalem. Jeroboam became the king of the northern kingdom of

Shoshenq I

Pharaoh Shoshenq I was the founder of Egypt's 22nd Dynasty. Since he is linked to the Shishak account in the Bible, he is conventionally dated to 943-922 BC

279

Israel, which contained ten tribes.

There was war between Israel and Judah throughout the reigns of Jeroboam and Rehoboam. In the southern kingdom of Judah, Rehoboam fortified a string of cities in preparation for the attack he knew was coming. In the fifth year of Rehoboam's reign, Pharaoh Shishak – the one who had helped Jeroboam – came up and attacked Judah with a huge army. He captured Judah's fortified cities, but the text says that as he approached Jerusalem, its leaders humbled themselves so that the Lord granted that they would not be destroyed. Pharaoh Shishak was content to sack the city, and he seized all the great treasures of Solomon's Temple to bring back to Egypt. [100]

I turned to Rohl and asked, "So this was the story that Champollion believed he had found depicted on the walls of Karnak, correct?"

"Yes, it was. But if we look at those three rows up there, the top rows, we have the third row down. You see the third figure from the right?"

"I do. It's an enemy name ring." The wall before me was lined with rows of defeated peoples.

"Do you see the name there?"

I nodded.

"When Champollion came to Egypt for the very first time in the 1820s, he read that name there as 'Judah the kingdom.' So he thought that this was proof of the biblical story of Shishak coming and taking the treasure from Jerusalem."

"What effect did this have?" I asked.

"Ever since he read this inscription and suggested that this was Shishak's invasion of Judah, his interpretation has become one of the foundations for the chronology of Egypt."

So this was where the conventional view of Egypt's timeline had begun. In England I asked Professor Bimson about Champollion's finding. "This connection between the biblical Shishak and the Egyptian Shoshenq, was it pivotal?"

"The chronology of that period has been constructed with that identification always in mind," Bimson said with a serious look. "It's become a tie around which a whole load of other stuff has been reconstructed."

IV. Taking a Closer Look

The connection seemed obvious. The two names of the pharaohs were remarkably similar – Shishak mentioned in the Bible, and Shoshenq the name recorded on the wall at Karnak. Both led a military campaign into the Holy Land, and both seemingly defeated the kingdom of Judah because Champollion had read the name "Judah" as one of the enemies defeated by Shoshenq I. But were they really the same pharaoh?

Bimson lowered his voice. "The problems emerge when you start to look at the details."

At Karnak I continued to question Rohl. "What was so critical about this story?"

"Well, this is the weird thing people today don't realize. The Bible was used to date the Egyptian Pharaoh Shoshenq I to the time of 925 BC. That's the biblical date."

"I find it hard to believe it actually happened that way."

"I am telling you that the whole edifice of Egyptian chronology is hooked onto that

The list of cities (numbered in black) defeated on Shoshenq I's campaign wall, shows that he did not defeat Jerusalem or the 15 fortified cities (lettered in red) mentioned in the Bible as being defeated by Shishak. Instead, Shoshenq avoided Judah and attacked Israel.

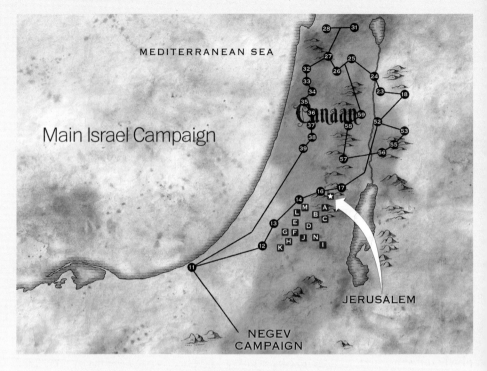

Biblical Account

A	Bethlehem
B	Etam
C	Tekoa
D	Beth-Zur
E	Soco
E	Adullam
G	Moresheth-Gath
H	Maresha
I	Ziph
J	Adoraim
K	Lachish
L	Azekah
M	Zorah
14	Aijalon
N	Hebron

Egyptian Account

01-09	Nine Bows	**25**	Shunem	**47**	Bethsabu[ma]
10	"List [of the towns...]*"	**26**	Tanaach	**48-51**	[Lost]
11	G[aza]	**27**	Megiddo	**52**	Abel[meholah?]
12	Makkedah	**28**	Adar	**53**	[P]enuel
13	Rubuti	**29**	Yachamelek	**54**	Hedeshet
14	Aijalon	**30**	[Heb]el?	**55**	Succoth?
15	Kiriathaim?	**31**	Honim	**56**	Adam[ah]
16	Bethhoron	**32**	Aruna	**57**	Zemaraim
17	Gibeon	**33**	Borim	**58**	[M]igdol (Shechem?)
18	Mahanaim	**34**	Gathpadalla	**59**	[Ti]razah
19	Shaud[y]	**35**	Yahma	**60**	[...]nar
20	[Lost]	**36**	Betharuma	**61-63**	[Lost]
21	Adoraim	**37**	Kekry	**64**	H[...]pen
22	Hapharaim	**38**	Socoh	**65**	Pa-Emek ("The Vale")
23	Rehob	**39**	Bethtappuah		
24	Bethshan	**40-46**	[Lost]		

one link. The Shishak/Shoshenq link is the lynch pin on which all the other dates are dependent."

If Shoshenq really was the Shishak of the Bible, then dating him to around the time of Solomon's death would make sense.

"Why is that a problem?"

"Well, significant questions arise when you try to connect this Shoshenq with the pharaoh of the Bible, Shishak, who plundered the Temple of Solomon."

"What type of questions?"

Rohl pointed to one of the enemy name rings on the wall. "The initial mistake occurred when Champollion incorrectly read one of the name rings in Shoshenq's campaign list. He read that name there *Iouda-ha-malek*. He thought it meant 'Judah the kingdom.' He believed that to be the story from the Bible. And a very important connection."

"Was it not?"

"Well, since then, we've managed to reread that heiroglyph in a different way. We now read it as *Yad-ha-melek,* which means 'hand of the king.' It means something completely different. And it's close to all the places like Megiddo and Taanach and Aruna. Now they're all in the Jezreel Valley, much further north than Jerusalem. So, this can't be Judah because it's too far north."

"So there really wasn't a connection?"

"There wasn't. Champollion got it wrong. But remember he had just started to use hieroglyphics and scholars have learned much more about the language since that time."

Rohl had more to say. "There is also a serious question about the target of the military campaign depicted on the wall. In the Bible, Shishak attacks the kingdom of Judah in the south and he takes the treasure from the Temple in Jerusalem. The golden shields are taken back to Egypt. So it's the south that's attacked by Shishak."

"What's different about this Egyptian wall inscription?"

"On the wall inscription, it's the northern kingdom of Israel that's attacked by Shoshenq. He goes up to the Jezreel Valley. He goes up to Megiddo. He goes into the Jordan Valley. He's not going to the southern kingdom of Judah. He's missing Judah. There's no Judah in here."

"And that is very different from the Bible's story." I was starting to understand.

Rohl continued, "In the Bible, Shishak is attacking Judah and not attacking the

Salah el-Masekh making the point that many of the name rings on Shoshenq's wall contain unknown locations.

north. The Egyptian Pharaoh Shoshenq on this wall inscription is attacking the north and not attacking Judah. It's the opposite."

El-Masekh had been patiently listening to the conversation. I knew he accepted the conventional view that Shishak and Shoshenq were the same person, and wasn't convinced by Rohl's reasoning.

I turned to him. "So Salah, what do you think is the story here?"

"Shoshenq mentions all the cities won by his hand," el-Masekh replied. "We have more than 180 names of the cities. If we compare names from our list with these names on the wall from the archaeological sites, we know only 50 names of these cities – only 50 names."

Rohl added, "So what you mean is that two-thirds of these cities are unknown to us. We don't know where they are?"

"Yes," said el-Masekh. "Only one-third we actually have the records for. The rest of them, we just don't know where they are – if they are in Judah or not."

"What do you make of that point?" I asked Rohl.

He was shaking his head in disagreement with el-Masekh's argument. "The point is that we *do* know the names of the fortified towns in Judah that Shishak *did* capture according to 2 Chronicles 12 – because they are listed in 2 Chronicles 11. And only one of them appears in Shoshenq's list – the town of Aijalon, located on Judah's border and on the route over into the Jordan Valley. So Shoshenq did not capture Rehoboam's fortified towns of Judah as the Bible states.

"Moreover, Jerusalem is not listed amongst Shoshenq's subjugated cities – and yet Jerusalem was the main target of Shishak's campaign! The story in the Bible is about the pharaoh going and taking the gold away from the Temple and from the palace, and bringing it back to Egypt. But Jerusalem is not here on this inscription. Of all these names here, it's missing. It should actually be up there in the second row, about the fourth of the rings along. But it's actually not there."

I thought for a minute. "So all of the cities here are listed in geographic order? They are in groups, and Jerusalem is not mentioned in its geographical grouping?"

"Correct. We have Gibeon mentioned and Mahanaim, and Jerusalem should be between those two. And it's perfectly clear. It's not destroyed. Yet it is simply not there!"

I had to agree. If Shoshenq is one and the same as Shishak, why did he fail to mention the chief target of his campaign? Would the plundering of Solomon's famous treasure from the Temple not merit a mention in the Shoshenq list?

When I asked Bimson, he said, "There's no doubt, any pharaoh would have mentioned it. If Jerusalem had capitulated, it would be in the list. As the capital city, it would have deserved mention."

"People should look at this for what it really means," I said thoughtfully.

Bimson agreed. "If Shoshenq I is not the biblical Shishak then that undoes one of the lynch pins of conventional Egyptian chronology. And if that tie is dismantled, then it becomes very plausible to reconstruct Egyptian chronology on a very different basis."

I asked David Rohl, "In your opinion what's the bottom line?"

"I think what's happened here is, we've got a mix-up because the names are so similar – Shoshenq and Shishak. They sound the same. So Champollion in a way was justified to think that Shoshenq and Shishak are the same. But the problem is the campaigns are different. I don't think Shoshenq is the same as the biblical Shishak. I think it's a different ruler from a different time because of the contradictions in the inscription," said Rohl.

"And what does that mean in terms of relating the Bible's history to Egypt?"

"Early Egyptologists used the Bible to date an Egyptian pharaoh, which in fact formed the foundation for Egyptian history. So the Bible was used to date Egyptian history, and then somehow or another, Egyptian history today is used to deny the biblical story. I think that's just ridiculous."

I was fascinated by this whole account of how Egypt's conventional dating system had gotten started. Originally, Champollion leapt to the Shoshenq = Shishak connection because he believed he had three solid pieces of evidence. But today we can see that the basis for that connection was flimsy at best and the only factor that remains to support the claim that the two pharaohs are the same is the similarity of the two names. Not long after Champollion's interpretation, it was found that the word "Judah" (the target of Shishak's campaign in the Bible) was actually not mentioned on the campaign wall of Shoshenq I at Karnak. Additionally, the campaign listed on the wall does not really fit the story of Shishak in the Bible. In fact, it's the opposite. The biblical Shishak came to the aid of Israel, its ally, by capturing all of Judah's fortified cities and sacking Jerusalem. Shoshenq's wall has the pharaoh attacking Israel and avoiding Judah and its capital, Jerusalem.

However, modern scholarship has never gone back to reexamine the foundations of the current timeline. They have just continued to build on the old assumptions they have inherited.

V. Reevaluating a Basic Assumption

If Pharaoh Shoshenq is not the biblical Shishak, that fact would remove a foundational anchor point for all of Egyptian chronology and challenge the basic assumption that 1450 BC must be in the New Kingdom. Could it really be somewhere else, perhaps at the end of the Middle Kingdom?

This possibility seemed to have considerable potency.

When I talked with Professor Hoffmeier about the need to reexamine Egypt's dating, he was suspicious of the motives of someone wanting to revise the conventional timeline. He said, "If a person is revising chronology because they want to fit a particular theory, I find that very suspect. People often want to revise chronology because they want things to fit a particular theory they have about the way things ought to be. And I'm a bit skeptical of that kind of motivation."

I agree with Hoffmeier's point. We do need to be careful not to go against the status quo just because we want a theory to be true. As Hoffmeier has said, "Very good, very competent historians have been working for decades and decades on Egyptian chronology and Near Eastern chronology." I'm sure they have reasons to support the status quo.

"The public can judge if you are a scientific man."
– Mansour Boraik

However, the argument that almost all scholars follow the conventional view, is something I have heard over and over again. Is this an appeal to authority and not an appeal to facts and evidence?

The fact is, Champollion revised the thinking of his day regarding Egypt's history in order to fit his theory that Shishak and Shoshenq I were the same pharaoh. Standing on Champollion's assumption were the founders of Egyptology. Upon their shoulders stood the great scholars of the 20th century. And upon their shoulders are the scholars of today.

But what about Champollion's basic assumption? Haven't crucial facts for that assumption been proven inaccurate? If so, a truly scientific approach would follow the evidence wherever it leads. Perhaps after a rigorous reexamination, the standard timeline would still be found to be correct. But an objective approach should not be intimidated by the majority view; that approach should concern itself with the evidence.

This brings me back to Ze'ev Herzog, the Israeli archaeologist who said that "the Exodus story is a legendary compilation about the people of Israel, but it has no real historical basis." When I'd asked him what caused him to take that position, he said that early in his career he and his colleagues had "considered the biblical stories as historical events." But after trying to do their best to see the evidence as fitting the stories, the accumulation of data contrary to the early history in the Bible finally made them stop and come to a new realization – the Bible's account is not real history.

But there is a question I now feel is fair to ask scholars like Ze'ev Herzog. Could it be that they came to their negative conclusions because they were standing on the shoulders of a faulty assumption? If that assumption created an inaccurate timeline, then perhaps it prevented them from seeing evidence for the Exodus and Conquest that has been in plain sight all along.

VI. Conclusion

I'm not an Egyptologist; I'm a filmmaker. And I'm not endorsing any one particular dating theory out there. I'm just searching for the truth. Because isn't that what the pursuit of both science and faith should be – a search for truth?

For me, it's been a 12-year journey that at first challenged me with great doubts. I've met a number of amazing people and have explored places I never dreamed of visiting. Today I can say it's been worth the effort. I have answered some questions, but there is still so much more to explore.

When I thought about how to wrap up this journey, I remembered the advice given to me by Egyptologist Mansour Boraik as we stood in the hall of the mortuary temple at Luxor. He laid out the basis for how my investigation should be judged. He said, "At the end, the audience – the people themselves – they will judge. They will know. The public can judge if you are a scientific man, with a logical theory, or if you are exaggerating, or if you have some story from your own mind."

Now you can judge for yourself. Are these findings illogical? Are they just an exaggeration? Or is looking for the Exodus at the earlier date the key step in bringing the Bible out of the shadows of myth and into the light of true history?

It's something to think about.

VII. Epilogue

After the Israelites left Egypt, it was written that they miraculously crossed a mighty sea and traveled on to Mount Sinai where they received the Ten Commandments and built the Tabernacle with the Ark of the Covenant. No trace of their journey has ever been found – or has it? If there really was an Exodus, then the mountain was somewhere out there. I had heard fascinating reports from Exodus explorers who claimed they had found new evidence for Mount Sinai and the sea crossing. But again, they were stirring up controversy. I could see that my journey was not over. It was about to get more interesting.

The Gulf of Aqaba, one of the candidates for the lost sea of the Exodus.

ACKNOWLEDGEMENTS

Once you have worked on a project as comprehensive as *Patterns of Evidence: The Exodus,* you realize that no one does this alone. This book tells the story of creating a film, and many people have helped to make both the film and the book realities. Here are some of those I would like to acknowledge.

My wife, Jill, thank you for all the patience that you've shown from the very first time we met in 1977 when I asked if you'd like to run an errand to a film lab. I am grateful for your patience as you have endured so many late nights, missed dinners, long distance trips, and risk-taking adventures. You are the one who believed, you are my encourager, you are my best friend.

My children, thank you for going to all the film conferences on our vacations. I love you all dearly and hope I have set a good example for you to search for truth, to live kindly, find your purpose, and pursue it with no regrets.

David Wessner, thank you for your vision and trust. Without you it's very probable that this project would never have happened. I'm glad I wasn't the only one who was interested in this journey of investigating the Bible's historical reality. You are one of my closest friends, a fellow steel guitar and Dobro player, and the one who gave me the creative freedom I needed to lead and direct this project.

David was a visionary leader in the health industry, running a hospital network in Minnesota. David is the Executive Producer, and it was through his family's help and eventually through the help of others that I was able to pursue this project.

Peter Windahl, thank you for being a loyal, true, and faithful friend. I appreciate your positive attitude and your tremendous ability to resource anything. When you heard about the film investigation, you left your job to join the team. You always wanted to be an archaeologist and little did you realize you'd manage a massive film project all about archaeology.

Pete and I were both on the high school ski jumping team in Minnesota. Pete plays two roles. He is Co-Producer for *Patterns of Evidence: The Exodus* and is also the Chief Manager for the initiative. Forty years later, here we are still taking flying leaps into the unknown.

Steven Law, thank you for taking a risk, bringing your family back to Minnesota from another state with no guarantees, no job, just because you wanted to be a part of this project. You are a valuable part of our writing team. Your thorough research and logical approach has actually made me look intelligent at times. I trust you and appreciate how you support my creative vision.

Steve is our researcher and my co-writer on the project. He didn't ski jump but was a competitive cross-country skier and coach.

Chad Greene, thank you for pursuing creative excellence in editing and graphics. But also thank you for being so organized. Despite the massive amount of material we have collected, you know where it is and have created the systems to use it effectively. You have supported, improved, and guided the film through the editing and finishing phases and onto the screen.

Chad is head of post production for Thinking Man Films and the primary film editor.

Diane Walker, thank you for being courageous with the realities of finances and the lack of them. Many times throughout this project you dug in, set and tracked budgets, and made the best of the situation. You took care of business and you took care of our vendors: film crews, museums, and interviewees around the world.

Diane performs two roles: Co-Producer of the film and Business Manager for Thinking Man Films.

Matt Pankratz, thank you for taking on all the other production duties in editing. And thank you for supporting Chad whenever and with whatever he needed.

Matt works as a film editor and graphic designer.

Crystal Mahoney, thank you for keeping us cheered up and for getting all the supplies and shipping handled. Thank you, too, for being a strong supporter of me, your brother.

Crystal serves as a member of our administrative support staff.

291

Lisa Batdorf, thank you for helping Diane with accounting and Pete with everything else. You managed to do a lot.

Lisa served as a member of our administrative support staff.

Chris Ray, thank you for coming in as the production manager on the last lap and making sure the post production – including an enormous amount of animations – was completed on time and with excellence.

Chris is the post production manager on the project.

Kim Dulas, thank you for being my right-hand producer on so many projects. You helped bring many of the re-creations together and have always been there for our team.

Kim is our USA field producer.

John Burch, thank you for excellence in cinematography and lighting. You gave many scenes an international production quality that matched the tone of those filmed in other parts of the world.

John is one of our primary cinematographers.

Dorian Vandegrift and C.J. Olsen, thank you for taking on this massive project. Dorian, you've always had a positive attitude. You said, "Yes," even when we weren't sure how. That didn't stop you from trying. And C.J., you figured out how to make amazing city and plague effects beyond anything I thought we could do. You both helped all of us visualize this ancient world and brought cities like Avaris, Jericho, and Shechem to life. I knew that if people didn't see the locations referenced in the biblical stories, it would be very difficult for them to understand them or to consider the possibility that they might have existed. You also helped us communicate complex concepts by building the Wall of Time that educates and guides the viewer through the film. You both have made some of the biggest contributions to this project. I couldn't have done this without your talents. Your images can be viewed throughout this book.

Dorian and C.J. are the lead animators for the film and supplied all the animated re-creations for the book.

Michael Medved, thank you for believing in the project and for participating in the numerous efforts to refine the language and approach of the story. Thank you for your input and your patience.

Michael was the narrator for earlier versions of the film, and is also a content advisor.

Kevin Sorbo, thank you for bringing your great baritone voice and acting talents to the film. It was a pleasure to work with you, and I hope to see you again back in Minnesota when the ice leaves Lake Minnetonka.

Kevin is the narrator of the final version of the film.

Bart Gavigan, thank you for suggesting that my voice be the one to tell the story in the film. You planted the idea in my mind that "having a conversation with the world" was the best way to communicate my journey. You guided our team creatively in the early stages. Thank you for introducing us to composer Jonathan David Neal and the Budapest Film Orchestra who performed many of the themes in our soundtrack.

Bart is a creative and script advisor.

Rick Garside, thank you for being my first producer when I traveled to Egypt and England. You managed our team and took photos. You have encouraged me for over a decade as I wandered through the filmmaking and storytelling process.

Rick was our overseas and LA producer.

Jonathan Neal, *Rob Barrett*, *and David Rohl*, thank you for a wonderful collaborative body of music that has set a unique tone for the film. This music is now a part of the ethos of the project. It brings the audience along in the storytelling process, delivering themes of the ancient past, themes of the journey, themes of questioning and despair, and themes portraying the grandeur of the biblical narrative. The music is international in scope, at times epic in nature and at other times gently inspiring. It has motivated me as I have worked on the writing of this book.

Jonathan, Rob, and David are the main composers for the film.

Kevin O'Neill, thank you for your friendship, your positive attitude, and your constant willingness to tackle the difficult tasks. Your talent to take complex ideas and make them into something visually wonderful has completed the storytelling process and brought the book and the film to another level of excellence. Your art direction can be seen throughout the pages of this book.

Kevin is in charge of all branding, art direction, and web development for the project.

Grace Kosloski, thank you for jumping into the thick of the writing process, assisting Steve and me as we worked out the poetry and prose of this book. Your editing and organizing freed us to focus on telling the story. Your positive and supportive help was essential as we expanded the film script into the manuscript for the book.

Grace is the editor for the book.

Karen Fullerton, thank you for helping us review the manuscript. Your ideas were welcomed and your understanding of the audience respected. Your feedback has made this a better product.

Karen Fullerton is a writer and a publicist for Thinking Man Films.

Scott, Ruth, Rick, Doneetsa, Mark, Colleen, Madan, and Brett, thank you for your encouragement every week. Your support has been enormous to our team.

These people are friends of the project.

To all the Scholars, Archaeologists, and Participants, thank you for giving me the time to interview you and for sharing your research, your opinions, and your findings. The film and the book are based upon my interpretation and editing of your contributions. If I didn't have them, then this would be a very short story. I hope that this project is a platform that introduces you and your work to new people, allowing them to understand your ideas. Let's keep the dialogue going.

BONUS CHAPTER A:
A CONVERSATION WITH
DAVID ROHL

The ideas and research of David Rohl have played an important part in the debate over the Egyptian timeline and its relation to the events of the Bible. And, indeed, his work has contributed significantly to the new direction *Patterns of Evidence: The Exodus* took after a series of interviews with him. However, David's initial approach was not to start with the Bible and then look to see if there was a fit to be found somewhere in Egypt's history. That was the approach taken by my team during the film's investigation, but David had begun his research decades earlier and had come to his conclusions about the timeline of ancient history from a purely Egyptological standpoint.

David Rohl regards himself as an agnostic, initially with little interest in the biblical text. His passion, from early childhood, has always been focused on the extraordinary civilization of the pharaohs. Back in the 1970s he began to realize that there were disturbing anomalies in the Egyptian dating system when he first read the important book by Kenneth Kitchen entitled *The Third Intermediate Period in Egypt* (published in 1973). He told me how he studied that little blue book, crammed with chronological data for the 21st to 25th Egyptian dynasties, and began the process of trying to work out an alternative chronology, which solved the problems that he saw in Kitchen's reconstruction of the Third Intermediate Period. He felt strongly that the only solution was to propose a shorter chronology for Egypt, lowering the dates of the New Kingdom by around three centuries. Only then did he look to see if his revision of the Egyptian timeline provided fresh links with the Bible. What he found amazed him, and that same set of discoveries has subsequently led my team to confirm, at least to our satisfaction, a pattern of evidence in the Egyptian records and the archaeology of the Holy Land that appears to match the biblical account.

In my numerous interviews with David Rohl, I gained more insight into his controversial and often misunderstood theories. If you have seen the film, you will know that he was a key interviewee. Here is more from the conversations I had with David Rohl.

Mahoney: Who is David Rohl?

Rohl: David Rohl is an Egyptologist and an ancient historian – a trained scholar with the proper degrees in his subject – but also a bit of a maverick, as some might say. I came to university with a lot of ideas, which I developed over decades of studying ancient Egypt, and gradually laid them before the professors, who responded in a very positive way. I was presenting these ideas at postgraduate seminars, even in my first year as an undergraduate student! So I had a great time in the scholarly environment of University College London and, upon graduation, was recruited as a tutor in the History Department. So I got on very well with both my tutors and fellow students. But the problem that I have subsequently had is with the scholars who don't know me as an individual who, without that interaction, tend to think of me as a rebel because I have dared to question established orthodoxy.

Mahoney: Yes, I have gotten that reaction when I've asked scholars about your New Chronology.

Rohl: Correct. I'm now in a situation where I am suggesting some revolutionary new ideas to resolve some of the most tenacious problems of Old Testament history and archaeology, and those academics who don't know me are resisting those ideas very strongly. They just don't want me to upset the apple cart or rock the boat as it were. So I'm fighting for a new way of thinking and I'm getting the cold shoulder from some academic quarters because my ideas are just too revolutionary for them. If I had kept my head below the parapet and just nibbled at the Orthodox Chronology, I might have been more acceptable to my peers, but because I am trying to change things in a dramatic way – not by just simply pushing the envelope slightly – I now have this rebel, non-conformist label, which I have to say I wear with some pride! I have always wanted to go beyond the envelope and take us all to a completely new way of thinking.

Mahoney: And yet your hypothesis has been pretty successful outside academia and has become popular with ordinary people. Tell me the story of how that came about.

Rohl: Even before I went to university, like-minded scholars and colleagues had this sort of debating situation going on, and people were coming up with all sorts of ideas as to how we might revise the timeline of ancient history to solve the anomalies. This is how the New Chronology, as we call it, was born – and it is still forever evolving. Nothing is set in stone as new discoveries are coming to light all the time. I then took this new approach to university and got the postgraduate students of Egyptology involved in testing it all out. These guys were a bunch of very clever people, who have gone on to become the new generation of Egyptologists within UK academia. Discussing and debating the timeline of history with those students and post-grads, with the professors often joining in, was a great experience and provided the knowledge to fine-tune the New Chronology theory to the degree that, somewhat ironically, it became even more of a threat to the establishment. The New Chronology theory could not simply be ignored as the ravings of an amateur historian because it had undergone a rigorous testing within scholarly circles, and its principal proponent – me – had learnt the tools of academia to put up a viable case for its consideration as an alternative to the Orthodox Chronology.

Mahoney: What happened to you though? Why did you suddenly leave the university and give up your PhD research?

Rohl: Well, it was rather amazing actually and certainly not anticipated. In my second year of postgraduate studies, I was asked by the Egypt Exploration Society to present my New Chronology theory at a public lecture in London. Unbeknownst to me, sitting in the audience was a literary agent, who came to me at the end of the lecture and said, "Do you mind if I represent you?" So I signed a contract with him a couple of weeks later and within a month I was over in Washington signing a TV deal with Discovery Channel, and doing the same in England with Channel Four, to make the three-part documentary series *Pharaohs and Kings*. Book contracts were flying at me as well, as different UK publishers vied for the rights to publish the book of the TV series. That book, entitled *A Test of Time* in the UK and *Pharaohs and Kings* in the USA, ended up sitting at number two in the *Sunday Times* Best Seller List for eight weeks. So I ended up being dragged away from university to write popular books and do various TV series about my research. And unfortunately in that situation you can never go back to do your PhD afterwards.

Mahoney: Why was that?

Rohl: Well, one of the rules of University College London is that you're not allowed to pre-publish your thesis. Only ten percent can be in the public domain prior to submission of the PhD dissertation. In my case, of course, it was on television all over the world and already published in a best-selling book. So I simply couldn't go back to finish the PhD thesis on that basis.

Mahoney: So your sudden success had been both a good and a negative thing.
Rohl: Absolutely. It just sort of happened, and I found myself in quite a dilemma – either start again with a new PhD topic and live off a very low assistant tutor's salary, or accept the six-figure advances being offered for follow-up books, as well as for further TV series. Actually, it wasn't much of a dilemma as I am sure you realize – just a matter of common sense. But there was another motive, which was basically the realization (due to the popularity of both the TV series and book) that I had to take this directly to the people, to see how the world would react to this big new idea.

Mahoney: And how have they reacted?
Rohl: Fantastically well. The ordinary members of the public love it, because they can see the satisfying truth of it.

Mahoney: What do other archaeologists say to you about your ideas?
Rohl: Well, to my face not very much. Okay. Many are not specialists in chronology so they tend to ignore the New Chronology in the hope that it will simply disappear and not disturb their existing world of accepted wisdom. On the other hand, there are a few whose careers have been built on the Orthodox Chronology, and they have been quite vociferous – especially in the 1990s when the book and TV series came out. So in reviews and in written works, of course, they criticized it heavily. It's all quieted down now, since these defenders of the old chronology think they have succeeded in quashing the revolution. Now it's a matter of starving the thesis of the oxygen of publicity. They think that if they don't write about it, if they don't talk about it, it might go away. But it's not going away because your film is going to re-ignite the debate and bring it to an even bigger audience.

Mahoney: When did it dawn on you that you could actually question the standard chronology for Egypt?

Rohl: As I said earlier, I suppose the first point was when I was studying the Third Inter-mediate Period in Egypt, which is the era at the end of the New Kingdom, when the great pharaohs like Ramesses II were all dead and gone. Egypt fell into a period of decline – a very severe decline for several centuries. This was an era I was fascinated by, because it was so complicated and interesting – and there were so many questions to be answered. I just wanted to dive in there and get to work on it. Somewhat ironically, I was inspired by my chief critic, Professor Kenneth Kitchen, who published his wonderful book in the early '70s, entirely dedicated to a detailed analysis of the Third Intermediate Period in Egypt. For the very first time a scholar had put all the data from this quagmire of history into a single volume for researchers to get their teeth into. That was like ten birthdays coming all at once for someone like me!

Mahoney: What was it in that book that you found so interesting?

Rohl: The contents were like a giant chronological jigsaw puzzle. I loved moving dates around and looking at how bits of evidence might work and synchronize with each other in different ways. And that was my challenge – to look at that material and try to create a timeline that removed the majority of the anomalies. As you can see, all this had nothing to do with the Bible at all. This was pure Egyptological material that I was dealing with.

So here I am looking at this great pile of material and finding all sorts of problems with the way the timeline had been constructed – how the dynasties were working – or not working – within Kitchen's chronology of this particular period – from around 1069 BC down to 664 BC. That's the era of the 21st to 25th Dynasties following the end of the New Kingdom empire period. And I found that it could be shorter. It looked like the timeline could be compressed by well over a century in this period. And the result of that was that everything before the Third Intermediate Period had to be lowered. All the dynasties before the 21st Dynasty must come down in time. It's like if you remove rows of bricks in a wall, so that all the rows above have to drop down (come later in time) in order to fill the gap.

Now that is a fascinating thing because, if the chronology of Egypt is lowered, then the archaeological levels in Israel also come down. Why? Because in the Holy Land – if you go to the site of Megiddo, for instance – you might find an object like a statue or a scarab (a little seal), with the name of Ramesses II carved on it. That dates the stratum or level at the site to the time of the 19th Dynasty in the New Kingdom. So if you're lowering the dates of Ramesses II by centuries, then the levels in the ruin-mounds of Israel containing Ramesses II inscriptions – for instance at Megiddo and Hazor – are also lowering as well. This changes the whole ball game in terms of the archaeology of the Holy Land compared to the timeline of the Bible, which is independent of both the Egyptian chronology and the archaeology of the region.

Mahoney: So basically your Egyptological research impacts the Bible. In other words, if you can get Ramesses' dates right, then it will help you get things in Israel right as well.
Rohl: That's right. It's like a domino effect. If one thing changes down in the later time period, everything above or earlier than that has to change as well. And that has led to a whole new phase of research, introducing the key question as to whether the Bible itself is historical. Can we actually find evidence in archaeology for the biblical stories? And that's what I set out to do in the 1980s.

Mahoney: But then you have archaeologists like Ze'ev Herzog, who says the Old Testament stories never happened. It was all just made up.
Rohl: Yes. Well, there are two classic quotations. Professor Bill Dever (an American archaeologist) famously stated that "Joshua destroyed a city that wasn't even there" because Jericho had long been an abandoned ruin by the time of Ramesses II – the so-called Pharaoh of the Exodus. Then the Israeli professor Ze'ev Herzog said that the Exodus was "a history that never happened." Again, because the accepted timeline is wrong.

Mahoney: So the entire understanding or even belief system in a book can be denied –
Rohl: – by a single mistake of chronology.

Mahoney: Fascinating. So what are you proposing?
Rohl: My whole thesis is that we have to look for the Israelite sojourn and slavery in Egypt and the subsequent Exodus from Egypt in a much earlier time period than is normally considered. Most Egyptologists would place the Exodus in the 19th Dynasty. I, on the other hand, would place it at the end of the 13th Dynasty, when we have the archaeological evidence to match the story. The Ramesses Exodus theorists have no archaeological evidence to match the story in the 19th Dynasty. So, many of the non-

religious or secular scholars then say the story must be fictional. They say the epic events of Exodus didn't really happen. Can you see the circularity in this position? Using the reference to the store-city of Ramesses in the Bible as your starting point, you place Exodus in the wrong time (the time of Ramesses II) when there is no evidence, and then you argue it never happened (that the Exodus is a myth) because there is no evidence! What a weird way to do history.

Mahoney: Well, the Exodus is such a significant event in biblical history, and the impact of it has shaped Western civilization. What events in Egyptian history are so sacred that they can't adapt to the Exodus evidence?

Rohl: The sacred cow of Egyptology is its chronology – its timeline. You cannot dare change it. That's the problem we're up against here. Just let's suggest for a moment that we've got the timeline wrong, and what we should be doing is revising that timeline – shortening it by say around three centuries, something like that. And all of the sudden the archaeological evidence in Egypt and the Holy Land that appears to match the biblical story but used to be too early, now becomes contemporary with the events in the Old Testament. They sync up again. Everything links together. That's the exercise we're involved in here. But, of course, I'm up against people who don't want to change the Egyptian timeline, and that's my problem.

Mahoney: And why don't they want to change it?

Rohl: They don't want to change the timeline because it's been established for the last 100 years or so, something like that. You've got respected scholars who have spent their whole lives – their professional careers – explaining away this chronology – this timeline – with all its anomalies. So Bible stories that don't match the history of Egypt become awkward anomalies. These then get put to one side. We try to forget about them because we're not comfortable with the consequences. And that's why we get other secular scholars saying, "Well, having done that, we might as well dismiss the Old Testament before the Divided Monarchy completely, and say it's a work of fiction."

Mahoney: I know that some have looked at the Brooklyn Papyrus and the Ipuwer Papyrus, for example, and they say, "Well, it's amusing that these historical documents seem to have narratives similar to some of the Bible stories, but that's all it is – just a coincidence."

Rohl: Well, that's what we find all the way through history. We find that there are so many "coincidences" that match the biblical story, and yet they can only be coincidences. They're not actualities – that's the nub of it all. And here I am trying to explain that, if you have so many of these coincidences one after another, then why not believe they are historical. Why are you saying that they are fiction?

But it's very difficult for scholars who have been working within what was accepted chronology for the last 100 years to change their ways. It's understandable. And so when someone like me comes along and says, "Hang on a minute, you've got your timeline wrong. I want you to rethink it," it's very hard for them, psychologically, to do that.

Mahoney: If we talk about Ken Kitchen, he has a chronology that has been accepted by most Egyptologists, but you've come along and upset the apple cart.

Rohl: That's me, that's the way I am. If I see the evidence taking me in a particular direction, I will follow that direction. The problem is that over the last 100 years people have got used to this idea that things are not working properly in history. So we have a chronology with all these anomalies – all these problems – but they're forgotten about, they're pushed to one side because this thing has become established. It's set in stone now. We have a history that cannot be changed. We have a chronology that can't be changed. I'm saying we have to take the edifice down. We have to dismantle the edifice and start building the ancient timeline from the foundations again – with what we know today as opposed to what we knew 100 years ago, and build the whole thing upwards.

What we have at the moment is an archaeology that has grown out of a timeline that doesn't work. So what we've got to do is adjust the timeline to fit the archaeology properly – and the traditional histories we have, like for instance the Old Testament narratives.

Mahoney: What's at stake?

Rohl: At stake are reputations. For instance, history books that have been written in the past that people are still reading, standard university textbooks, encyclopedias. All those things are going to have to change.

Mahoney: That's an incredible amount of change.

Rohl: It's a big task for sure.

Mahoney: Yeah, and you've got a lot of people who don't want to do that.

Rohl: Of course they don't. They're comfortable with what they've got. They've got this edifice, which they've got used to and now find quite attractive. Why would you want to pull that down? But what happens if the knowledge behind this edifice – the pillars of its chronological structure – are wrong?

Mahoney: And those pillars right now – the way they've been established – deny the stories of the Bible?

Rohl: Not because it's intentional. Okay, let's understand this. It's simply the way things have worked out. Over the last century of scholarship, anomalies have been revealed through what people have discovered. They've not understood what's happened here, and they've quietly put those anomalies away, into the bottom drawer, to forget about them. But then, of course, somebody like me comes along and says, "I want to open that drawer. I want to find out what those anomalies are and I want to see how we can explain them in a different way." And that's what we're doing here. What we've found is that scholars have overstretched the timeline by roughly 300 years. You take those 300 years out, and suddenly the artifacts that we're finding in the ground fit with the biblical story.

Mahoney: Let's repeat that, but from a different angle. So people like Israel Finkelstein, Ze'ev Herzog, William Dever – are they intentionally trying to deny the stories of the Bible?

Rohl: No, of course they're not. These are honest, intelligent scholars. What they're looking at in the ground is what they're telling us they're seeing. And they're not wrong. None of them are wrong about this. There is no evidence for the Israelite Conquest of the Promised Land at the end of the Late Bronze Age. That's a fact. Okay. And that's where the problems arise. It's simply a matter of time. They're looking in the right places for the Conquest stories, but they're looking in the wrong time period.

Mahoney: Are there other types of anomalies that this standard chronology or conventional chronology has created?

Rohl: The history of Egypt is full of anomalies. We have them from all periods, and they're basically anomalies of time, when things don't fit into the time structure that we have assembled.

Mahoney: How did the problem get started?

Rohl: What early scholars did to construct the ancient history of Egypt was to use a text by a priest named Manetho who wrote for one of the Ptolemaic pharaohs in the third century BC. He constructed a history of Egypt, basing it on dynasties, and he gives the lengths of the reigns of each of the kings. Now he warns us that some of these dynasties overlap one another, but scholars have literally added one dynasty upon the other to work backwards in time in order to get a date for the beginning of Egyptian history or for the building of the pyramids or whatever it might be – Ramesses II for instance. So what they are doing is they are simply adding the dates together in a simplified way when in fact some of these dynasties and some of these reigns overlapped each other. As a result, they get an artificially old chronology, older than it was in reality. And I think that's what's happened. Something like 300 years of history has been artificially added to the timeline, pushing Ramesses II back in time to make him much earlier in date than he really was.

Mahoney: Okay, so if the timeline's been stretched back and you shift it forward again, won't you create other anomalies?

Rohl: You will always create anomalies, because anomalies are unknown things. Okay? But gradually we begin to understand those anomalies. And what you've got to do is get a history with fewer anomalies. A history that's been constructed by a historian, after all, is not "the past." A history is only our best guess at what happened in the past. And that's what we're trying to do – reconstruct a history from the archaeological record, which fits the stories we know of – the historical stories – better.

Mahoney: Well, some people are saying that, you know, they can't go that way because there will be consequences for history that are unacceptable.

Rohl: Why unacceptable? Why is it unacceptable to find archaeological evidence to match the biblical stories? Why's that unacceptable?

Mahoney: I don't have an answer for that.

Rohl: I don't have an answer either. You go and ask them.

Mahoney: I will.

Rohl: Good.

Mahoney: People are afraid to talk about these things, though. I mean, I've experienced that when I go speak to them. They're willing to talk about it off camera, but once the camera turns on, then they change.

Rohl: Yes, that's reputations again. That's all about academia imposing upon scholarship a rigid framework, which you cannot move out of.

Mahoney: Yeah, but that really irritates me.

Rohl: It irritates the heck out of me, too. I think it's very, very important that scholars are not frightened to put forward ideas. Most scholars are afraid to do it because they're afraid of peer pressure. They are afraid of being ridiculed because they suggested something that isn't part of orthodoxy. The trouble is you never move scholarship forward if you do that. If you nibble at knowledge, you never get anywhere. Sometimes you have to take a giant bite, and that's what I and other scholars have done, and we are ridiculed for it. That's the world heterodox scholars exist in.

As you can see, I'm not scared of proposing a new suggestion or idea in order to explore it. If I'm wrong, I'm wrong – and I'm really not worried about that. But most scholars are petrified of being wrong. Academics are so immersed in this process that they have somehow become tunnel-visioned. They are potentially digging in the wrong chronological furrow and they're not looking outside that furrow to see what alternative possibilities exist. It's a psychological issue. Professor Max Planck, the famous German physicist, said basically that when a new idea is brought forward, the generation in whose time that idea is brought forward will reject it utterly and will go to their graves rejecting it. It takes a new generation of scholars, familiar with the idea, to accept the proposition or amend it and move on. That's the truth of the matter. Very few academics will be convinced by my arguments because they have their own perspectives enshrined in the established dogma.

Mahoney: My understanding is that your approach is evidential. You're looking for evidence that corresponds to historical events and saying, "Well, why are we ignoring all of this?"

Rohl: When you follow a process of logic, and you work from small clues, and you piece them all together, you end up with a big theory. And usually big theories are not accepted by academia, by the establishment – that's inevitable. Some of the greatest minds of the last 300 or 400 years have come across this problem. The 16th-century scholar Giodarno Bruno, who said to the Vatican scholars, "Hey, wait a minute, the Earth actually goes around the Sun and the stars are other suns," well, he was burned at the stake for his heretical views, because everybody used to think, of course, that the Earth was the center of the universe. So many revolutionary ideas have been obstructed by the community of academics of the time. I just have to be patient and see how things work out – hopefully without the involvement of stakes and burnings!

Mahoney: So then, does the Bible give an accurate historical account of the Exodus?

Rohl: This is the fundamental question I am asking myself as I write my new book *Exodus – Myth or History?*, which was instigated by my involvement in your movie. Can we treat the biblical story as an historical record? I think the answer to this question is yes, we can. I would treat the Bible like any other historical document. Let's analyze it, let's look at what evidence we can find to corroborate it. If the corroboration is there – if we can find the archaeological evidence and the contemporary textual evidence to confirm the stories – then the Bible is likely to be a reasonably sound historical record. If, on the other hand, we find no evidence for the Bible stories in archaeology, then it is much more likely to be a work of "pious fiction." The fact of the matter is that it can't be fiction because the evidence really is there!

BONUS CHAPTER B: A CONVERSATION WITH JAMES HOFFMEIER

James Hoffmeier is an Egyptologist and an archaeologist. As a supporter of the idea of a historical Exodus at the time of Ramesses II, Hoffmeier believes that we should not expect to find much direct archaeological evidence for these ancient events. Instead, he stresses certain linguistic features in the biblical account that he believes indicate the authenticity and ancientness of the text. He also emphasizes clues in the background information found in the stories that fit the general realities seen in the archaeology of Egypt and Canaan. Hoffmeier is a professor of Near Eastern Archaeology and Old Testament at Trinity Evangelical Divinity School of Trinity International University, in Deerfield, Illinois. Here are excerpts from my interviews with him that help to further explain his views.

Mahoney: Who is James Hoffmeier?

Hoffmeier: James Hoffmeier is a practicing archaeologist. I work in Egypt and I've excavated there for the past ten years in Sinai. Before that, I worked with the Akhenaten Temple project at Karnak Temple in southern Egypt. I've spent a good deal of my life researching in Egypt. I'm very much interested in Egyptian history, whether it's the Old Kingdom, a thousand years before the time of Abraham, or those periods where the Bible and Egyptian history intersect – but those are especially interesting to me.

Mahoney: What role does archaeology play for students of the Bible?

Hoffmeier: Archaeology is a wonderful tool to provide background information, provide a context for the narratives of the Bible, whether it's in the New Testament or the Old Testament. We live thousands of years removed from those events talked about in the

Bible. We live, many of us, thousands of miles away from that part of the world. So it actually places us in the world of the Bible. And so it provides a contextual picture that we would not know just sitting in our living rooms or in our classrooms or reading the Bible.

I have my four *c*'s. Archaeology provides a **context** for reading the Bible. Sometimes it **complements** the Bible, that is, it provides information not in the Bible about certain events and people and places. The third *c* is it **challenges** erroneous theories and interpretations of the Bible by providing new data. And lastly, in some cases, archaeology can actually **confirm** the historicity of events. It can confirm the presence of certain people and certain events in history. So four *c*'s – very important background information to the study of the Bible.

Mahoney: You wrote *Israel in Egypt* and *Ancient Israel in Sinai.* Why did you write those two books?

Hoffmeier: I wrote these two books because biblical scholars and Syro-Palestinian archaeologists were questioning the ethnic origins of Israel – had largely written off the sojourn/Exodus/Sinai tradition – and I felt that they were doing so without having a full command of how the data in Egypt could expand the picture, and round out the picture, and provide additional background information. So that's why I subtitled the first book *The Evidence for the Authenticity of the Exodus Tradition* – coming at them from the Egyptian vantage point. Most Egyptologists could care less about biblical history and biblical archaeology, and there are only a handful of Egyptologists who have that interest and I was one of them. So it seemed to me that this was a contribution to make to the debate by bringing an Egyptian perspective, an Egyptological perspective, to a burning historical debate.

Mahoney: There's a trend, though, to put a deeper requirement on the Bible. The Bible has to have a secondary source before they will take any of the information from it. Can we talk about that?

Hoffmeier: Well, there are those who have adopted the erroneous historical methodology of saying that the Bible must be viewed skeptically: one must be cautious in how one applies it, or accepts it. In essence what they've done is said the Bible is guilty until proven innocent. My preference is to treat the Bible like I do any other ancient text, and that is to treat it as innocent until proven guilty. That is, if we're talking about an ancient Egyptian text, like the annals of Thutmosis III, who talks about battles in Canaan against the city of Megiddo – I'm prepared to accept that as historically reliable unless there's some compelling evidence to the contrary. So I treat the Bible methodologically, as a historical document, the same way I would treat other ancient texts. So I try to treat it innocent until proven guilty, not guilty until proven innocent.

But the tendency to hold the Bible to a different standard than other documents is obviously based on the fact that the Bible is not just another ancient historical document. The Bible still shapes the religious traditions of both Jews and Christians. So I think that because of its function in the community of faith, the Bible is viewed with a more skeptical eye than if no Jew or Christian believed in its message.

Mahoney: Lately the Bible has been challenged greatly by people like Israel Finkelstein. Tell me about what's going on there.

Hoffmeier: Professor Finkelstein is a very good archaeologist, but he interprets his data differently than I do. I believe that the Bible, just like archaeological data, has to be properly interpreted. And I think when you interpret the archaeological data correctly and you interpret the biblical data correctly, you'll get a connection between them. So I would say that it has to do with different assumptions about the text.

Mahoney: Is the trend of recent scholarship continuing toward increased skepticism?

Hoffmeier: I think the trend goes back and forth. How people view the Bible sort of swings back and forth like a pendulum. And we've been on a pretty negative move for the last 30 years in what we call the "minimalist" historical direction. That is, deriving the minimal amount of historical worth or information from the Bible. I think it's gone as far in that direction as it can possibly go, and it's beginning to move back, ever so slightly, in a more moderate direction.

Mahoney: If we talk about the patriarchs in the Bible, what is the feasibility of characters like Abraham or Jacob, or the story of Joseph?

Hoffmeier: Well, the Genesis patriarchs play a very important role in Bible history and the history of the faith of the Jewish people. From a Christian perspective, Abraham is viewed as sort of the father of the faithful, as the paradigm of faith and trusting God. So these are very important stories. Now can we prove that these are historical characters?

No, we can't. Archaeology can't do that and probably never will. We probably will never find an inscription that said that Jacob slept here. We'll probably never find a similar document saying that Abraham rode a camel or rode a donkey on this road. We have no direct archaeological evidence to confirm the reality of the individuals or the events the Bible talks about in the books of Genesis and Exodus. But these are unrealistic expectations of what archaeology can and cannot do. What archaeology can do is provide what I call contextual or background information, which enables the story to come across as very realistic and authentic. And basically what we do see in the Genesis narratives seems to fit what we know about pastoralists in the second millennium BC. There are many things that can point to the authenticity of these Genesis narratives.

Mahoney: What would be an example of that?

Hoffmeier: One example would be that we have names like Ishmael and Isaac. These are called the Amorite imperfective. This is a grammatical analysis, but it basically shows us that these names that begin with a "yuh" vowel is a type of name that was very common in the early second millennium BC coming out of north Syria, which happens to be where Abraham comes from. His family lived in the land of Haran. Before that, they had lived in Ur of the Chaldeans, but they seemed to be of Amorite, Syrian stock and their names reflect that kind of tradition. So their names fit the kind of characters and personalities one would expect in a story set in the second millennium BC.

Mahoney: Are there other clues in the language used in the Bible that hint at the origin of the story?

Hoffmeier: As somebody who works with the Hebrew Bible and is also an Egyptologist, I try to read these narratives looking for any Egyptian words that have been borrowed by, or are a part of, the Hebrew that is in the text. And interestingly enough, in the Joseph story we have Joseph being decked out in linen before he goes to see Pharaoh. The word that is used there for linen is the actual Egyptian word for linen – it's the word *shesh*. This same word pops up with reference to the Tabernacle and the priesthood. The priests coming out of Egypt in Sinai are wearing linen gowns and part of the Tabernacle uses linen. This is the Egyptian word for linen. But this is not the same word that's used later on in the Bible for linen, where we have the actual Hebrew word *buwts* used. So it's interesting that this Egyptian word is used in narratives in Egypt or just after the people came out of Egypt. So again, that is the sort of very small detail that people would not recognize when reading the English Bible. But when you see it in Hebrew and you know Egyptian, you say, "Can this just be a coincidence?"

Mahoney: So you're saying these words are significant because someone possibly inventing the Bible 500 or 1,000 years later wouldn't know what those words were?

Hoffmeier: It would seem very doubtful that some Jewish scribe writing in Babylon, hundreds of years later would know what the Egyptian word for linen was. Certainly in texts from the monarchy period, this word *shesh* is no longer used for linen. So we have to account for how this gets in there, unless it is part of a very old memory, part of a very old strand of tradition.

Mahoney: If we think about the character of Joseph, is the story of Joseph even feasible in Egyptian culture?

Hoffmeier: The Egyptological evidence can flesh out the picture and provide the context and background information that enables us to look at the story of Joseph and say, "Yes, this rings true."

The idea of foreigners serving in Egypt, we have ample evidence for that in the Brooklyn Papyrus. But then we are talking about somebody who advances to a very high position – namely what probably would be considered the prime minister of Egypt. People often think that this rags-to-riches-in-the-palace kind of story just doesn't happen in reality. Well, just in the 1980s, the French archaeologist, Alain Zivie, discovered a series of tombs covered over in sand at Saqqara, the famous metropolis of Old Kingdom Egypt, located just outside of Cairo. But one of the tombs was of an Egyptian official named Aper-El. Aper-El is not an Egyptian name; it's a Semitic name. And as it turns out, this man, Aper-El, had become the Prime Minister of Egypt under Pharaoh Akhenaten. What's amazing is that he is a foreigner who advances to be the highest-ranking official in Egypt in the14th century BC.

We also find out that Aper-El was trained as a prince in the court of Pharaoh, and that he was elevated to this position of importance – the number two man in the land, if you will. This is roughly the time of Moses. So the idea that a foreigner could advance to such a high position in Egypt is documented – it's attested. We didn't know about this until about 1986. So it's a relatively recent discovery. But it's a perfect fit for the sort of person Joseph was, who was likely serving in a similar capacity at an earlier time.

Mahoney: Now David Rohl is suggesting that Manfred Bietak has found a palace of a Semitic ruler. What are your thoughts on that palace and the idea that Joseph came from that period and that his family belonged to that earlier group?

Hoffmeier: There have been important discoveries made at Tell el-Dab'a, and we know that there was this foreign population. We have a tomb of a high-ranking Hyksos Period official that some have suggested could be Joseph. Well, it would be wonderful if there were some evidence that we could tie to Joseph such as an inscription with the name. So in the absence of that kind of direct correlation it's best to leave such theorizing aside. Because if future excavations reveal the name of this person and it turns out not to be Joseph, then the speculation was not very helpful. It's certainly an intriguing thing to think about, and who knows? That's a wonderful thing about archaeology. New evidence is always just around the corner. So I prefer to be cautious and not to jump to conclusions until we have firm archaeological data.

Mahoney: Moses became a prince of Egypt, as it were. Is there any evidence fitting that?

Hoffmeier: The pharaohs of Egypt had an institution connected to the palace called the *Kap;* it's usually translated "the Royal Nursery." This was the place where the princes of Egypt were educated, learned how to read and write, were trained in other aspects such as learning archery and so on, the things that a young prince might need to know. And this institution actually goes back to the 19th and 18th century BC, so it goes back to the Middle Kingdom. What's interesting is when we get to the 15th century BC, we have the first evidence that foreign princes were brought by Thutmosis III from Canaan, from other parts of the Middle East, and were brought in and educated and reared in this institution. Aper-El, the prime minister of Egypt under Akhenaten – who might be likened to Joseph, whose tomb was found at Saqqara – he proudly claims to be a graduate of this institution. He was a foreign prince. That's probably where he was educated. That's where he was noticed, and that probably contributed to his rise to this position of prominence.

So it is interesting that the very time period – the 15th, 14th, and into the 13th century – the very period when we believe the Israelites were there, the oppression was beginning, and Moses would have been reared in the court of the pharaoh according to the tradition, and therefore would have learned to read and write Egyptian along with his

Hebrew Canaanite language. This is the period when foreign princes were being trained in this institution. So that suggests to me that, again, the timing of this can't be coincidental. This fits a particular period of time, not earlier and certainly not later.

Mahoney: Some people, such as David Rohl, say that you should look for an Exodus during a time of a collapse of Egyptian culture – you wouldn't look in the time of Ramesses II because that was the height of Egyptian culture. You should look at the earlier Middle Bronze Age when you have a dark age. What do you say to that?

Hoffmeier: Well, we still have the reality of the text as we have it. I don't think, even if we went with the so-called biblical chronology and a 1447 Exodus date – and David Rohl wants to push it back even earlier, so that's not according with any biblical chronology. I think it's really dangerous to create a scenario where you say, "This must be when this event took place," and then adjust the biblical text or the historical text to fit that reconstruction. So I'm dubious of that. I would also say, again from the theological standpoint of Scripture, that it's trying to make it clear that this is a great triumph over a very powerful pharaoh, not over a wimpy pharaoh at a time of weakness. In the biblical story we have a major Egyptian chariotry, and really chariotry becomes very important in the middle part of the 18th dynasty and in the time of Ramesses it reaches its zenith. We have the stables at Per-Ramesses discovered by Edgar Pusch that can house 500 horses. We have no possibility of that size of a chariotry in the Hyksos period. They may have had a few horses and chariots, but to have a major chariotry where they could send 600 chariots after the Israelites, I don't think that fits that earlier period.

If Exodus had simply told us the name of the pharaoh that Moses deals with, we would be able to settle this issue probably with some certainty. And it's not that the author of Exodus didn't know. In Exodus chapter one we know the name of the midwives but we don't know the name of Pharaoh. And you have to ask, "Why?" And I think there's an intentionality in that omission because it is a story about who's the God of the Exodus, not who is the pharaoh of the Exodus. And I think historians sometimes get too carried away either trying to answer the questions *when* and *who*, but they are not trying to answer the question the text is trying to answer for us, mainly, "Who is the God of the Exodus?" That's the question posed by Pharaoh and that is what the book of Exodus is trying to tell us. And so there is almost an irony that we look for who is the pharaoh of the Exodus and we are left in the dark. But who is the God of the Exodus? That's what the whole story is about.

313

Mahoney: Can you tell me more about the confrontation with Pharaoh?

Hoffmeier: We have this battle going on between the God of Israel and Pharaoh, the god of the Egyptian state. Egyptian temples are replete with pictures of Pharaoh with his conquering arm bashing the heads of his enemies. So it's interesting that we have this language of the arm of God and the arm of Pharaoh in the Exodus narratives. And this goes right through the Torah – this image of God's arm defeating the arm of Pharaoh. This is classic because that's how Pharaoh likes to present himself – as the one with the strong arm. And we have this contest in which, in the end of course, Pharaoh is defeated, his armies are ruined, and the people of Israel are able to escape into Sinai.

And there are close to ten times in the Exodus narratives where we're told that God is doing this plague or doing this action "that you might know that I am the Lord" or "that the Egyptians might know that I am the Lord" and in Exodus 9 "that the Earth might know that I am the Lord." So this is the agenda of the text. It's not trying to answer all of the questions we modern historians would like to have answered. But having said that, it doesn't mean it's not a historical document. It's talking about real events and real people that took place somewhere around 34, 33, 3200 years ago. And even though I'm an historian and that's what I'm interested in, the story of the Exodus is about the God of the Exodus.

Mahoney: Why is the Bible important?

Hoffmeier: The Bible is important because it has two roles. It has its historical and cultural information that is a great boon to Western civilization. On the other hand, it also has a religious and theological dimension to it. Western civilization is founded on those legal principles of "Thou shalt not kill," "Love your neighbor as yourself." These are the ethical dimensions and the religious dimensions of the Bible. And what we can't do is separate these two. We cannot separate the God who is active in history from the commands and the ethical demands that he has on people. They go together. It's a God who has acted in history. And that's what makes the Bible and the Judeo-Christian faith different than other religions because this is a God who has acted in history. His people and their faith are based on what God has done. As Saint Paul says, these things happened. And because these things happened, they have theological importance and ethical importance to us.

BONUS CHAPTER C: HOW MANY ISRAELITES IN EGYPT?

The question of the population of the Israelites at the time of the Exodus is important because it determines what sort of evidence we should be looking for in Egypt. A few thousand Israelites might be able to be hidden in the archaeological record, and a small population could fit at many times in Egypt's history. However, if there were hundreds of thousands of Israelites settled for an extended time in Egypt, it would become one of the great distinctives of the biblical sequence. We should then be looking for archaeological evidence indicating the potential of those kinds of numbers in the **Multiplication** step, and it should not be hard to find.

Likewise, the size of the population would strongly affect how severe the **Judgment** step of the biblical sequence was. The loss of two million slaves and their herds would have greatly contributed to the chaos and collapse of Egypt. Additionally, the large amounts of silver, gold, and other valuables taken out by over two million Israelites who had asked for them from their Egyptian neighbors would have hurt Egypt far more than the much smaller quantity carried out by 20,000 would. This would add to the degree of trouble we should be looking for. If there were that many Israelites, then we should look for evidence of a collapse in Egyptian society associated with the **Judgment** step. Losing just a few thousand might be no more than a blip on Egypt's radar.

A population of 20,000 is less than one percent of over two million. So determining the number of Israelites involved could completely change what is considered matching evidence for the biblical steps of **Multiplication** and **Judgment**.

The idea that the biblical account is describing an exodus of more than two million people can be seen for the first time as they leave Egypt. Exodus 12:37 says: "The Israelites traveled from Rameses to Succoth, about 600,000 soldiers on foot, besides their families."

Later texts indicate that this number was based on men who were 20 years old and upward, which qualified them to serve in the army, for instance, or do other things. If there really were 600,000 Israelite men of military age during the Exodus, this would suggest a total population in excess of two million if women and children were added in. The Bible also speaks about a mixed multitude of others leaving Egypt with the Israelites. However, many scholars are uncomfortable with such large numbers. This is largely due to the fact that evidence for this large of a Semitic population is currently lacking. In some, an anti-miracle bias may also be a factor in not accepting this large of a population.

This has led many to argue that this reference in Exodus should not be understood as 600 "thousand" men but rather as 600 "companies" or "troops" of men since the Hebrew word *'eleph* translated here as "thousand" can also mean squad, division, unit, troop, clan, or even chief. This would change the interpretation from 600 "thousand" Israelite men to 600 "squads" or "units" of Israelite men. A squad in Israelite military history was about four or five men, so some proponents of this thinking put forward figures of about 3,000 fighting men and around 12,000 - 20,000 Israelites in total. Others propose different numbers, both higher and lower.

So is the Bible claiming 600 "thousand" men or 600 "squads" of men? I raised this issue with Bryant Wood. "If we go back to the fact that the Bible states that there were 600,000 Israelite men that left, a lot of people have a hard time with the Exodus and the Conquest and all this because they say there's just not evidence for that number of people. So is the Bible right or wrong in this regard?"

Wood responded, "This matter of large numbers in the Old Testament is a very, very thorny issue, and I don't pretend to have the answers to it. But I think clearly it has to do with our understanding of the Hebrew word *'eleph,* which is translated "thousand." I believe that in these early accounts it must have another meaning. We find, in fact, that there are some places in the Old Testament where it's translated "chief." It's translated "clan." It has a number of meanings. The theory I kind of like is that in the early history of Israel, the tribe was subdivided into various sub-tribal units, and one of them was called an *'eleph.* And this *'eleph,* which would be composed of a number of families or extended families or something, was responsible for providing a military contingent in a time of war. That seems to make the most sense, and we don't know exactly how many would be in that contingent. It depends on the size of the *'eleph* and how many men they had available. But I think something like that has to be the answer because when you begin to look at these very large numbers they just don't stack up. With our site of Ai, it talks about 30 or 40,000. I mean, it's a little fortress of less than three acres, and I don't think we could have such large numbers of people involved in the fighting there. Now, I will say that when you get into the later part of the Old Testament, it's clear *'eleph* does mean "thousand" there. So, I think it changed meaning through time, and we kind of lost what the original meaning was and how to understand it."

"But what number do you think it meant at the time of the Exodus?" I asked.

"A lot of people wonder about how many people left Egypt, and of course if you use the translation of "thousand" for *'eleph,* you come up with 600,000 men, which means several million Israelites leaving Egypt, and I think that's an impossibly large number," said Wood. "One scholar who looked at this recently was Colin Humphries in England, and I think he has a reasonable approach. What he came up with is that it was about 20,000 people who left Egypt, and I think that's a reasonable figure. I mean, it's a huge number and a miraculous number to take through the wilderness. You don't need three million. It's difficult just for a small group to survive in Sinai, and 20,000 would be incredible. But it's more realistic perhaps than three million."

"Do you know how he came up with the 20,000?" I asked.

"Well, you'd have to read his article. He goes – it's very mathematical."

"Okay, in other words the text says there were 600 *'eleph.*"

"It's always speaking in terms of *'elephs.*"

"*'Eleph* is a thousand?"

"Yes."

"So if it says 650 *'elephs,* then that would mean 650,000?"

"If you take *'eleph* to mean 'thousand.'"

"Right, right."

"I like the translation "unit" better," Wood concluded.

My conversation with Bryant Wood illustrates a view that is very dominant among scholars today. However, as my team looked further into the matter, additional information was found in the details of the text that strongly indicates that "thousand" is in fact the intended meaning for *'eleph* in this verse and in almost all of its early uses.

If Exodus 12:37 were the only reference to the number of Israelites in the Exodus, it would seem justifiable to suppose that it meant 600 "squads" of men rather than 600 "thousand" men. However, the first chapter of the book of Numbers records a census

Numbers Chapter One

TRIBES		
Reuben		46,500
Simeon		59,300
Gad		45,650
Judah		74,600
Issachar		54,600
Zebulun		57,400
Ephraim		40,500
Manasseh		32,200
Benjamin		35,400
Dan		62,700
Asher		41,500
Naphtali		53,400
TOTAL		**603,550**

Numbers Chapter Two

North Camp	Dan	Asher	Naphtali	Total
	62,700	41,500	53,400	157,600
South Camp	**Reuben**	**Simeon**	**Gad**	**Total**
	46,500	59,300	45,650	151,450
East Camp	**Judah**	**Issacher**	**Zebulun**	**Total**
	40,500	32,200	35,400	108,100
West Camp	**Ephraim**	**Manasseh**	**Benjamin**	**Total**
	40,500	32,200	35,400	108,100
TOTAL				**603,550**

The census of Israel recorded in the first two chapters of the book of Numbers records the number of adult males for each tribe. It also contains several different tallies, each reaching totals exactly in line with the idea that the populations are recorded in thousands and not some other unit.

taken in the year after the Exodus for men over the age of 20. The numbers for each of the 12 tribes are listed individually and then tallied in the text to gain a total of 603,550. Additionally, in the second chapter of the book of Numbers, four Israelite camps – of three tribes each – are designated, with the subtotals of each camp given in the text. The text then adds those camp subtotals together to reach the same grand total of 603,550.

In all of these calculations, straight from the text, it is clear that the term *'eleph* means "thousand" since it is functioning precisely as the word *thousand* would. There appears to be no other value for *'eleph* that would add up to these totals in such an exact way. For instance, if we supply the meaning of "squads," it would read that Reuben had 46 squads plus 500 (or 46 squads = 500). If the figures for all 12 tribes were added in this manner, it would result in a total of 598 squads plus 5,550 – not the 603 squads plus 550 that is recorded. Many attempts have been made to come up with systems of counting that use meanings other than "thousand" in these verses and still equate to the stated totals, but no proposal has succeeded in providing a credible solution. The simplest and best explanation is that *'eleph* in this situation has its usual meaning of "thousand."

There are many other evidences that the Bible is describing an Israelite population of hundreds of thousands of adult men. One example related to these numbers has the

Hebrew word for thousand (*'eleph*) functioning exactly as "thousand" should, just as the term for "hundreds" is functioning as "hundreds." In Exodus 18:21, 24, Numbers 31:14, 48, 52, 54, and Deuteronomy 1:15, the leaders of Israel are referred to as commanders of tens, fifties, hundreds, and thousands. This indicates that some number greater than 100 was how the term *'eleph* was used when addressing the numbers of the Israelite military – the most obvious candidate being "thousand" as it is normally used.

Another census is taken near the end of Israel's 40 years of wandering in Numbers chapter 26, and again the calculation of the population comes out exactly to the total when the normal use of "thousand" is used. This time the total reached is precisely 601,730. This seems to make it virtually impossible that the term used for "thousand" could mean anything other than "thousand." In this case, meanings for *'eleph*, such as squads, clans, units, chiefs, or groups of any type, just don't qualify.

While *'eleph* can sometimes mean something other than "thousand," it almost always carries the meaning of "thousands" in the Bible. Of the 505 uses of *'eleph*, in the text, the King James Version of the Bible renders it as "thousand" 504 times. Other versions replace "thousand" a couple dozen times, usually in phrases that could either mean "thousands" or something else. For example, it could mean either "among Israel's thousands" or "among Israel's divisions."

Exodus chapter 38 gives further evidence that there were more than 600,000 adult Israelite males. At Mount Sinai a collection was taken up for the construction of the tabernacle. Each man was to contribute one *beka* of silver (a half *shekel*) and the number of *bekas* collected was more than 600,000 – not the 3 or 4,000 that would have been collected if there were only 600 units of Israelite men.

> The silver from those of the community who were registered was 100 talents and 1,775 shekels, according to the sanctuary shekel – a beka per man, that is, half a shekel according to the sanctuary shekel, from everyone 20 years old or more who had crossed over to the registered group, 603,550 men. (Ex. 38:25-26)

One *talent* = 3,600 *shekels*, therefore "100 *talents* and 1,775 *shekels*" = 360,000 +1,775 *shekels* = 361,775 total *shekels* donated or 723,550 total *bekas* (half shekels) donated.

The text says that 723,550 *bekas* were donated and that one *beka* was given by each of the 603,550 men. This fits with 600,000 men but not with 600 squads of men. The greater total of 723,550 *bekas* (120,000 more than the census figure) may be accounted for by men from the tribe of Levi and the mixed multitude who were not included in the census totals (Num. 1:47-49, 2:33).

Many other places in the biblical account stress the great size of the Israelite population at the time of the Exodus:

> He [Pharaoh] said to his people, "Look, the Israelite people are more numerous and powerful than we are." . . . But the more they oppressed them, the more they multiplied and spread so that the Egyptians came to dread the Israelites. (Ex. 1:9,12)

Even if this was an exaggeration, the populations of Israel and Egypt must have been comparable on some level or the Egyptians would not have had reason to fear them so greatly. Many experts estimate the population of Egypt at this time at two-four million based on the amount of dwellings that have been uncovered. But it must be noted that there can be no way of confirming how much larger this population might have been, because we don't know how much of Egypt's archaeology remains undiscovered. Also, tents and huts usually leave little or no trace and the Bible refers to Egyptians living in tents (Psalm 78:51). If many Israelites were living in tents, this might help explain why evidence for their great totals is currently lacking. The annual flooding over the Delta also eliminates all but the most solid materials over time.

Here are more passages that stress the great numbers of Israelites:

> But the Israelites were fruitful, increased rapidly, multiplied, and became extremely numerous so that the land was filled with them. (Ex. 1:7)

> The people multiplied and became very numerous. (Ex. 1:20)

> The LORD your God has so multiplied you that today you are as numerous as the stars of the sky. (Deut 1:10)

Furthermore, the entire army of the pharaoh was needed to retrieve the unarmed

Israelites. This included much more than 600 picked chariots. Among the complete army were all the other chariots, the horsemen, and the army who are said to have marched (Ex. 14:6, 7, 9).

At Mount Sinai 3,000 and more Israelites were killed (Ex. 32:28). Then in the rebellion of Korah, 250 captains of fame and renown (Num. 16:2) rose up against Moses and all were killed, along with 14,700 of the congregation (Num. 16:49). Later, 24,000 were killed (Num. 25:9) in a plague when they committed whoredom with the daughters of Moab and joined themselves to Baal. This is all difficult to reconcile with the total of around 20,000 available Israelites that has been proposed by some, especially if after these deaths, the entire people remained more or less intact. Additionally, 250 captains of tens, fifties, hundreds, and thousands would require a large number of subordinates, and these captains and their units were only a fraction of the whole congregation.

From their wars, the Israelites were able to absorb huge amounts of spoil, which would have outfitted an army numbering in the hundreds of thousands. In Numbers 31, Israel is ordered to arm some of the men among them to war against Midian. The text says that one "thousand" warriors were recruited from each of the 12 tribes to fight. The men of this army (totaling 12 "thousand") each end up carrying out gold as booty from the battle. These men then made an offering from the golden armlets, bracelets, rings, and earrings they had taken. The total gold from this offering was 16,750 shekels. For an army of 12,000 men, this would have meant that each man would have given an average contribution of a little more than half an ounce of gold – or the equivalent of about three gold rings each. If the army instead had been 12 squads of 5 men each, then every individual would have offered about 7 pounds of gold. Verse 48 indicates that this army consisted of leaders of "hundreds" and leaders of "thousands" (or "units"). This would not make sense if the entire army consisted only of about 60 men (12 "units" of men instead of 12 "thousand" men). Additionally, a raid of about 60 men does not have the capabilities to take and manage spoil consisting of 675,000 sheep, 72,000 cattle, 61,000 donkeys, and 32,000 unmarried females as described in this event.

The Hebrews conquered the nations on the far side of the Jordan as well as most of Canaan, a land filled with very great high-walled cities. They had victories over 31 kings and their armies. This does not fit an army of only about 3,000 (Num. 13:28, Num. 21:21-35, Deut. 1:28, 3:4-6, Josh. 12:1-24).

Joshua 11:3-4 describes the Israelites defeating the Canaanites, including the Hittites:

They went out with all their armies – a multitude as numerous as the sand on the sea-shore – along with a vast number of horses and chariots. (Joshua 11:4)

In Joshua 8:3 a single elite unit of the bravest Hebrew soldiers numbered 30,000 men.

The people of Israel needed a huge area of land for the tribes to settle in. The area described in Numbers 34 is roughly the size of today's Israel plus the areas on the far side of Jordan that were occupied.

In Numbers 35:1-8 the smallest tribe of Levi that served in the tabernacle, and who were not farmers or shepherds, received 48 walled cities as their share in Canaan. Each city was, with its surroundings outside the wall (for the cattle), approximately 1 x 1 km.

When looking more closely at the example of Ai (Josh. 7:1-5 and 8:1-29) that Bryant Wood used to argue against 'eleph meaning "thousand," I saw that it was not a very strong point. I could see that the remains of Ai do show that it was in fact a small fortress, just as Wood is suggesting. However, fortresses were extremely difficult to capture, and the number of defenders at Ai was likely swelled by Canaanites living in the surrounding areas who would flee to the fortress in times of invasion. The Israelite scouts initially advised that 2,000 or 3,000 Israelite warriors were enough to defeat Ai, and 3,000 were sent to the first attack. This seems completely appropriate to deal with a fortress containing several hundred defenders. But 36 Israelites were killed, and they fled in terror from the Canaanites. Later in the account it speaks of men from the nearby large city of Bethel working in accord with Ai, and says that 12,000 men and women of the Canaanites ended up being killed by the much larger Israelite army in the final battle that defeated Ai. Three "squads" of Israelites in the initial attack actually does not fit this narrative nearly as well as three "thousand" does. [101]

Whether these large numbers are believed or not, there does seem to be clear indication that the text portrays in many places that the Israelites had more than 600,000 men of fighting age. This yields very distinct criteria to look for in Egypt. More than two million Semites in total, many of them settled for extended periods of time, could not be completely hidden in the archaeological record. Based on the evidence we have today, the only period that demonstrates anything like such massive numbers of Semites in Egypt is during the late Middle Kingdom and the Second Intermediate Period that followed. This span also contains a unique major collapse of Egypt at the end of the Middle Kingdom (late 13th Dynasty) as well as conditions in Canaan that match the Conquest. This is why the late Middle Kingdom/Middle Bronze Age seems to stand alone in strongly matching the biblical account.

BONUS CHAPTER D: FOUR HUNDRED YEARS OF SLAVERY?

Another crucial factor involved in investigating the Exodus is determining the length of the Israelites' stay in Egypt, commonly called the sojourn. An effective search for the Exodus in the history of Egypt only becomes possible after the timeline for the Bible has been worked out properly. This goes beyond just establishing an accurate date for the point of departure from Egypt. Equally important are the windows of time for the other biblical events both prior to and after the date of the Exodus itself.

In what time period should evidence for each of the first three steps of **Arrival, Multiplication,** and **Slavery** be looked for? Should evidence that fits Joseph and the arrival of the Israelites be considered valid if it exists about 430 years before the date of the **Exodus?** Having an accurate picture of the biblical timeline is needed to produce an effective measuring tool, which can then be used to determine what evidence fits and what does not. In order to create this timeline, we first need to address the question of how long the Israelites were in Egypt before the Exodus occurred.

The problem is that there are two different interpretations of the Bible's information on this issue. The most popular view today favors a 430-year stay in Egypt based on Exodus 12:40-41 and Genesis 15:13. Most modern English translations render these verses this way:

> The time that the Israelites lived in Egypt was 430 years. At the end of 430 years, on that same day, all the Lord's divisions went out from the land of Egypt. (Ex. 12:40-41)

> [to Abraham] Your offspring will be foreigners in a land that does not belong to them; they will be enslaved and oppressed 400 years. (Gen. 15:13)

However, the consensus view among Jewish and Christian scholars up until the last 150 years was that the 400/430 years recorded in these verses should be understood as the time from Abraham to the Exodus, not just the time that Jacob's family lived in Egypt. This would mean that the time in Egypt would only be about half of the 430-year period.

To see how this could be so, it is important to begin by looking more closely at Exodus 12:40. The original Hebrew wording of this verse actually contains two terms for the concept of living or dwelling or sojourning. The King James Version of the Bible reflects this reality:

> Now the sojourning of the children of Israel, who dwelt in Egypt, was 430 years.
> (Ex. 12:40 KJV)

Because most modern translations summarize this verse, they miss the fact that it contains two different terms for dwelling or sojourning. Rather than restricting the meaning of the 430 years to just the time in Egypt, the original Hebrew as rendered in the King James Version seems to open up the possibility that the 430 years mentioned could be referring to either the shorter time just in Egypt or to the broader sojourn period from Abraham to the point of Exodus. It may be that the clause "who dwelt in Egypt" was not the main point of the verse but merely a parenthesis adding a detail that clarified who the Israelites were. In that case the time in Egypt would just be a subordinate aspect of the larger sojourn. The main idea was the larger sojourn – the time Abraham and his descendants spent in Canaan as well as the later time in Egypt.

Do the books of Genesis and Exodus elsewhere portray the sojourn of that people who ended up in Egypt (God's chosen people) as just the time in Egypt, or do they portray it as including the time that Abraham, Isaac, and Jacob spent in Canaan and Haran when away from their homeland in Mesopotamia? The following verses seem to indicate that the second option is indeed the case:

> [Abraham speaking] I am a stranger and a sojourner with you: give me a possession of a burying place with you, that I may bury my dead out of my sight. (Gen. 23:4 KJV)

> And Jacob said to Pharaoh, "The days of the years of my sojourning are a hundred and thirty

years. Few and evil have been the days of the years of my life, and they do not attain to the days of the years of the life of my fathers, in the days of their sojourning." (Gen. 47:9 DBY)

The structure of Genesis 15:13 can be understood as follows:
A) Your offspring will be foreigners in a land that does not belong to them;
> B) they will be enslaved
> B) and oppressed
A) 400 years.

This can be seen as a list of events with their total time of 400 years listed at the end. It can also be viewed as a literary form known as an introversion – where the main idea flows from *A* to *A* and the *B*'s also go together but are a parenthesis of additional information. [102]

So in this way of thinking, the 400 years would be the time that Abraham's offspring would be foreigners in a land not their own, waiting for the Covenant promises to be fulfilled. The number of years would not be referring only to their time as slaves in Egypt. Although Abraham and his offspring were promised the land, they remained foreigners and never gained possession of it until the Conquest of Canaan (Gen. 23:4, 28:4, 47:9, Heb. 11:8-13). The two main verses that support the 430-years-in-Egypt view (Ex. 12:40 and Gen. 15:13) can then both be seen as allowing for a 430-year broad sojourn in Canaan and Egypt.

The earliest translations of the book of Exodus support this way of thinking about the timeline of Israel's early history. The Greek translation of the Hebrew Bible known as the Septuagint (believed to be originally penned about 250 BC) renders Exodus 12:40 as: "The sojourn of the sons of Israel, which they sojourned in the land of Egypt **and the land of Canaan** was 430 years." The Samaritan version of the Pentateuch (450-150 BC) also includes the stay in Canaan in this verse.

All the oldest known Jewish sources held the view that the 400 and 430 years reported in Genesis and Exodus were meant to include the time in Canaan as well as Egypt. These sources include Josephus in the *Antiquity of the Jews,* Jose Ben Halafta (writer of *Seder Olam Rabbah,* ca. 150 AD), the *Book of Jubilees* (ca. 100 BC), Philo (ca. 30 AD), Demetrius (the earliest Jewish author to write in Greek, ca. 250 BC), writings found in the Dead Sea scrolls (some written about 100 BC), and the Babylonian Talmud (ca. 400 AD). The

Jewish Midrash, in *Genesis Rabbah,* interprets Genesis 15:13 by stating that "this means, until four hundred years after seed shall be granted to thee." Rabbi Jacob Neusner, one of the most published authors in history, commented on this: "The Israelites will not serve as slaves for four hundred years, but that figure refers to the passage of time from Isaac's birth." In the Babylonian Talmud in Megillah, it states, "And the abode of the children of Israel which they stayed in Egypt and in other lands was four hundred years." [103]

The Christian church also long held this view. The apostle Paul in the book of Galatians wrote:

Now the promises were spoken to Abraham and to his seed. . . . And I say this: The law, which came 430 years later, does not revoke a covenant that was previously ratified by God and cancel the promise. . . . but God granted it to Abraham through the promise. (Gal. 3:16-18)

The book of Exodus records that the law was given at Mount Sinai just months after the Exodus. So according to this passage, it was 430 years from Abraham to Exodus, not 430 years from the entry of Jacob's family into Egypt to the Exodus. Another indication of this view is seen in Stephen's speech in the book of Acts chapter 7, which begins with the same 400-year promise to Abraham as seen in Genesis 15. Later in the passage, after covering the period of Isaac and the early patriarchs, it states:

As the time was drawing near to fulfill the promise that God had made to Abraham, the people flourished and multiplied in Egypt until a different king who did not know Joseph ruled over Egypt. He dealt deceitfully with our race and oppressed our ancestors . . . . (Acts 7:17-19)

This makes it clear that for Luke, the author of Acts, the period after Joseph died and before the slavery began was "near" to the time of the fulfillment of the promise made to Abraham. If the 400 years determined for Abraham's descendants (Acts 7:6 and Gen. 15:13) was referring to the time in Egypt only, then the period before the slavery began would be near the beginning of the 400 years – not near its end. Since this verse says that this period was, in fact, near the end of the 400 years, it must have been treating the time of the sojourn as from the time of Abraham's first descendant of promise (Isaac) until the point of Exodus, not Jacob's entry into Egypt to the Exodus.

The early Christian Church Fathers also held the view that the 430-year time span began with the original promises to Abraham and continued until the initial fulfillment of those promises in the Exodus. Important theologians throughout Christendom – Saint Augustine, Saint Thomas Aquinas, Martin Luther, John Calvin, John Wesley, and Jonathan Edwards – also accepted this understanding. Even Sir Isaac Newton, who wrote more on the Bible than on physics and mathematics, calculated his biblical calendar in agreement with this thinking. It was only after modern translations started summarizing Exodus 14:40 in the 1800s that views regarding the length of the Israelite sojourn began to change.

Other important clues show that the Hebrew text itself mandates that the 430 years were not meant to be understood as the time in Egypt alone. First of all, if the 400 years of Genesis 15 is instead taken as the time of slavery in Egypt only (which is the popular modern view), and not the broader sojourn, it creates several problems within that chapter and with other information in the Bible.

That the Israelites were "enslaved and oppressed in Egypt for 400 years" (which is the common modern interpretation of Genesis 15:13) does not fit a 430-year stay in Egypt because other biblical information demands that the Israelites were free in Egypt for about 100 years before they were enslaved. For example, consider the first few verses of Exodus. These verses say that a new pharaoh arose to enslave the Israelites only after Joseph and his brothers and the rest of that generation died. The text states that Joseph was 30 at the beginning of the seven years of plenty followed by the seven years of famine (Gen. 41:46). It also says that Jacob and his family moved down to Egypt in the second year of the famine (Gen. 45:6) when Joseph would have been 39. Joseph is said to have died when 110 and his brother Levi died when 137 (Gen. 50:22, Ex. 6:16). Other biblical information suggests that Levi was at most about 10 years older than Joseph. This means that after Jacob's family moved down to Egypt, Joseph lived another 71 years and Levi another 88 years, and then the rest of that generation had to die before the pharaoh who enslaved the Israelites came to power.

If the Israelites lived for a century or more in Egypt before becoming enslaved, then this does not fit with the idea that they were slaves 400 years and in Egypt for a total of 430 years. If there were 400 years of slavery, it would equate to 500 total years or more in

Egypt (based on the life of Joseph) – not precisely 430 as is stated in Exodus 12:40. This shows that there is something wrong with the popular modern view.

Another problem for the 400-years-as-slaves interpretation is that the coming out of Egypt to conquer Canaan was to occur "in the fourth generation" (Gen. 15:16) – not after 430 years in Egypt. There appears to be no way to stretch three and some fraction generations into a 430-year period.

The genealogy of Levi to Moses in Exodus chapter 6 is the one place in the Bible that matches and verifies God's fourth generation promise made in Genesis 15. However, the ages attached to each of the members of this family tree show that the time spent in Egypt was at most 350 years, making a 430-year time frame in Egypt mathematically impossible. Kohath is said to have arrived in Egypt as a boy with his father Levi and to have lived to age 133. Kohath fathered Amram, who lived to 137, and Amram fathered Moses. Moses was 80 years old at the time of the Exodus out of Egypt (Gen. 46:8-11, Ex. 6:18-20, Ex. 7:6).

Kohath	133
Amram	137
Moses	80
Total	350

Even if Levi's son Kohath was a newborn when entering Egypt and he and Amram fathered their sons in the last year of their lives, the maximum time in Egypt could only be 350 years, and it would likely be at least a century less than this. Although the line from Levi to Moses was following the pattern recorded in the Bible of the older patriarchs living long and fathering children at older ages, the biblical account also records that the rest of the Israelites were multiplying exceedingly. Two of the 12 sons of Jacob were grandfathers despite being in their 40s when entering Egypt. Benjamin in his mid-twenties at this same time already had 10 sons, and in Joseph's 71 years in Egypt after Jacob's entry, he saw his son Ephraim's children to the third generation (Gen. 46:12, 17, 21 and 50:23). These factors show that there was plenty of opportunity for exceedingly great multiplication among the Israelites. These points and others also favor the view that the 430 years was meant to apply to the entire sojourn from Abraham to Exodus. Since we know Abraham fathered Isaac at age 100 and Isaac fathered Jacob at 60 and Jacob entered Egypt at 130 (Gen 21:5, 25:26, 47:9), only about half the 430 years would have actually been spent in Egypt.

Assigning a 430-year total stay in Egypt based on Jacob's entry creates numerous contradictions between the primary sojourn references and other important chronological realities reported in the Bible. However, the points above show that the Hebrew Bible is actually not in conflict with itself or with the Greek translation in the Septuagint. Those who adopt the interpretation that the apostle Paul was referencing the Septuagint to make his point concerning the 430 years in the book of Galatians (rather than the Hebrew manuscript) are unnecessarily creating a contradiction between the Old and New Testaments. A closer look at the evidence reveals that the New Testament writers are in complete agreement with the Hebrew text, the Septuagint translation, and all the early Jewish and Christian writers, and that the 430 years defines the grand sojourn from Abraham to the Exodus.

With about 210 or 215 years spent in Egypt, and a period of slavery of about one century (all the time that was left in the sojourn after the death of Joseph's generation), an accurate timeline for the biblical events including all these factors can be produced. This gives a better understanding of the history related in the Bible and provides a much more precise and powerful measuring tool for examining the archaeological record in Egypt and Canaan for signs of the Exodus.

Using the 1450 BC "Early" Exodus date
yeilds the following timeline:

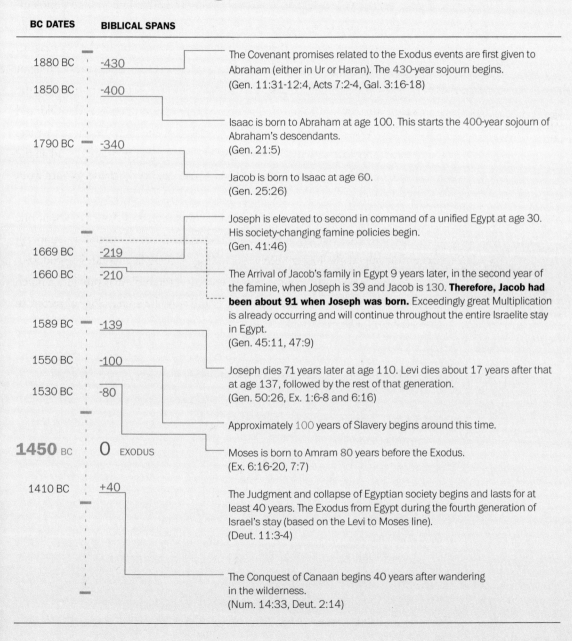

BC DATES	BIBLICAL SPANS	
1880 BC	-430	The Covenant promises related to the Exodus events are first given to Abraham (either in Ur or Haran). The 430-year sojourn begins. (Gen. 11:31-12:4, Acts 7:2-4, Gal. 3:16-18)
1850 BC	-400	
		Isaac is born to Abraham at age 100. This starts the 400-year sojourn of Abraham's descendants. (Gen. 21:5)
1790 BC	-340	
		Jacob is born to Isaac at age 60. (Gen. 25:26)
		Joseph is elevated to second in command of a unified Egypt at age 30. His society-changing famine policies begin. (Gen. 41:46)
1669 BC	-219	
1660 BC	-210	The Arrival of Jacob's family in Egypt 9 years later, in the second year of the famine, when Joseph is 39 and Jacob is 130. **Therefore, Jacob had been about 91 when Joseph was born.** Exceedingly great Multiplication is already occurring and will continue throughout the entire Israelite stay in Egypt. (Gen. 45:11, 47:9)
1589 BC	-139	
1550 BC	-100	Joseph dies 71 years later at age 110. Levi dies about 17 years after that at age 137, followed by the rest of that generation. (Gen. 50:26, Ex. 1:6-8 and 6:16)
1530 BC	-80	
		Approximately 100 years of Slavery begins around this time.
1450 BC	0 EXODUS	Moses is born to Amram 80 years before the Exodus. (Ex. 6:16-20, 7:7)
1410 BC	+40	The Judgment and collapse of Egyptian society begins and lasts for at least 40 years. The Exodus from Egypt during the fourth generation of Israel's stay (based on the Levi to Moses line). (Deut. 11:3-4)
		The Conquest of Canaan begins 40 years after wandering in the wilderness. (Num. 14:33, Deut. 2:14)

BONUS CHAPTER E:
THE CONQUEST DEBATE

Over the years, the search for evidence related to the events of Exodus has actually been focused on the Conquest in Canaan. In fact, the current state of skepticism about the Exodus among mainstream scholars was largely generated from their findings in Israel related to the Conquest of Canaan. This is because the Bible says this event happened just 40 years after the Exodus from Egypt, and the Bible also gives a specific list of cities involved – many of them major cities – that were said to be heavily fortified and defended but suffered defeat to the Israelites. Several of these cities are explicitly said to have been burned. This provides a distinct set of criteria to look for when searching for a match with the Bible's account. It is also the kind of criteria that would not likely remain completely hidden in the archaeological record – a group of specifically named, high-walled fortifications in Canaan that were defeated, with some burned, should be apparent in the remains.

However, after initially promising results, it became increasingly apparent during the second half of the 20th century that the archaeological remains (found in Canaan for the assumed dates of the Conquest) painted a very different picture than the Bible's account of these events. Because of the problems with the evidence, most mainstream scholars conclude that the Bible's account is largely fiction. Those scholars who do support the validity of the history found in the Bible's account of the Conquest fall into several camps. These groups have come up with different approaches to explain the problems with the evidence in Canaan. This chapter will briefly cover some of the approaches taken by the main pro-Conquest camps in this debate.

There are four main camps among Exodus supporters that can be described as follows:
1. Those who hold to an Exodus date in the Ramesses period around 1250 BC (Conquest around 1210 BC),
2. Those who hold to an Exodus date around 1450 BC (Conquest around 1410 BC),
3. Those who hold to an Exodus date around 1600 BC (Conquest around 1560 BC),

4. Those who hold to an Exodus date around 1450 BC (Conquest around 1410 BC) but with an unconventional timeline shift for Egypt/Canaan.

The first three camps use the conventional timeline for Egypt/Canaan with no major adjustments. The fourth camp includes various proposals that retain a traditional biblical timeline but adjust the dates assigned to Egypt and Canaan's archaeological levels, which produce better alignments with the biblical data.

As covered in the main Conquest chapter of this book, the mainstream view is that the archaeological landscape for a period of several hundred years seems to yield no time when the evidence matches the Bible's account. In fact, several of the Bible's Conquest cities seem to have been completely abandoned or largely abandoned throughout the entire Late Bronze Age (conventionally dated to about 1550 – 1200 BC). This causes most scholars in camps 1 and 2 to focus on three main sites, Jericho, Ai, and Hazor, which are said in the book of Joshua to have been burned. To gain a better overview of the issues involved, the following chart maps out the general condition of Conquest sites from the period in question.

The archaeological condition of major cities in Canaan. Some cities were destroyed around 1200 BC, but these destructions were spread out over a century or more, causing the skepticism of many scholars. There is only one time that appears to fit the biblical account well— near the end of the earlier Middle Bronze Age (1550 BC under conventional dating).[104]

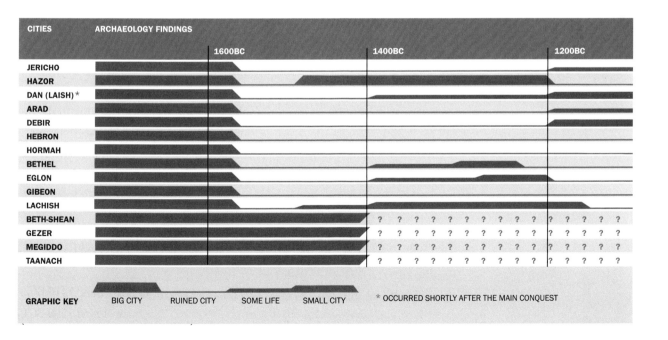

Remember that most mainstream scholars such as Israel Finkelstein, Ze'ev Herzog, and Norma Franklin assume that the Bible depicts the Exodus happening in the time of Ramesses in the 13th century (1200s) BC. Some even go a bit later than that. However, the archaeological scene in Canaan a few decades after that date does not provide a good fit with the Conquest story based on the evidence available today.

As a supporter of the historical Conquest happening around 1210 BC, James Hoffmeier stresses the finds at Hazor, while pointing to other realities at Jericho, to explain the apparent problems with the evidence there.

Mahoney: When we talk about Kathleen Kenyon and Jericho, my understanding is that Kenyon actually stated some things that a lot of people have somehow left out.

Hoffmeier: With the story of Jericho we have a lot of confusion and a lot of uncertainty, and this stems from the fact that in the 1930s the British archaeologist John Garstang from Liverpool excavated and found a very clear burn destruction layer that he had attributed to Joshua and the Israelites. Twenty years later when Dame Kathleen Kenyon came along and excavated, she dated that level not to the time of Joshua, say 1400 BC, but rather 150 years earlier, marking the end of the Middle Bronze Age. Now a lot of people have simply said, "Well, Kenyon has proven that this couldn't have been Joshua's Jericho either in the 14th century or the 13th century – or the 15th century – so the story of Jericho must be made up, maybe an etiology" – that is, a story made up to tell the origin of something – "but surely there's no corresponding history behind it."

Now sadly, what many archaeologists have done is not read all of what Kenyon has said. And, in fact, we do know that her excavations produced ample evidence for a Late Bronze occupation, that is, a level of occupation in the 15th and 14th centuries, and in fact one colleague has written a book called *Jericho in the Late Bronze Age.* So very clearly there was some sort of Late Bronze settlement at Jericho, and Kenyon herself acknowledges that the Late Bronze community may well have used the defense walls from the Middle Bronze Age that were still standing or at least enough standing to be the ramparts of the city. So if you really read what Kenyon has said, I think many scholars would be surprised to find out that what she actually said and what she has been reported to have said by others are two different things. So clearly there was something there in the Late Bronze Age, the general period of Joshua.

Mahoney: But does the site during that time match the Bible's story?

Hoffmeier: The question is how much and how large it was, and we may never know the answer to that because according to the biblical tradition the city lay fallow for several centuries, and during that period of three, four hundred years until the days of Ahab, the city was unoccupied, we're told in the Bible, because Joshua put a curse on it. So, Kenyon argues, based on what she found, that there was considerable erosion because the site had lain fallow – no occupation for hundreds of years and much erosion had occurred, and she claims this accounts for the loss of much of what was the Late Bronze site of Jericho, although there is pottery, there are other finds. There are tombs from the Late Bronze Age, no doubt about it. So the reality is, there is something there in the Late Bronze Age. It may not have been the largest settlement, but there was something there. And I think people have gone too far in writing off Jericho or trying to redate Jericho to fit different theories. But there clearly was something there in the 15th and 14th centuries.

Mahoney: What about other Conquest sites?

Hoffmeier: Now there are issues, there are problems with Jericho, which archaeologists are well aware of. But the most important city being excavated right now relevant to the Exodus and Conquest, of course, is the city of Hazor in northern Israel, where Amnon Ben-Tor has been uncovering a powerful destruction of a city at the end of the 13th century BC that he believes is the destruction of Joshua. And what's amazing about this is not only do we have a destroyed palace and temple areas, but we have statues of deities that have been decapitated, defaced. So there's clearly aggressive attacks against the religious paraphernalia of these people. That is unparalleled. Most foreign invasions do not go in and destroy the gods. Yet that was the command that Joshua had in Joshua 7, to go in and destroy their high places, their altars, their pillars, tear all this down. And that's what we see going on in the excavations at Hazor.

* * *

Hoffmeier's evidence of idols being destroyed at Hazor matches passages in the Bible such as the following:

You must drive out all the inhabitants of the land before you, destroy all their stone images and cast images, and demolish all their high places. (Num. 33:52)

This is what you are to do to them: tear down their altars, smash their sacred pillars, cut down their Asherah poles, and burn up their carved images. For you are a holy people belonging to the Lord your God. (Deut. 7:5-6)

However, the Israelites occupied areas of Canaan for more than 800 years, so the question is (granting that the destruction at Hazor may have been caused by the Israelites), was the destruction there, near the end of the Late Bronze Age, a result of the Conquest, or one of the judges such as Deborah, or from a later figure such as King David (1 Chron. 18) or even afterward? The possibility also exists that this destruction was not caused by the Israelites. It is interesting to note that in 1 Kings 9:15 Solomon's fortifying of Hazor is listed as one of his major building projects, so it was not abandoned during his reign.

Hoffmeier would designate an earlier destruction at Hazor (around the time of the Middle/Late Bronze transition) as being pre-Exodus. He would equate the second Hazor destruction near the end of the Late Bronze Age with Joshua's Conquest. The conventional dating of this second event would fit well with a Ramesses Exodus date around 1250 BC, which results in a 1210 Conquest date. According to David Rohl, during the first major excavations of the site in the 1950s, renowned Israeli archaeologist Yigal Yadin dated the Late Bronze burning of Hazor to around 1300 BC. Since that time, archaeologists, such as the current excavator Amnon Ben-Tor, have lowered the estimate to 1200 BC, give or take a couple decades.

While this destruction at Hazor fits the Ramesses Exodus Theory well, there remain other major problems. The archaeology shows that, after this second destruction, the site was abandoned and empty for several centuries. Yet the Bible has the Israelites, under the judge Deborah, defeating the army from a major Hazor, perhaps about 200 years after the Conquest. Additionally, many of the other Conquest sites on the chart don't match the biblical description of fearsome, fortified cities with walls reaching to heaven in 1200 BC. It also seems questionable whether the eroded remains of a highly fortified Jericho from 1200 BC could remain hidden from archaeologists searching near the base of the tell.

Camp 2: A 1450 BC Exodus (conventional timeline)

Proponents of an approximately 1450 BC Exodus date using the conventional timeline of Egypt include Bryant Wood, Charles Aling, and Clyde Billington. They use the verse of 1 Kings 6:1 to date the Exodus 480 years before the conventional dates for Solomon's reign. This camp points to the earlier destructions of Hazor and Jericho as evidence for a 1410 BC Conquest. However, dating those destructions to the end of the Late Bronze 1 period – around 1410 BC, goes against the consensus of mainstream opinion. Most scholars place those destructions at the very end of the Middle Bronze Age, conventionally dated to around 1550 BC. However, there are conflicting claims about the destruction layers at Hazor, as well as a minor shift of opinion over the last 50 years as to what dates mainstream archaeologists should assign to the various layers.

Members of Camp 2 would link the second destruction at Hazor with the time of the judges when Deborah and Barak battled forces from Hazor. In his discussion with Bryant Wood, Tim Mahoney asked him about various issues related to the Conquest including Wood's proposal for shifting the date of the main destruction at Jericho from about 1550 BC (held by most archaeologists) to around 1400 BC in order to fit the biblical record.

Mahoney: Many scholars are suggesting a date around 1200 BC for the Conquest. What are the consequence of that?

Wood: Well, if you're looking in the wrong century for the Conquest, you're not going to find evidence for it obviously. If we look at the archaeological evidence around 1400 BC, we find evidence that supports the biblical account, particularly the cities that were burned by fire – the cities of Jericho, Ai, and Hazor. We're told in the book of Joshua that the Israelites burned those three places. If you go to those sites, and all three of them have been excavated, you find that there is evidence for burning. If you go to those sites and look at the 1230 or 1200 BC time period, which is this later dating of the Exodus Conquest, there is no evidence. One exception you could say is Hazor. We do have a destruction around 1230 BC, but that one has to be ascribed to Deborah and Barak in Judges 4.

Mahoney: So you're saying there's two burnings at that city?

Wood: Yes.

Mahoney: And that is what the biblical story says?

Wood: Yes. It matches exactly, and in fact at Jericho we have a similar situation. We have a massive destruction around 1400 and then, built on the ruin of the destruction, we have this what you can call a residency which dates to the latter part of the 14th century, which would be exactly the time of Ehud and Eglon and the story in Judges chapter 3. And so it matches perfectly with the biblical history we have, as does Hazor with its two destructions. Now the people who favor the later dating of the Conquest, they say, "Oh, that later destruction in Hazor is the Joshua destruction in 1230 BC. There's evidence for our late date Conquest." But if you ascribe that to Joshua, there's no city after that for Deborah and Barak to conquer. And so it just doesn't fit.

Mahoney: What about the earlier destruction at Jericho? Do Joshua and Jericho go together?

Wood: When we come to the site of Jericho, the problem (in trying to correlate the archaeological findings there with the biblical record) is that the destruction level at Jericho has been misdated by Kathleen Kenyon who excavated there in the 1950s. From my interpretation of the dating evidence that we have, we can date that destruction to the end of the Late Bronze 1 period, around 1400 BC. And that's based on mainly pottery. But we do have in the cemetery some Egyptian scarabs that Garstang excavated in the 1930s, and these are scarabs of pharaohs who ruled in the 15th century BC. And so that is supporting evidence from a documentary source, you could say. But the strongest evidence is the actual Canaanite pottery that's in the destruction layer, and that is Late Bronze 1 pottery.

Mahoney: What made you investigate Jericho? What caused you to take notice and change your mind about the dating there?

Wood: I got interested in Jericho when I was working on my PhD thesis. The subject of my thesis was the pottery of the Late Bronze period, the Canaanite pottery, local pottery, not the imported pottery. And so I was going through all the excavation reports, and studying that Late Bronze Age pottery, and I came to Garstang's report on Jericho. I looked at his report and I said, "Wow. He's got Late Bronze 1 pottery here. That's odd. No occupation in Jericho during this time period, the time period of the Exodus and Conquest? What's happening here?"

Mahoney: So you're saying that this was a different opinion, different than the standard view. Is that correct?
Wood: Yes.

Mahoney: What happened then?
Wood: Well, then I was invited to give a paper at a symposium on the Exodus and Conquest. And I thought, I think I'll look into this Jericho question. This was after I'd completed my PhD and had a little more time. So I did. I went through all of Kenyon's articles and writings concerning Jericho and the date of the destruction. And I learned a very interesting thing – that she did not ever analyze the local Canaanite pottery in the destruction level. She based her dating on the fact that she did not have imported Cypriot bichrome ware in that destruction level. Now this was a type of pottery imported from Cyprus that was indeed in use in the 15th century BC, but she based her argument on the fact that it wasn't there. It was absent. So she was making an argument from silence, from something she did not find. "It's not there, so it must be that nobody was living in this city in the Late Bronze 1 period." Well, she should have looked at the local Canaanite pottery because that's all Late Bronze 1.

Mahoney: Is there something unique about this particular type of pottery that she was looking for that the common person didn't have?
Wood: The Cypriot pottery was imported. Therefore it was more expensive. It was nicely decorated, so it was kind of a fine ware, Grandma's fine china, so to speak. So it wasn't all that common. It's found mainly in tombs as grave goods. When someone died, they would put this in the grave with them as kind of a memorial gift or something. But it's not that common in the domestic levels.

Mahoney: So what you're saying is that the average person wouldn't have it in the first place.

Wood: Usually not, and in particular the area that Kenyon was excavating at Jericho, and Garstang dug in the same area, was a poor part of town. Kenyon noted this in her own reports. This was a very poor area, the houses were small and the pottery was just common everyday cheap pottery, you might say. She made that observation and yet expected to find expensive imported pottery in that destruction level. It just was not logical thinking, really.

Mahoney: Another important part of your work is the city of Ai. Can you talk about that?

Wood: Ai was the second city that the Israelites conquered. It's described in Joshua chapters 7 and 8, and scholars have decided that the location of Ai is at et-Tell. This is a large ruin about ten miles north of Jerusalem. It's been excavated by several expeditions over the years, and what they have found there is a large Early Bronze Age city. This would go back to roughly 2300 BC, even to the days before Abraham. And then there's a big gap with no occupation at the site all the way until about 1100 BC down in the time of the Judges. So no matter which date you might choose for the Exodus and Conquest, there's no evidence at et-Tell to support the biblical account. There was no city there. This has led scholars to conclude that, as they did with Jericho, that the biblical story is legendary – it never really happened.

Now in our organization, the Associates for Biblical Research, we don't accept this interpretation. We've been doing field work for many years to locate the real site of Ai. I began working at a site called Khirbet el-Maqatir, which is only 1 kilometer, six-tenths of a mile, west of et-Tell. I began working there in 1995, and from the very first season we began discovering evidence that matches the biblical record, and we're still working there many years later.

Mahoney: So because they had the wrong location it was another mark against the Conquest.

Wood: Yes. So these two places, Jericho and Ai, have pretty much provided the evidence the scholars use to say that there was no Conquest. In the case of Jericho, the difficulty there is misdating the finds from the destruction. In the case of Ai, the problem is they had the wrong site identified as Ai.

Mahoney: What type of evidence are you finding?

Wood: Well, we have discovered a small fortress there, which dates to the time of Joshua. It's a Late Bronze 1 fortress. We have found the gate of that fortress, actually half the gate. The other half has been robbed out. They've taken the stones away for building something else. But, at least we have half of it. We found two lower gate socket stones. These were stones that the pivot of the gate turned in, and we even have an upper socket stone, a very rare find in Israel. And so that was very important because there's no question but what the structure was the gate, can't be anything else. The gate figures very prominently in Joshua 7 and 8. The gate is very interesting because of its location. We read in Joshua chapter 8, when Joshua brought the army up to Ai, that he camped in front of the city, on the north side of the city. Well, that's very indicative of where you would find the gate, because what is the front of a city or a fortress? It's where the entrance is. It's where the gate is. The front of your house is where your front door is. And so, it very specifically says on the north side. So we should expect to find the gate of Ai on the north side of the site, and that's exactly where our gate is located, on the north side of the site.

Mahoney: Okay. And was that site burned?

Wood: Yes, we have evidence for burning. We have found it all over the site actually, in some cases ash. Not much because the site was left abandoned and exposed to the elements, and there's been a lot of rebuilding. So, much of that evidence is gone. But we have found stones, and particularly the limestone bedrock has been discolored and subjected to very high temperatures, making it kind of decompose, almost turn to lime. It becomes very chalky.

Then perhaps the strongest evidence that wouldn't be recognized by the normal person, but to an archaeologist it's significant that we find pottery from the time of the fortress, Late Bronze 1 pottery, that has been what we call "refired." In other words, it's been subjected to a second burning, subjected to extremely high temperatures which has turned that pottery rock hard. It's like cement – obviously it's not the original firing – it's whitish, what we call "metallic" in consistency. And we find this pottery all over the site, and that is indicative that the whole place was burned with an intense fire that has made this pottery rock hard.

Mahoney: Okay, Jericho, and this location that you're suggesting is Ai, and Hazor.

Those three cities, do you have evidence that they were destroyed around the same time?
Wood: Jericho, Ai, and Hazor were all destroyed at the end of Late Bronze 1 as we can tell from the pottery that's in the destruction level. It's very similar in all three sites.

Mahoney: Now, you're going against the trend here. I mean, most of the archaeologists in the world have bought into a completely different date for these finds.
Wood: Yes, that's true. But I go back to my original thesis, that we must base our conclusions on the evidence and on the data. And if these scholars will look at the evidence and the data, I think they will be forced to come to the correct conclusion concerning the biblical dating of these events and concerning the destructions that we have found.

* * *

It should be noted that Wood's attempt to redate Jericho's destruction to a Late Bronze date around 1410 BC does not address an important problem Wood needs to overcome. When we look at the Conquest cities listed as defeated by the Israelites in the Bible, the archaeology shows that more than half of them were either completely abandoned or mostly abandoned at the conventional date for the Conquest around 1410 BC. So even if Wood can show some evidence that Jericho may have been destroyed around 1410 BC, against the consensus view of its demise near the end of the Middle Bronze Age, his proposal still does not address the other dozen or so Conquest cities (about half of the total) that were empty around 1410 BC. Since they were empty ruins, they couldn't have been defeated by the Israelites as the Bible describes. In order for Wood's proposal to match the biblical account, he would need to produce convincing evidence that the final destructions of all these major Conquest sites have also been misdated by 150 years. All of this can be reviewed in the chart at the beginning of this chapter.

Another problem for a 1410 BC destruction date for Hazor is the Amarna letters, which record the correspondence between Canaanite rulers and the pharaohs Amenhotep III and Akhenaten between about 1390-1340 BC. We learn from these letters that Hazor was thriving during this time, which is not consistent with a city that had just been completely destroyed and its armies wiped out. Wood associates the marauding Habiru of the Amarna letters with the Hebrews. But the letters indicate that Hazor was an ally of the Habiru at this time, not their enemy as would be the case if these Habiru were Joshua's Israelites.

Perhaps new information will help resolve the difficulties with a 1450 BC Exodus in the conventional time frame. But for now, the problems with the evidence for the **Conquest** in Canaan join other problems with the six steps to weaken this view. It only can fit with Joseph/**Arrival** evidence by using the 430-years-in-Egypt scenario, and even then it is not an exact fit. It has the last century of the **Multiplication** step happening after the Delta had been emptied of much of its Semitic population (based on archaeological remains as well as historical records). It puts the **Judgment** and **Exodus** steps at a time in history when Egypt was experiencing an unbroken period of wealth and power with no sign of major problems.

As with the other parts of my investigation, the only place that a pattern of evidence matches all the steps of the biblical sequence is in the Middle Kingdom/Middle Bronze Age.

Camp 3: A 1600 BC Exodus (conventional timeline)

Camp 3 considers the biblical dating of the Exodus from the book of 1 Kings 6:1 to be symbolic. It claims that there is other information in the Bible that suggests the time between the Exodus and Solomon is greater than 480 years, and this would push the Exodus back from the 1450 BC date by more than a century. Much of the basis for this view comes from the book of Acts 13:16-22, which recounts the early history of Israel. Several translations interpret this passage in a way that seems to stipulate that there were actually 450 years of judges.

> And when he had destroyed seven nations in the land of Chanaan, he divided their land to them by lot. And after that he gave unto them judges about the space of four hundred and fifty years, until Samuel the prophet. (Acts 13:19-20 KJV)

This view of Acts 13 would result in an apparent contradiction between these verses and 1 Kings 6:1 – Acts 13 with 450 years of judges and 1 Kings with 350 years of judges as depicted below.

> Solomon began to build the temple for the Lord in the four hundred eightieth year after the

Israelites came out of the land of Egypt, in the fourth year of his reign over Israel, in the second month, in the month of Ziv. (1 Kings 6:1)

480	(Exodus to Solomon's 4th year)
- 40	wanderings after the Exodus
- 6	Conquest
- 40	Saul
- 40	David
- 3.1	Solomon
= 350	years of judges

To solve this problem, the 450-years-of-judges view maintains that the 480 years of 1 Kings 6:1 does not include the 114 years of oppressions of the Israelite tribes in Canaan by foreign forces. When these are added to the 336 years of peace and judgeships depicted in the book of Judges, a total of 450 years for the judges is reached. Other slight variations of this equation are sometimes used to reach the 450-year figure. Since many in this group go with the classic dating of Solomon (about 45 years older than the current standard) this produces an Exodus date around 1600 BC and a Conquest around 1560 BC.

This method would indeed provide a good fit with the conventional dates for the destruction of Conquest sites in Canaan near the end of the Middle Bronze Age. However, at present there are several factors that seem to challenge this view. First of all, a 1600 BC Exodus would not align as well with evidence for the first 5 steps of the biblical sequence.

One example of this problem is that an Exodus happening around the 1600 BC time frame would not coincide with a major collapse of Egyptian society as suggested by the **Judgment** step. Instead, Egypt at this time was slowly increasing in power and would soon become unified again after a long period of splintered dynasties simultaneously ruling from different places. Egypt was already in a condition of weakness at this time in the Middle of the Second Intermediate Period and had been for more than 50 years. This therefore does not match a relatively strong Egypt being plunged into weakness and chaos.

An arrival happening 210 or 215 years before 1600 BC would put Joseph's famine relief at a time when the pharaohs were declining in power at the end of the 12th Dynasty, not at a time when they were sharply rising in power. An Israelite entry into Egypt

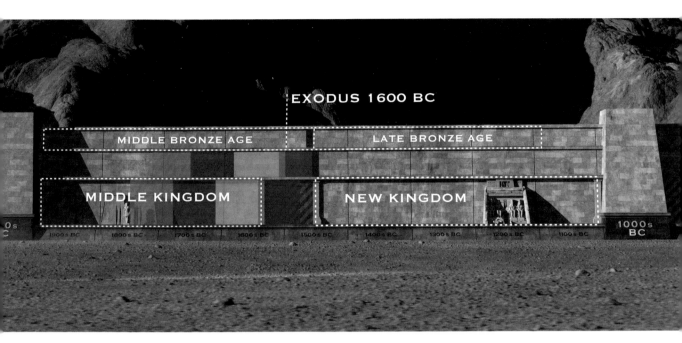

EXODUS 1600 BC

MIDDLE BRONZE AGE   LATE BRONZE AGE

MIDDLE KINGDOM   NEW KINGDOM

1900s BC   1800s BC   1700s BC   1600s BC   1500s BC   1400s BC   1300s BC   1200s BC   1100s BC   1000s BC

at 1810 BC would also mean that the slavery would not have begun until several decades after the Brooklyn Papyrus with its Hebrew slave names. The shifting of Egypt's timeline that would be needed to resolve these differences would then begin to make this proposal look more like Camp 4, only with a different Exodus date.

Perhaps more significantly, the biblical case for the Exodus happening much longer than 480 years before Solomon is not compelling. It is questionable whether the 450 years of Acts 13:19-20 is talking about the judges at all. There are two possible interpretations of this passage in Acts, and the majority view is that the "450 years" pertains to the early phase of Israel's history from Abraham to the dividing of the land after the Conquest.

A 1600 BC Exodus with a 210-year Israelite sojourn still has problems lining up the archaeological evidence with some of the six steps.

Interpretation Option No. 1:

Then after destroying seven nations in the land of Canaan, He gave their land to them as an inheritance. This all took about 450 years. After this, He gave them judges until Samuel the prophet. (Acts 13:19-20 HCSB)

The second option is that the "450 years" refers to the time of the judges.

Interpretation Option No. 2:

And when he had destroyed seven nations in the land of Chanaan, he divided their land to them by lot. And after that he gave unto them judges about the space of four hundred and fifty years, until Samuel the prophet. (Acts 13:19-20 KJV)

But several difficulties arise in the second option if the 450 years does refer to the judges. One problem is that the symbolic interpretation of 480 years from Exodus to Solomon's fourth year does not really equate to 336 (or 339 in some calculations) years of symbolic judges (all of the judges period minus the times of oppression) plus the rest of the biblical events in that period as defined by Paul in Acts 13. The total reached would actually be 465 years, not 480.

40	wanderings after the Exodus
6	Conquest
40	Saul
40	David
3.1	Solomon
+ 336	Judges (not including oppressions)
= 465	(not 480 as 1 Kings 6:1 records)

If the time spans recorded in the book of Judges really do run end to end (as maintained by this view), then the judges period as defined by Paul in Acts 13 would actually not add up to 450 years but instead would be much longer. In contrast, there are clear indications in the text that many of the periods reported in the book of Judges overlapped each other, which would allow for the accuracy of 350 years of judges as required by 1 Kings 6:1.

Another check to the 450-years-of-judges view shows that a problem is caused by the genealogies such as the one of Salmon (the fifth generation below Judah) to King David recorded in Ruth 4: 21-22, 1 Chronicles 2:10-15, and Matthew 1:5-6. In a 450-years-of-judges view each of the three consecutive generations in this family line would be required to have fathered their children when over the age of 140, which seems much too high – even when compared to the norms of the patriarchs. You have to go back to Noah to see a greater age recorded for the fathering of children.

In Judges 11:26, one of the last judges of Israel, Jephthah states that the Israelites had been living in the land for 300 years at that time. This fits 350 years of judges and 480 years between Solomon and Exodus, rather than 450 years of judges.

These factors combine to caution against an interpretation of Acts 13 that stipulates 450 years for the judges. It seems that more research needs to be done and new evidence would need to be uncovered for some variation of this option to become a leading candidate.

Camp 4: A 1450 BC Exodus (unconventional timeline)

The family line from Salmon and Rahab down to David argues against the 450-years-of-judges view.

While all of the four main pro-Exodus camps can point to some evidence that matches the Exodus account, Camp 4 is the only one that seems to hold the promise of produc-

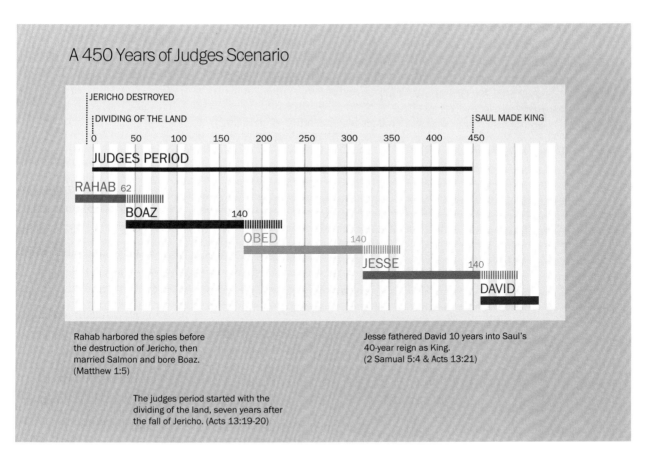

A 450 Years of Judges Scenario

JERICHO DESTROYED

DIVIDING OF THE LAND

SAUL MADE KING

0   50   100   150   200   250   300   350   400   450

JUDGES PERIOD

RAHAB 62

BOAZ   140

OBED   140

JESSE   140

DAVID

Rahab harbored the spies before the destruction of Jericho, then married Salmon and bore Boaz. (Matthew 1:5)

Jesse fathered David 10 years into Saul's 40-year reign as King. (2 Samual 5:4 & Acts 13:21)

The judges period started with the dividing of the land, seven years after the fall of Jericho. (Acts 13:19-20)

ing a consistently good match between the archaeological evidence available today and all six of the major biblical steps for Exodus (both in the big picture of the archaeological landscape and in specific and detailed finds). Therefore, this view has been the main focus of this book. While there are a variety of differing ideas within this camp, all hold to the common opinion that mainstream scholarship puts far too much confidence in the current reconstruction of the timeline for ancient Egypt. They seek to reevaluate the ancient timeline of Egypt/Canaan and reconstruct it based on a fresh treatment of all the archaeological evidence. They believe that major shifts to Egypt's timeline are in order, which would help align the dates of the Bible's Exodus account with the archaeological evidence found earlier than expected on the timeline. The amount of shifting has many possible variations, but proposals range from about 150 years to nearly 1,000 years for the period that may be related to the events of Exodus (2500 BC - 1000 BC). Proponents of these views generally have a high regard for ancient historical texts such as the Bible and seek to coordinate those accounts with the available hard evidence, but they vary in regards to their knowledge of Egyptology.

Additional support for this option is gained by the fact that evidence exists having nothing to do with the Bible, from Egypt and the nations surrounding it, which also points in the direction of shifting the timeline for Egypt's New Kingdom forward by centuries. However, Camp 4 faces stiff challenges from mainstream scholars because it runs counter to the conventional timeline for ancient Egypt, whose general framework has been used by scholars for more than a century.

In regards to the Conquest, it can be noted that one major reason for dating the multiple destructions in Canaan to the very end of the Middle Bronze Age was to match the theory that the destructions were the result of the Egyptians pursuing the Hyksos after they expelled them from Egypt at the beginning of the 18th Dynasty around 1550 BC. But there is no solid evidence that the Egyptians were responsible for these destructions. If it was the Israelites who actually caused these troubles, then it would open the door wider to the possibility that the demise of the Canaanite cities occurred somewhat before the end of the Middle Bronze Age. More work is needed to better determine how close to the end of the Middle Bronze these destructions occurred. This question underscores the difference between David Rohl and John Bimson, with Bimson putting the destructions within a few decades of the end of the Middle Bronze, and Rohl proposing a more gradual ending to that period with the destructions occurring more than a century before the very end of the Middle Bronze Age.

Although there are many possible variations that need further research, there are three very major realities late in the Middle Kingdom of Egypt and in the Middle Bronze Age of Palestine that seem to make them stand out above all the other factors. These factors seem to paint the general archaeological landscape in a way that allows the Exodus to fit best. The convergence of these three elements is unique in the whole period of ancient history that includes the Old, Middle, and New kingdoms of Egypt:

- The rise of a massive Semitic population at Avaris and other Delta sites during the only period when the archaeology shows this kind of Semitic domination matching the **Multiplication** step of the biblical sequence,

- The first time in Egypt's history since the establishment of the Old Kingdom, where the archaeology shows Egypt's entire society suffering a dramatic and prolonged collapse to the point where they are dominated by foreign powers matching the **Judgment** step,

- The only time in the second millenium BC when the archaeology of Canaan matches the Bible's description of specific cities having high walls and being destroyed in the same short period matching the **Conquest** step.

Radiocarbon Dating

One argument that is frequently made against Camp 4, and its support for shifting Egyptian dates, utilizes radiocarbon dating, which employs the radioactive decay rate of carbon-14 atoms to determine the age of ancient organic matter. It is often claimed that carbon-14 tests have confirmed the general reliability of the conventional timeline so that a major shift is not possible.

Two main points can be offered in response. First, most people might be surprised to learn that, typically, the dates reported for carbon-14 test results are not the raw numbers from the lab but rather they are adjusted numbers based on a process that is suspect. The raw numbers themselves for the period before about 500 BC are actually understood by the academic community to be invalid. This is what *Cambridge Encyclopaedia of Archaeology* has to say about this issue:

"When the radiocarbon method was first tested, good agreement was found between radiocarbon dates and the historical dates for samples of known age (for example, from ancient Egyptian contexts). As measurements became more precise, however, it gradually became apparent that there were systematic discrepancies between the dates that were being obtained and those that could be expected from historical evidence. These differences were most marked in the period before about the mid-first millenium BC, in which radiocarbon dates appeared too recent, by up to several hundred years by comparison with historical dates. Dates for the earliest comparative material available, reeds used as bonding between mud-brick courses of tombs of the Egyptian Dynasty I, about 3100 BC, appeared to be as much as 600 years, or about 12 percent, too young." [105]

So generally speaking, the raw numbers from radiocarbon testing actually fit the idea of a younger Egyptian timeline rather well. However, instead of questioning the histories that have been reconstructed for the ancient world, scholars attempt to solve the problem by adjusting the results given by the radiocarbon testing process. There are a number of assumptions that are inherent to this method of dating that need to be true if it is to be accurate. If any of these assumptions are wrong, the dates produced by the test will be wrong. One of those assumptions is that the amount of carbon in the atmosphere has been steady over the last thousands of years. Since scientists know this is not the case, they attempt to compensate by applying a "calibration curve" to the raw carbon-14 results to produce an older and hopefully more accurate number. So it is these adjusted figures that are published, not the raw numbers from the tests.

The accuracy of this calibration equation is checked by a method known as "wiggle matching." Wiggle matching uses tree-ring sequences that have been constructed by the process of matching patterns of growth rings in trees that appear to be similar to one another in order to make a single long sequence. Increasingly ancient sections of wood are combined together to extend the record of rings back over many thousands of years. Carbon-14 tests (the very process that the tree rings are attempting to validate) are then done on the ancient parts of these tree-ring sequences to gauge the accuracy of the calibration curve. The 2,500th ring in the sequence should test as being 2,500 years old in a carbon-14 test.

One big question is whether these lengthy tree ring sequences have been assembled properly. Another question is whether radiocarbon tests can legitimately be used to help verify the accuracy of radiocarbon testing. Although other dating methods are used in the attempt to get multiple verifications, they all suffer from having to rely on a list of unverifiable assumptions. It may be the case that one questionable method is being used to validate another questionable method. This is far from an exact science and claims of recent advances in the "accuracy" of these tests ignore the underlying problems of the method.

The second major point is that even after all the adjustments, the results from radiocarbon testing still do not actually match the timelines constructed by mainstream historians and archaeologists. There is a split between members of this group and the scientists doing radiocarbon dating.

This is what the eminent Egyptologist Manfred Bietak wrote: "In order to apply such a scheme with absolute dates, we still have the problem of two chronologies: the historical chronology, based mainly on Egyptian and Assyrian chronologies and their interrelationship, and radiocarbon chronology. Despite all attempts to discuss these differences away or at least to minimize them, one has to realize that there are periods with a considerable difference between radiocarbon and historical chronology, which cannot be denied nor be reconciled at the moment. However, other sciences being involved, we hope for decisive results."

Bietak would rather set aside the reliance on radiocarbon dating in favor of the approach of using inscriptions, texts, and artifacts to work from known dates backwards to the unknown, as has been done in the conventional reconstruction of the Egyptian timeline. He wrote that this approach "is today the preferred method of arriving at a historical chronology" for Egyptian history. [106]

The farther back in time you go, the less confident is the ability of carbon-14 measurements to produce accurate calendar dates. Bietak is not claiming that radiocarbon dates are off from the conventional timeline by centuries, but the principle remains the same. If the method is not trustworthy and believed to be off by 1-2 percent, is it really inconceivable that it may be off by as much as 10 percent? Perhaps the raw numbers are a good general indicator after all. Despite the claims of some scientists, carbon-14 dating is not a settled issue, and allowing it to trump ideas that are based on strong patterns of historical evidence is a practice that should be strongly questioned.

ENDNOTES

Chapter 1

[1]   Christopher Hitchens, *God Is Not Great: How Religion Poisons Everything*
     (New York: Hachette Book Group, 2007), 102.

[2]   *Ibid.,* 8.

[3]   Richard Dawkins, *The God Delusion* (New York: Houghton Mifflin, 2006), 237.

Chapter 3

[4]   The 19th Dynasty of Egypt's New Kingdom included the first pharaohs
     named Ramesses.

The Family of the 19th Dynasty

These New Kingdom pharaohs were the first to
reign with the name Ramesses

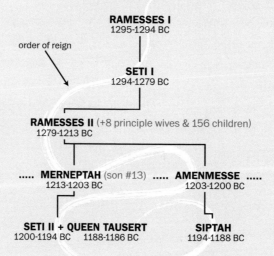

RAMESSES I
1295-1294 BC

order of reign

SETI I
1294-1279 BC

RAMESSES II (+8 principle wives & 156 children)
1279-1213 BC

..... **MERNEPTAH** (son #13) ..... **AMENMESSE** .....
1213-1203 BC   1203-1200 BC

SETI II + QUEEN TAUSERT   **SIPTAH**
1200-1194 BC   1188-1186 BC   1194-1188 BC

5   The Bible describes the Israelites as shepherds with flocks and herds in Genesis 47:
1-4. Genesis 47:5-6 recounts Pharaoh giving permission for the family of Israel to
settle in Goshen, the best land for grazing in Egypt. The Israelites multiplying
exceedingly is found in the book of Exodus 1:7-10, 12.

So Joseph went and informed Pharaoh: "My father and my brothers, with their sheep and
cattle and all that they own, have come from the land of Canaan and are now in the land of
Goshen."

He took five of his brothers and presented them before Pharaoh. Then Pharaoh asked his
brothers, "What is your occupation?"

And they said to Pharaoh, "Your servants, both we and our fathers, are shepherds." Then
they said to Pharaoh, "We have come to live in the land for a while because there is no grazing land for your servants' sheep, since the famine in the land of Canaan has been severe.
So now, please let your servants settle in the land of Goshen."

Then Pharaoh said to Joseph, "Now that your father and brothers have come to you, the
land of Egypt is open before you; settle your father and brothers in the best part of the land.
They can live in the land of Goshen. If you know of any capable men among them, put them
in charge of my livestock." (Gen. 47:1-6)

But the Israelites were fruitful, increased rapidly, multiplied, and became extremely numerous so that the land was filled with them.

A new king, who had not known Joseph, came to power in Egypt. He said to his people,
"Look, the Israelite people are more numerous and powerful than we are. Let us deal
shrewdly with them; otherwise they will multiply further, and if war breaks out, they may join
our enemies, fight against us, and leave the country." (Ex. 1:7-10)

But the more they oppressed them, the more they multiplied and spread so that the Egyptians came to dread the Israelites. (Ex. 1:12)

[6] The foundational importance of the events related to the Exodus in the Bible can be seen in many places, including Deuteronomy 4:33-35, and for the Christian in Mark 12:26-27 and John 5:46-47 of the New Testament.

"Has a people heard God's voice speaking from the fire as you have, and lived? Or has a god attempted to go and take a nation as his own out of another nation, by trials, signs, wonders, and war, by a strong hand and an outstretched arm, by great terrors, as the Lord your God did for you in Egypt before your eyes? You were shown these things so that you would know that the Lord is God; there is no other besides Him." (Deut. 4:33-35)

Now concerning the dead being raised – haven't you read in the book of Moses, in the passage about the burning bush, how God spoke to him: I am the God of Abraham and the God of Isaac and the God of Jacob? He is not God of the dead but of the living. You are badly deceived." (Mark 12:26-27)

"For if you believed Moses, you would believe Me, because he wrote about Me. But if you don't believe his writings, how will you believe My words?" (John 5:46-47)

Chapter 4

[7] The land promises given to Abraham, initially recorded in Genesis 12:7 and 13:14 17, are repeated in Genesis 15:18-21. All six of the major steps of the biblical sequence for the Exodus period can also be derived from the foundational chapter of Genesis 15 where God ratifies the Covenant with Abraham:

Step 1   **Arrival** from Gen. 15:13

Step 2   **Multiplication** from Gen. 15:5

Step 3   **Slavery** from Gen. 15:13

Step 4   **Judgment** from Gen. 15:14

Step 5   **Exodus** from Gen. 15:14

Step 6   **Conquest** from Gen. 15:16

⁵ He took him outside and said, "Look at the sky and count the stars, if you are able to count them." Then He said to him, "Your offspring will be that numerous."

¹³ Then the Lord said to Abram, "Know this for certain: Your offspring will be foreigners in a land that does not belong to them; they will be enslaved and oppressed 400 years. ¹⁴ However, I will judge the nation they serve, and afterward they will go out with many possessions. ¹⁵ But you will go to your fathers in peace and be buried at a ripe old age. ¹⁶ In the fourth generation they will return here, for the iniquity of the Amorites has not yet reached its full measure."

¹⁸ On that day the Lord made a covenant with Abram, saying, "I give this land to your offspring, from the brook of Egypt to the Euphrates River." (Genesis 15:5, 13-16, 18)

These events are then fleshed out over the following six books of the Bible.

Chapter 5

8. The account of Joseph being sold to traders who take him to Egypt can be found in Genesis 37:12-36. Joseph's rise to power and his subsequent rescue of Egypt from the famine is recounted in Genesis 41:37-57.

9. Many consider the first major writer of history in Western literature to be the Greek historian Herodotus, who traveled extensively in the fifth century BC investigating the traditional accounts of the wars and major events in the cultures surrounding Greece. Herodotus recorded his findings in a book called *The Histories*. The Bible attributes Moses, who lived during the time of the Exodus, as the author of the first books of the Bible. Many scholars today doubt this and claim that the books of the Bible were written many hundreds of years after the time of the Exodus. However, if Moses really did author the early Bible, this would make him earlier than Herodotus by about 1,000 years.

10. The land of Goshen, where the Israelites settled, is first mentioned in Genesis 45:10 and described in verse 18. Similar mentions can be found elsewhere, such as in Genesis 47:1, 4, 6, and 27.

> Israel settled in the land of Egypt, in the region of Goshen. They acquired property in it and became fruitful and very numerous. (Gen. 47:27)

[11] How do we know that the second mention of Ramesses in the Bible was about 100 years after the first? The first mention of Ramesses is "the land of Rameses" that Jacob's family moved to in Genesis 47:11. The second mention of Ramesses is the supply city built by the Israelite slaves in Exodus 1:11.

We know that there were at least 100 years between the two references because Joseph was 30 when he stood before Pharaoh (Gen. 41:46). Then came seven years plenty followed by two years of famine before Jacob and his family arrived in Egypt (Gen. 45:6):

- Therefore, Joseph would have been 39 when Jacob arrived and settled in Ramesses.
- It was 71 years later that Joseph died at the age of 110 (Gen. 50:26).
- After this, all of Joseph's brothers died. Levi lived to 137 (Ex. 6:16) and was at most ten years older than Joseph, so he died at least 17 years after Joseph.
- After an unspecified number of years, the remainder of that generation died, and after that point the new pharaoh arose who did not know Joseph, and at some point he enslaved the Israelites who eventually built the city of Ramesses (Ex. 1:6-11).

So it seems likely that more than 100 years passed between the initial settlement of Jacob in the land of Ramesses and the building of the store city of Ramesses after the **Slavery** step began.

[12] The Bible itself clearly shows other cases of anachronisms in the form of updated city names. The city of Dan is referenced in Genesis 14:14. However, we know from Judges 18:29 that the city was originally called Laish and not named Dan until after the Conquest, when the tribe of Dan took over the city and renamed it. The renaming of the city occurred decades after the death of Moses, who is credited with writing Genesis. Therefore, the city could not have had the name Dan at the time of Moses and certainly not at the time of Abraham. Several other passages also use later city names even though they happened in earlier periods of the story,

before the more recent version of the name was instituted. For example, the name of the city of Luz was changed to Bethel in Genesis 28:19, but the name "Bethel" is used for this city back in Genesis 12:8 and 13:3 with no mention of its former name.

13   The family of Jacob had strong connections to Haran, which today is located near the border between Turkey and Syria:
   • Jacob's grandfather Abraham lived in Haran before he came to Canaan (Gen. 11:31-32, 12:4-5).
   • Jacob's father, Isaac, got his wife from Haran. Abraham had insisted that he marry from among his relatives, so he sent his servant back to Haran, where he found Rebekah, the sister of Laban, and brought her to Isaac. (Gen. 24:2-4, 29).
   • Jacob also had strong ties to Haran. He went back to Haran, where he married the daughters of Laban (Gen. 27:43, 29:19-20).
   • Jacob ended up living in Haran for 20 years and had 11 sons and a daughter during that time (Gen. 31:41).

14   Genesis 41:37-46 tells of Pharaoh rewarding Joseph for his wisdom in interpreting his dreams that warned of the coming famine.

15   Jacob's 12 sons are listed in Exodus 1:1-5. The story of their births by four different mothers can be found in Genesis 29:31 - 30:24 and also Genesis 35:16-19.

16   The story of Joseph's multicolored coat can be found in Genesis 37:3-4. We know from the Bible that Joseph's original coat never made it to Egypt (Gen. 37:29-33). However, it is certainly possible that Jacob had a new coat made for his favorite son after they reunited in Egypt.

Now Israel loved Joseph more than his other sons because Joseph was a son born to him in his old age, and he made a robe of many colors for him. When his brothers saw that their father loved him more than all his brothers, they hated him and could not bring themselves to speak peaceably to him. (Gen. 37:3-4)

17   Joseph's dreams of his family bowing down to him, and the account of his brothers selling him as a slave to Midianite traders, can be read in Genesis 37:5-11 and

37:18-28. The detail of 20 shekels is referenced in the last verse.

18 Joseph interprets Pharaoh's dreams and is made second in command of Egypt in Genesis 41:1-46. In Genesis 45:6 it is made clear that there will be neither planting nor harvest during the seven years of famine.

> For the famine has been in the land these two years, and there will be five more years without plowing or harvesting. (Gen. 45:6)

19 The Bible records that seven years of plenty were followed by seven years of famine. Eventually, everyone in Egypt was forced to sell their land in order to continue buying grain for their survival. A 20 percent tax was levied on all the produce of the land, and only the priests were exempt from selling their land and paying the tax.

The stone on Sehel Island mentioning seven years of famine and a tax that the priests were exempt from.

Interestingly, very similar conditions are recorded on a large rock face in the middle of the upper Nile River at the First Cataract below Aswan. The stone resting on Sehel Island is called the Joseph Stone by some. It may preserve the faded memory of a seven-year famine just as described in the Bible. It is believed to have been made in the Ptolemaic period, perhaps between 332-180 BC, by a group of Egyptian priests who claimed ownership of the surrounding land and exemption from paying the tax as overseers of its collection. To make this claim, they appealed to an ancient story.

The inscription purports to be an account from the time of Pharaoh Djoser of the Old Kingdom's Third Dynasty (conventionally dated to around 2660 BC) and speaks of a great famine caused by seven years of extreme drought, followed by a time of plenty. This is followed by an official decree enacting a 10 percent tax on all the harvest and commerce in the land.

While this is very similar to the biblical account, the dates of the inscription as well as the various details it describes, come from a wide variety of time periods. These hieroglyphs may represent a historical composite, echoing events from the distant past. The account on this stone perhaps combined the Bible's great famine with various details from other parts of ancient history that were superimposed one over the other. Scholars find such telescoping of history in other Egyptian documents.

20 A chart depicting these years of high floods can be found here: David M. Rohl, *Exodus – Myth or History?* (Minneapolis, MN: Thinking Man Media, 2015), 96.

21 The Bible depicts Joseph being favored in several places:
- Joseph was his father's favorite son (Gen. 37:3-4)
- Joseph gained favor with Potiphar (Gen. 39:2-5)
- Potiphar's wife loved Joseph (Gen. 39:6-7)
- Joseph gained favor with keeper of the prison (Gen. 39:21-23)
- Joseph gained favor with Pharaoh (Gen. 41:37-40)

22 The account of Joseph's Famine Policy (storing grain and then selling it to the Egyptians and all the neighboring lands) can be found in Genesis 41:47-49, 41:53-57, 45:6-7, and 47:13-26. Joseph's efforts brought all the wealth of the nations into Pharaoh's hands, and that wealth and power were sustained by the policy of an on-going 20 percent tax on Egypt's produce.

23 An example of the opulent tomb of one of the last powerful nomarchs can be seen at Beni Hasen, which is covered in chapter 6, section 1.

24 An article about the super-forts (*The Middle Kingdom Egyptian Fortresses in Nubia* by Brian Yare, published in January 2001) can be found here: http://www.yare.org/essays/fortresses.htm

25 The account of the burial of Joseph's bones in Shechem can be found in these verses:

Joseph said to his brothers, "I am about to die, but God will certainly come to your aid and bring you up from this land to the land He promised Abraham, Isaac, and Jacob." So Joseph made the sons of Israel take an oath: "When God comes to your aid, you are to carry my bones up from here." (Gen. 50:24-25)

So He led the people around toward the Red Sea along the road of the wilderness. And the Israelites left the land of Egypt in battle formation.

Moses took the bones of Joseph with him, because Joseph had made the Israelites swear a solemn oath, saying, "God will certainly come to your aid; then you must take my bones with you from this place." (Ex. 13:18-19)

Joseph's bones, which the Israelites had brought up from Egypt, were buried at Shechem in the parcel of land Jacob had purchased from the sons of Hamor, Shechem's father, for 100 *qesitahs*. It was an inheritance for Joseph's descendants. (Josh 24:32)

[26] Abraham's first stop when he arrived in Canaan was Shechem, where God again promised him the land and Abraham built an altar to the LORD (Gen. 12:5-7).

[27] Information about Joseph's Tomb throughout history can be found here:
http://en.wikipedia.org/wiki/Joseph's_Tomb

[28] The story of Joseph forgiving the treachery of his brothers can be read in Genesis:
- Joseph is betrayed, thrown into a well, and sold to slave traders (Gen. 37:16-36).
- Joseph forgives his brothers (Gen. 45:1-15).
- Joseph reassures his brothers after Jacob's death (Gen. 50:15-21).

Chapter 6

[29] The Israelites' great multiplication, and their wealth as they lived in the best of the land of Egypt, is depicted during and after Joseph's life in Genesis 47:11, 27 and in Exodus 1:6-7. Jacob's family, numbering 70 members at the time of their arrival in Egypt, can be seen in Genesis 46:26-27.

[30] This quote and more information about Father Lucien Galtier can be found here:
http://en.wikipedia.org/wiki/Pierre_Parrant

31 It is clear that Ramesses (Avaris) continued to be a center for the Israelites because they departed Egypt from there after the plagues of the Exodus (Ex. 12:37 and Num. 33:3, 5).

32 The accounts of a new pharaoh enslaving the Israelites and their hard labor making bricks with straw are covered in Exodus 1:8-14 and 5:6-21.

33 The great multiplication of the Israelites, despite oppression, and their "spread" throughout the land can be found in Exodus 1:12. The episode of the drowning of the baby boys, Moses' birth and hiding, as well as his being found and adopted by Pharaoh's daughter is in Exodus 1:22 - 2:10.

34 James Hoffmeier commented on why we don't find remains of writings on papyrus from the Delta:

"It would be wonderful to have direct archaeological evidence, but we don't. And that's in large part because written documents, papyrus that might have told us about these people and who they were and what was going on, have not survived. The Delta is muddy, it has the annual flood, and the tombs just do not survive. The tombs that do survive, of course, are in the desert, out of the flood plain. Amazingly, Professor Bietak is digging in some cases below the water table. They have to pump out the water to lower the water table so that they can access the brick walls. In fact, in the Delta of Egypt, let's say at Tell el-Dab'a, where Manfred Bietak is excavating, from the period of Joseph and the Hebrews in Egypt, not one papyrus document has survived. He's found numerous clay seals that at one time did seal papyrus documents. Only the seals have survived. The papyrus is gone. It's a moist environment. It's not like Qumran, dry, or up in the deserts of Saqqara and Giza where papyrus can survive. So we actually have no surviving papyri from the Pharaonic period in the Delta. So if we had them, we might have more background information. The reality is we don't have that, so we have to go with what we do have."

35 The Israelites are said to have spread throughout the land (Ex. 1:12). This matches the evidence of many Semitic settlements in the Delta as well as the Brooklyn Papyrus, where nearly two-thirds of the 95 slaves were Semitic and from a single estate in southern Egypt. It also fits with the settlement at Kahun in central Egypt where there were many western Asiatic slaves. Not all the Asiatic population in Egypt during this period need be Israelite to fit the Bible's account. It says that a

"mixed multitude" or an "ethnically diverse crowd" joined the Israelites as they left Egypt (Ex. 12:38).

> But the more they oppressed them, the more they multiplied and spread so that the Egyptians came to dread the Israelites. (Ex. 1:12)
> An ethnically diverse crowd also went up with them, along with a huge number of livestock, both flocks and herds. (Ex. 12:38)

Chapter 7

36 The account of Moses fleeing to Midian, where he lived with Jethro, a priest of Midian, can be found in Exodus 2:11-15. Moses approaching the burning bush is in Exodus 3:1-10.

37 This Bible passage reveals the personal name of God.

> Then Moses asked God, "If I go to the Israelites and say to them: The God of your fathers has sent me to you, and they ask me, 'What is His name?' what should I tell them?"
>
> God replied to Moses, "I AM WHO I AM. This is what you are to say to the Israelites: I AM has sent me to you." God also said to Moses, "Say this to the Israelites: Yahweh, the God of your fathers, the God of Abraham, the God of Isaac, and the God of Jacob, has sent me to you. This is My name forever; this is how I am to be remembered in every generation. (Ex. 3:13-15)

38 The first two confrontations between Moses and Pharaoh can be read in Exodus 5:1-4 and 7:10-13.

39 Beginning with the fourth plague, God protected the Israelites from the effects of the plagues (Ex. 8:22-23). In Exodus 10:7, Pharaoh's servants said that Egypt was already devastated before the eighth plague.

> Pharaoh's officials asked him, "How long must this man be a snare to us? Let the men go, so that they may worship Yahweh their God. Don't you realize yet that Egypt is devastated?" (Ex. 10:7)

40 This covenantal relationship between God and the Israelites can be seen in the proclamation that was made in Exodus 20:1-2, right before the Ten Commandments begin in the third verse. The Covenant had first been made to Abraham (Genesis 12:1-3 and chapter 15) and passed through Isaac (Gen. 17:19-21) and then to Jacob, whose name was changed to Israel (Gen. 27:36-37 and 35:10-12). The nation of Israel under Moses entered into a special aspect of this Covenant at Mount Sinai (Ex. 19:5-6).

I am the Lord your God, who brought you out of the land of Egypt, out of the place of slavery. Do not have other gods besides Me. (Ex. 20:1-3)

41 The tenth plague of the death of the firstborn and the first Passover night are covered in Exodus chapters 11 and 12.

42 These aspects of the story of the Israelites leaving Egypt are found in the following places:
   • Pharaoh's son dying, resulting in the command to leave (Ex. 12:29-32)
   • The Israelites gaining gold and silver from the Egyptians (Ex.12:33-36)
   • Pharaoh changing his mind and pursuing (Ex. 14:5-9)
   • The destruction of the Egyptians in the sea (Ex. 14:26-31, 15:19)

43 Today the Passover commemorating God's protection of the Israelite people and their liberation from slavery in Egypt is the central celebration of Judaism. The command to remember this day was given in the book of Exodus.

"The blood on the houses where you are staying will be a distinguishing mark for you; when I see the blood, I will pass over you. No plague will be among you to destroy you when I strike the land of Egypt. This day is to be a memorial for you, and you must celebrate it as a festival to the Lord. You are to celebrate it throughout your generations as a permanent statute." (Ex.12:13-14)

Then Moses said to the people, "Remember this day when you came out of Egypt, out of the place of slavery, for the Lord brought you out of here by the strength of His hand." (Ex. 13:3)

[44] The extent of the devastation that would have been suffered by Egypt if the biblical account is accurate is often overlooked. Additional aspects of the judgment include the following points:

- Even if there were no plagues and the Israelites were not slaves, the single factor of losing such a significant proportion of a country's population would be enough to cause tremendous disruption and chaos in Egypt.
- The agricultural loss was not just that one year's crops and would be felt for many years, which meant prolonged hardship – fish, cattle, fruit trees, and vines destroyed.
- Not only did the Egyptians lose their cattle by plague but they lost the Israelites' huge herds as well (Ex. 12:32).
- The Egyptians also lost much of their liquid assets of gold, silver, and clothing (Ex. 12:35-36). A simple tunic could cost 3 days of a laborer's wage in the ancient world, and fine clothing such as silks could be more than 100 times more expensive.

http://ancientcoinsforeducation.org/content/view/79/98/

- God's stated purpose was to severely judge Egypt (Ex. 3:20-22, 6:1, 7:3-5, 9:14-18, 10:1-2, 11:6-9, 12:12, 14:17-18).
- Pharaoh's servants said that Egypt was devastated even before the eighth plague (Ex. 10:7).
- If the firstborn male of every Egyptian woman was killed, this would have been 33 percent of the male population, if women had an average of three sons who were living at the time.
- Firstborns typically dominated positions of leadership and authority at every level of ancient society.
- Moses' reference to Egypt still being in a state of defeat 40 years after the Exodus comes just before Israel was about to begin the Conquest of Canaan in Deuteronomy 11:4.

- After this point in the narrative, Egypt is not mentioned in the present tense again until the time of King David 400 years later.
- A devastated and weak Egypt would invite foreign invasion, lured by the riches in the tombs and the fertile production of the Nile basin, since power abhors a vacuum.
- Certainly, this is one of the elements of the Exodus story that is too big to remain hidden in the archaeology.

[45] Miriam Lichtheim, *Ancient Egyptian Literature* (Berkeley and Los Angeles: University of California Press, 1973, 2006), 149.

[46] *Ibid.,* 150.

[47] The dating of the Ipuwer Papyrus is a crucial matter. Many publications display confusion when writing about the date of the *Admonitions.* Two problems are commonly seen. First, some list the date of the copy housed at the Leiden Museum (19th Dynasty). However, since this is known to be a copy of a much older document, it is the date of the original composition that is of more importance to any possible connection to the Exodus. A second tendency is to list dates for the period that the story may be speaking of. Often the calamities during the decline of the 6th Dynasty through the First Intermediate Period (ending around 2050 BC) are postulated as the possible setting. But again, various theories about what period the story might be set in are not the initial concern of an objective inquiry. Of first importance is the date of the original composition of the story. After that is determined, ideas related to what event it is referring to can be addressed.

Nearly all linguistics experts today date the original composition of the Ipuwer Papyrus to late in the Middle Kingdom. They are basing their conclusion on the characteristics of the language used in the papyrus, as well as the style and historical realities revealed in the text. But there are differing views on exactly what "late in the Middle Kingdom" means. The end of the 12th Dynasty in Egypt is conventionally dated to around 1800 BC, and some consider this point as the end of the Middle Kingdom. But many scholars include the majority of the 13th Dynasty within the Middle Kingdom as well, since there is no archaeological evidence of major problems in Egypt for much of the 13th Dynasty. Subsequently, many of these experts also date the *Admonitions of an Egyptian Sage* a little later than Raven does, by a century or more:

- Vincent A. Tobin in *The Literature of Ancient Egypt* (Yale University, 2003, 188) writes that the composition of the text in the *Admonitions* is unlikely to have been as early as Gardiner's original estimate of the 12th Dynasty. Tobin says the more widely accepted date is "late Middle Kingdom."
- Miriam Lichtheim in *Ancient Egyptian Literature* (149-50) writes that the text is "late Middle Kingdom" and is the last composition on the theme "order versus chaos."
- John van Seters argues that the original Ipuwer text belonged securely in the late Middle Kingdom or early Second Intermediate Period. He wrote: "One date seems to fit all the requirements: late 13th Dynasty" (*The Hyksos: A New Investigation*, Yale University, 1966, 115).

One historical indication of the date of the original composition is the mention of pyramid builders in the present tense. Pyramids were built by pharaohs from the 3rd Dynasty onward throughout the Old and Middle Kingdoms. There were no large royal pyramids built in the New Kingdom. The construction of pyramids ended late in the 13th Dynasty, showing that this would be the latest time this document would have been written.

Chapter 8

48 This famous sonnet, "Ozymandias," written by Percy Bysshe Shelley in 1817 was inspired by the British Museum's acquisition of a statue remnant of Ramesses II. The ancient Greek version of Ramesses II's throne name was Ozymandias.

I met a traveller from an antique land
Who said: Two vast and trunkless legs of stone
Stand in the desert . . . Near them, on the sand,
Half sunk, a shattered visage lies, whose frown,
And wrinkled lip, and sneer of cold command,
Tell that its sculptor well those passions read
Which yet survive, stamped on these lifeless things,
The hand that mocked them, and the heart that fed:
And on the pedestal these words appear:
"My name is Ozymandias, king of kings:

Look on my works, ye Mighty, and despair!"
Nothing beside remains. Round the decay
Of that colossal wreck, boundless and bare
The lone and level sands stretch far away.

49 There are numerous places in the Bible that hint that the text was updated, besides the apparent anachronisms of geographical names such as the city of Dan (see note 12 above). Deuteronomy credits Moses as its author, but chapter 34 recounts the death and burial of Moses (obviously not written by Moses after his death). Verse 6 says that "no one to this day knows where his grave is." Most readers of the text might assume that Joshua wrote the postscript, but the text does not claim this. Additionally, verse 10 says, "No prophet has arisen again in Israel like Moses." This appears to have been written from the perspective of someone who knew about a long history of prophets in Israel, all of whom could not be compared to Moses. Accounts of the prophets in Israel did not become common until the time of the kings, hundreds of years after Moses.

It may be that a later prophet in Israel put the writings of Moses and other authors into their final form and included the updated terms. Other verses that show signs of being written long after the events occurred include the following:

That is why, **to this day**, the Israelites don't eat the thigh muscle that is at the hip socket: because He struck Jacob's hip socket at the thigh muscle. (Gen. 32:32)

Jacob set up a marker on her grave; it is the marker at Rachel's grave **to this day**. (Gen. 35:20)

The Horites had previously lived in Seir, but the descendants of Esau drove them out, destroying them completely and settling in their place, **just as Israel did** in the land of its possession the Lord **gave** them. (Deut. 2:12)

Joshua also set up 12 stones in the middle of the Jordan where the priests who carried the Ark of the Covenant were standing. The stones are there **to this day**. (Josh. 4:9)

And raised over him a large pile of rocks that remains **to this day**. Then the Lord turned from His burning anger. Therefore that place is called the Valley of Achor **to this day.** (Josh. 7:26)

Joshua burned Ai and left it a permanent ruin, desolate to this day. He hung the body of the king of Ai on a tree until evening, and at sunset Joshua commanded that they take his body down from the tree. They threw it down at the entrance of the city gate and put a large pile of rocks over it, **which remains to this day.** (Josh. 8:28-29)

He had 30 sons who rode on 30 donkeys. They had 30 towns in Gilead, which are called Jair's Villages **to this day.** (Judg. 10:4)

That is why, **to this day**, the priests of Dagon and everyone who enters the temple of Dagon in Ashdod do not step on Dagon's threshold. (1 Sam. 5:5)

And it has been so **from that day forward**. David established this policy as a law and an ordinance for Israel and **it continues to this very day.** (1 Sam. 30:25)

[50] An Exodus date derived from 1 Kings 6:1 in turn depends on the dates assigned to Solomon. Based on the majority view for Solomon's dates, his fourth year would equate to 966 BC, resulting in an Exodus date of 1446 BC, which is the Exodus date most commonly cited by recent scholars who use this verse for their calculations. The dates for Solomon's reign are arrived at by starting with the date for the fall of the kingdom of Judah and the destruction of the Temple in 587 or 586 BC. Then the reign-lengths of kings listed in the Bible are used to work back to Solomon. However, traditional views among theologians and chronologists (prior to the mid-20th century) actually put Solomon's reign about 45 years earlier than the current conventional dates because the Bible appears to lay out 45 more years for the kings of Judah. This would also push the Exodus 45 years earlier.

The current or modern conventional view adjusts the Bible's timeline of Israel's kings. This is because the Assyrian chronology is preeminent in the minds of many scholars. There are historical links between Assyrian kings and Israel's kings. Because Assyrian dates are preferred, they are used to date the Israelite kings even though this goes against the Bible's timeline. But could the Assyrian lists in this early period be in error rather than the Bible's report? For the sake of simplicity, and since the year 1446 for the early Exodus date has been so widely held, this book uses a general Exodus date of 1450 BC based on 1 Kings 6:1.

[51] The Pharaoh who built Ramesses died before the Israelites left Egypt. The building of the city of Ramesses occurs in the narrative around the time of Moses' birth (Ex. 1:11 and 2:1-10). Moses fled to Midian as an adult (Ex. 2:11-15). During his stay in Midian before the Exodus, the text in two places says that the pharaoh who had sought Moses' life had died (Ex. 2:23, 4:19).

> Now in Midian the Lord told Moses, "Return to Egypt, for all the men who wanted to kill you are dead." (Ex. 4:19)

[52] Did the pharaoh die in the sea crossing? When the passage describing the Egyptian army's attempt to cross the sea in Exodus 14:27-28 is looked at in isolation, it is evident that the pharaoh is not explicitly said to have died. This has caused many scholars to argue that he was not killed. In fact, famous Exodus films such as DeMille's *The Ten Commandments* depict Pharaoh surviving the destruction at the sea. However, a broader look at the information in the Bible seems to require Pharaoh's death along with his army.

Perhaps the strongest indicator is seen when comparing Exodus 14:27 to Psalm 136:15. Here, the Hebrew word for "threw" in Exodus 14:27 is the identical Hebrew word used for "hurled" in Psalm 136:15. This Hebrew word is *na'ar*, which means to shake off or to shake out. Other English translations use the words "overthrew" and "swept" in these spots. So according to these two texts, what happened to the "Egyptians" in Exodus 14 is exactly what happened to "Pharaoh and his army" in Psalm 136 – and that means destruction.

> So Moses stretched out his hand over the sea, and at daybreak the sea returned to its normal depth. While the Egyptians were trying to escape from it, the LORD **threw** [na'ar] them into the sea. The waters came back and covered the chariots and horsemen, the entire army of Pharaoh, that had gone after them into the sea. None of them survived. (Ex. 14:27-28)

But [He] **hurled** [*na'ar*] Pharaoh and his army into the Red Sea.
His love is eternal. (Psalm 136:15)

Second, the Bible paints the picture of Pharaoh personally leading his army in the pursuit. In ancient times, the normal role of kings in battle was to lead the army from the front, not stay in the rear. Scenes and accounts of kings leading their forces are common in Egypt as well as in the Bible. What follows is the account that makes clear that Pharaoh personally led his troops.

When the king of Egypt was told that the people had fled, Pharaoh and his officials changed their minds about the people and said: "What have we done? We have released Israel from serving us." So he got his chariot ready and took his troops with him; he took 600 of the best chariots and all the rest of the chariots of Egypt, with officers in each one. The LORD hardened the heart of Pharaoh king of Egypt, and he pursued the Israelites, who were going out triumphantly. The Egyptians – all Pharaoh's horses and chariots, his horsemen, and his army – chased after them and caught up with them as they camped by the sea. As Pharaoh approached, the Israelites looked up and saw the Egyptians coming after them. Then the Israelites were terrified and cried out to the LORD for help. (Ex. 14:5-10)

The text then explicitly says that the entire army went in – and all who went in were destroyed.

But Moses said to the people, "Don't be afraid. Stand firm and see the LORD's salvation He will provide for you today; for the Egyptians you see today, you will never see again. (Ex. 14:13)

The Egyptians set out in pursuit – **all** Pharaoh's horses, his chariots, and his horsemen – and went into the sea after them. (Ex. 14:23)

The waters came back and covered the chariots and horsemen, the entire army of Pharaoh, that had gone after them into the sea. **None of them survived.** (Ex. 14:28)

The reason that the Israelites were not to fear is that they would never see these Egyptians again. That is because God was about to destroy the Egyptians, and Pharaoh was the chief Egyptian. Not just some of the Egyptians were to be destroyed, but all of them. The one whom the Israelites feared most was Pharaoh himself, and there is no exception made for him in the text. In fact, if he had survived, the Israelites still would have had cause to fear. The Jewish historian Josephus, in his *Antiquities of the Jews II*, xvi, 3 (343-44), also writes that not a single Egyptian escaped the disaster to return to Egypt. In Exodus 15:19, the word "horses" in the phrase "Pharaoh's horses" is just as likely to be singular as plural. It is used in a singular sense in 15:1 and 15:21 and several translations of the Bible use the singular form for this verse as well. This renders the statement as "Pharaoh's horse with his chariots and horsemen went into the sea."

When Pharaoh's horse(s) with his chariots and horsemen went into the sea, the LORD brought the waters of the sea back over them . . . . (Ex. 15:19)

A final point to make is that in many places God states that his intention is to judge Pharaoh and the Egyptians. In chapter 14 alone, Pharaoh is distinguished from his troops three times when God states that he would gain glory by means of Pharaoh and by means of his army. There is no indication that the army received one kind of justice (destruction in the sea) and Pharaoh received another. Quite the opposite.

I will harden Pharaoh's heart so that he will pursue them. Then I will receive glory by means of Pharaoh and all his army, and the Egyptians will know that I am Yahweh." So the Israelites did this. (Ex. 14:4)

I am going to harden the hearts of the Egyptians so that they will go in after them, and I will receive glory by means of Pharaoh, all his army, and his chariots and horsemen. The Egyptians will know that I am Yahweh when I receive glory through Pharaoh, his chariots, and his horsemen." (Ex. 14:17-18)

A plain reading of the text strongly favors the idea that Pharaoh is depicted as being destroyed in the sea crossing along with his entire army. Attempts to argue otherwise appear to be motivated largely by a desire to fit the story with some New Kingdom pharaoh, almost all of whose mummies have been found intact in Egypt. As with many other factors in debates about the Bible, the details of descriptions in the text are often downplayed in order to fit the various theories of scholars, which don't really match the text at all.

[53] The length of the Judges Period poses another problem for the Ramesses Exodus Theory. The judges ruled in Israel between the Conquest and the time of the first kings – Saul, David, and Solomon. David was known to be reigning before 1000 BC and Saul was before him. This would mean the Judges Period in the Ramesses Exodus view would be limited to only about 150 years. However, the Judges ruled for about 350 years, based on other evidence in the Bible. When the details of the book of Judges are reviewed, there appears to be no way that its history can be compressed into a 150-year period. Besides the 480-year reference in 1 Kings 6:1, the declaration of one of Israel's later judges, Jephthah, also seems to indicate that during the Judges Period the Israelites had been living in the land of Canaan for about 300 years, far more than the 150 years allowed by the Ramesses Exodus Theory. Here are Jephthah's words:

"While Israel lived 300 years in Heshbon and its villages, in Aroer and its villages, and in all the cities that are on the banks of the Arnon, why didn't you take them back at that time?" (Judg. 11:26)

[54] Kent Weeks gave more information about the sons of Ramesses who may be buried in KV5: "We have four names of these sons from son number one up through son number twelve. Those are the potential candidates for burial in KV5. We have four, I think, with certainty because we have their names. We have their canopic jars. We have, I think, their bodies. But there are another eight here who also could have been buried in the tomb."

[55] References to the Israelites spending 40 years in the wilderness after the Exodus can be found in Numbers 14:26-34, Deuteronomy 2:7, and Joshua 5:6. For most

of the Judges Period, a span of about 350 years that followed the Conquest, the tribes were fairly independent and not an established and unified nation, sometimes even warring against each other (Judg. 20:20).

56 The Berlin Pedestal mentioning Israel was discovered by the German archaeologist Manfred Gorg. An excellent article by Gorg, with colleagues Peter van der Veen and Christoffer Theis, can be found here:

http://goo.gl/HPcvAd

57 When we examine the Bible closely, an important relationship between the Shasu of Yahweh inscription and the Exodus becomes apparent. The Bible indicates that the pharaohs of Egypt, and even the Israelites, were not aware of the name Yahweh before the time of the Exodus. This fact is supported by the scene at the burning bush where Moses is not aware of the personal name for God (Ex. 3:13). In Exodus 5:2 Pharaoh denies knowing who Yahweh is. Exodus 6:2-3 says that God had not even revealed his name to the patriarchs.

Then Moses asked God, "If I go to the Israelites and say to them: The God of your fathers has sent me to you, and they ask me, 'What is His name?' what should I tell them?" (Ex. 3:13)

But Pharaoh responded, "Who is Yahweh that I should obey Him by letting Israel go? I do not know anything about Yahweh, and besides, I will not let Israel go." (Ex. 5:2)

Then God spoke to Moses, telling him, "I am Yahweh. I appeared to Abraham, Isaac, and Jacob as God Almighty, but I did not reveal My name Yahweh to them. (Ex. 6:2-3)

Later, God said to Pharaoh,

"I have let you live for this purpose: to show you My power and to make My name known in all the earth." (Ex. 9:16)

The Shasu of Yahweh inscription was written by the 18th Dynasty Pharaoh Amenhotep III (conventionally dated to 1390 BC). If the name of Yahweh was truly not known until the time of the Exodus, it means that this inscription naming Yahweh must have come **after** the Exodus. Yet this inscription was made nearly 150 years **before** the middle of Ramesses' reign and the Ramesses Exodus date. This would mean Ramesses reigned long after the Exodus and could not be the pharaoh who confronted Moses.

Chapter 9

[58] The swift expulsion of the people of Israel from Egypt is seen in Exodus chapter 12:

> Now the Egyptians pressured the people in order to send them quickly out of the country, for they said, "We're all going to die!" So the people took their dough before it was leavened, with their kneading bowls wrapped up in their clothes on their shoulders.
>
> The Israelites acted on Moses' word and asked the Egyptians for silver and gold jewelry and for clothing. And the Lord gave the people such favor in the Egyptians' sight that they gave them what they requested. In this way they plundered the Egyptians.
>
> The Israelites traveled from Rameses to Succoth, about 600,000 soldiers on foot, besides their families. An ethnically diverse crowd also went up with them, along with a huge number of livestock, both flocks and herds. The people baked the dough they had brought out of Egypt into unleavened loaves, since it had no yeast; for when they had been driven out of Egypt they could not delay and had not prepared any provisions for themselves. (Ex. 12:33-39)

[59] It should be noted that the other Semitic sites in the area of Goshen mentioned by John Bimson also seem to have experienced significant abandonments of their Semitic population in the same general time period as Avaris.

James Hoffmeier writes that the zenith of Semitic presence in Egypt's Nile Delta occurred from about 1800 BC - 1550 BC. This presence was represented by such sites as Tell el-Retabeh, Tell el-Yehudiyeh, Inshas, Tell Farasha, Tell el-Kebir and Tell el-Maskhuta. Along with Avaris, some of these sites show an occupational hiatus of large numbers of Semites during the New Kingdom/Late Bronze Age (*Israel in Egypt,* New York: Oxford University Press, 1996, pp. 53, 67-68).

60 A. R. David, *The Pyramid Builders of Ancient Egypt* (London: Routledge, 1986, 1996), 59.

61 Like Avaris, we don't know precisely when Kahun was abandoned, but the end of the Middle Kingdom also fits well with the evidence. Only one scarab from the 13th Dynasty was found at Kahun – that of Pharaoh Neferhotep I, meaning the abandonment of the village happened at some point after his mid-dynasty reign. Interestingly, the early partial abandonment of Avaris' Semitic population also occurred late in the 13th Dynasty. Rosalie David writes in her book that an evacuation date for Kahun in "the later reigns of the 13th Dynasty" can be concluded from papyrus documents and artifacts discovered there. Professor David wrote: "It seems that the town continued to prosper without interruption throughout the whole of this period [12th and 13th dynasties], and the local situation would have reflected the general conditions throughout Egypt at this time" (*Ibid.,* 115, 197).

62 *Ibid.,* 4, 199.

63 *Jewish Antiquities,* Book 2, Chapter 14, Loeb 311-12 found in *The New Complete Works of Josephus* (Grand Rapids, MI: Kregel Publications, 1966), 105.

64 David, *Pyramid Builders,* 246.

65 *Ibid.,* 121.

66 David found her information on page 11 of an excavation report by Petrie entitled *Illahun, Kahun and Gurob, 1889-90.*

67 David, *Pyramid Builders,* 241.

68 There appears to have been a mysterious takeover of the super-forts. Late in the 13th Dynasty a number of monuments at Buhen (including the stela of Ka) have the commander at the fortress proudly declaring that he serves the new king in control of the region, King Nedjeh of Kush. The Egyptian commander at the fort had come from a long line of rulers whose authority had been passed down from father to son, making this shift in allegiance even more striking.

http://wysinger.homestead.com/nedjeh.html

[69] Two ancient historians that are relevant to this part of the story are Manetho, an Egyptian priest, and Artrapanus, an early Jewish writer. Both wrote in Greek during the third century BC, and there are no surviving copies of either of their writings. We know parts of their work only from other ancient writers quoting them.

Egyptologists originally used Manetho as the basis for their reconstruction of Egyptian dynasties. Manetho's story of the Hyksos invasion of Egypt is recounted by the first century AD Jewish historian Josephus in his *Against Apion,* 14, 73-92, where he quotes a part of Manetho that fits the conditions that would be in Egypt after the calamities surrounding the Exodus:

"Tutimaeus [Dudimose]. In his reign, for what cause I know not, a blast of God smote us; and unexpectedly, from the regions of the East, invaders of obscure race marched in confidence of victory against our land. By main force they easily seized it without striking a blow; and having overpowered the rulers of the land, they burned our cities ruthlessly, razed to the ground the temples of the gods, and treated all the natives with a cruel hostility, massacring some and leading into slavery the wives and children of others."

The historian Artrapanus is important because he actually gives the name of the pharaoh who raised Moses. He is paraphrased by Eusebius (Book 9, Chapter 27:1-37) as saying that the pharaoh during Moses' time as prince of Egypt was Khenephres, which equates to the Egyptian throne name of Khaneferre taken by Pharaoh Sobekhotep IV, who followed shortly after Neferhotep I of the 13th Dynasty. If Artrapanus had invented the story, it seems far more likely that he would have chosen a famous pharaoh rather than the obscure name of Khenephres (Khaneferre). This dating is significant because it also fits an Exodus happening in the late 13th Dynasty. Sobekhotep IV (Khaneferre) reigned several decades before Pharaoh Dudimose (Tutimaos), during whose time Manetho wrote that a blast of God smote the Egyptians. The Bible places Moses' birth 80 years before the Exodus.

David M. Rohl, *Exodus – Myth or History?* (Minneapolis, MN: Thinking Man Media, 2014), 156-60, 375-78.

Chapter 10

[70] Major events during Israel's 40 years of wilderness wandering include:

- The miraculous sea crossing (Ex.14)
- The giving of the law at Mount Sinai (Ex.19 - 20)
- The construction of the tabernacle, the Ark of the Covenant, and all the other furnishings (Ex. 36 - 40)
- Israel refusing to enter the land because of the bad report of the spies at Kadesh Barnea, which resulted in the judgment that they would spend 40 years in the wilderness (Num. 13 - 14, Deut. 1:3 and 2:14)
- And the transfer of authority to Joshua, followed by the death of Moses, just before the Israelites entered the land of Canaan (Deut. 34)

[71] The walls Garstang tagged as being from Joshua's Conquest were found to actually be from the Early Bronze Age. His city IV, which he also associated with Joshua's Conquest, was found to be from the end of the Middle Bronze Age. (Taken from Thinking Man Films' interview of Bryant Wood.)

[72] The account of Rahab hiding the spies can be found in Joshua 2. According to the book of Matthew (1:4-6), Rahab would go on to marry Salmon, the son of Nahshon, who was the leader of the tribe of Judah during the Exodus. Their great-great grandson would be King David of Israel.

[73] The Bible describes the major cities of Canaan as being great and having high walls reaching up to heaven (Deut. 1:28, 9:1). It can also be seen that Jericho was a fortified city with a gate and walls in Joshua 2:5, 2:15, and 6:1.

[74] The Ark of the Covenant represented God's presence within Israel. The two tablets of the Ten Commandments were kept inside. The Ark is described in Exodus 25 and 26. The passage in Numbers 4:4-6, 15 explains how it was transported.

[75] Jericho's defeat and destruction is found in Joshua 6, the walls coming down in 6:20, and the burning of the city in 6:24.

[76] Kathleen Kenyon concluded that the fire accompanying the final destruction of Jericho was intentional and due to enemy attack. She wrote that the three-foot-thick brushwood fire layer – consisting of streaks of black, brown, white, and pinkish ash – was testimony to the intense temperatures and the enormous quantity of brushwood that must have been used to burn the city (*Digging Up Jericho: The*

Results of the Jericho Excavations 1952-1956, London: Frederick A. Praeger, 1957, 177, 229, 259). The tactic of piling brushwood high and then igniting it is evidenced at other burned cities in Canaan as well as in the Bible, where every man in a renegade army is ordered to take up a bundle of brushwood on his shoulder to burn a stronghold.

So Abimelech and all the people who were with him went up to Mount Zalmon. Abimelech took his ax in his hand and cut a branch from the trees. He picked up the branch, put it on his shoulder, and said to the people who were with him, "Hurry and do what you have seen me do." Each person also cut his own branch and followed Abimelech. They put the branches against the inner chamber and set it on fire around the people, and all the people in the Tower of Shechem died – about 1,000 men and women. (Judg. 9:48-49)

[77] It is interesting to note that at several points in her book, Kenyon dates the final destruction at Jericho to around 1580 BC, not 1550 BC (*Digging Up Jericho,* 48, 171, 229).

[78] Several details in the biblical narrative point to the battle of Jericho being a very short springtime siege:
- The fact that there was flax drying on the rooftop indicates that the spring harvest had just come in (Josh. 2:6).
- The Israelites crossed the Jordan River at the time of the harvest (Josh. 3:15).
- They crossed the Jordan on the tenth day of the first month, and for the Israelites the first month started with spring and is equivalent to our March/April (Josh. 4:19, Ex. 12:1-6, Num. 33:3, Ex. 16:1, and Ex. 19:1).
- They celebrated Passover shortly after crossing the Jordan River (Josh. 5:10).
- The siege only lasted seven days (Josh. 6:14-16).

[79] The value of food was much greater in ancient times. Unlike much of today's world where an average person might spend less than 20 percent of their income on food, the average person in antiquity would normally spend more than 50 percent of his wages on food.

(http://ancientcoinsforeducation.org/content/view/79/98/)

80 Leaving the grain in place to be burned fits both the record of the Israelites' actions and the instructions they were given for how to deal with Jericho.

> But the city and everything in it are set apart to the Lord for destruction. . . . They burned up the city and everything in it, but they put the silver and gold and the articles of bronze and iron into the treasury of the Lord's house." (Josh. 6:17, 24)

81 Rahab living in the wall and marking her home is found in Joshua 2:15-21 and 6:25.

82 Joshua curses Jericho in Joshua 6:26. The prophecy of this curse is said to be fulfilled when Jericho was rebuilt in the days of Ahab, the seventh king of the northern state of Israel, about 550 years after the Conquest (1 Kings 16:33-34). Apparently there was some minor development at Jericho in the time of King David (2 Sam. 10:5).

83 Spies reported a land flowing with milk and honey but also filled with very large fortified cities (Num. 13:27-28). The original use of "milk and honey" occurred in Exodus 3:8. The fortified cities were described as having walls reaching up to heaven in Deuteronomy 9:1.

84 The northern campaign of Joshua is covered in Joshua 11:1-15. King Jabin is mentioned in verse 1 and Hazor is burned in verse 13. A century or more after Joshua destroyed Hazor, the narrative mentions another king called Jabin, who is again defeated during the time of the judge Deborah (Judg. 4:1-2, 23-24). Jabin could have been a dynastic (or family) name like Ramesses was during the 19th and 20th dynasties of Egypt, with several Jabins reigning in that part of Canaan's history. For the multiple burn layers at Hazor, see Bonus Chapter E.

85 The Conquest is said to have occurred years after the Exodus because the Israelites wandered in the wilderness for 40 years due to their unwillingness to fight the Canaanites in the year following the Exodus (Num. 13:25 - 14:38).

86 The way the Merneptah Stele presents the term "Israel" in its account also matches the idea of nomadic Israelites, which is the apparent state of many of the Israelites in the biblical narrative during the wandering period, the Conquest, the time of the judges, and even the early kings of Israel.

Your children will be **shepherds** in the wilderness for 40 years and bear the penalty for your acts of unfaithfulness until all your corpses lie scattered in the wilderness. (Num. 14:33)

So Gideon sent all the Israelites to their **tents** but kept the 300, who took the people's provisions and their trumpets. (Judg. 7:8)

So the Philistines fought, and Israel was defeated, and each man fled to his **tent**. (1 Sam. 4:10)

David answered Saul: "Your servant has been tending his father's **sheep**. (1 Sam. 17:34)

One of Saul's servants, detained before the Lord, was there that day. His name was Doeg the Edomite, chief of Saul's **shepherds**. (1 Sam. 21:7)

I hear that you are shearing. When your **shepherds** were with us, we did not harass them, and nothing of theirs was missing the whole time they were in Carmel. (1 Sam. 25:7)

They took Absalom, threw him into a large pit in the forest, and piled a huge mound of stones over him. And all Israel fled, each to his **tent**. (2 Sam. 18:17)

When all Israel saw that the king had not listened to them, the people answered him: What portion do we have in David? We have no inheritance in the son of Jesse. Israel, return to your **tents**; David, now look after your own house! So Israel went to their **tents**. (1 Kings 12:16)

[87] The Israelites did not push out all the Canaanites but dwelt among them. This can be seen in many verses, including the following:

But, **they did not drive out the Canaanites** who lived in Gezer. **So the Canaanites live in Ephraim** to this day, but they are forced laborers. (Josh. 16:10)

The descendants of Manasseh **could not possess these cities, because the Canaanites were determined to stay in this land**. (Josh. 17:12)

At the same time **the Benjaminites did not drive out the Jebusites who were living in Jerusalem. The Jebusites have lived among the Benjaminites in Jerusalem to this day**. (Judg. 1:21)

When Israel became stronger, they made the Canaanites serve as forced labor **but never drove them out completely**. At that time Ephraim failed to drive out the Canaanites who were living in Gezer, **so the Canaanites have lived among them** in Gezer. Zebulun failed to drive out the residents of Kitron or the residents of Nahalol, **so the Canaanites lived among them** and served as forced labor. Asher failed to drive out the residents of Acco or of Sidon, or Ahlab, Achzib, Helbah, Aphik, or Rehob. **The Asherites lived among the Canaanites who were living in the land**, because they failed to drive them out. Naphtali did not drive out the residents of Beth-shemesh or the residents of Beth-anath. **They lived among the Canaanites who were living in the land**, but the residents of Beth-shemesh and Beth-anath served as their forced labor. (Judg. 1:28-33)

88 The book of Joshua 24:13 affirms that what Deuteronomy 6 had spoken of had actually taken place. The Israelites acquired intact homes filled with good things during the Conquest.

89 The Bible indicates that more than three cities were destroyed in the Conquest. It uses a certain term for the "curse of destruction" (or *charam* in Hebrew) that was placed upon the people of Canaan (Deut. 7:2) because of their wickedness (Gen. 15:16 and Deut. 9:4-5). But out of more than 300 Canaanite cities mentioned as being divided among the Israelite tribes in the Conquest, there are times when the text indicates that particular cities themselves, not just the people, were included in the destruction and in this curse. This leads to a higher number of cities that the archaeology should show were destroyed, if the story is true. See Bonus Chapter E for more information.

90 Even if some of the 19 cities on the list were not destroyed or not burned in the Conquest, they were great cities protected by high walls at that time according to the biblical account (Num. 13:28, Deut. 1:28, 9:1). The fact that nearly half of the cities on this list show no archaeological evidence for occupation – or evidence for only meager occupation with no walls in the Late Bronze Age – is opposite of the picture painted by the biblical account.

Hazor was said to be the only city in the northern phase of the Conquest that was burned. The way the text mentions this suggests that just a single isolated burning was different from the tactics used in the south. So the archaeological remains of 20-30 major fortified cities destroyed (most of which were burned) or abandoned in the south at the end of the Middle Bronze Age would then seem to fit the biblical picture very well. Conversely, there is a Late Bronze Age gap in occupation (activity or population) of Jericho, Hebron, Gibeon, Hormah, and Arad that goes all the way from the end of the Middle Bronze Age to the start of the Iron Age.

The information on the gap in occupation is taken from:

John J. Bimson, *Redating the Exodus and Conquest* (Sheffield, England: *Journal for the Study of the Old Testament*, 1978), 230-32.

[91] Most of the southern campaign to conquer Canaan is covered in Joshua 10:28-43, 11:21-23, and Judges chapter 1. The northern campaign including Hazor is found in Joshua 11:1-15.

[92] Additionally, the Bible gives a list of cities that it says were not defeated by the Israelites during the Conquest, including Megiddo, Taanach, Beth-shan, and Gezer (Judg. 1:27-33). In every case where a city from this group has been excavated, the archaeology shows evidence of continuous occupation going from the Middle into the Late Bronze Ages with no sign of destruction or abandonment. This further matches the biblical account. Bonus Chapter E shows a chart of this information. Bimson, *Redating the Exodus and Conquest,* 231.

[93] A brief biblical history of Shechem follows:

- Abraham's first stop in Canaan was at Shechem, where God spoke to him and he built an altar (Gen. 12:6).
- Jacob lived a while in Shechem where he bought land and built an altar (Gen. 33:18-20).
- Joshua called Israel to Shechem after the Conquest to renew the Covenant made at Mount Sinai (Josh. 24).
- Joseph's bones were buried in Shechem (Josh. 24:32).
- The tower of Shechem was where a terrible massacre occurred with about 1,000 people burned alive a couple hundred years after the Conquest (Judg. 9:46-49).

- Shechem at that time was demolished and sown with salt, meaning it was cursed and ruined (Judg. 9:45).

94 The tomb that many believe to be Joseph's is located within 200 meters of the remains of the migdol (fortress) temple and within 500 meters of Jacob's well at Shechem, modern Nablus. The tomb is ancient and was mentioned in Christian sources from the fourth century AD. Alan D. Crown, Reinhard Pummer, Abraham Tal, *A Companion to Samaritan Studies* (Tubingen, Germany: J. C. B. Mohr (Paul Siebeck), 1993), 139.

95 The "Tower of Shechem" is mentioned in Judges 9:46-49, the House of Millo Beth-Millo in Judges 9:6, 20, and the house of Baal-Berith in Judges 9:4. In Judges 8:30 - 9:57 the text relates the story of Abimelech, the son of Gideon, who brutally destroyed the city and trapped a thousand souls in the tower of the temple. There he burned them alive. The city was cursed, sown with salt, and abandoned.

96 Joshua challenging the people is found in the book of Joshua 24:14-15. Later in Joshua 24, it records his setting up the covenant renewal stone.

> Joshua recorded these things in the book of the law of God; he also took a large stone and set it up there under the oak next to the sanctuary of the Lord. And Joshua said to all the people, "You see this stone – it will be a witness against us, for it has heard all the words the Lord said to us, and it will be a witness against you, so that you will not deny your God." (Josh. 24:26-27)

97 G. Ernest Wright, *Shechem: The Biography of a Biblical City* (New York: McGraw Hill, 1965), 84-85.

Chapter 11

98 A few scholars have proposed that the Exodus may actually have occurred more than 100 years before the mid-1400s BC. They suggest that the 480 years between the Exodus and the building of Solomon's temple, referenced in 1 Kings 6:1, is not meant to be interpreted as 480 total years. Rather, they claim the 480-year figure does not include the times of foreign oppressions of the Israelites in Canaan listed in the book of Judges (the total time under oppressors being more than a century).

This would allow the Exodus to be dated earlier, perhaps around 1600 BC. This idea, which uses conventional dating for Egypt, fits quite well the dates for the evidence matching the Conquest but would create difficulties for matching the other steps of the biblical sequence. See Bonus Chapter E.

[99] Among those who question Egypt's standard chronology, John Bimson disagrees with David Rohl on how close to the end of the Middle Bronze Age the city destructions in Canaan occurred and therefore exactly how much of an adjustment is needed to the dates assigned to the Middle and Late Bronze Ages. Others propose a variety of somewhat different Exodus dates – but all within the general idea of looking earlier than expected. One proposal is that the Exodus actually occurred at the end of the 12th Dynasty instead of late in the 13th Dynasty, but the hard evidence for this does not seem to provide a good fit with the six steps of the biblical sequence.

Chapter 12

[100] The context of Pharaoh Shishak's war against Judah can be found in 1 Kings 11:26 - 12:24, 1 Kings 14:21-31, and 2 Chronicles 10:1 - 12:16. Highlights of the story include:

Jeroboam rebelled against Solomon. . . . Therefore, Solomon tried to kill Jeroboam, but he fled to Egypt, to Shishak king of Egypt, where he remained until Solomon's death. (1 Kings 11:26, 40)

When all Israel heard that Jeroboam [after Solomon's death] had come back, they summoned him to the assembly and made him king over all Israel. No one followed the house of David except the tribe of Judah alone. When Rehoboam arrived in Jerusalem, he mobilized 180,000 choice warriors from the entire house of Judah and the tribe of Benjamin to fight against the house of Israel to restore the kingdom to Rehoboam son of Solomon. (1 Kings 12:20-21)

There was war between Rehoboam and Jeroboam throughout their reigns. (1 Kings 14:30)

Rehoboam stayed in Jerusalem, and **he fortified cities in Judah**. He built up Bethlehem, Etam, Tekoa, Beth-zur, Soco, Adullam, Gath, Mareshah, Ziph, Adoraim, Lachish, Azekah, Zorah, Aijalon, and Hebron, which are fortified cities in Judah and in Benjamin. He strengthened their fortifications and put leaders in them with supplies of food, oil, and wine. He also put large shields and spears in each and every city to make them very strong. So Judah and Benjamin were his. (2 Chron. 11:5-12)

Because they were unfaithful to the Lord, in the fifth year of King Rehoboam, **Shishak king of Egypt** went to war against Jerusalem with 1,200 chariots, 60,000 cavalrymen, and countless people who came with him from Egypt—Libyans, Sukkiim, and Cushites. **He captured the fortified cities of Judah and came as far as Jerusalem**. . . . So King Shishak of Egypt went to war against Jerusalem. He seized the treasuries of the Lord's temple and the treasuries of the royal palace. **He took everything**. He took the gold shields that Solomon had made. (2 Chron. 12:2-4, 9)

Bonus Chapter C

101 Examples of the difficulty of capturing a fortress defended by resolute forces include Pharaoh Thutmose III of the 18th Dynasty besieging the fortress city of Megiddo for seven months before overcoming it. In the siege of Masada in 72 AD, 960 Jewish defenders resisted 15,000 Roman soldiers for several months before it fell.

Bonus Chapter D

102 This idea of introversion can be found in the Gen. 15:13 note from:
E. W. Bullinger, *The Companion Bible* (Grand Rapids, MI: Kregel Publications, 1990), 22.
103 References for these works can be found in Dr. Stephen C. Meyers' article, *Biblical Archaeology: The Date of the Exodus According to Ancient Writers,* at the following address:
http://www.bibleandscience.com/archaeology/exodusdate.htm

Bonus Chapter E

[104] The information on the chart is taken from:

Bimson, *Redating the Exodus and Conquest,* 52-53.

[105] Andrew Sherratt, *The Cambridge Encyclopaedia of Archaeology* (New York: Crown Publishers, 1980), 24.

[106] Manfred Bietak and Felix Hoflmayer, "Introduction: High and Low Chronology" in *The Synchronisation of Civilizations in the Eastern Mediterranean in the Second Millennium BC III* (Vienna: Österreichische Akademie der Wissenschaften, 2007), 13.

The quote can also be found on page 13 of this link:

http://www.academia.edu/226890/Introduction_High_and_Low_Chronology

PAGE 136 (Wall of Time) © Copyright, 2014 Patterns of Evidence, LLC.

PAGE 137 (Amenemhat III) © Copyright, 2012 David Rohl

PAGE 137 (Typical pharaoh) © Copyright, 2012 David Rohl

PAGE 138 (Joseph's Death) © Copyright, 2011 Mahoney Media Group/ Patterns of Evidence, LLC.

PAGE 139 (Shrine) © Copyright, Collections of the Library of Congress –Jericho – Matson 07374

PAGE 139 (Nablus) © Copyright, 2008 Mahoney Media Group / Patterns of Evidence, LLC.

PAGE 140 (Central Park) © Copyright, 2008 Mahoney Media Group/ Patterns of Evidence, LLC.

PAGE 141 (Mason) © Copyright, 2008 Mahoney Media Group /Patterns of Evidence, LLC.

PAGE 143 (Wall of Time) © Copyright, 2014 Patterns of Evidence, LLC.

Chapter 6

PAGE 145 (Rabbi Friedman) © Copyright, 2014 Patterns of Evidence, LLC.

PAGE 146 (Hill House) © Copyright, 2011 Mahoney Media Group /Patterns of Evidence, LLC.

PAGE 146 (Donkey) © Copyright, Photo: OeAI, Austrian Archaeological Institute, used with permission

PAGE 146 (Skeleton) © Copyright, OeAI, Austrian Archaeological Institute, used with permission

PAGE 147 (Avaris recreation) © Copyright, 2014 Patterns of Evidence, LLC.

PAGE 147 (Daggers) © Copyright, David Rohl, used with permission

PAGE 148 (Beni Hasan) © Copyright, David Rohl, used with permission

PAGE 149 (Gavigan) © Copyright, 2005 Mahoney Media Group / Patterns of Evidence, LLC.

PAGE 152 (Bimson) © Copyright, 2012 Mahoney Media Group / Patterns of Evidence, LLC.

PAGE 153 (Semitic Map) © Copyright, 2014 Patterns of Evidence, LLC.

PAGE 154 (Wall of Time) © Copyright, 2014 Patterns of Evidence, LLC.

PAGE 155 (DeMille) © Copyright, DeMille Family, used with permission

PAGE 155 (Bricks) © Copyright, 2012 Mahoney Media Group / Patterns of Evidence, LLC.

PAGE 156 (Mud Bricks) © Copyright, 2012 Mahoney Media Group/ Patterns of Evidence, LLC.

PAGE 156 (Tomb Painting) © Copyright, 2012 Titus Kennedy/ Mahoney Media Group/ Patterns of Evidence, LLC.

PAGE 157 (Hartman) © Copyright, 2007 Mahoney Media Group/ Patterns of Evidence, LLC.

PAGE 158 (Baby Moses) © Copyright, 2011 Mahoney Media Group/ Patterns of Evidence, LLC.

PAGE 159 (Graphic – Graves) © Copyright, 2014 Patterns of Evidence, LLC.

PAGE 159 (Graphic – Mortality) © Copyright, 2014 Patterns of Evidence, LLC.

PAGE 162 (Brooklyn Papayrus Graphic) © Copyright, Images Brooklyn Museum, used with permission from book *"A Papyrus of the Late Middle Kingdom"*

PAGE 165 (upper middle image skeleton) © Copyright, Photo: OeAI, Austrian Archaeological Institute, used with permission

PAGE 165 (upper right tomb) © Copyright, Photo: OeAI, Austrian Archaeological Institute, used with permission

PAGE 165 (Book Image) Photo from page *"A Papyrus of the Late Middle Kingdom"* © Copyright, 2011 Mahoney Media Group / Patterns of Evidence, LLC.

PAGE 165 (upper left image of Avaris) © Copyright, 2014 Patterns of Evidence, LLC.

PAGE 165 (Wall of Time) © Copyright, 2014 Patterns of Evidence, LLC.

PAGE 165 (Slavery photo) © Copyright, 2011 Mahoney Media Group/ Patterns of Evidence, LLC.

Chapter 7

PAGE 166 (Moses Flight Map) © Copyright, 2014 Patterns of Evidence, LLC.

PAGE 167 (Moses) © Copyright, 2011 Patterns of Evidence, LLC.

PAGE 167 (Rabbi Friedman) © Copyright, 2014 Patterns of Evidence, LLC.

PAGE 169 (Nile into Blood Animation of Plagues) © Copyright, 2014 Patterns of Evidence, LLC.

PAGE 169 (Death of Livestock Animations of plagues) © Copyright, 2014 Patterns of Evidence, LLC.

PAGE 169 (Hail Animations of plagues) © Copyright, 2014 Patterns of Evidence, LLC.

PAGE 170 (Avaris) © Copyright, 2014 Patterns of Evidence, LLC.

PAGE 171 (Pillar) © Copyright, 2012 Mahoney Media Group /Patterns of Evidence, LLC.

PAGE 172 (Tenth Plague animations) © Copyright, 2014 Patterns of Evidence, LLC.

PAGE 172 (Death Passover animations) © Copyright, 2014 Patterns of Evidence, LLC.

PAGE 220 (Kahun Map) © Copyright, 2014 Patterns of Evidence, LLC.

PAGE 221 (Rosalie David) © Copyright, Jonathan Kent, used with permission

PAGE 221 (Kahun Animation) © Copyright, 2014 Patterns of Evidence, LLC.

PAGE 223 (Kahun Abandonment Animation) © Copyright, 2014 Patterns of Evidence, LLC.

PAGE 224 (Rohl) © Copyright, 2013 Mahoney Media Group /Patterns of Evidence, LLC.

PAGE 225 (Wall of Time) © Copyright, 2014 Patterns of Evidence, LLC.

PAGE 226 (Columns Luxor) © Copyright, 2012 Patterns of Evidence, LLC.

PAGE 229 (Four Wall of Time (Timeline examples) © Copyright, 2014 Pattern Of Evidence

Chapter 10

PAGE 230 (Franklin) © Copyright, 2011 Mahoney Media Group / Patterns of Evidence, LLC.

PAGE 230 (Canaan Map) © Copyright, 2014 Patterns of Evidence, LLC.

PAGE 231 (Wall of Time) © Copyright, 2014 Patterns of Evidence, LLC.

PAGE 232 (Finkelstein) © Copyright, 2012 Mahoney Media Group/Patterns of Evidence, LLC.

PAGE 233 (Megiddo Dig Site) © Copyright, 2012 Mahoney Media Group/Patterns of Evidence, LLC.

PAGE 234 (Jericho Ruins) © Copyright, 2013 Titus Kennedy/ Mahoney Media Group/ Patterns of Evidence, LLC.

PAGE 234 (Sellin Team) Photo from the estate of Professor Carl Watzinger in Tubingen, reproduced with the kind permission of Prof. Dr. Thomas Schäfer, University of Tübingen, Institute of Classical Archaeology.

PAGE 235 (Garstang) Reproduced by the permission of the Palestine Exploration Fund, London.

PAGE 235 (Kenyon) University College, London, used with permission Stuart Laidlaw

PAGE 236 (Jericho animation) © Copyright, 2014 Patterns of Evidence, LLC.

PAGE 237 (Jericho Map) © Copyright, 2014 Patterns of Evidence, LLC.

PAGE 237 (Jericho Wall) Collections of the Library of Congress, Jericho, Matson 09110

PAGE 238 (Animation mud brick walls of Jericho) © Copyright, 2014 Patterns of Evidence, LLC.

PAGE 239 (Revetment walls) Public domain Sellin and Watzinger Jericho Book 1913

PAGE 239 (Animation walls burning) © Copyright, 2014 Patterns of Evidence

PAGE 240 (Burn Layer) © Copyright, 2013 Titus Kennedy/ Mahoney Media Group/ Patterns of Evidence, LLC.

PAGE 241 (Pot filled with grain) Reproduced by the permission of the Palestine Exploration Fund, London.

PAGE 241 (Pot with archaeologist) Reproduced by the permission of the Palestine Exploration Fund, London.

PAGE 242 (Mahoney) © Copyright, 2013 Patterns of Evidence, LLC.

Page 243 (Conquered Cities Map) © Copyright, 2014 Patterns of Evidence

PAGE 244 (Aerial view Hazor) © Copyright, David Rohl, used with permission

PAGE 245 (Jabin Tablet) © Copyright, David Rohl, used with permission

PAGE 246 (Wood) © Copyright, Michael Luddeni, used with permission

PAGE 251 (Bimson/Mahoney) © Copyright, 2012, Mahoney Media Group/ Patterns of Evidence, LLC.

PAGE 252 (Cities of Canaan Graphic) © Copyright, 2014 Patterns of Evidence, LLC.

PAGE 253 (Biblical Cities Graphic) © Copyright, 2014 Patterns of Evidence, LLC.

PAGE 255 (Rabbi Friedman) © Copyright, 2013 Mahoney Media Group/ Patterns of Evidence, LLC.

PAGE 257 (Entrance ancient site of Shechem) © Copyright, David Rohl, used with permission

PAGE 257 (Alt View archaeological site of Shechem) © Copyright, David Rohl, used with permission

PAGE 257 (3D animation alt view of Shechem) © Copyright, David Rohl/ Patterns of Evidence, LLC., used with permission

PAGE 258 (Animation Joshua) © Copyright, 2014 Patterns of Evidence, LLC.

PAGE 259 Photo from the estate of Professor Carl Watzinger in Tubingen, reproduced with the kind permission of Prof. Dr. Thomas Schäfer, University of Tübingen, Institute of Classical Archaeology.

PAGE 259 (Alt View archaeological site of Shechem) © Copyright, David Rohl, used with permission

PAGE 259 (Standing Stone) © Copyright, David Rohl, used with permission

PHOTOGRAPHY AND ILLUSTRATION CREDITS